Sexual Offenders and the Criminal System

This book demonstrates that the criminal justice system in the United States has allowed the natural emotions surrounding sexuality to allow the minority of sexual offenders who are truly dangerous to be merged with the majority of offenders who pose little, if any, risk to be at large. Such aggregations force the system to exhaust resources while ignoring the burgeoning research into the assessment and treatment of such offenders. Relying on research in the literature combined with his many years of experience, Barry Maletzky details how the system operates at present and offers suggestions for change to re-align what we know about sexual offending with how such offenders might be better managed within the criminal justice system.

The work provides an overview of the process from the original apprehension of sexual offenders through the determination of their guilt, their detention in prisons or jails, and their supervision following incarceration. Allowing scientific advances to inform decisions in these matters will not only enhance public safety but will spare unnecessary expense, save taxpayers' money, and actually serve to prevent future recidivism among such offenders.

This work is thought-provoking for attorneys, prosecutors, legal assistants and law clerks, members of the judiciary, those who teach or are students of the administration of justice, those who assess or treat sexual offenders, and offenders and their families affected by the system.

Barry Maletzky M.D., graduated from Columbia University with a B.A. in psychophysiology and from Stony Brook Campus, with an M.D. He completed a residency in psychiatry at the Oregon Health Sciences University. Following two years of service in the military, he entered the practice of psychiatry in Portland, Oregon. Dr. Maletzky began specializing in several fields in psychiatry, including the treatment of severe depression and the assessment and treatment of sexual offenders. In 1975 he founded the Portland Sexual Abuse Clinic to treat sexual offenders and their victims. Since that time, the clinic has become one of the largest such clinics in the world. He is the author of more than 65 articles in peer-reviewed medical journals, ten chapters in edited textbooks, and six original textbooks of psychiatry in various subspecialties. He served as editor of a medical journal from 1994 through 2004. Dr. Maletzky is the recipient of numerous military and civilian awards, including the Dean's Award from OHSU. He partially retired in 2007 in order to devote more time to his teaching, research, volunteer, and consulting activities, including membership on the boards of non-profit organizations working with those just released from prison, those who subsist below the poverty line, and those within the LGBTQ community.

Sexual Offenders and the Criminal System

Perceptions, Beliefs, and Science

Barry Maletzky

Routledge
Taylor & Francis Group
NEW YORK AND LONDON

Designed cover image: © Getty Images

First published 2025
by Routledge
605 Third Avenue, New York, NY 10158

and by Routledge
4 Park Square, Milton Park, Abingdon, Oxon OX14 4RN

Routledge is an imprint of the Taylor & Francis Group, an informa business

Library of Congress Cataloging-in-Publication Data
Names: Maletzky, Barry, author.
Title: The burden of truth and sexual offenders : how emotions trump science in our criminal justice system / Barry Maletzky.
Description: New York, NY : Routledge, 2025. | Includes bibliographical references and index.
Identifiers: LCCN 2024057900 (print) | LCCN 2024057901 (ebook) | ISBN 9781032874210 (hardback) | ISBN 9781032874227 (paperback) | ISBN 9781003532590 (ebook)
Subjects: LCSH: Sex offenders. | Sex crimes. | Criminal justice, Administration of.
Classification: LCC HV6556 .M35 2025 (print) | LCC HV6556 (ebook) | DDC 364.15/30973–dc23/eng/20250218
LC record available at https://lccn.loc.gov/2024057900
LC ebook record available at https://lccn.loc.gov/2024057901

ISBN: 978-1-032-87421-0 (hbk)
ISBN: 978-1-032-87422-7 (pbk)
ISBN: 978-1-003-53259-0 (ebk)

DOI: 10.4324/9781003532590

Typeset in Sabon
by Taylor & Francis Books

To Michelle, among the smallest women I know but with the biggest heart

Contents

Acknowledgements

No such text could have seen the light of publication day without the benign guidance of the clinical staff with whom I've been privileged to work throughout my many years of practice. I owe a dept of gratitude to those who helped me establish the first clinic devoted exclusively to the treatment of sexual offenders in 1972 in Portland, OR. These include brave therapists such as Ronald Price, Dennis Cliff, and George Miller who forsook practices in potentially more lucrative positions to assist in designing, often from scratch, the equipment and locations for assessing and treating sexual offenders. Their assistance and devotion provided the fuel to pursue techniques which, at the time, were unproven therapies, and an uncertain future. Nonetheless, they persisted and eventually, we began to realize our approaches were working to reduce or eliminate harmful and often unwanted sexual misbehaviors.

My deepest appreciation goes to my most consistent and effective therapist, Cynthia Steinhauser, Ph.D., LCSW, who, over the past 27 years has accepted the most refractory and alienated clients, even those in complete denial and disdain, for treatment. She has been accepted almost entirely by these recalcitrant souls through her exuberance, nonjudgmental manner and welcoming persistence. I know that many such men might well have been expelled from other such clinics but she has held them both close yet responsible, accepting that we all make mistakes and it is those from which we can learn the most. Dr. Steinhauser is now Director of our Clinic, simply known as The Sexual Abuse Clinic. She, along with others, brought in new therapists and helped us train several postgraduate fellows in forensics from the Department of Psychiatry at the Oregon Health and Sciences University.

I would be delinquent in not also singling out Will Brown for his ingenious use of the penile plethysmograph, not only in devising aversive conditioning techniques but in designing novel and individualized biofeedback programs for many of our clients. He spent countless hours, often on his own time, in developing methods of utilizing the plethysmograph that are widely recognized today as standard in the behavioral part of treatment for many sexual offenders.

With the growth in the numbers of clients referred, often after failing at other clinics, we expanded to other locations in Oregon and Washington. Through constant dialogues with attorneys, district attorneys, and probation and post-prison supervisors, we have been able to create a network for the therapy of sexual officers that is well-recognized as performing responsible and effective treatment in successfully reducing the incidence of repeat offending in the vast majority of sexual offenders who have completed our programs.

I should also acknowledge our steadfast, long-term business manager, Andrea Murdoch. Without her business acumen, it would have proven impossible to function, given the logistics problems she has been able to resolve. I am certain her management skills have allowed us to assess and treat the multitudes of offenders as we already have. In that way, she has helped to make the Portland metropolitan area, and indeed all of Oregon and Southwestern Washington, safer from sexual predation throughout these many years.

I am also grateful to the Association for the Treatment of Sexual Abusers (ATSA) for establishing guidelines, now internationally accepted, for the assessment and treatment of such offenders. Those of us still breathing can take pride in the knowledge that this Association, now including thousands of therapists world-wide, originated through our efforts to organize a statewide alliance over 50 years ago, at first composed of just a handful of courageous therapists meeting in our homes and offices here in the oft-neglected State of Oregon. Through those efforts sprung the Safer Society Press, now renowned for their publication of numerous workbooks we all find so helpful in structuring treatment and ensuring that lessons are well generalized to the outside world.

I am equally in debt to the attorneys and supervisory officers who helped proofread the text and correct my frequent errors of misinterpretation and set me on the correct course of describing their roles in the entire system of criminal justice. They have provided invaluable guidance in formulating changes they would like to see within this overburdened field.

I cannot end without praising the perseverance of those at Taylor and Francis, especially Ellen Boyne, who graciously accepted the publication of a text not without controversy, and to the editors who parsed my overly complex sentences and who rendered my often purple prose less colorful and less inflammatory. I remain hopeful that some of the ideas presented herein will prove of some help in furthering the main aim of this text: to emphasize and put into practice the science-based rehabilitation and treatment techniques we are certain will reduce the incidence of sexual abuse and thereby heal the souls of those who otherwise might be hurt by its continuance.

Introduction

This book is not an *apologia* for sexual offenders. Some are dangerous and require confinement, a few even for their lifetimes. Many others require incarceration until they reach an age generally inconsistent with re-offending. The criminal justice system, however, has not kept pace with scientific advances in the assessment and treatment techniques which allow us, with an excellent degree of accuracy, to predict the likelihood that any particular offender will commit another sexual crime. Moreover, such advances largely ensure that each such offender will remain offense-free in the future.

In addition, the roles are challenging in the extreme for those tasked with the evaluation of risk, such as psychologists, social workers and other treatment providers; the determination of which charges are brought by the district attorneys and grand juries; the determination of sentences imposed by the courts, that is, the judges or, more frequently the District Attorneys (DAs) and defense attorneys who arrange plea agreements; the conditions within penal institutions, overseen by corrections officials within state or federal jurisdictions; and the probation officers (POs) and parole officers (now termed post-prison supervisors–PPSs), tasked with managing offenders following their release from confinement. The duties for each set of these officials are formidable. Yet, due to their distance from each other in location and timing, as well as the sheer numbers of all types of offenders, they only rarely communicate directly about any single case or about distinctions amongst the types of sexual offenders.

Because there is a need for regulations concerning the roles of DAs, courts and corrections divisions, many sexual offenders are bundled together into groups that may not match their risk for re-offense, termed recidivism. It is typical of our species to group items and people into separate subdivisions and for good reason: it is easier to learn, compare, teach, and conceive of a single collection, a congregation of sorts, than it would be to attempt to categorize each individual; this is especially so when many such individuals, such as sexual offenders, share a number of traits.

Problems arise, however, when such offenders are herded together as if all warranted equal disposition when, in fact, they are distinct in levels of risk

DOI: 10.4324/9781003532590-1

and modes of rehabilitation for optimal growth. We tend to form groups based on shared characteristics so as to reduce the burden of isolating each individual and specifying his or her needs.

Please note that I have referred to all sexual offenders in the male gender; this is not based upon misogyny but rather on clinical practice and statistics. In our 60 years of experience with over 35,000 sexual offenders, 98% of them are male. I am certain this represents a bias based on the reluctance for women offenders to be identified or treated. Moreover, the majority of such "offenders" actually have been either coerced or manipulated into a sexual offense by a male accomplice. Hence the pronouns "he" and "his", are, in the main, employed in the text. A separate section devoted to female offenders will be found in Chapter Six. I hope no one is offended.

For example, a man who repeatedly rapes women is quite distinct in terms of needs for incarceration, supervision, and treatment than an 18-year-old teen who has consensual intercourse with his 15-year-old girlfriend. Yet both are labelled sexual offenders and both will have to bear that stigma, including the requirement to register as a sexual offender, often for the remainder of their lives. There is a mechanism for the latter to achieve relief from this last obligation but not without considerable time, effort and expense. We must acknowledge that each sexual offender is unique and all such offenders should not serve as uniform avatars for their group identity.

Consider this example: that of a man lured into a sexually tinged chat with an adult police officer posing as a 16-year-old "teenage girl" on common social media sites such as Snapchat. Merely discussing sexual topics could lead to a charge of *Online Sexual Delinquency of a Child* despite any actual contact with the underage individual. Should the adult male (95% to 98% of all charged sexual offenders are male. I will use the male pronoun in this text; I hope no one is offended) arrange a meeting with the "minor", then drive to an arranged location, he will be immediately arrested with a variety of charges, including the one above and, more commonly, *Luring a Minor for Immoral Purpose* or *Communicating with a Minor for Sexual Purposes*. Who is the victim in such cases? The police officer? The DA would prosecute such a case based on the *assumption of intent*, which is impossible to prove in any scientific manner. In the absence of a victim, has a crime been committed?

Contrast these cases to one in which a man seeks out the company of prepubescent boys for the purpose of grooming them, isolating one or several, and forcing them, by a variety of means, into sexual activity. He may have created, in his life span of offending, a number of victims and they may suffer for years with symptoms of anxiety, dread, insomnia, vivid nightmares, sexual and relationship difficulties, fears of committing to potential partners, difficulty concentrating, and flashbacks of the abuse – all signs of post-traumatic stress disorder (PTSD). The danger of this type of offender is immediate and palpable. Of greater scientific import, his risk can be measured; he must somehow be punished when apprehended, but he is classified as a sexual offender, exactly as in the less dangerous examples cited in the above paragraph.

Of course, the justice system would treat these various types of offenders in a different manner. But, as in life, there are gray areas, both in the notions of punishment and the manner in which such individuals are perceived by the general public. Most people in a community population are poised for prejudice when all they can know is that a man has committed a sexual crime. Indeed, in a popularity contest sexual offenders would probably lose to Satan. Debates about punishment for sexual offenses resemble a dialogue of the deaf, leaving both sides impoverished. Moreover, many people would prefer not to discuss sexual offending. We are thus fed silence.

Such cases, differ vastly in severity and serve as examples that judgement must be limited to what the offender has actually done rather than the entirety of a person's lifetime of actions and the totality of his personality. The actual example cited of a man who has molested many boys is surely dangerous and he must be both incarcerated and treated. Yet this same human being, living in a northern clime, once jumped into a freezing lake to rescue a drowning girl, an action which could have taken his life. Is he a monster or a hero? The real world is not inhabited by angels and demons, as popular media portrays; instead, each of us carries the potential to commit kind acts and destructive ones, especially given difficult and variable situations.

Most people are primed to notice the awful rather than the admirable. News channels rarely report acts of beneficence or charity. War and destruction predominate as their audiences are attracted to conflict as opposed to compromise, cohesion, and compassion. On social media, this tendency is amplified. Evolution has rendered it more essential that we humans, indeed almost all animals, are more keen to discern danger rather than decency. Most people will notice and judge a sexual crime, even if that offender has otherwise lived a life filled with good will and kindness. In a 2023 study of lay-people among a general population and professionals treating sexual offenders, a group from Brandies University noted that the general public's ratings of a repeat sexual offense were significantly higher than those of the professionals who actually work with these offenders and follow them throughout and following therapy.

We do not live in a black and white binary world. By judging our fellow human beings by one abominable act or a pattern of such acts, we are ignoring the remainder of the other days in their lives, during which they acted as kind fathers, were faithful husbands, generous and helpful companions to their friends, and were excellent workers. By those standards, we are all sinners. Yet behind every shadow, there has to be a light.

In this book, I hope to convey how the science of assessing sexual offender risk has advanced, thus allowing professionals to correctly predict who, among all such offenders, presents greater or lesser degrees of risk, which of them are most amenable to treatment, and which are safe to be at large in their communities. I hope to outline how the justice system has responded (or not) to these advances, and how we can render the system more efficient and equitable, less costly, and more beneficial to our civilization. "Common sense" is often used to justify opinions in these matters but, in the arena of sexual offenders, it may be an oxymoron: there is nothing common amongst opinions of everyone in our species and much of it makes little sense.

This will not be a technical scientific report, replete with obscure journal citations and complex statistical analyses. These can be accessed through the annotated bibliography at the end of the text for those interested in the research basis of my comments, ideas, suggestions and conclusions. My purpose is not to disparage any particular branch of our justice system, but to illuminate, by the light of scientific endeavor, the murky corners within which the justice system often victimizes certain types of benign sexual offenders while failing to adequately protect the public from the most dangerous among this lot.

In addition, viewing the system from an overall perspective can help inform future policy. Differing perspectives lead to a variety of opinions; however, we should embrace dissent, though without discord. I am hopeful this book will both inform the public in these matters as well as alter, in some small way, the manner in which certain sexual offenders are managed within our justice systems. In a compromise, no one believes the final decision is completely satisfactory.

It is important to note that I am in no position to criticize any individual or portion of our justice systems. Within each of the segments comprising this system ther are prosecuting and defense attorneys, courts, corrections officers, or even therapists who have their own perspectives and have been extensively trained to carry out their duties. Each individual within these systems, in my experience, attempts to execute their tasks in the sincere belief they are helping to make our communities safer for their citizens.

Nonetheless, many of these opinions cannot be viewed through an absolute lens of right or wrong. These are complicated issues and conclusions must be examined based upon their source. A district attorney (DA), parole officer (PO), or post-prison supervisor (PPS) may have a completely different view on any of these factors and, from her or his perspective, that view may make good sense. My basic concern is that the system arrives at decisions which are based not solely upon any single actor's experience within it nor upon the copious literature in this field. It also should, indeed must, take into account what we can learn from the science of sexual offending and the impact the justice system has had upon both offenders, their families, their victims, and their probabilities of re-offense.

Unfortunately, the punitive atmosphere which permeates the criminal justice system, combined with the lack of awareness of recent research findings in the area of criminal justice reform and in the rehabilitation and treatment of sexual offenders, forces the system into inequalities, erratic judgements, arbitrary punishments and inequitable sanctions such that it accomplishes less than its potential in preventing future sexual crimes.

Experts in criminal justice have urged reforms in recent years, reinforced by research findings, yet few have yielded any effective changes, especially in regard to sexual offenders. True, modest improvements have been achieved. Nonetheless, our criminal justice system remains in relative stasis. Politicians and those who occupy positions of oversight within the system are much like Odysseus, who fought many minor battles for decades in the Mediterranean Sea only to realize that his greatest challenge was finding his way home.

Should a psychiatrist have the hubris to address the criminal justice system about its operations? I do believe that a view from outside the system can sometimes prove helpful. In my 50 years of psychiatric practice, including evaluating and treating over 35,000 sexual offenders, and publishing over 60 peer-reviewed journal articles and five books concerning the assessment and treatment of sexual offenders, the qualified opinions offered herein are worth considering. Of greater consequence, I am more than familiar with the sexual offender and criminal justice literature, which should inform important decisions about how each offender should be judged, sentenced, punished, and supervised.

I have also testified for both the defense and prosecution in countless cases, though I would quickly acknowledge there are undoubtedly areas within the system I may have misinterpreted or misrepresented. Moreover, each jurisdiction may prosecute and supervise sexual offenders in a different manner. I would be more than happy to be corrected from readers or entertain alternative views as no single specialty or individual within it can be correct under all circumstances. Please offer criticisms or corrections through the publisher and I will address these in an unopinionated and timely fashion. Controversy and debate form the wellsprings of fruitful discovery.

Those embedded within the magnitude of the criminal justice system may not be as keen to alter it; a certain comfort, even anomie, arises from stability. Yet the clinical and scientific aspects of criminal behavior, and specifically sexual offending, demand not only observation but a mindset of reform, especially in the areas of punishment, supervision, and rehabilitation. When the system finds itself in a hole, the best advice would be to stop digging. The United States imprisons more individuals per capita than any other country in the world. Nonetheless, over 45% of former inmates will return to prison within five years after release, either on a new conviction or a violation of their conditions of probation or post-prison supervision. Professor Giane Silvestre of the University of São Paulo commented recently that, in many countries, including the United States, "Overcrowding means that many prisoners are simply placed in cages."

In fact, America has one of the highest rates of incarceration in the world: 629 people per 100,000 of the total population. Even autocratic regimes and theocracies incarcerate fewer persons, in absolute numbers (except for China) and per capita for any other country. The costs of this system are staggering and run into the billions of dollars each year, funded in the main by individual citizens' taxes. Some countries are beginning to recognize that too many inmates are not only overcrowding prisons but are not dangerous to be at large. Of Latin American countries, six have recently reduced their prison populations since 2018, as reported by the World Prison Brief, a nonprofit organization. Despite this reduction in their prison populations, there has been no concomitant increase in the rates of any types of crime in those nations.

At present our criminal justice system refers to an organized governmental entity comprised of a number of elements, including the idea of "Corrections." That grand title and the idealistic vision it implies has been tarnished by the reality of conditions within this system. There are significant inequities and inconsistencies when the system is applied that are not only erratic but are incorrect. Moreover, *correcting* criminal behavior implies that one of the most crucial elements of the system should be the rehabilitation of those who break the law, such as sexual offenders, so as to prevent future criminal behavior. However, many of the processes and regulations surrounding sexual offending appear to suffer from strategic ambiguity.

Unfortunately, the means by which the system could reduce such uncertainties currently ignores the input of scientifically proven techniques which could achieve that goal. This text hopes to address these problems and suggests alternative policies which, I believe, will provide remedies to significantly reduce, to a large extent, not only sexual offense recidivism, but may also be applied in general to save time and money in the pursuit of justice for all offenders and victims alike.

Authorities and legislators in our criminal justice system appear to rely upon dogma rather than data. Congressional bodies appear moribund, ignoring any legislation which might appear to lessen the burdens imposed on sexual offenders. These legislators find it easier to ignore such matters out of fear of political self-harm. They conveniently disregard the effects of progressive changes which would reduce recidivism, save money and allow the promotion of human rehabilitation. The effects of these changes are not experienced by legislators, but rather by those who suffer the effects on their cowardice: offenders and their families as well.

Many of the opinions and suggestions herein are not absolute; they may not be clear-cut about what is right or wrong. This text clearly reflects my own notions and priorities, background, experiences and the culture in which I was raised. Even in science, and especially so in that domain, conflicting perspectives and divergent beliefs do not indicate argument as much as an avenue towards understanding varying points of view and compromise or consensus. It is only through dialogue and debate that enrichment and verification can be realized.

I believe, with the humble appreciation of an outsider, that this book can both inform an understanding of how sexual offenders differ one from another, while emphasizing the significance of familiarity of the scientific literature, now abundant in these fields and growing on a steady basis. My narrative is based upon this literature but it is, of course, incomplete, as is any scientific undertaking. It includes research featuring scientific advances, discoveries now known yet also mysteries left to solve. The value of these empirical studies demonstrates how the criminal justice system can adapt to more adequately guide the management of offenders who pose no risk to their communities in contrast to those who prey upon vulnerable victims and thus seek to satisfy the darkest of their desires.

Chapter 1

The Four Pillars of Justice Defined

Although I have testified in over 750 trails involving sexual offenders; read thousands of pre-sentence and judicial reviews; am familiar to some degree with the correction's literature; and have held countless meetings with district attorneys, judges, probation and parole and post-prison supervisors, and legislators in Washington and Oregon, I cannot pretend to be an expert in the field of jurisprudence. I have never attended a class in law school nor served in any law office as an official employee. Nonetheless, based on my experience in not only assessing and treating many thousands of sexual offenders as well as involvement in hundreds of other felony cases, including homicide and kidnapping, I have come to appreciate the foundations upon which our justice system lies and the reasons why, for centuries, these have changed to only a slight degree.

There exist four pillars of justice that district attorneys (DAs), defense attorneys, juries, judges, corrections officers, and policy makers must take into account in devising what constitutes the appropriate administration of justice. Should a crime have been committed and an individual is either determined guilty of that crime by a judge or jury, or accepts a plea arrangement admitting to have committed the offense, the four pillars consist of:

(I) Punishment
(II) Justice for the victim(s)
(III) Supervision
(IV) Rehabilitation

This classification is arbitrary as certain of these processes merge over time. Moreover, I have touched only in brief in this opening Chapter on the detection and investigation of a sexual crime, as I wish to focus in the main on what occurs *after* a conviction takes place. Although I will mention police tactics briefly in later chapters, the four areas of the criminal justice system noted above are where the strengths and deficiencies of this system are most apparent, its impacts most acutely experienced, and its aims most conflicted.

DOI: 10.4324/9781003532590-2

These categories are, to some extent, artificial and can overlap. For example, incarceration can be considered as both punishment and part of recompense for victims, while supervision often includes treatment and rehabilitation by corrections officers following incarceration. Nonetheless, I will provide the rationale upon which the system is based as often perceived by different segments of the judicial system as well as the public at large, with the recognition that each official may differ between, and even within, departments.

For example, prosecutors (the DAs) may disagree about which charges to bring in similar cases even within their own county. Judges may well differ on matters of sentencing. Victims may feel more or less satisfied with the punishment meted out while, following incarceration, corrections officers such as POs or PPSs, may disagree about how strict the rules of supervision should be in similar cases. (Please see Appendix A at the rear of this book for a complete list of abbreviations.) Lastly, even therapists will often offer widely varying techniques in attempting to treat convicted sexual offenders and hence, reduce the risk of an offender repeating his offense (commonly referred to as recidivism). The valleys between these professionals are as deep as a desert canyon and cannot be easily bridged without fundamental changes in the system itself. However, before these chasms can be spanned, it would be worthwhile to provide a brief overview in this initial chapter about how most sexual offenders are apprehended and the processes involved in the determination of their guilt.

The Apprehension of a Sexual Offender: Many sexual crimes are not reported by the victim(s) out of fear of retribution, embarrassment, uncertainty about whether what occurred was illegal, qualms or anxiety lest a family becomes fractured. A few may be dismissed by the police or the DA has not chosen to prosecute because of insufficient evidence. Unfortunately, many rapes may fall into several of these categories. Estimates of failure to report a rape by the victim vary widely, from 25% to 60%, alarming figures, in part the fault of therapists, teachers, academic institutions, parents or religious leaders, most of whom are mandatory reporters to authorities. However, it appears that a larger reason for a victim to not report a rape is probably a fear of not being believed, apprehension about having to testify in a trial, or anxiety about the perpetrator seeking revenge.

Police are to be congratulated for a rapid response in most sexual abuse cases. Their reports are invaluable if the offender eventually enters therapy. Most often, police refer child victims to a specialized center with therapists well-trained and highly skilled in gaining information from both pre- and post-pubescent youth, while detectives usually limit their investigations to interviews with witnesses, family members or others familiar with what occurred.

They also are tasked with collecting evidence. I will spare the reader a tedious discussion of evidence collection as most people these days are almost too familiar with crime scene investigations via the popular media, including blood and semen sampling, electronics investigations, and DNA evidence. Witness testimony is occasionally helpful but recent studies call into question facial recognition as being unreliable. But even here, artificial intelligence (another oxymoron) can be helpful in facial reconstruction along with artists' renderings, which have proven a bit more trustworthy.

Despite the fact that all attorneys would have told the alleged offender not to provide any information, most sexual offenders either deny complicity and only a few ask to speak to an attorney until after they have provided their version of what occurred. Police are human and we have encountered a tendency toward bias against the offender even before any guilt is determined. Detectives are as disgusted as anyone in the general population by a variety of sexual crimes and realize that their reports can sway a grand jury and frighten the offender to the extent that many such offenders offer their own version of what occurred in an effort to appear cooperative in the vain hope such willingness will impress authorities and ease whatever disposition they will receive. This assumption is rarely effective.

Once an arrest is made, the offender may be released on his own recognizance if the crime was a minor one, or placed in custody pending a bail hearing. Many offenders prefer to pay for bail instead of spending many months in jail pending a definitive outcome. Bail for most alleged sexual offenders can range from US$50,000 to $500,000, 10% or 15% percent of which is payable before release. That amount is not returnable. Many offenders rely on family for funds; some take out a second mortgage on their homes or even sell their dwellings to raise the cash required. A few sexual offenders are deemed a potential risk to their communities and can be placed on an ankle monitor and given strict conditions, such as where they cannot go (usually parks, schoolyards and playgrounds). Those who have committed computer-based crimes can have their electronics confiscated; these are often placed into evidence.

Thus, depending upon the nature and severity of the crime, a long waiting period now begins as attorneys, DAs and the offenders conduct a dance in determining what charge(s) will be brought and, in 97% of cases, what plea deal can be struck. Few sexual offenders dare face a judge or jury in the knowledge that the victim(s) will almost always be believed. In our experience, fewer than 1% of victims say that what occurred is an outright lie.

The Determination of Guilt: Even prior to the determination of whether a crime has been committed, an entire host of events must take place, including detection of an offense, generally by police officials; an investigation and the accumulation of evidence; the transmission of such facts to the office of the governing DA's office; a separate determination by this office of whether there is sufficient material proof and documentation to make charges against an individual or group; and, the likelihood that there is adequate evidence to convince a jury or judge to find the parties guilty.

I am not an expert in these areas but I have been involved in reading and evaluating thousands of police reports and pre-sentence evaluations, then in reviewing with the alleged offender their versions of what actually occurred. In such cases, I have also been privy to what are termed "discovery materials." These often include not only the original police reports but secondary police actions, including interviews of the suspect(s); victims' accounts of the crime(s); witnesses' statements; interviews of family members and friends of the accused; reviews of electronic activity, including text messages and access to pornography; DNA evidence; and recordings, video or auditory, of those interviews and statements.

In addition, also included in discovery are "secret" indictments by the DA, following a grand jury determination of whether a case should be brought by the DA. However, by law, all materials pertinent to the case and the grand jury's findings must be made available to those who will be involved in the prosecution and defense in the case. These include: warrants authorized by a court; interviews of victims in child abuse cases by Departments of Human Services, Children's Welfare Programs (DHS); victim interviews conducted by specialized clinics and recordings of these; the criminal histories of accused offenders; transcripts of communications conducted by and between a suspect and victim, generally these days via electronic means; and, usually after a finding of guilt or a plea arrangement is agreed upon, the pre-sentence evaluation prepared by a corrections officer trained to review the evidence and familiar with sentencing guidelines. This officer can review the results of a trial or plea agreement, and make suggestions about an appropriate sentence in the matter at hand.

As noted above, while most police officers attempt to report their interviews and subsequent written descriptions in an objective manner, they are simply human and, faced with the possibility that a sexual crime has been committed, may, consciously or not, exaggerate or even falsify their reports. I believe they may do so as sexual offenses are considered, regardless of the facts, among the most heinous of crimes and no officer wishes to be seen as lenient in such investigations. To be fair, they may also be swayed by the very valid concern that public safety is at stake, especially if the alleged victim is a child.

One area of concern for us as clinicians is the accuracy of initial police reports. Most contain factual information which cannot be disputed, as, for example, child pornography (CP) on a computer, text messages between individuals, and victims' descriptions. However, in interviews with the offender himself, clear bias is often present. Individuals express emotions in a variable manner; some police reports appear to emphasize a dark and inimical version of the offender and the crime(s) allegedly committed. Yet some sexual offenders have a mental or biological illness, such as attention deficit hyperactivity disorder (ADHD) or an autistic disorder which renders them inconsistent in their manner, which others might misinterpret as defiant or uncooperative. This is rarely taken into account as police officials are not diagnosticians. However, subsequent evaluations must allow for these conditions and the effects they may have upon initial police reports.

Several case examples, taken from real-life materials, may illuminate the inconsistency, ambiguity, and frank prejudice apparent in a selected minority of such cases:

> An IT executive, Aaron, diagnosed with a mild autistic disorder, and his wife were engaged in marital counseling when he described what he thought was an innocent, even amusing incident. After showering, his four-year-old daughter entered what he thought was the locked bathroom as he was exiting the shower stall. His wife usually shaved her pubic hair so she wondered aloud about his pubic hair and asked if she could touch it. Without much hesitance or thought, he complied. She touched his hair for a brief few seconds, then remarked, "It felt like fur." The marriage counselor was uncertain but, out of an abundance of caution, as an obligate reporter she informed DHS of the incident. The detective who interviewed Aaron noted that he occasionally smiled as he described the incident. This officer inferred that this constituted proof that Aaron enjoyed some sort of sexual contact with his young daughter and wrote a report advising that sexual abuse might have occurred. He may have believed that Aaron was aroused by this incident, despite the fact that his daughter, subsequently interviewed by DHS, both denied that she ever made contact with Aaron's genitals and that he did not have an erection. Nonetheless, Aaron was accused of a number of charges of *Sexual Abuse in the First Degree*, and was considered to have molested his daughter.

I will return to this case in future chapters when discussing sentencing and supervision but, in reviewing interviews with Aaron's wife and daughter, and his lack of any criminal record, I regarded such charges as an egregious overreaction to an innocent encounter. A problem often exists in the initial police investigations. When an officer first learns that she or he will be investigating a sexual offense case, a bias may already exist. Police officials, usually detectives in such investigations, are simply human and may overreact to allegations of sexual abuse. In Aaron's case, the initial police report made statements that were simply untrue, such as that the girl said her father touched her vaginal area when she said nothing of the sort. He inferred, incorrectly, that when Aaron smiled at various points, he was secretly coveting sexual activity with a prepubescent child. In fact, due to Aaron's autism, his emotions would be expected to be different and they could appear odd to others.

In other words, this officer (who might be an otherwise excellent examiner) made his own inferences, based perhaps on prior biases, and basically did the work of the District Attorney in assigning guilt even before a thorough evaluation. Police authorities claim that they always pursue the path of due diligence in investigations, including multiple interviews with alleged perpetrators, victims and witnesses but, as Aaron's case demonstrates, this is not always true. The detective built a house on a foundation which did not exist. The failure to closely scrutinize sexual abuse cases and provide these with as much painstaking examination absent any preconceived prejudice, which any case deeply deserves, often results in a presumption that a sexual offense did occur.

Similar examples of what most therapists and other experts in criminology and the law consider prosecutorial overreach abound:

> Brian, a truck driver, had several children, ranging in age from 3 to 14, both girls and boys. He had no prior record of criminal acts, though I should always add, "of which we are aware." I usually won't because very few sexual offenders escape detection; although a common belief is that many cases of sexual abuse do go unreported, in current times this is fortunately becoming increasingly uncommon. Brian, as is typical in many households, enjoyed physical contact with his children and they would often play-wrestle on a couch or the floor, often with his wife present. In discussions with several male co-workers, he admitted that sometimes, in wrestling with his children, he would experience an erection. A female driver was within hearing range and reported this to a friend, who convinced her to report this to police. In several police interviews, Brian was open about this occurring but denied any sexual arousal despite his stiff penis. He was subsequently charged with several counts of *Sexual Abuse* and, somewhat confusingly, *Contributing to the Sexual Delinquency of a Minor*. The investigating officers failed to take into account the scientific evidence that a male can have an erection based on physical contact without the slightest degree of arousal or gratification. Indeed, many men experience an erection when a child squirms about on their laps. Were this not so, cases in which females rape a male would be impossible. The erection is a physical reaction absent any arousal.

Admittedly, these are unusual cases but unfortunately, they are not unique: both Aaron and Brian subsequently faced charges of *Sexual Abuse* and had to accept a plea bargain to avoid the embarrassment of a trial, with the risk of actually being found guilty of some crime. The mere accusations alone struck fear into both, and their attorneys had to be honest in that a jury or even a single judge might agree with the charges. In most such cases, we, as therapists, cannot provide legal advice but frankly, we remain distressed that such men might accept a plea when they did not commit a sexual crime.

Moreover, such a plea requires them to be labelled a sexual offender and will require them to register as such, many for the remainder of their lifetimes. A few will be able to receive relief from registration but the assignation as a sexual offender will likely impair their ability to maintain or obtain employment in their fields or their ability to advance should they do so. They may have trouble finding a place to live, may be hounded by adverse publicity, and will carry the unnecessary stigma of such a label, in most cases forever.

In the few cases where the accused and his attorney agree to fight the charge (s), we often recommend trial by a judge rather than a jury as most jurors will be biased against any suspicion of a sexual accusation while we would hope a judge, more schooled in such matters, could be impartial and rely on the facts. This must be balanced against the requirement of unanimity in jury decisions; just one of 12 individuals has to disagree with the charge(s) to acquit. It's a gamble most of the accused are unwilling to make; I cannot blame them.

The consequences of a finding of guilt in a sexual case cannot be underestimated. One would like to believe that all discovery materials are prepared with the patience and lack of bias required to render an objective opinion. But, as the examples above demonstrate, that is not uniformly true in cases involving sexual abuse. In our country, an individual accused of a crime is presumed innocent until a determination of guilt is reached. Hence the burden of proof should lie with the government, via the DA or prosecuting attorney, who must prove, in most cases beyond a reasonable doubt, or in other cases a greater than a 50% likelihood, that a crime occurred; that is, that the suspect is more likely than not to have committed the offense.

However, there exists a distinction between an individual accused of a nonsexual crime and one being indicted on charges of sexual abuse. Simply being *suspected* of a sexual crime is, in all truth, considered evidence itself, absent the usual responsibility of proof on the prosecution; the assumption that one is innocent until proven guilty in sexual abuse cases is turned upside down. Partly this belief begins with some police reports that demonstrate obvious bias against the suspect. Because no individual desires to be an apologist for sexual offending, least of all the prosecuting attorney and the judge or those on juries, the assumption of the accused as being innocent until proven guilty is, in sexual offender cases, reversed; the onus of proving innocence lies squarely on the defense as, in our considerable experience, the burden of proof shifts to the offender and his attorney.

Unfortunately, to prove that some deed did *not* happen establishes a high bar and in sexual abuse cases, that bar is too high to surmount. In other words, the burden of proof in such cases is set lower than the burden of truth. This is amplified by the fact that fewer than 1% of all sexual abuse cases have been proven to stem from false accusations. This is not to say that the charges may not be exaggerated but, in the main, youngsters who have been sexually abused or women who have been raped, have little motivation to report embarrassing total fictions to authorities, then undergo extensive judicial investigations.

Yes, there are isolated cases in which a mother may coach a child to provide a false story out of spite toward a former abusive spouse, although it is difficult to imagine a mother instructing a child to concoct a sexual narrative.

There is also probably a narrow minority of women who seek revenge after being jilted by an ex-lover and then claim rape. In our extensive experience such cases are about as common as a deer attacking a wildcat.

Proving a negative – that is, something that didn't happen – is difficult not only within the legal system but in the discipline of science as well. Proving the veracity of the assertion that a higher power exists, for example, or that living organisms are present on extrasolar planets, is beyond the realm of science at present, not because these beliefs are in error, but because we lack the means by which to prove them correct or wrong. Astronomers are currently exploring means to test this latter premise but, as in both such cases, we must remain agnostic: we simply do not know, nor can we discover the truth at present.

In most sexual offender cases we are fortunate in having solid evidence, but there remain a number, though small, where questions linger. This does not diminish the fact that the manner in which the case is reported by police and in which the DA weaves a story often assures the most incriminating interpretation. This can result in penalties extreme and disproportionate to the criminal acts which were actually committed. The hardships borne not only by the offender, but by his family as well, can be not only devastating in the present, but long-lasting as we have found.

Whether an individual is found guilty of a sexual crime is a matter of an adversarial process known as a trial. In the case of sexual offenders, fewer than 2% of those accused of a sexual crime, regardless of its severity, ever face a judge or jury to determine guilt or innocence. This is due to a number of factors:

a Most often, men who commit a sexual crime realize the evidence is overwhelming against them.
b Fewer than 1% of accusations of sexual abuse are found to be false, despite the many initial denials or claims that the victims concocted a story out of anger, jealousy, or were prompted to manufacture an accusation. Moreover, only a tiny number of accusations spring from a hope that a civil case can be brought against the accused and therefore financial gain is possible. Very few sexual offenders, after conviction, would have sufficient assets for a civil penalty to be worth the expense of initiating a civil proceeding.
c Victims rarely benefit from bringing false allegations of being sexually abused. In doing so, they may experience fear, shame, and embarrassment or retaliation. Often, a story of sexual abuse, especially in younger victims, emerges after many months or years of the crime(s) being committed, when a precipitating event takes place. At times, only trusted friends are privy to what has occurred and they subsequently report to school authorities; at other times, an adult, after being abused as a child, begins to remember the trauma and experiences symptoms of PTSD. The statute of limitations only begins at that point in time, even if the abuse occurred years in the past.

d Few men wish to risk a harsh sentence by a jury or even a judge in a sexual matter when a plea agreement offering a lesser sentence is reached between their defense attorneys and the DAs.
e Fewer wish to undergo the agony of awaiting a trial, which can take many months or even years to be scheduled.
f None relish the thought of the adverse publicity a trial might bring down upon them. Indeed, often the harshest epithet hurled by conspiracy theorists is that some politician is a "pedophile."
g Delays in the process are common. It is not unusual for many months, and even years, to pass from the time of charges being brought to the variety of hearings and, eventually, a determination of sentencing. Often, victims only bring charges long after a sexual offense took place, either because of embarrassment or the realization, in adolescence or adulthood, that what occurred to them as children is now causing symptoms of fear, anxiety, depression, or relationship difficulties.
h The expense of a defense in an actual trial is by and large beyond the means of most men accused of a sexual offense.

When first accused, most sexual offenders will offer minimizations ("I was just teaching her about sex", or "It was just an accident when I went to change her clothes"); justifications ("She started it by wearing revealing clothing", or "She was flirting with me and secretly wanted it"); distortions ("She still likes me so it wasn't that bad", or "She's fine now – it didn't bother her at all"); or outright denial ("Her mother coached her to make it up to gain custody", or "She's just saying it now because her parents would be mad if they learned she really wanted it"). As noted above, is it possible to imagine a mother sitting down with her four-year-old daughter and saying, "We're going to make up a sexual story about your dad"? I can't, though I admit it is possible, but only in the sense that anything is possible.

The ubiquity of such distortions underscores how troubling it would be for a man to admit to molesting a child or raping an intoxicated female. These denials are offered not only to preserve some sense of immediate innocence but to avoid having committed among the most foul of deeds, at least in the eyes of the general public. During the course, often protracted, of discussions with attorneys, DAs and therapists, the vast majority of accused offenders will eventually admit they did do *something* wrong, though many, although not most, will maintain, even throughout their course of punishment and treatment, that the charges were exaggerated in some fashion.

As therapists, we are surprised yet pleased if an offender admits to what he actually did but we neither expect a full admission nor are we bothered by even outright denial. That is an issue to be addressed during treatment, after which the majority of offenders do admit to what occurred. In the scientific literature, surprisingly, denial has not been correlated with either success in treatment nor with the rate of recidivism. If interested, you might consult some of the literature in the bibliography as this factor seems contrary to common sense, but that's what science is for: differentiating what appears to be true from what is actually the truth. It is not that science can, as yet, provide all the answers. Its importance is that, in science, we are continuing to question and probe for a more accurate result through experimentation, even when we wish something to be correct, only to find our biases were in error.

It is appropriate here to distinguish truth from fact. As an example, as a mountain climber planning an expedition, I invited a well-known climber to my home in Portland who lives in Alaska along with another expert ascensionist who had spent the winter months in Florida. The fellow from Alaska complained that the room we were in was too hot; the Alaskan chap said it was too cold. In fact, the temperature registered 72 degrees. Were these climbers telling the truth? Yes, in their perception of a comfortable temperature; they were not lying. It was *their* truth based upon their belief. They were prejudiced because of their different prior living conditions. None of us is completely unbiased as we all have experienced the world in a different and unique manner.

The lurid tales of predatory sexual offenders cannot help but lead to such biases and beliefs. Nonetheless, it is incumbent upon us to measure, evaluate, experiment and study, employing the scientific method as objectively as we are able, to isolate what we believe is true from what science tells us, regardless of those preconceived notions. I hate it when a promising drug trial fails; I accept it and must move on with further inquiry.

Delays in the process can include:

The procedures of investigation, which often involves obtaining warrants

The time then taken by a busy DA's office to determine what charges should be proposed

The need to then convene a grand jury to confirm there are sufficient grounds (probable cause, not the more demanding criterion in an actual trial of beyond a reasonable doubt) for a formal charge(s) to be brought

The multiple consultations the accused must undertake with an attorney

An initial arraignment, during which the prosecution and defense explain their perspectives on the case

The determination by the prosecution of whether the accused represents an immediate threat to the community

The need for a remand to immediate incarceration before a hearing

The court finds that the offender can be allowed to post bail and be released to the community pending a resolution of the case.

One of the first steps the accused offender must take is to obtain an attorney. However, in many cases, this proves almost impossible for well over half of all sexual offenders. The initial cost, as of 2023 in the Portland area, is representative of most locations in America, and stands at about $30,000. However, many top-notch attorneys are increasing their initial fees, some up to $50,000. These are to be paid before any work on the case proceeds. But those fees simply cover the assistance an attorney would offer in the lead-up to a trial, including studying the case materials, conferences with the defendant, and meetings with the DA (usually a deputy DA – a DDA) to discuss whether a plea deal can be arranged. Should the offender decide to risk a trial, the total fees could exceed $100,000, yet without any assurance of a positive outcome; should he lose at trial, he will, in all likelihood, face stiffer sentences than if he had accepted a plea agreement.

Once arrested, a sexual offender is most often offered the opportunity to post bail, although, in certain states, bail has been deemed to be in violation of the 14th Amendment as it discriminates against those too poor to post it. Federal cases still require it. A subset of offenders deemed by a judge to have committed a particularly heinous crime, or who are repeat offenders, or are deemed a flight risk, may well be denied bail pending further hearings. A serial rapist or a man accused of repeatedly torturing boys sexually would likely not be granted the privilege of waiting at home until his case is settled.

The majority of sexual offenders are given bail, though some may not be able to post the 10% required. Bail for many cases of a situational offender, such as a child porn-only case (CPO), extortion or a Romeo and Juliet-type crime (R&J) revolving around age of consent, is usually in the range of $50,000 to $100,000. Ten to fifteen percent is required but many offenders have difficulty paying, while others are fortunate to have family help. Even when released and the case is completed, the bail bondsman will require 10% to 15% of the actual cash for "handling fees."

Faced with all these initial financial charges, many of the accused call upon family assistance. Some have had to assume the burden of a second mortgage while many others must sell their homes, vehicles and other belongings to afford these legal fees. Few attorneys accept partial payment options; who could blame them? Their client may well be imprisoned and thus unable to continue any prolonged schedule of payments.

In addition, family support is not guaranteed. More often than not, families, even those previously close, hold reservations in offering support. Although many try to offer comfort and financial help, others are frankly judgmental and some spurn the accused and cast him out entirely. This occurs especially in families rigid in their religious beliefs. They may fail to recognize that we all make mistakes; in our experience, those who spew the most hatred toward their accused relative may harbor their own grievous errors from the past. Those who eat misery for breakfast and dinner rarely enjoy lunch.

I am not in a position to criticize financial dealings, especially as a private psychiatrist such as myself could charge $450 to $500 per session for individual treatment. (Disclaimer: I have not practiced clinical psychiatry in a number of years, to the disservice of my family.) Nor am I pleading for sympathy for any sexual offender. If guilty, such deeds call for some form of legal intervention. Moreover, should the accused prove unable to pay for a private attorney, the law provides for a public defender to assume the responsibility for such assistance.

In populous urban areas, public defenders are well-organized and operate under the auspices of the county. They employ attorneys who should be admired for forgoing staggering salaries in order to help those not fortunate enough to afford private counsel. Many, in my experience, perform in as apt and proficient a manner as a private advocate might. Nonetheless, many public defenders, good-hearted as they may be, have difficulty remaining in that office for lengthy periods and, at some point, will accept the reality of present-day life in America and accept a position in a private or commercial practice.

In mostly rural areas, counties cannot afford the benefits of a formal public defender's office and, by law, require private attorneys to accept indigent cases for a pittance. As with public defenders, in such cases they are deemed by the media, and thereby the public, as somehow deficient in advocating for such impoverished clients. This has not been universally true in my experience. I continue to be impressed by their ardor, thorough investigation, and powerful advocacy, even in the most difficult of cases, which almost automatically include the defense of sexual offenders.

Less impressive have been, at times, the tactics of detectives in their investigations of cases in which a man is accused of a sexual crime or crimes. Aside from prejudicial interviews replete with leading or ambiguous questioning, inferences unsupported by actual victim and witness statements, and a too-cozy relationship with prosecutors, charges are sometimes brought based on evidence as thin as a runway model and as nebulous as the fog rising from a street after a rare summer rain in the Pacific Northwest:

> A 40-year-old man on disability due to a bipolar illness, Curtis experienced rather regular recurrences of a manic state in which he experienced delusions of grandeur. In two such states, separated by four months, he began to view child pornography with the belief that he could discover who was creating it, and thereby help the police eliminate it from the internet. Back on his prescription medications, Curtis realized the insanity of such an impossible endeavor. He had neither arousal to children nor any history of criminal activity in his past. Indeed, he served as a trusted babysitter on numerous occasions without any implications of abusing any child in his care. The time he accessed child porn amounted to about five minutes. Nevertheless, he was charged with multiple counts of *Possession and*

> *Distribution of Child Pornography* and accepted, on the advice of his attorney, a plea agreement to two years of house arrest with ankle monitoring. He was prohibited from entering any stores and had to have his elderly parents arrange expensive delivery services for his meals. The expert clinician's opinion that Curtis was not a danger to children nor a pedophile and acted only out of a delusional illness that was treatable was ignored, as was the suggestion that he could receive his medications by injection, thus eliminating the threat of a repeat manic episode.

The topic of child pornography will be dealt with in Chapter Six as it is unique amongst sexual crimes in a number of ways: it is one of just two sexual crimes that are increasing throughout our country; the other is one of entrapment (also see Chapter Six). The increases are due not to their actual prevalence but are a result of increasing sophistication in electronic surveillance techniques. Moreover, most men accused of accessing child porn *are not attracted to children* but are simply bored with regular porn and seek out increasingly exotic material. Over 50 studies in the scientific literature demonstrate that such men, with no prior history of a sexual crime, have almost no chance of ever committing a hands-on sexual act with a child after initial detection. (See the Bibliography if interested in further research.)

> In what is known as a police sting, a detective posing as a 16-year-old female initiated a chat with a 52-year-old insurance executive, David, who was seeking "companionship" online, which we perhaps cynically believed was in reality the hope of a sexual encounter. The detective employed increasingly sexual suggestions, including statements that "she" was eager to see sexually explicit pictures and was increasingly "wet." She invited David one night to a dark parking area. Upon arrival, David was immediately taken into custody and charged with multiple counts (don't ask why) of *Online Sexual Corruption of a Child* and *Luring*. Out on bail, he accepted a guilty plea with some charges eliminated. He received a three-year probation. However, as part of the conditions of his supervision, he was not allowed to see his 16-year-old son, a questionable restriction given that he had raised the boy from infancy and posed no threat to him based upon expert psychological testimony. He had no prior criminal history.

The issue of such "sting" operations will also be a subject of a later chapter but it is of interest to question whether, in such cases, a victim exists. If there is no victim, has a crime been committed? The arrest was based upon the *assumption of intent* that David would have followed through with sexual activity with an underage female. If I announced to a police officer that I intended, via the popular media, to rob a bank but never did so, would I be guilty of a crime?

Such matters are beyond the main thrust of this book, which concerns itself with what occurs *after* a person is found guilty or accepts a plea of guilt in a sexual crime. However, in dealing with sexual offenders over such an extensive period of time, I would be remiss in not devoting some time in later chapters to the issues of accessing and especially *distributing* child pornography and the equally vexing matter of entrapment. In point of fact, in California, David would not have been the subject of a "sting" as entrapment has been deemed unjust.

This chapter has dealt with issues which pertain to what happens when a man is accused of a sexual crime. A background in such matters is of importance in understanding how a person is detected, charged and either found guilty or accepts a plea agreement. But in keeping with the main thrust of exploring issues of how justice is meted out thereafter, I must return to the pillars underlying our criminal justice system. While I may be perceived as too negative in some of these matters, our system of justice, just as our system of government, is probably the best conceived across all nations in many ways. That does not mean it cannot be improved.

The true scientist never rests; she or he always seeks to go a step further, constantly questioning the way things appear to be, and asking how results can be extended, improved and verified...or not. Certainty is the enemy of knowledge and of the opportunity to improve and expand systems of operation. This will prove to be essential in order to enhance our ability to devise something even better than the way it has always been.

Chapter 2

The First Pillar

Punishment

As the phases in the journey of a sexual offender continue to the point of rendering a finding of guilt at a trial or, in the vast majority of cases, when a plea arrangement is reached, sentencing must be determined. The actual sentence must be approved by a judge, regardless of any plea deal arrived at by the DA and the defense. A judge may either consider a deal too lenient, not well-considered, or too harsh. However, in over 97% of cases of which I am aware, the court will allow the plea deal to stand.

(For the sake of continuity, I will repeat some of the content here that was offered in the preceding chapter so that this narrative flows in a more chronologically understandable manner.)

The justice system could be faulted for several flaws, failures, muddles and misfires in sentencing, though none are the fault of any one sector of this system.

a The statute of limitations does not apply to cases of rape but even in child abuse situations, a sexual crime that took place many years earlier can be prosecuted once a victim *begins to realize its impact* upon her. The record for such latencies in such a case involving a disclosure of which our clinic (The Sexual Abuse Clinic in Portland, OR) is aware was a crime which occurred almost half a century earlier.

The 40-year-old daughter of Earl, a 76-year-old retired carpenter with no prior criminal record, was in therapy when she related an incident which occurred when she was 13. She claimed that her stepfather had spied on her while she was showering by observing her through a sun-light window over her bathroom. Earl recalled the incident with shame and pled guilty to a single charge of *Voyeuring*. Although he received a sentence of a three-year probation, his family was aghast. At a family meeting soon after his admission of peeking at his daughter, his entire family rejected him as a sexual predator. They insisted he leave the Portland area, never to return. (He had to gain approval for moving to a different jurisdiction from his probation officer.) They ceased all

DOI: 10.4324/9781003532590-3

communications with him; his wife divorced him; he was excommunicated from the church he had attended for many years; has not seen any members of his family, including his children or grandchildren since the crime became known, even after his period of supervision has now ended.

b. There exists an imbalance in sexual abuse cases when compared to other crimes. Simply being accused of a sexual offense reverses the old saw that the accused is innocent until proven guilty. The accusation itself reverses the matter and it is on the shoulders of the subjects and their attorneys to prove innocence. It is not the job of the prosecution, judge or jury to find a sexual offender not guilty.

This places a huge burden on attorneys, who must plow through many documents, invest a great deal of time, listen to victims who, they realize in all honesty are probably telling the truth as they see it, and then have to face them, their families, and what is likely to be a hostile jury. The opprobrium of being labelled a sexual offender impels the man thus charged and his attorney to agree to a plea deal in order to avoid a public trial. This bias proves too powerful for most sexual offenders to risk leaving a decision in the hands of a jury or a judge.

This tendency is understandable for a number of reasons. For example, the average federal prison sentence (based on the US Sentencing Commission of the Federal Sentencing Statistics, Department of Justice (DOJ)) for manslaughter is 86 months; for kidnapping, 823 months; for deadly assault, 65 months; for drug trafficking, 78 months. However, the average sentence for any sexual crime is 227 months; and for accessing child pornography only (CPO), where no physical contact with a child had ever occurred CPO), it is 108 months, although more recently, minor CPO offenders have been given shorter jail terms or at times, only probation.

The only crimes receiving lengthier sentences exist for murder (231 months). Even money laundering, regardless of the amount involved, is just 69 months. Yet many money laundering crimes have cost victims millions of dollars. CP is a special case as this charge has increased over 200% over the past five years; this will be discussed in Chapter Six. What of voluntary manslaughter or vehicular homicide? Despite the horror and grief their perpetrators create, the average sentences are lower than that of a man convicted of molesting a child just once, exposing himself in public, or peeking into windows at night.

Moreover, a variety of penalties are meted out in different judicial districts which encompass wide levels of severity. There is no unanimity across county and state borders about the charges brought against similar crimes nor is there any federal guideline on sentencing except in federal courts. Most sexual offenses are adjudicated in state courts but those involving many internet crimes and extortion become federal matters as the internet crosses state boundaries.

c. No one wants to be seen as "soft" on sexual offenders. DAs are sometimes elected; politicians are always so. Being regarded as tough on crime is the narcotic to which these officials are addicted. Thus, sexual abuse cases are prosecuted with more vigor than most other offenses, many of which might have created more harm. Sex is still, in our so-called "enlightened age", equated, sometimes unconsciously, with being a taboo topic; a private matter not to be discussed in furtive conversations, except under specified circumstances; a concession to temptation; an act in which we engage at our most vulnerable moments; and at its most basic level, prurient, licentious, and even at times sinful except under the "correct" circumstances and within "proper bounds."

In the 21st century, we have come some way from the Draconian penalties meted out centuries ago. Nonetheless sexual activity may be among the last endeavor to be cleansed in the march toward a more liberal society. This is most manifest in a prison environment, where sexual offenders are considered the most vile of inmates, even below those who have committed murder.

d. The actual risk an offender poses to his community is only considered in a peripheral manner in sentencing. As therapists and scientific researchers, we can predict, with acceptable accuracy, the risk that any offender poses in recommitting a sexual crime (called recidivism). Yet our recommendations to DAs and courts are rarely taken into account when a plea arrangement is made or a court determines the actual sentence an offender receives. This represents an abdication not only of science but of morality. It is not that DAs or judges are prejudiced against sexual offenders; it is far worse: they simply do not care.
e. Sentencing guidelines are not within the exclusive province of the DAs or even the Attorney General of a state. They are promulgated by elected legislators; few campaigns emphasize criminal justice reform, even though in private, some lawmakers agree that the sentencing system is flawed. Such guidelines also, in many cases, remove the discretion we would ordinarily place in the hands of a judge, limiting the flexibility that would appear to be within the court's province. This is particularly significant in sexual crimes due to the vast differences in severity, consequences, and risks of re-offending amongst sexual offenders. Punishment of sexual offenders and their subsequent supervisory restrictions should not be based on idiosyncratic anecdote or even any one expert's experience but on the scientific literature, which is abundant, especially in judging risk.

Following a 2023 meta-analysis, The American Council on Criminal Justice has noted exactly what we find in assessing and treating sexual offenders: "People have not been shown to be deterred from any crime based upon the severity of punishment." The length of incarceration is not correlated to the presence or absence of a repeat for any particular crime.

Minimum and maximum allowable sentences, enacted by state legislators, often conflict with our scientifically determined assessment of actual risk. **Situational offenders** are most often at little to no risk of repeating their crime whereas **preferential or predatory offenders**, often pedophiles, are at higher risk. Yet the sentencing guidelines are not well-informed in these matters. Most therapists, who actually get to know an offender best as a human being who made a terrible mistake, believe sentences for situational sexual offenders are too harsh. Lengthier sentences are often assigned especially for those who are in positions of authority over children, such as youth pastors, teachers and child care workers.

Examples of **situational offenders** might include:

A 15-year-old boy who convinces his cousin, several years younger than him, to engage in sexual play on several occasions but uses no force nor threats to act on his urges.

An uncle whose 15-year-old niece is visiting and who then "accidentally" brushes up against her breasts.

A boyfriend moving in with a woman who has a seven-year-old daughter, who then molests her on a number of occasions but has had no other sexual victims.

An 18-year-old senior in high school having sexual activity with his 15-year-old girlfriend, a sophomore at the time. It is common for younger female adolescents to be attracted to older teen males. Chapter Six will discuss such "Romeo and Juliet" (R&J) cases. Several other states use the age of 16, in my opinion a more reasonable consideration of maturity. However, a three-year difference in their age makes this a crime by statute regardless of consent. Our State, Oregon, considers a teen under the age of 18 to be too young to provide informed consent. Across the Columbia River, Washington considers the age of consent to be 16, as does Montana, Nevada, and all the New England States. In all, 28 States have enacted ages of consent as 16 or even later; that is more than half of all states.

Males at a party who take advantage of an intoxicated female, too unaware of her condition to be able to provide knowledgeable consent; this is a situational offense only if this offender commits this act just once; a serial offender preying on vulnerable women would be considered predatory.

A man who attempts sexual activity with a disabled woman, handicapped either physically or intellectually, if she is judged to be unable to provide consent, if this is *not* a pattern of behavior.

A man communicating sexual content with a female under the age of consent via electronic means but who never makes physical contact with her.

A man who communicates with a "female minor" by electronic means but is actually the victim of a "sting" in which a detective is posing as the minor. If a meeting is arranged and the man arrives, he can be arrested, usually for *Luring* or *Communicating with a Minor for Illicit Purposes*. This offender would be considered a situational offender unless this proved to be a *pattern* of behavior. (Again, this issue of entrapment will be discussed in Chapters Six and Seven.)

A man caught urinating in a public park, even with no children present. (Yes, he would be considered by our antiquated laws as a sexual offender; it's best to hold it until you get home.)

A man who becomes bored with the usual adult pornography and wanders onto a child porn site, finds it exotic and different, but is not now, nor had ever been, attracted sexually to children.

As an example of a situational offense, consider the case of a man moving in with a female partner, the mother of an 11-year-old daughter. He did not raise her from birth but now they inhabit the same living quarters and she is maturing. As she develops secondary sexual characteristics such as breasts and wider more-defined hips, how many men might begin to notice her and even think about or fantasize about her in a sexual manner? We simply do not know. Such research has never been conducted and probably never will be as most men, even in anonymous surveys, will not answer truthfully. From my experience, that number is over 50% but it is not infinitesimal.

However, had these particular situations never occurred, for example if the boy in example 1 above had consenting sexual play and his cousin was one year younger; or the man in number 3 above moved in with a woman with no daughters; or the boyfriend in example number 4 above waited until his partner reached the age of 18; no crimes would have occurred. We consider these as situational offenders.

As an aside, it is important to note that in the main, such men are not *preferentially* attracted to teenage or prepubescent girls. We would not, nor could we, according to the *Diagnostic and Statistical Manual of the American Psychiatric Association, Fifth Edition* (DSM-V) diagnose any of such offenders as having a *paraphilia*. That would necessitate a prevailing arousal to, or a number of hands-on offenses against, an unwilling victim. But, if truth be known, the majority of adult males *are* sexually attracted to adolescent females who have developed secondary sexual characteristics. Studies utilizing the penile plethysmograph, admittedly not a perfect indicator, demonstrate that men with no history of sexual crimes show arousal to adolescent females.

This should not be surprising. When a man raises a girl from birth, a taboo occurs which prevents sexual arousal to that child. Evolution has ensured such inhibition in order to prevent matings within biological families, which also include siblings. These can frequently produce offspring with birth defects, especially within the second generation. For the sake of species' preservation, such a taboo exists in many higher primates, including *homo sapiens*, our own. It even extends to plants, which have evolved mechanisms to inhibit self-fertilizations as they carry both male and female organs within the same blossom.

There are a few men who molest their biological children, though the majority do so after long periods of separation, especially when they are absent from the family during the child's earliest years. Men who have sexual activity only with a child from infancy or only with a child whom they have adopted who was younger than 2 or 3, should be considered, in my opinion, to have committed *true incest*. Such men have broken the evolutionary taboo which prevents close relatives from engaging in intercourse as such unions can result in future fetal abnormalities. Men who have sexual activity after they enter into a child's life by co-habiting with a woman who has a child older than 2 or 3 might technically be charged with incest but must be differentially regarded as a child molester. These men should, in my opinion, not be charged with, or regarded as having committed, *incest*. The difference is of importance when considering treatment and sentencing. Such offenders may require more intensive and lengthier therapy than the former. Among men who have molested a biological child, fewer than 1% have been present throughout all of that youngster's formative years.

Aside from the typical situational cases described above, other offenses can be considered to have occurred only because a certain set of circumstances co-existed to cause criminal sexual behavior. Here are some examples.

> One evening, a mildly autistic 27-year-old man, Frank, still living with his parents, wandered into his step-sister's room while she was undressing. She had failed to lock the door. She screamed in anger at him and he tried to reassure her by touching her arm. The following morning, this 12-year-old girl disclosed to her parents what had occurred the night before. Their parents were both teachers at a school for disabled children and, as such, believed they were mandatory reporters. They subsequently reported the incident to the Department of Human Services (DHS) – Child Welfare Division, who made a cross report to the county sheriff's office. Detectives there conducted an investigation and reported their findings to the DA. A DDA brought an indictment charging Frank with one count of *Voyeuring* and one count of *Sexual Abuse in the Second Degree* (because he touched her). Fearful of the impact a trial would have upon him, he and his parents agreed to a plea deal

which included a 364-day jail term (any longer would have required prison) followed by a five-year period of probation. In jail, he was bullied due to his naiveté and designation as a sexual offender. After three months, he was found hanged in his cell. No mention of his autism was included in any official report.

George, 25 years of age and working as a technician at Intel, was hosting a party for family members from California. Everyone in attendance became intoxicated. George's 22-year-old female cousin began flirting with him and, in a mutual state of inebriation, they eventually had intercourse. All appeared to go well the following morning but when his cousin returned to California, she claimed he had raped her and that she had screamed during the assault. George, however, had filmed her initiating hugging him, smiling and engaging in some foreplay; in addition, no one in attendance heard her scream. Nonetheless, he is now being charged with *Rape*; the outcome is still uncertain as she has altered her story a bit and proceedings have been delayed due to the distance between the parties involved. The charge of *Rape* remains, however, and, if he is convicted or a plea deal is reached, his future will be permanently impaired, including his ability to work at the level to which he was trained, to live wherever and with whom he wishes and, for a time, he will likely be incarcerated. The case was initially brought three years ago and still its outcome is uncertain, leaving George in a state of constant severe anxiety, partially eased through therapy.

Although there may be some overlap, by and large, predatory and situational offender are as different than the sun is from the moon.

Situational offenders such as Frank are considered less dangerous than predatory offenders and generally receive lighter sentences; they also have better treatment outcomes than predatory offenders. Nonetheless, they will carry the stigma of being defined as a "sexual offender" and may have to register as such for the remainder of their lifetimes. They will, in the vast majority of cases, most certainly be forbidden to have their record expunged, that is, removed from official archives. It is the most unusual low-level sexual offenders who can ever hope to be blessed with expungement. Even a person committing homicide or a money laundering charge stands a better chance to gain erasure from official court and internet annals.

A similar situation faces a male high school teacher, the leader of a church youth group, or a camp counselor authorized to tutor junior counselors, many of whom may be in their later teenage years. How many men teaching a class with a number of attractive teen females would at least notice their faces and bodies? A rhetorical question at best as we lack data. But I would hazard a guess that, throughout a male teacher's career in even middle school as well as in high school, many men would have thought about a teen (male or female) in a sexual manner. He may even have masturbated with the girl's image in mind.

I realize this is not a comfortable subject but reality in sexual matters often brings about an uneasy feeling, uncomfortable even to contemplate and especially awkward to discuss. However, whatever the number of such men placed in a position of authority over teens, the vast majority have the self-control to never allow sexual attraction to lead to concrete action. They may also have been aware of what might occur should they have done so.

> At a church camp, Howard, 21 years of age at the time and a senior counselor there, was assigned to mentor a 16-year-old female junior counselor. They became close friends at first but a genuine mutual attraction soon developed. He was an accomplished artist and she asked him to draw a portrait of her. She suggested a partially nude picture, baring her breasts as she did so. Their relationship progressed to mutual fondling and, toward the end of summer, they made plans to meet at a local motel with the unspoken but clear intention of engaging in intercourse. Suspicious of their interactions over the past months, a camp leader notified police, who met Howard at the motel. At first denying any sexual intent, he later admitted to their relationship after detectives interviewed the tearful girl. On advice from his attorney and from our therapists, Howard accepted a plea agreement even though we thought it unduly harsh: a five-year prison sentence followed by five years of post-prison supervision (PPS). Of particular concern was Howard's history. From an upstanding family, he had excelled academically and was well on his way to a prestigious law school. He had always dreamed of becoming an attorney but, with this sexual charge, that life path will now be forever thwarted.

Prosecutors are particularly unsparing in cases in which an adult becomes involved with a youth over which he exerted some authority. Perhaps this is just, but in many such cases, these sentences appear to be overly harsh. Some justification for such severe penalties may be an acknowledgement that many men, such as teachers, are placed in similar situations and that rigorous punishment is necessary to prevent others from committing such crimes. Nonetheless, we consider such offenses to be situational in nature rather than predatory. Unfortunately, strict punishments have never been shown to affect the rate of any crime.

On the other hand, punishment can be anything but evenhanded, as shown in the following examples.

> Isabel, a high school teacher in Seattle, developed an attraction to a 15-year-old boy. In this nationally publicized case, this movie-star blonde, already married, engaged in an affair with the boy over a period exceeding one year. Their relationship became common knowledge, not surprising in a school environment. Of little surprise,

> multiple charges of *Sexual Abuse in the First Degree* were preferred against her. She had little choice but agree to a plea deal, including a prison term. What then occurred was both unexpected and almost unique in our experience with sentencing: the judge in the case threw out the deal and sentenced her to a period of five years of supervision, with no jail or prison time included. His reasoning might shock feminists of today: he opined that *she was simply too physically attractive* to be in a women's prison as she would be easy prey to other female inmates. Compare Howard's sentence with that of Isabel's to witness the yawning inequality and unpredictability with which the punishment phase of our judicial system is out of balance. In our opinion, one was unduly harsh, the other too lenient.

This case was followed with some interest in the national media. I was asked to evaluate Isabel and testify for the prosecution that, indeed, sexual abuse had occurred, though on cross examination, I had to admit that this was a situational offense and that she posed no real danger to the community. Its irony however was manifest. Once the teen reached the age of 16 (the age of consent in Washington State), he and Isabel, his former teacher, married and subsequently had two children. Unfortunately, their marriage ended in a divorce. In fact, the majority of unions between either an older man and a subordinate younger female or an older female and a subordinate younger male are eventually doomed to end in failure. To speculate on all the reasons why is beyond my capacity as no scientific study has investigated the fate of such relationships, but I suspect they begin on an uneven footing, although a multitude of other explanations are possible.

The facts of re -offending are well-known throughout the scientific community through years of research on recidivism and the assessment instruments employed to determine risk. Regardless of whether a sexual offender is guilty of a situational or predatory crime, the overall recidivism rate for *all* sexual offenders is relatively low at 13.4%. In comparison, the DOJ has estimated that the odds of any criminal re-offense, regardless of type of crime, can be quite a bit higher: 45% of men, incarcerated for any offense will re-commit either a similar crime or one of a different sort within six months to three years following release. In contrast, for situational offenders the chance of reoffending is quite low: based on a bevy of long-term studies in the psychology and legal literature, we estimate the risk, depending on type of offense, at 1% to 3%. For "Romeo and Juliet" (R&J), statutory crimes, those involving entrapment and for those who view child pornography but have never committed any hands-on crime, the risk approaches zero. (See Chapter Six for a more thorough discussion of these types of offenders and the bibliography for specific references.)

It should also be noted that the prepubescent and adolescent victims of sexual abuse were most often known to the offender. Hence, in many cases of situational offenders against young children, the crime is an intrafamilial one. Common examples include the perpetrator being a boyfriend living with a woman who has children, or an uncle who shows a sudden interest in one among several of his nieces as she matures.

Since the odds of any situational offender repeating a sexual offense are low, one would expect, upon sentencing, lesser time in prison. This is not always the case. For example, situational offenses with a low probability of recidivism, such as child pornography with no history of ever molesting a child, have been sentenced to an average of 102 months in prison as compared to men convicted of arson (78 months) or assault (66 months), illegal possession of firearms (48 months), money laundering (56 months), stalking (29 months), vehicular homicide (57 months), or drug distribution to children (27 months).

I would submit that these other crimes pose infinitely more risk to individuals and communities than men watching child porn. It is also more likely than not that a driver who is intoxicated is a much greater risk of harming himself and others than most situational sexual offenders. Yet a single DUII [Driving while Under the Influence of Intoxicants] offender is rarely imprisoned; indeed, most are let go (though minus their driving license) and the few who are repeat DUII offenders spend an average of seven days in jail (roughly the shelf life of a cabbage), before being mandated into a substance abuse program.

Predatory offenders, sometimes referred to as **Preferential offenders**, on the other hand, have *patterns* of sexual misbehaviors that, with even more certainty, can create excruciating and persistent anguish and which may affect multiple victims. These are cases in which apparent affection turns into deception. Examples of such cases include the following.

a Heterosexual pedophiles: To qualify as a pedophile, a man must have a *pattern* of molesting girls under the age of 13 or be proven, usually by a plethysmograph test, to be aroused to stimuli featuring sexual activity with such girls. This latter is of interest in that this diagnosis can be made for a person who has never committed a crime, though this would be rare. A predatory offender in this category often will "groom" a young girl, providing gifts and attention. He may lure a young girl into his home, show her pornography, and slowly progress to innocent touching and hugs, but will eventually progress to fondling her genital areas.

Most horrific, he may even attempt intercourse. In the main, the victims in such cases do not know what is happening or may attempt to fight the offender off, but they are rarely successful; if force is required, the pedophile may not hesitate to employ it. Most often, he will warn his victim not to tell, that "it's our secret," or she or he will get into trouble if others become aware of their sexual activity. Since the odds of a situational offender committing a new sexual crime are low, one would expect, upon sentencing, lesser time in prison than that given to predatory offenders. This is not always the case. For example, child pornography-only offenders (CPO) have been sentenced to an average of 102 months in prison (although this is now being reduced) as compared to men convicted of arson (78 months) or assault (90 months).

Homosexual pedophiles: These men are either gay or bisexual, but many live quite ordinary lives, often with females who are unaware of their partners' sexual desires. Many such offenders prefer boys but can have sexual relations with women as well. A minority never engage in long-term relationships. The majority of such offenders prey upon boys, especially vulnerable ones or those with unsatisfactory relationships with their parents. They attempt to befriend them, may isolate one or several boys, buy them special gifts or encourage them to distance themselves from their parents so that they may appear to be more supportive, becoming a special confidante in whom they can trust. This process is known in the field as "grooming".

> James, a 47-year-old divorced construction manager, had always preferred the company of boys 6–9-years of age. He volunteered at youth camps, and clubs, selecting certain boys as "special." He would befriend them, ask them about their home lives, and eventually turn the topic to sexual activity. He would teach them about masturbation as a "healthy" practice, then show them pornography. He might well also get to know their families to obtain their trust, then suggest special trips for camping or to amusement parks. His habit was to fondle the boys' genitals as he was teaching them about masturbation, but at times he would also commit fellatio on them. Although he told the boys the sexual activity was "their secret." one of the boys, growing older and no longer of sexual interest to the offender, reported his sexual behaviors to authorities. He was charged with multiple counts of *Sexual Abuse in the First Degree* and received a penalty of 20 years in prison, where he remains to this day.

Pedophiles who molest boys have been among the more difficult to treat offenders, although with modern techniques as further described in Chapter Five, the majority of such offenders (in our studies, about 70%) who have completed a certified sexual offender-specific treatment program will not repeat their sexual crimes. An interesting case had been made decades ago for the supposed legitimacy of men having sexual relations with boys. Indeed, a national association of such pedophiles was formed as a valid nonprofit organization: the Man–Boy Love Association (MBLA) was based on the notion not only that the government should not criminalize positive emotions such as love, but that, of even more importance, the boys being lured into a sexual relationship with an adult male could result in positive effects on that child.

I had the opportunity of interviewing its leader and found him to be sensitive, well-informed, intelligent (not the same thing), and sincere. He identified numerous purported benefits a boy might gain through a "loving relationship" with an older mature male adult, including companionship, positive modeling, affection, sexual education, and even nurturance.

However, although he could cite several examples of boys molested in their prepubescent and teen years, he could not believe that so many such boys, either during or following their sexual activity with adults, suffered ill effects, including guilt, shame, and PTSD-like symptoms. Reports of such, he claimed, were "politically motivated," despite my attempting to acquaint him with the research literature on the subject. I testified for the prosecution in his San Francisco trial, at which he was found guilty of multiple counts of *Sexual Abuse in the First Degree* and sentenced to 30 years in prison, where he passed away several years later.

The man–boy problem was brought into harsh light in the 1980s and the decades following when priests were discovered to have molested thousands of boys. The continued suffering of these victims and their bravery in finally coming forward garnered national attention about the harm such sexual relations can create in their aftermath. MBLA disintegrated thereafter, split into small local and very private groupings. We have not discovered any well-organized remnants of it on the West Coast during the present century but they may well be active, though quite fragmented and secretive, abandoning their efforts to normalize such pedophilic activities.

Make no mistake: these men are a danger to their communities and many should be prevented from living outside of a residential setting, including prison. Even following release and even after reaching old age, they must be monitored closely and never allowed to be alone with any child regardless of their gender; several homosexual pedophiles have been demonstrated to be attracted to prepubescent girls as well.

By the way, despite the common belief that sexual offenders are marked for physical abuse in prison, in fact, many are placed in special units for such prisoners and are relatively well-protected, if not actually treated. A host of in-prison treatment programs gave way to fiscal restraints in the 1990s and it is rare to find, in jails or prisons today, an actual treatment program utilizing the modern methods of reducing recidivism in use in modern times.

b Serial rapists:

> Long diagnosed with schizophrenia, Kevin would follow women walking alone in parks or on jogging trails in the Seattle area. He disparaged women, delighted in humiliating them, and would not only often urinate on them after completing a rape, but on several occasions, he would choke them in such a savage and unrelenting manner that they

died of asphyxiation. He rarely took his medications but even when receiving them by intravenous injection, he would fail to keep his appointments and thus essentially remained unmedicated for months at a time. Thus his rapes continued. When I evaluated him, he was surprisingly honest, saying he would probably continue to rape if he were to be released into the community. At his trial, I recommended commitment to a mental institution for life, even though, were he to live beyond 80, his likelihood of completing a rape would be diminished. Still, we have encountered several men who have committed rapes in their eighties. He remains in a Washington State Psychiatric Facility to this day, 36 years after his case was adjudicated. I am hopeful that he will never be released.

Serial rapists are less common than the streaming media or movies would make it appear. But they do exist, especially in high-density urban settings. Some will break into homes, others await joggers in a park, but most will use some measure of force to compel compliance. These men are dangerous, particularly if they have bonded aggression with sexual arousal. Some of these offenders are not only preferential rapists, they are obligatory ones as well. For such culprits, it is the *violence* that is as sexually satisfying as the sexual acts themselves. They may fantasize torturing a woman and become aroused simply by instilling that look of fear in the eyes of their victims.

Unfortunately, this is one group in which treatment techniques have been less effective. Nonetheless, approximately 72% of serial rapists who have completed a scientifically based treatment program do not re-offend. However, this is a selected group as they have been discharged from prison and are under severe restrictions about their whereabouts. In egregious cases, such as a man who has inextricably bound arousal to aggression, we almost always recommend long-term incarceration.

Lawrence, 37 at the time of his apprehension, had admitted to over 20 rapes. These were not, however, simple sexual acts forced upon his victims. At the same time, he was raping them, he would also be dissecting them as would a first-year medical student, except they were alive throughout much of this ordeal. I cannot to this day, erase the memory of drawings he made and, with pride, displayed for all in court to see: Women with their bowels hanging out, others hung like a side of beef, preparing to be sliced. He fortunately remains in a mental facility near Seattle, from which we are certain he will never be released.

Such an example is not pleasant to contemplate but it is sometimes necessary for us clinicians to be aware of such evil, and for all within the criminal justice system to realize such men should never be set free. Still, the conditions under which many are held are abominable: a number of them are placed in solitary confinement for long periods of time, ostensibly for their own safety. Yet, as noted above, most sexual offenders are not subject to physical violence absent any sexual component. Instead, such long-term prisoners may never see the sun again; for them, there is but a single season: A cold, dark winter without the prospect of receiving treatment which might render them less dangerous, especially as they advance into their graying years. Many people believe this is what they deserve, and the examples above fit into this category, though they are but a slim minority amongst all sexual offenders. In selected cases, however, I don't think, regardless of past crimes, most human beings do.

It is unfortunate that the current DSM-V neglected the request of several clinicians treating sexual offenders across a variety of national settings to include a separate category for men attracted to violence alone. This manual also omits men who are hypersexual. These latter frequently get into trouble approaching women whom they do not know well with lewd suggestions or inappropriate touching. They may have experienced difficulty maintaining employment by accessing porn at work. They commonly spend increasing time watching porn at home instead of attending to their tasks. Troubles are frequent in their relationships with partners and cheating in such relationships is common. Some of these men find themselves in trouble with the law as more and more women, especially in the work environment, call them out to managers. Treatment is usually successful and many of these men seek it on their own. Further discussion of this phenomenon is discussed in Chapter Six.

d. Hebephiles: This term is used to differentiate men who prey upon teens, usually adolescents, from pedophiles who prey upon children younger than 13 (*Hebe* is the Greek root for youth). In such cases, hebephiles are more often attracted to teen boys rather than girls. It is of value to distinguish these men from pedophiles as their predatory patterns can be different than men who prefer children younger than teens. They more often befriend a family, take adolescent boys on trips, buy them presents, drugs and alcohol and pretend to select boys who are having troubles at home. They often select boys who are vulnerable and who may enjoy the attention of men who appear to serve as a supportive friend as opposed to strict or harsh parental figures.

The form of a treatment program is similar to that used with pedophiles but results are a bit less effective. In our series, hebephiles following completion of a treatment program have a 65% success rate over a follow-up period of 20 years. During that time period, 35% of such offenders will commit another sexual crime, requiring a cry for additional and novel treatment techniques.

e. Exhibitionists. While a few men either masturbate in their cars or urinate in public by necessity, men who habitually expose their genitals, usually an erect penis, to women are often thought to be harmless pests and often the butt of jokes. But to certain female victims, the act itself is traumatic and not a few (we lack studies of percentages here) experience fears of going out alone, frequenting parks, using jogging or hiking trails, experience trouble with sexual relationships, have difficulty sleeping, suffer with nightmares and general anxiety; these are all potential symptoms of PTSD. For them, being exposed to is not a laughing matter.

For most such men who only occasionally expose, long prison sentences make little sense, nor does the treatment literature support extended periods of incarceration. Most such exhibitionists are generally reserved, non-aggressive and lonely men who may lack the social skills to initiate contact with appropriate females even for routine purposes, such as introductions, questions about work, or asking permission to sit near them on a bus. This, however, does not describe all men who expose themselves. We lack knowledge, and research reports attempting to explain exhibitionism, although lofty theories about lack of attachments at early ages have often been posited in the literature, absent any actual research. Fortunately, most such men (in our studies, about 89%) will not expose again after successfully graduating from a sexual offender treatment program.

f. Serial voyeurs: Men who habitually spy on women can do so in a variety of ways: some sneak about in yards at night but this proves to be a false stereotype. These days, we find more voyeurs employing hidden cameras, now available in such miniaturized form as to be easily hidden in girls' locker rooms or in the bedrooms or bathrooms of friends or roommates with daughters. No longer are drilled holes as common as in the past when you can now purchase a camera as small as a pen.Michael worked as a manager of a construction company. Being familiar with home-building he managed to specify skylights over bedrooms and bathrooms in several residences. He had advanced knowledge that these were ones already purchased by young married women or older families with adolescent teen females. After a family had moved in he would climb up to these roofs, often at night, and peer into those rooms hoping to catch a glimpse of females in states of undress or engaged in sexual activity. If discovered, he would offer the pretense that he was merely "inspecting the roof for defects." Although we recognized that this was a preferential problem which had been ongoing for a number of years, prosecutors offered a plea deal of just three years of probation, yet no treatment was mandated. Following his period of supervision, Michael soon resumed his peeking behavior, though this time he would steal

> about neighborhoods at night to find windows unblinded, again in the hopes of viewing sexual scenes. He is now serving five years in a federal penitentiary as he engaged in voyeuring in several adjoining states.

Such simple taxonomic divisions cannot hope to neatly categorize every sexual offender. Although about 90% of such offenders remain true to form, others are not so sharply subdivided.

> Now 76 years of age, Norman was recently accused of molesting his step granddaughter Heidi. He would groom her first by inviting her, but not her brother, to the movies or the zoo, buying her gifts and showering her with attention. He would babysit for the family and, on several occasions, would isolate nine-year-old Heidi by pretending to "tuck her in at night"; such "tuck-ins" consisted initially of inspecting her genital area by making her pull down her underwear, then rubbing her vaginal area. He told her this was "our secret" but, if she told, he might have to go to prison and, because he was so old and had a weak heart, he would die and it would be on her conscience forever. Brave Heidi summoned the courage to tell her parents about the molestations in front of him on a subsequent visit and in a family meeting but Norman denied all, pretending she had dreamt these fantasies. It was then that Norman's grandniece Lori, 12 at the time and in attendance, jumped up and forcibly confronted Norman, proclaiming "I know you did it because you did the same thing to me." Although quiet at the time, Norman's own stepdaughter then realized she also should have had the strength to disclose her own sexual abuse at Norman's hands years before. Because this represented a pattern, we would classify Norman as a heterosexual pedophile. Following a five-year term in federal prison, Norman is now on post-prison supervision and enrolled in both individual and group therapy.

In addition, cases are encountered in which an offender molests both girls and boys, or exposes to children of both genders. These represent, in our extensive experience, rare exceptions. The majority of sexual offenders adhere to a single pattern of behavior (despite one and only one report that found diversity in victims in a subset of offenders). The vast majority of sexual offenders are habitual, even compulsive, in preferring their type of victims and are aroused by a single category of victim, although mixtures occur, particularly men who are aroused by aggression alone and also molest young girls. For the purposes of this text, these are sufficiently unusual as to not overly complicate the narrative. Punishment, many believe, should fit the nature of the crime but it should also fit the offender himself and his history. Were the criminal acts repetitive? How many victims have been affected? How heinous or forceful were the details?

We must therefore learn well the offender's history. Has he committed other types of crimes and were these sexual or nonsexual in nature? Did substance abuse play a role in the crime? Does he have a history of ongoing substance abuse? How stable has his employment been? Does he have a history of durable relationships? Is there any history of domestic violence? Is he a loner or does he maintain a group of close friendships and, if so, are his friends law-abiding or of criminal bent? These factors are of importance to know as they have been demonstrated to play a role in whether or not the offender poses a high or low risk of re-offending.

From the perspective of sexual abuse cases, we would like to learn 1) the probability that the offender will repeat this crime, and 2) can he be treated so that this likelihood is markedly reduced? The answers to these questions bear directly on the offender's danger to be at large and his amenability to treatment, as amply demonstrated in the scientific literature. Yet these historical factors are rarely taken into account when a plea deal is arranged or a sentence determined. Nonetheless, the rate of recidivism for sexual offenses is a measurable quantity and the subject of extensive research, which is being studied even more intensively than ever before. Unfortunately, the criminal justice system most often fails to take such factors into consideration when meting out punishments.

We can, at present, and with excellent accuracy learn what type of offender we are dealing with and gauge their likelihood of reoffending (but not with 100% certainty). However, to be honest, we have no single test, physical or psychological, that can reliably diagnose sexual preferences or arousal. The assessment instruments in current use, such as the *STATIC-99R* and the *STABLE-2007R*, employ historical factors, such as number and types of past sexual offenses and stability of personality types, such as antisocial or avoidant lifestyles. These often, but not always, correlate to a diagnosis or likelihood of committing future sexual crimes. Combined with other historical factors and with measurements, as described in Chapter Five, we are becoming increasingly confident we can reach a conclusion about the likelihood of an offender repeating a sexual crime.

The most recent validity and reliability of risk for the *STATIC-99* comes from a number of studies carried out since 2020, as for example a large 2023 study from Carleton University in Ottawa. This research merely repeats over 25 studies of similar structure since 2009. The *STABLE-2007* has a similar record of over 30 such studies in the literature. This latter test claims to concentrate on factors which are changeable or "dynamic." It is difficult, however, to alter many of the factors included in the *STABLE-2007*, such as ability to lead a reliable and responsible lifestyle, maintain employment, accept women in roles of authority, and enjoy trouble-free relationships. Moreover, these elements are as predictable for antisocial behavior as they are for sexual offending. Indeed, many sexual offenders hold highly responsible jobs and have satisfactory and stable social commitments.

Nonetheless, these instruments in combination with physiological tests, as described on p.00, have proven of significant value in accurately estimating the risk that an offender will commit a similar crime in the future. History informs: a situational offender is unlikely to recidivate; a preferential one, without treatment, most often will. And treatment is much more effective than the received wisdom that once a sexual offender, always a sexual offender. Chapter Five will, in brief, describe treatment methods, although their technical aspects and the research documenting their efficacy must be sought by those interested, in references in the Annotated Bibliography.

Therefore, many therapists in this field try to determine whether a man has a condition termed a paraphilia: an habitual persistent preference for deviant behavior. Clearly, this fits the man who grooms prepubescent girls or boys (or both), rapes repeatedly, exposes in public or commits voyeurism on a repeated basis. It might also include a man who has a fetish for leather or bondage but only if, in the pursuit of those behaviors, he creates a victim, or these attractions interfere with his responsibilities, or cause him or others distress. The issue of consent is the crucial variable in most of such latter cases.

Throughout the years attempts have been made to measure, in a physiological sense, whether a man is sexually attracted to children, here defined as prepubescent and lacking secondary sexual characteristics, typically under the age of 13. Most of those working in this field, such as psychologists, social workers, or other clinical therapists, are keen to demonstrate a bona fide physical test so as to place their assessment and treatment techniques within a legitimate scientific framework. These have included the polygraph ("lie detector"), penile plethysmograph, viewing time tests, and distraction tests. Fortunately, all have proven helpful but only when combined with historical factors correlated to an offender's actual *pattern* of offending. There remain gaps, fortunately small, which only future research can fill.

The *polygraph* has been proven, in a number of well-documented scientifically sound studies to accurately measure anxiety but little else, especially the ability to distinguish truth from deceit. One can go online to learn interesting techniques to defeat the polygraph's instruments, which measure heart rate, blood pressure, skin conductance, and respiratory rate. But that is hardly necessary. The studies soundly defy the premise that a lie can be detected by measuring anxiety; indeed, often the opposite is true. Nonetheless, while clinicians only rarely employ the polygraph to determine much of anything, supervising officers are religious acolytes of the procedure and utilize it often. Men on parole or probation are scrutinized by this instrument repeatedly once released, then every six months thereafter throughout their period of supervision, no matter its duration. It is costly to offenders but is employed so frequently that it has made millionaires of many polygraphers.

There are three types of polygraphs. The first is known as a single-issue test in which a specific question is asked regarding the crime itself. A full-disclosure polygraph seeks a full sexual history in order to determine (to the extent to which the test is capable) whether the subject has committed other crimes, especially of a sexual nature, of which we were previously unaware. A third type of polygraph is a maintenance test, usually ordered by the supervising officer to determine whether the offender on probation or post-prison supervision has committed a crime or violated his conditions of supervision.

A single-issue polygraph is often demanded even before conviction, often by the defendant's attorney to "demonstrate" that the client is being honest about a charge. A maintenance polygraph is often required of the offender by his supervising officer every six months during the course of supervision.

Woe to the anxious but honest client. The cost, mostly borne by the accused or convicted, can be $400 for a specific-issue polygraph or maintenance polygraph (which takes about ½ to ¾ hour), in which a supervisor is interested in a particular set of actions. The purpose of a full-disclosure test (about one hour) is undertaken to determine whther the offender has *ever* committed crimes, and this will cost $500. The burden of payment for these tests lies, in the main, with the offender. In summary, clinicians, by and large, do not lend much credence to the polygraph. It is an instrument designed to determine not much of anything except that the client is nervous when taking the test, especially so when crucial questions are asked.

In the opinion of most professionals in this field, and relying on the preponderance of scientific research, this test does not, in many cases, distinguish between a deception and the truth. Nonetheless, we employ it for a different and valuable purpose: we tell the offender in advance that a polygraph is scheduled for a certain time and that now would be the best time to let us know the full extent of his sexual offending, not only in the present crime but anything else he has omitted in the past. We are constantly surprised about the amount of additional information this has yielded and therefrom, how treatment should be tailored to everything we can know about this particular offender.

The first and most informative test employed to determine arousal is the hard-to-pronounce plethysmograph. This test requires the patient to place a flexible ring around the shaft of his penis, then view scenes on a screen of various sexual activity to determine if blood flow increases to his penis, thus increasing its diameter. The clinician conducting the test remains out of view of the client, thus hopefully reducing embarrassment. It is employed in only a few clinics as it is cumbersome, intrusive, expensive and induces shame and discomfort. Nonetheless, it is still the test which can provide the most valid results of sexual arousal, if positive. Conducted in an artificial laboratory setting, however, as might be expected, false negatives are common.

The plethysmograph has largely been replaced by viewing time tests (VT), the most common being the *Abel Assessment* or *viewing time test*. In contrast to the plethysmograph, a viewing time test measures interest rather than arousal. In this test the dependent variable is the amount of time a man views photos of children as opposed to the time he views photos of adults.

All such photos depict frontal views of individuals in clothes, though some are in underwear or bathing suits; none are engaged in any sexual activity.

VT Tests covertly measure, to the millisecond, the amount of time the alleged offender spends viewing each photograph on a computer screen before clicking to proceed to the next photo. They have largely replaced the plethysmograph in most clinics as they are easy to administer, especially since a computer does most of the heavy lifting. However, many people not particularly aroused by children might be influenced by factors other than sexual interest and thus spend more time viewing children for a variety of nonsexual reasons: children gain our attention as cuter, more colorfully dressed, and are usually more active than adults. In reality, although a few studies have indicated that *VT Tests* are weakly predictive of actual sexual interest and can predict recidivism, those studies have been, in the main, carried out by authors in the same laboratory aligned with the test's manufacturer.

Therefore, it is not surprising that a number of studies have raised questions about *viewing time tests* as to their predictive accuracy in identifying any pattern of arousal or being predictive of sexual offense recidivism. In our experience, combined with the opinions and data provided by several large clinics nationwide (Portland, Seattle, Phoenix, etc.), they have not proven of value. In addition, most offenders already are aware of the test's purpose and quickly go through the photos in a routine manner, rarely lingering on photos of children, especially if they had offended against children. Therefore, the test is a bit too transparent to render any determination of actual arousal to children. At best, it can serve to demonstrate *interest*, which is not equivalent to *arousal*. It also lacks any validity in cases of men accused of crimes against postpubescent females, such as rape, hebephilia, exhibitionism, or voyeurism. In truth, both the plethysmograph and the viewing time tests have too many false negatives to be of utmost significance regarding clinical or predictive value.

Another viewing time test has been mooted. This would time *microsaccades*. These are tiny eye movements which occur in microseconds and of which we are unaware. Our pupils are in constant motion; were they not, we would never be able to focus on a single object. This somewhat counterintuitive finding, replicated in a variety of studies at Arizona State and Harvard Universities, formed the basis of a proposal we made in a grant for a research project to the National Institutes of Health. We proposed to measure pupillary fixation in photos of both adults and children, or of aggressive and nonaggressive scenes of sexual activity, thus effecting comparisons. We were not surprised at its rejection; the NIH has greater priorities, such as heart disease, cancer, and major psychiatric illnesses than to be bothered funding any research on sexual offenders. This is a pity given that victims of sexual abuse may suffer from as much agony as those afflicted by many other well-funded medical conditions.

It would be of major benefit if the current interest in functional MRI scans and PET scans could isolate brain areas which signify sexual arousal. In fact, researchers at John Hopkins Medical School, amongst several others, have indicated that PET scans showed increased activity in the limbic area of the central nervous system, which they believed correlated with sexual arousal. However, when approached in an attempt to interest them in further research, they demurred. The issue of sexual abuse and the work with sexual offenders may well prove unpalatable to governmental and academic scientists but we can always hope for future research in this neglected area, especially now that intra-brain recording techniques are becoming less intrusive. This, of course gives rise to ethical questions of mind-reading, but in my opinion, such probes would be worthwhile as determining true sexual arousal which might harm victims or exonerate the innocent; I believe these would be well worth further exploration.

A more recent development has employed *distraction techniques* in an attempt to discover sexual arousal. These tests measure the time it takes (the latency) for a person to note, on a computer screen, characteristics of a stimulus while a distractive stimulus is simultaneously displayed. For example, a screen displaying a young girl or an adult female might be paired with a color, such as orange, but the pairing is very brief, in milliseconds. The person tested would then have to identify the color briefly presented. The theory is that a pedophile would be distracted longer by the photo of a young girl than would a non-pedophile. Therefore, latency times to correctly identify the color would take a more extended period of time and contain more errors.

Such tests are based upon the same premise of a viewing time test: that a sexually deviant individual would fixate on a deviant stimulus for a longer period of time than would a non-offender and hence be distracted to the extent he would take longer to identify the alternate stimulus and make more errors when he did. However, many non-offenders prefer to view children for reasons other than sexual interest, such as that children are in general more interesting to observe, more active, dressed in a more colorful fashion, etc.

A more sophisticated *distraction test* has recently been tested and reported in the literature from Switzerland. It also displays computer-generated photos comparing, for example, a man and a woman, though it could be extended to include children in the future. However, this assessment adds a measure of physiology, in an attempt to render it more "scientific." A central nervous system (CNS) measure has been tentatively identified as associated with sexual arousal: *event-related brain potentials (ERPs) on an EEG*. Studies, not yet widely replicated, have measured enhanced ERPs in men secondary to exposure to sexually explicit stimuli.

In a recent study, two photographs each, one of a naked and a clothed man and another of a naked and fully dressed woman have been used side-by side, with a dot placed around various axes in between these images. The test consists of measuring how long it takes the person tested to subsequently correctly identify the exact location of the dot.

It is called the *dot-probe test*, at least for now. Groups of 40 heterosexual and 40 gay men were tested while their EEGs were measured simultaneously. Results confirmed, though not in a robust fashion, that it took longer (in milliseconds), for heterosexual men to correctly identify the exact location of the dot when a picture of a naked woman was present and this correlated with higher ERPs on the EEG. The same was demonstrated with homosexual men when a photo of a naked man was presented.

Intra-brain electrodes have recently demonstrated sexual drive correlated to certain CNS areas that appear to enhance sexual arousal; unfortunately, such methods are in the preliminary phase of human testing (Phase III) with special emergency exceptions and approval from the Federal Drug Administration for use in egregious cases of suicidal patients who have failed to improve with medications and electroconvulsive therapy. As is typical in such studies, sexual offenders have not been targeted, though these techniques, albeit intrusive, have demonstrated excellent and long-lasting positive results in eliminating major depressive disorder with minimal side-effects.

Such studies, unfortunately, have not yet been employed with sexual offenders. One problem is that the apparatus and specialists necessary are expensive and require a laboratory setting. Funds will not be forthcoming from governmental resources so an academic setting is required, but researchers do not see studies of sexual offenders as much of a priority.

In addition, more significant problems exist.

- Pornographic images are available for adults but, in the US, we cannot legally obtain any representation of a naked child (minus babies). We have repeatedly requested reassurances from a wide variety of district attorney's offices and attorneys general that a drawing or a photoshopped image be utilized but they have been adamant that even drawings to be used solely for research purposes would be prosecuted as child porn. The DAs would probably delight in accusing a treatment provider of accessing child porn should we attempt such tests.
- The correlation between ERPs and sexual arousal has not been firmly established; direct visualization of limbic areas for event-related potentials would be helpful but would require more extensive funding than we have, as yet, been able to obtain.
- No study, to date, has employed pornographic images with sexual offenders in distraction tests.

Nevertheless, to summarize: our ability to identify recidivism risk, employing present tests such as a combination of the *STATIC-99* and the *STABLE-2007*, along with VTs and the individual's history, have proven more than adequate to predict the risk of re-offending in sexual offenders. Therefore, while it would be more satisfying to have a physiological test to verify risk, such an expensive assessment is unlikely to be achieved in the near future due to lack of funds. At any rate, it might merely provide a pseudo-scientific veneer in verifying what we already can achieve with the standard psychological tests already mentioned.

Because we can reliably predict risk through history and testing, such scientific findings ought to be taken into account in sentencing decisions, especially if the issue is the deprivation of a man's liberty to remain at large. Unfortunately, the science is ignored and emotions over-rule decisions that will impact an individual human being, and his family, for the remainder of his lifetime.

In this chapter on punishment, we should also examine the conditions of incarceration. Both prison and county jails were constructed to be inhospitable. Rough-hewn and monochromatic, they cast a gray atmosphere, almost a pall of noxious inhabitants, not limited to inmates but to the guards as well, often dull-eyed and rarely supportive. Isolation is not all-encompassing except in solitary confinement, yet much time is still spent caged in cells, the antithesis of optimism, fresh air and sunlight. Studies show that it is just such an environment that may actually promote antisocial behavior. The lack of anything approximating enjoyment is sadly absent while many prisoners endure the stench of criminality, gloom, and, in some cases, ultimately death.

Moreover, incarceration may result in lifelong stigma, decreased opportunities for family reconciliation, difficulty finding housing and employment after release, and difficulties in reintegration into the community. It also evokes social isolation, and exposes the sexual offender to harassment at best or physical aggression at worst. Developmental and life course criminological research stress the value of meaningful social relationships, while the absence of such affiliations in punitive deprived circumstances may be related to repeat offending and result in dynamic risk factors that have been linked to the maintenance of sexual offending.

There are other problems with incarceration, especially in prisons. Despite the reduction over the past three decades in violent crimes (approximately 25% across national studies), prison populations have soared and new prisons seem somehow always to be financed, accompanied by the cheerleaders of such institutions. A 2019 report by the Department of Justice's Inspector General described many federal prisons as having abominable conditions, such as:

A crumbling infrastructure

The lack of adequate sanitation

Overcrowding

The absence of appropriate temperature adjustments

The disturbing presence of mice, rats, and insects

Inadequate medical facilities and the lack of qualified professional staff to administer necessary care

Several studies emphasize the relationship between inadequate cooling in summer, rising temperatures and aggression among inmates.

There exist intermediate steps in assigning sexual offenders to penal institutions. One step below a prison is what could be termed a "Correctional Institution." The Oregon State Correctional Institution is one example. It first is constructed with less brutal architecture, both in its external appearance and in providing more space per individual prisoner. Inmates are allowed to roam about in larger open communal spaces, for watching TV, socializing, and eating. Many inmates are allowed greater freedom, such as gardening and even visits for family gatherings such as funerals, after demonstrating good behavior over a long period of time. Such institutions also offer a greater of choice of work opportunities for inmates and they often provide more outdoor time for recreation.

Of course, these facilities are provided for those who have committed less severe crimes and often those who do not have a long criminal history. Unfortiunately, sexual offenders, regardless of risk and recommendations from specialists, rarely are allowed entry as the majority, even of low risk, such as child porn-only offenders, are almost automatically barred from these more tolerable institutions.

However, many sexual offenders are often housed in specialized areas in prisons and even jails where space and prison populations allow. This is based upon the concerns that such offenders might be singled out for mental and physical abuse once the nature of their crimes becomes known – and it is almost always discovered by guards and fellow prisoners. Such specialized units often offer greater freedom than the more severe state and federal prisons; unfortunately, they only infrequently, if at all, offer any specialized treatment for these inmates.

A handful of sexual offenders who are imprisoned are granted brief sentences if their crimes indicate low risk and they lack any other history of criminality. Occasionally, they are considered for shorter sentences if they confess that they did commit a sexual crime, although it is a minority of such individuals who confess to everything victims allege actually occurred. They may also be sent to a specialized half-way house, usually for a 6 to-12-month period. Most are under strict supervision during that period, but this does allow them to leave for medical and attorney appointments and, if obtained, attendance at a community college or employment. They are generally allowed access to electronics but only for work or education.

Even so, overcrowding is almost universal in all such units across the country, both in state and federal institutions. This can even expose the public to a dangerous offender being on a wait list and allowed to be in the public until a space opens. Of recent reviews (2023), Great Britan's Ministry of Justice has noted its prison population has achieved "an all-time high." In our country, many states report there are prisons constructed to house 1,000 inmates but whose actual population now exceeds 1,900 individuals. This not only creates unhealthy crowding and gang formation, it places pressure on the administrators and guards of such packed institutions. As a result, there is insufficient staff to monitor illegal activity and to oversee prisoners in work or recreational activities.

As a result, inmates can spend up to 22 hours each day locked in their cells. According to a report by the Howard League for Penal Reform, by the end of 2023, the number of individuals in prisons has risen by 24%. They recommend reducing sentences for low-level offenders, a definition which would apply to a majority of sexual offenders. As noted before, community-based sentences result in less recidivism and lower expense. One flaw in such a scheme, however, would necessitate a greater burden on supervisory personnel and guards, already in short supply. One must only look at the compensation these officers endure to understand why there exists, across the Western world, a lack of applicants for such positions.

It is estimated, however, that increasing the pay of such officers and prison guards could result in better overall supervision; this in turn might lead to a lower incidence of institutional crime and brutality, mitigate the power of prison gangs, and allow for a reduction of recidivism. There is scant evidence that inmates spending more time in their cells has any effect on lowering the rate of all crimes in general. This would especially apply to low-level sexual offenders. But politics plays a powerful part in determining sentencing guidelines. And politicians appear enamored of promoting building even more prisons; they may appear modern on the outside but these are mere cosmetic changes as conduct, whether a prison built a century ago or a week ago, remains a dungeon not even fit for an animal. I have never found any politician, from the county, state, and federal levels, who would promote the reforms needed to reduce overcrowding in prisons, except for building more of them.

But shuttering prisons is politically unpopular as they provide employment for locals and provide a (false) sense of security. In many federal cases, the prison to which an offender is assigned is located at a considerable distance from his home, rendering family visitations prohibitive. Partly this may be due to availability of space within any one institution. While the general public may believe sexual offenders do not deserve better, a recent study found that visits from family reduced subsequent recidivism. But it is possible that being closer to home in some fashion lowers the odds an offender will repeat his crimes.

The international figures underscore this to an even greater extent. Nations with lesser penalties, such as Sweden and Denmark, actually have a lower incidence of sexual crimes than those with a stricter set of punishments, such as Hungary or Kenya. Of course, many other variables confound such simple comparisons. The nature of populations and the conduct of a nation's judicial system all may contribute to such comparisons. Yet statistics, which can be manipulated (North Korea claims to have *no* sexual offenders) can also enlighten. The strictest of punishments fail to deter the most dangerous of offenders.

It remains a paradox that, in America, the exponential increase in construction of new prisons, which always elicits the voters' delight, has been accompanied by a decreasing incidence of most crimes, including sexual ones (with the exception of child pornography and entrapment). Our government, which has stressed liberty as an inalienable right, feels little compunction in limiting it, regardless of the danger any individual may pose. In 2024 the DOJ reported that there are over 2,200,000 individuals incarcerated in the United States, the highest *rate* (per 100,000 inhabitants) of imprisonment in all the world. The bill to feed and house all these inmates exceeds many billions of dollars of taxpayer money each year, a sum which might be better spent in the prevention, both primary and secondary, of crime itself; this is especially true for sexual offenders, and more specifically, those who pose little to no danger to the public. The true crime is that we know which offenders do, and do not, pose such risks.

Moreover, a number of studies point out that incarceration itself may produce unwanted outcomes. Scientific research has demonstrated that jailed or imprisoned sexual offenders are more likely to commit another sexual crime, at least before a treatment program is completed. In a study cited by Nickel (2005) of over 8,000 sexual offenders entering treatment, time served in prison was positively related to reoffending. This is, of course, confounded by the type of sexual crime committed: the more severe the crime, the longer the sentence. However, parsing out severity of sexual crime did not affect these results. One possible explanation could be that the negative impact of deprived circumstances may be related to repeat offending. In prison, contact with other types of criminals, particularly those with repeated sentences and antisocial personalities, also may encourage repeat offending after release.

Another study area of interest is the prison environment itself. More recently, sexual offenders have been placed in less restrictive sections of prisons or even in prison camps. Their interactions, and the possibility of some group therapy, are thereby enhanced. While many would argue that sexual offenders "deserve" unsparing and stern conditions, studies are underway to discern whether less brutal placements by themselves are more effective in reducing sexual offense recidivism. Nonetheless, the draconian sentences and harsh punitive treatment in prisons have never been correlated with a reduction in recommitting a sexual crime.

Fortunately, our jails and prisons are not the hell-holes depicted in TV and movie shows, with constantly screaming inmates and corrections guards brutally beating prisoners. Nor are they similar to the horrendous conditions in autocracies around the world, in which any political dissent is squelched by imprisonment. Many situational offenders in prison can easily bond with hardened criminals, by choice or necessity, and can accumulate a coterie of antisocial criminals, which may be maintained even after release.

Nonetheless, the surge in prison populations, combined with the lack of funding for adequate infrastructure, easily can bleed into excessive hostility amongst inmates and, ultimately, reduced opportunities for rehabilitative efforts by prison staff. In addition, exposure to other criminals is detrimental, given that most sexual offenders have not committed any other crime and only between 10–15% are sociopathic. Moreover, the criminal and gang subculture prominent in most federal penitentiaries is antithetical to that of most sexual offenders, especially those committing situational offenses, as they are often naïve, young, and easily bullied and abused by more sophisticated inmates. Moreover, while rarely unmerciful, guards are usually neutral at best but, when they learn that the inmate is a sexual offender (and they always will), they can be as cold as winter in Siberia.

Racial disparities among incarcerated men have often been cited as an example of bias against the African American population. Indeed, the numbers for men currently in prison as of 2023 per 100,00 individuals in the United States was 332 for Caucasian prisoners, contrasted with 1,890 for African American men, and 837 for men of Hispanic origin. (The DOJ still employs the term "Hispanic" as opposed to the more recent "Latino".) These figures come from the latest DOJ statistics. However, DOJ figures for that year indicate that, amongst all sexual offenders in prisons, the rate of incarcerated Caucasians at 17.1% nearly doubled the rate for African Americans (7.3%) but almost matched the rate of Hispanic sexual offenders at 16.0%.

There are theories about the relatively low rate of sexual offenses amongst African American males. Some have argued that, within the Black Community, victims may be more reluctant to report a sexual crime for fear of retaliation or shame. It has also been suggested that many African American men are already in prison at a young age for other crimes and therefore may advance in age before release, thereby reducing their risk of committing a sexual crime. Neither of these hypotheses appears entirely convincing; it is probably best to admit that we simply do not know the reasons for the relatively lower numbers of African American men in prison for sexual offenses compared with Caucasians or Hispanics. Data are not provided for the number of men of Asian descent who are incarcerated for sexual offenses although, from clinical experience, this number would be lower than that of Caucasians, Hispanics and African Americans. It would be difficult, but not impossible, to examine these disparities by designing appropriate studies.

The final point to be made about punishment is perhaps the most important: does it work to prevent future sexual crimes? When you take away your teenager's X-box for a week for skipping school, when you put your toddler in a room alone for a time-out, do those efforts prevent such mischief in the future? The studies say no. Often, such intrafamilial retributions only encourage greater deception. The statistics are compelling: *states and countries which levy the harshest of penalties have a greater number of repeat sexual crimes than those which are more flexible and lenient.*

An alternative is possible in place of incarceration, especially for situational offenders: consideration of financial penalties. Compensation for the victim, such as the offender being ordered to pay for her treatment, could be considered, as could bringing a civil case against the offender. Even if the accused is acquitted, the victim or her family could bring civil charges for damages. Unfortunately, we have been witnesses to just a handful of such cases, whether the offender is found innocent or guilty. Most offenders are not millionaires or funded by large corporations. Therefore, the majority are convicted or accept a plea bargain, and are thus usually incarcerated for some time. No insurance company would indemnify against such an offence. Moreover, a repeated trial would only harm the victim again regardless of outcome, itself an uncertainty.

Yet another form of financial penalty could be considered: while no perfect form of retribution will ever be devised, what if a convicted offender, or one who accepts a plea agreement, were made to forfeit a portion of his future earnings, whether to the victim, her family, or to the government (as an additional tax) or to a nonprofit organization designated by the victim or her family, preferably one which promotes the safety and treatment of victims of sexual abuse? Since most of the chapters discuss serious problems, this book would be incomplete without Chapter Seven on potential solutions, in which some of these issues are further discussed.

Perhaps the most harsh of punishments is the death penalty. Many would argue its value, not for deterrence (a life in prison would accomplish that) but for retaliation for the most heinous of crimes. Here is one such example.

> A homosexual pedophile, Wesly Dodd (I can use his name as he is now deceased and the case was in the public domain) was brought to court for crimes almost too loathsome and revolting to contemplate. While molesting boys 5 to 7 years of age, he would cut their bodies when they were still alive, then retain their body parts for his masturbation fantasies. I was asked to evaluate him first for the prosecution. The question at that point was whether he was treatable; he frankly told me that, if released, he could not control this gruesome behavior and it would continue. I testified that he was dangerous and would be so, likely for the remainder of his life, regardless of treatment. I was subsequently asked to evaluate him again after the prosecutors asked for the death penalty. The issue then was whether, even with a lifetime sentence, would he be dangerous to other prisoners and thus would merit death. Mr. Dodd stood 5'7" tall and weighed about 135 lbs. In my opinion, he would not only not be a danger to other prisoners but would, in all probability, become a victim himself. My testimony did little to save his life. After 10 years in isolation on death row, he was executed by the State of Washington.

There have been several other such vile and sickening cases which do not bear repeating here. There are a slight minority of sexual offenders who should never be set free. David and Mr. Dodd, mentioned above, are two of those. They say that time heals all wounds but there remains one that never heals – the loss of a child. No parent should ever have to attend the funeral of their child. Many sexual crimes are never forgiven or forgotten, nor should they be.

It is true that a number, though only a small percentage, of those receiving a sentence of death or those actually executed have subsequently been exonerated by DNA evidence. Yet beyond that argument, there remain existential problems with the death penalty. The difficulty with government taking a life is of a wider scope: no matter the horrendous nature of the crime, executing the guilty teaches our children that violence should be met with violence. We cannot predict the future but perhaps in 100 years, historions may look back upon the death penalty (and perhaps even potentially injurious sports such as boxing and football) in the same manner we now condemn Roman gladiators fighting to the death for the amusement of spectators. By then, it is possible that capital punishment might be lost in the shadows of shame. I am unsure that the government putting an offender to death is a measure of a civilized society. An eye for an eye yields a world that is totally blind.

In summary, study after study, whether in US states or in countries across the globe, unfailingly find no link between the severity of punishment and the re-commission of a crime. This is not only true for sexual offenders, but for the majority of other criminals as well. All that money to put prisoners out of sight in cages, and then subject them to the harshest of supervisory requirements upon release, contributes to government treasuries at the taxpayer's expense: such large amounts for such worthless results. Yet this is the price we pay, not only in money and human beings suffering penalties far beyond the harm they may have caused, but in the misery their innocent families must endure; this is what occurs when science is ignored. In a symposium organized by The Association for the Treatment of Sexual Abusers (ATSA) in Mach, 2012, Pia Sinha, CEO of the Prison Reform Trust gave a presentation in which she noted that there is " a systemic problem" within prisons, both federal and state, and offered to suggest there is "a crisis" requiring "experts" in this area to form a taskforce and "take the politics out of it."

The DAs, attorneys, judges, and jurors are observers of what an offender has wrought. Keen and well-meaning as they almost always are, they do not go on to actually *experience* the long-term consequences of their decisions on the victims, their perpetrators and their families. They can simply leave and go home. In the end, I believe that we should prize humility and humanity over hatred.

Chapter 3

The Second Pillar

Justice for the Victim(s)

While it is completely understandable that victims, their families, and the community at large will desire justice, there is considerable variability in how justice is defined, operationalized, and meted out. The most common response to a finding of guilt in a sexual offense case is influenced most heavily by emotion, not the offender's level of risk nor his prognosis for change. Such an outcome may assuage the public's desire for retribution, but it is not informed by scientific information, is costly, and does little, if anything, to ensure community safety over the long term.

If incarceration is added to the significant costs of being stigmatized, along with the financial loss for the guilty offender, it will only serve to punish the sexual offender long after his crime has taken place. Studies demonstrate that punishment that is not applied at the time of deviant behavior is ineffective in deterring future criminal behavior; indeed, incarceration by itself may even increase the risk of recidivism.

If your daughter is raped or murdered, you would hardly be satisfied with a sentence in which the perpetrator would receive only a term of probation. In court, victims, if they are of a reasonable age, are encouraged to present, usually by reading a prepared statement, how the crime affected her or him. In many cases, the family involved may also deliver a similar presentation. These are powerful and, I believe, entirely appropriate pronouncements of the effects of a crime and they often provide the most devasting impact upon a jury or judge. This is especially true in sexual abuse cases, and particularly when the victim(s) is a child. One also hopes that the offender himself comes to an understanding of the burdens he has inflicted upon all those involved.

Unfortunately, we cannot separate the concept of justice from the fervor of revenge, a base but basic human sensation. The emotion of revenge is a human trait that cannot be expunged by logic or science:

> Oliver moved in with his girlfriend three years before committing a sexual offense against her 14-year-old daughter. At night, on two occasions, he slipped into her room after his girlfriend was asleep, and fondled the girl's breasts. She was too afraid and shocked to repel his advances nor was she

DOI: 10.4324/9781003532590-4

comfortable disclosing to her mother what had occurred, at least for a number of months. After all, he was in most respects an excellent stepfather, far better than her alcoholic biological dad. She had formed a bond with him, and was comfortable in his presence even when her mother was absent. To tell would have disrupted the family and jeopardized their financial future. However, after a health class in school, she told her best friend what had happened. This prompted a cascade of events: The friend told a teacher, who disclosed the abuse to the school's counselor. Both are mandatory reporters so DHS was notified, leading to a police investigation and two eventual charges of *Sexual Abuse in the Second Degree*. Had she resisted, or had he used force, the charges might have been elevated to the *First Degree*. In the sentencing phase of the judicial proceedings, the victim and her mother both read convincing disclosures of the effects these crimes have had upon her and her family. The mother had to separate from the offender; had she not, DHS would have considered her an unfit mother and removed this victim from her custody.

We testified in this case that Oliver posed no risk to the community as long as he was supervised and prevented from being alone with adolescent females. Our experience, combined with scientifically validated testing, demonstrated that the risk of his repeating this type of crime in the future was minimal, especially since it had been identified, sanctioned and he was already beginning treatment in an approved sexual offender-specific program. He had no prior history of criminality nor of substance abuse and had been steadily employed. His attorney advised him to accept a plea deal involving 364 days of incarceration followed by three years of probation. He has lost his job while we, the taxpayers, are supporting him; the jail offered no treatment for his sexual misbehavior.

Has justice been served? Certainly, the victim and her mother were moderately satisfied and that is no small thing. Yet Oliver was no more dangerous under supervision in the community than any random male. Can we separate the emotion of revenge from how justice is meted out? Probably not. Yet, when weighed against the financial burden to taxpayers and even to the offender and his victim, is such a sentence justified? Would incarceration in a case with a situational offender who, in all likelihood, would never be in that situation again, provide community protection? Of course, this is a rhetorical question. I doubt we can eliminate the need for a victim to seek revenge. But at what cost?

A day in jail costs the taxpayer between US$60 to $90. A day in prison could exceed $100. Should an offender complete a three-year sentence, the cost to society would surpass $140,000. But this fails to take into account the lost productivity of the imprisoned; nor does it cover the costs of supervision, treatment and polygraphs following jail or prison, which can add another several thousand dollars. Had Oliver been placed on probation and into a treatment program, he would have had to pay a certain amount in restitution and pay for his treatment. A fair estimate of his treatment costs over a two-year period, absent incarceration, including his supervision and polygraph testing, would have been around $3,500, the majority of which would have been the responsibility of the offender or his family. None of the amount would have been borne by the tax-paying public.

Although some insurance companies cover part of the cost for treatment, many do not. Nor are ex-convicts able to obtain the same level of employment as they once enjoyed; thus they sometimes struggle to pay for treatment; we always spread out the costs of treatment on a lengthy basis such that it does not unduly impoverish the offender or his family.

Violent crime peaked in the 1990s, although certain crimes involving gun-related murders have increased in 2023 and 2024 in certain urban areas, particularly those with a higher proportion of poor African American males. This may be attributed to poverty, the prevalence of criminal gangs, and compounded by the ready availability of rapid-fire weapons and the reluctance to reform access to such arms. An additional factor may lie in the brisk advancement of communications via electronic means, whereby vulnerable individuals may be persuaded by misinformation on a variety of media platforms which spread conspiracy theories or publicize and focus on those who commit mass murders such as school shootings.

Despite the overall abatement in crime, including sexual assaults, jail and prison populations have ballooned. Multiply the figures above by the thousands of situational offenders proven to be safe to be at large yet still needlessly incarcerated, and the costs to taxpayers amount to many millions of dollars, most of which could have been saved by simply referring these types of situational offenders to a treatment program with adequate correctional supervision.

We have had the opportunity to treat a number of victims of sexual abuse. Some have self-identified through disclosures as children while others only find the courage to tell what has occurred years later. In fact, in such cases, the statute of limitations does not apply in certain sexual offender cases.

> Paula, 24 years of age, began to experience nightmares, vivid flashbacks and anxiety when out alone at night. She had recently broken off an engagement with her long-time boyfriend, afraid she could not commit to a prolonged or stable relationship. Memories of being molested by an uncle when she was 7–9 years of age, including digital penetration, kept recurring even though she was conscious of, and had clear memory of, the abuse throughout the intervening years. The appearance of PTSD-like symptoms, triggered by her looming marriage, amplified and sharpened these memories to the point where she began to experience symptoms. It was at that point that the statute began. Regardless of when the trauma occurred, the point at which it begins to cause

symptoms has, by law, determined the time at which the clock begins running. The victim confronted her aged uncle with how the abuse at his hands had scarred her and might well prevent her from forming trusting relationships with men in the future. He was given the opportunity to address her and the court, during which he emphasized three points: that he had lived a life free of any crime since the abuse; that he had achieved a research position in a university and contributed to the advances made in his specialty; and, looking directly at his now-adult niece, said "I'm sorry." Her uncle, now well into his seventies, was charged with multiple counts of *Sexual Abuse in the First Degree* and subsequently sentenced through a plea bargain to 13 years in prison. He passed away in a federal penitentiary at the age of 78.

Three male youths had accompanied an adolescent female home after a high school basketball game. Two of the boys made sexual comments which embarrassed her, then each began to grab her breasts over her clothing as they walked together. The contact was brief but clearly distressed her. In tears as she walked away from them, she screamed, "You're all a pack of wolves." She failed to attend classes for the next week. When questioned, the boys described the incident as "no big deal." It was only after reading her written statement to the court that they realized the extent of grief and trauma such an act could cause. They were both charged with *Sexual Harassment* (dropped from *Sexual Abuse in the Third Degree*). Both boys were placed under the Jurisdiction of the Oregon Youth Authority but only one was placed under supervision for more than one year. They were also instructed to write their own letters of apology to be read in court to the victim. Part of one youth's note read:

I never understood how horrible what I did would affect you so much. I did it for my own sexual pleasure without the slightest idea of how it would affect you. I am glad you told the authorities what happened because it made me realize that what I did was illegal, but even more important, it was immoral because it hurt you. Because now I realize that and because everyone knows, I can promise that this will never happen again. I can only hope you can put this in your past as I am truly sorry.

The boy who wrote the note was a straight A student who went on to a prestigious university. Despite his sincere apology (yes, I believe it was sincere at the time), he was subsequently accused of raping an intoxicated female college student and expelled, sentenced to five years in prison, and, once released, has only been able to work at low-level jobs. The other boy wrote a similar note. He was also a stellar student, obtained a doctorate in microbiology from an Ivy League college, and eventually received international recognition in chemistry.

> I know this story because I was the third boy in that walking-home group. I never engaged in any sexual talk or acts with the victim but neither did I intercede. Not a day goes by that I do not regret my cowardice in being too afraid to intervene on her behalf.

Apologies can be helpful, but barely. What else can an offender say after he is apprehended: only the two weakest words in the English Language – "I'm sorry." Does this offer some sense of compensation to the victims? That is unlikely. Offenders may be sorry even before being apprehended as they may realize what they did was wrong, though but a handful understand the full extent of the horrid damage they may have caused. Especially in cases of child molestation, many offenders think very little of the effects their abusive behavior may have on a youth. This is especially true in cases, not uncommon, where the victim, perhaps a prepubescent female, still has contact with the abuser, such as a step-father. She may actually enjoy his presence as she may have received special attention or gifts from him. In other cases, he may be the more stable parent in the family and its main source of financial support. Again, young girls are often hesitant to reveal abuse for fear of embarrassment, punishment, or of not being believed.

In cases of rape, a victim may be intimidated by potential revenge if she knew the abuser, and may also fear the entire judicial process of police reports, doubting witnesses, her state of intoxication at the time, fears of a trial, and, in a few cases, she may not actually want the perpetrator to be imprisoned. We can only estimate how many rapes go unreported; the number is surely higher among women who knew their attacker than in stranger rapes. If at all possible, the offender should be considered a source of funds for the treatment of whatever trauma he has effected in the victim. Additional financial penalties (see Chapter Seven) might be considered. However, in only a few cases has a court or prosecutor sought to consider such arrangements. Sexual offenders are not universally poor, but they are rarely wealthy. After paying for legal fees, losing employment, and facing incarceration, they are in a precarious position to even afford treatment fees. Some might argue that if he can, at some point, enter treatment for himself, those funds might instead be diverted to the victim.

Sexual offender treatment in most cases can prevent the creation of another victim. Moreover, mental health therapy for the victim is usually covered by insurance, although insurance companies often limit the number of sessions. With modern legislation, however, there has been a fortunate reversal of such restrictive policies, and for good reason. An increasing number of insurance companies may offer ongoing support for the victim. The targets of sexual abuse may suffer PTSD-like symptoms over an extended period; even more to the point, such extended treatment for victims has proven successful in lessening the otherwise lifelong burden these victims might have suffered.

We are in a period of extended testing of new treatments for PTSD. Certainly, psychological approaches, ranging from merely talking it through to desensitization and guided visualization, can often help, along with eye movement desensitization and reprocessing (EMDR); such treatments are being constantly refined. Medications sometimes help, particularly the newer antidepressants. Controversial approaches actually have proven helpful in limited trials; these include the hallucinogenic drugs such as psilocybin and MDMA, along with the anesthetics ketamine and propofol. Such speculative and potentially dangerous approaches will require guided experiences in a controlled setting. Indeed, the FDA [US Food and Drug Administration] has recently approved a new medication, trade-named Spravato, a nasal spray which actually contains ketamine in small doses. Hopefully, advances will continue in the resolution of such troubling symptoms as flashbacks, nightmares and hypersensitivity. The victims of sexual abuse deserve just as much experimental analysis as do those suffering from the more fully subsidized areas of major depression and bipolar disorder.

But we have not answered the central issue posed here: What is justice? Is it simply a matter of revenge? Is a prison term sufficient to quell those feelings? No study of this issue, of which I am aware, has been published, yet it is a question that could lend itself to research. While our Sexual Abuse Clinic has not carried out such a study and thus simply has anecdotal answers, it is not surprising that the majority of victims, and even more so their families, do not believe the punishments meted out were sufficiently severe.

> Michael, referred to in Chapter Two, had molested several prepubescent girls of which we were aware at sentencing. His five-year sentence was followed by mandated treatment, during which we and his post-prison supervisor (formerly known as a parole officer) required a full-disclosure polygraph. When thus informed, Michael spontaneously admitted molesting three other young girls for whom he had babysat throughout his many years. You might believe this would have made little difference in his treatment as we already knew about multiple victims. However, the details of these additional young girls formed part of the basis for specific scenes used during aversive conditioning. Because we had an obligation to notify the DA about these other crimes, some of his victims were similarly informed. We had the opportunity of interviewing two of Michael's victims and their families. All of these individuals believed strongly that his five-year sentence was too lenient and many expressed their hope he would die in prison.

There is little mercy for sexual offenders, even among those who believe in the religious edicts recommending it. Many of the offenders we treat have been shunned by their families, who are revolted by their dire deeds. They often lose support from them as well as from former friends and co-workers.

Churches have cast out these men as unfit to worship within their congregations. Families, over extended periods of time, have refused to communicate with such offenders. While exceptions exist, and we have undertaken a fair share of family reconciliations, these have occurred when a single offense was committed and the victim reached a point, not of forgiveness (some acts are truly unforgivable), but of a wish to reunite and provide a second chance for the offender. In the majority of cases of those who have suffered sexual abuse, however, the offender should never be alone with his victim.

How then is justice defined? How can it be considered sufficient if its aim is to compensate the victim and her family? The *Oxford Dictionary* is of little assistance. It engages in tautology, defining justice as "the quality of being just." Does five years in prison, or even 20, make the trauma more tolerable? Is the victim compensated, at least in an emotional manner? From our experience, such recompence is never sufficient nor long-lasting. No amount of time in prison or sum of money will undo the harm wrought by a sexual offense. We must acknowledge that the prime merit justice holds for the victims, their families, and the community at large, is simply revenge.

Vengeance may be a base emotion, but it is inevitable in our species. Retribution for the offender is the major vehicle by which victims can recognize that some punishment can be effected. Sexual crimes can never be forgotten nor forgiven. But forgetting is for the past, which cannot be undone, while a focus on the future may hold better promise.

A secondary benefit of incarceration is isolation from the community. But such mandated separation is generally comparatively brief and, by itself, without treatment, rarely prevents another sexual crime in many offenders, especially in predatory men. Science does not lie: punishment doesn't prevent further crimes nor does the threat of negative consequences have a deterrent effect.

I have no perfect answer (although I do offer some recommendations in Chapter Seven). However, it is important to differentiate beliefs from facts: most people of any faith believe in a higher power, while a minority claim to be atheists. However, the true scientist should be honest: we do not have the ability to test this belief in a scientific manner. Therefore, my opinion is that there can be no true atheist as we cannot prove whether a god exists, at least by present means. It's often difficult, especially for physicians, to say "I don't know," but any rational thinker could assume less arrogance and would, in my opinion, adopt agnosticism.

Justice may be simply a synonym for revenge. And revenge is only a fancy word for payback. Revenge is considered a base emotion but that is what justice for all offenders really means. Is that so bad? Surely society has some right to moral outrage. We can never eliminate such basic human emotions. Though I hold no divine provenance for the Bible, I try to remind those families of my three favorite biblical passages (though I may misquote them as differing versions have been offered):

"Justice is mine sayeth the Lord."
"Do not judge lest ye be judged."
"Ye without sin cast the first stone."

Though not always true, I am sure it has often appeared to us as if those who worship at the alter of Adrasteia, the Greek Goddess of Vengeance, and are often the most spiteful and morally enraged by sexual offenses, may often be the very ones who have the most to hide. As a single species, each of us carries the potential within us for acts of beneficence or malignity. We all have committed mistakes, and hopefully learned from them. When has there been a prolonged period of time during which we have all been our best selves? There exists in us all the potential for good and evil given the circumstances. We should therefore not hate the person; only hate what they actually did. Judge the act, but not the actor.

Chapter 4

The Third Pillar

Supervision

The majority of sexual offenders face some type of incarceration after sentencing, whether by a plea agreement or being found guilty in a trial. Some of these men have endured long delays in the judicial process. This has been especially true during the Covid-19 pandemic in the early years of the 2020 decade. In our experience, delays from the first arrest to a final sentencing can range from one year to more than three years. These periods are marked for sexual offenders by the worry of what their sentence might be and often how they will manage the financial turmoil in affording attorney's fees while not being able to retain their jobs or even their homes. Justice delayed is not justice denied but rather justice suspended.

During that prolonged period, many offenders are advised by their lawyers to seek treatment. This not only presents a more favorable view from the court, it also can actually be effective in many situational cases, reducing their risk of a long period of incarceration. Still, many men who pose no risk to the community as they begin a jail or prison sentence will be locked away, at taxpayer's expense, for the purposes of punishment and justice, but such imprisonment accomplishes little in terms of safety.

> Quincy, a 74-year-old retired businessman, was undergoing treatment for his second offense, having molested several young girls 20 years earlier. The more recent offense was viewing and downloading child pornography. Because this was a second sexual crime, he faced rather strict sentencing guidelines, even though it was a hands-off offense. His attorney and the DA dithered about sentencing as it was complicated by several factors: Quincy was quite ill, requiring kidney dialysis, and had cardiac problems as well. At 74, were he to be imprisoned, the penal institution would be required to provide lengthy and expensive treatment. In addition, he had successfully completed a more modern treatment program while awaiting sentencing and his age and medical disabilities rendered him to be at low risk. The final agreement with his attorney, the DA and the court came as a relief – probation only with ankle-bracelet monitoring. The decision was reached more than four

DOI: 10.4324/9781003532590-5

years after the arrest, during which Quincy's medical conditions worsened, probably hastened by the anxiety of not learning his fate for all those years.

Admittedly, this was an unusually protracted case, but not an isolated or rare one. Attorneys and DAs are often overloaded with cases, many of which might be fraught with more danger than many sexual offenders would pose. In addition, the courts have been backlogged from before the pandemic. Still, many men waiting for sentencing must endure protracted periods and expensive delays before they know what they will face as penalties.

Should a sexual offender be sentenced to a period of incarceration that is less than 365 days he would be imprisoned but supervised upon release by a probation officer, a county employee. However, if the offender receives a sentence exceeding one year, after being set free he would be sent either to a state prison or, if a federal crime had been committed, a federal penitentiary would be his destination. Upon release, he would be supervised by a post-prison supervisor (or "officer" in some jurisdictions).

Since such supervision cannot begin until the offender has accepted a plea deal (he is presumed innocent before that time), some offenders whom we believe might act again with unlawful sexual behavior may be free in the community. However, the most dangerous of offenders are usually not granted the opportunity of bail. Nonetheless, some menacing cases slip through. If the court deems a person to be highly dangerous yet he is allowed to pay for bail, restrictions ought to be placed upon his liberty, such as house confinement and GPS monitoring (ankle bracelet), along with a constant trusted chaperone/supervisor.

The problem quite often seen, nonetheless, is that situational offenders, such as child porn offenders or those who have crimes related to age-of-consent only, are sometimes unduly restricted even before a plea arrangement or a trial and should theoretically be deemed innocent until proven guilty or accepting a plea agreement.

A 20-year-old college student, Rob, was arrested on a charge of downloading child pornography (hereafter referred to as porn). Even before any determination of guilt, however, he was restricted from living with his family as he had a 14-year-old sister. Moreover, he was placed on an ankle monitor, could not leave his house for anything other than to meet his attorney, attend classes and visit the doctor, nor could he utilize electronic equipment of any sort. Unfortunately, almost all his classes demanded assignments on a computer or other electronic device. His therapist in our Clinic and its Director argued on his behalf that there are programs which automatically block porn and can be monitored so that a supervisor can see exactly what he is doing online at all times. This carried little weight and, as a result, Rob had to drop

> almost all his classes. Following sentencing, he was placed on probation and many of these restrictions were lifted but he lost two semesters of college and had to repeat several of his classes, which caused substantial expense. While common sense is not often based on science, in this case, his earlier restrictions not only made no sense, they also flew in the face of scientific research on risk.

It is the erratic nature of presentence supervision that is, at times, maddening, as many restrictions are placed on the accused which do nothing to enhance community safety but are seen by a judge or a corrections officer almost as "pre-punishment." It can not only impair the individual affected from maintaining employment, thus hurting families; it may also limit where the accused can live; whether he can see his own children; where he can shop (no malls or fast-food restaurants are common constraints); or, in certain cases, whether he can even leave his house as ankle monitoring is frequently imposed. His family, as well as the offender himself, suffers what his therapists believed had been unnecessary, burdensome, and draconian limitations on all involved:

> Steven, an IT consultant to a local business, was suspected of molesting his four-year-old daughter by touching her vaginal area. Both he and his wife insisted nothing sexual had occurred. The charge stemmed from the girl making a statement in preschool that her "daddy" touched her "pee-pee." In a subsequent DHS interview there was some confusion as the alleged victim gave conflicting disclosures about baths and putting her to bed. When asked, in a second interview five months later, she appeared to have matured sufficiently to make a more direct statement, saying clearly that her father never touched her vagina but only washed her when bathing and both mother and father were always present when he participated.
>
> Nonetheless, he was compelled to agree to a plea arrangement and the pre-sentence restrictions were not immediately lifted even though DHS found the case "unfounded" – their way of saying there was no need to follow up on the case. (However, this is not the equivalent of a legal opinion of guilt or innocence.) Steven and his attorney, citing our Sexual Abuse Clinic's written reports, begged relief from severe constraints, including an ankle monitor; limited computer access; banishment from his home; and only supervised visits with his young daughter and five-year-old son. These latter conditions specified that an approved supervisor, a stranger to the family, would have to monitor these visits and the visits could only occur at a local corrections office. These restraints on Steven's liberty were only discontinued when, five months later, the charges were dropped. By that time, he had not been involved in raising his two children for two important years of their lives and had had to sell his home to afford his attorney's fees and incurred other costs connected to his period of supervision.

These pre-and post-sentence constraints on most *situational* offenders do nothing to protect the community but do inflict upon the offender additional expenses. Polygraphs can cost $500 for a full-disclosure test; the maintenance polygraphs required of all sexual offenders, mostly every six months during supervision, can cost between $250 and $400. Visits to a pretrial supervisor can cost $40 each month, but in certain cases can be required up to once each week. Blood and urine drug and alcohol testing can be ordered on an unannounced basis (to prevent cheating) and its cost, plus any sexual offender-specific treatment fees (our Clinic's average is lower than most at $500 per month) must be the responsibility of the offender.

Moreover, the offender's family is being punished yet they have committed no crime. Such penalties can be equally egregious, including time, effort and expense. These same burdens are also borne by corrections divisions and their already overburdened staff. Some larger counties designate a pre-sentence officer who does not have to carry an additional load of post-sentence offenders. But smaller, usually rural, counties, assign both pre- and post-sentence offenders to staff who may be overwhelmed with the number of offenders they must follow. Again, corrections' budgets can only be balanced by taxpayer funds. There are solutions (see Chapter Seven), but these are admittedly imperfect.

The main task of divisions of corrections occurs, however, in supervision after either a plea arrangement has been approved by a judge or an offender is sentenced, then released. The point at which post-sentencing commences is therefore either when the offender is placed on probation or is sent to jail (less than a 12-month sentence) or prison (a sentence exceeding 12 months). Sexual offenders can be charged locally within a county after an investigation by local police and county sheriff's offices, or in federal court after probes by federal police forces, such as the FBI. Such investigations recently have been prolonged by the rising number of electronic crimes as specially trained officers comb through hard drives, SIM cards and the rest. See Chapter Six for more details about this process. A common notion that you can delete any electronic data is false, no matter to what lengths you go and no matter how much you believe you are skilled in electronics. Once it's there, it can always be found, even on a damaged instrument. (Remember the Cloud.)

These days, there has fortunately been a tendency toward lesser sentences for noncontact offenders, such as those downloading child porn only or statutory crimes ("Romeo and Juliet" or R&J cases, as for example an 18-year-old youth having consensual relations with his 15-year-old girlfriend). Such statutory and some situational offenders will be either sentenced to a brief stint in a county jail, usually no more than three months, or go straight to probation, either of three or five years, depending on the extent of his porn collection, whether any noncontact coercion was used, how overcrowded the DAs caseload is, or on the judge's predisposition regarding sexual offenders in general.

Once released, most sexual offenders experience difficulty finding housing. Their supervisors can help but most apartment houses, condos, and even halfway houses refuse entry, either because children are present or due to a general bias against such ex-prisoners. Moreover, the importance of housing stability was documented in a 2023 study carried out at Arizona University on a sexual offender population of over 3,000 sexual offenders during incarceration, then released into the community under supervision. Results indicated that frequent changes in jail or prison locations as well as rapid turnover in housing placements, once released but under supervision, demonstrated an important indicator of an increase in sexual offense recidivism. These cases are usually handled within county systems but the federal government is also heavily involved in prosecuting child porn cases as these can be considered crimes which occur across state or even county boundaries. Federal prosecutors and courts often hand down more severe penalties than county jurisdictions but that is not true in all cases. If incarceration is part of a federal crime, the sentence must exceed 12 months and must be served in a federal facility (a prison, as opposed to a county jail), often at a distance from the offender's family.

A sexual offender, whether after incarceration or just serving a sentence of probation, will be supervised by a probation officer (PO) if his sentence was less than 12 months. If it exceeds that period, he will be supervised by what used to be called a parole officer; the correct term these days is a post-prison supervisor (PPS). Conditions vary depending upon the crime itself, but also include the offender's criminal history, if any, and the supervisor's impression of how compliant the offender is likely to be. This may also be influenced by the nature and frequency of his criminal history and assessment scales predicting compliance. In more populous counties, a number of supervisors may be assigned specifically to handle sexual abuse cases; in more rural counties, a single supervisor must assume that duty.

Corrections departments will switch some supervisors to other duties so as to provide all such employees with the monitoring of a variety of criminals, but often, even within urban districts, a specialized sexual offender supervisor may be tasked exclusively with sexual offenders for many years. There exist, however, huge discrepancies among POs and PPSs, even within the same jurisdiction, about the restrictions placed upon an offender.

> A 42-year-old married man, Thomas, had a history of grooming, then molesting boys between the ages of 5 and 10. His victims were, at first, strangers to him (a dangerous sign itself), and he had additional charges when under supervision in the past for several *Driving While Under the Influence of Intoxicants* (DUII) offenses, usually alcohol. He also had a habit of missing visits with his PO, failing to attend a diversion program for substance abuse, and once, *Failure to Appear* after being summoned to court for these parole violations. Following a 10-year

sentence, during which he served just six years, he was placed on PPS. His PPS officer at the time provided him with the standard list of prohibitions, known as the "Sex Offender Package." An example of this will be found in Appendix B at the back of this book.

Although there are a number of prohibitions in Thomas' set of "You cannots...", depending upon the severity of Thomas' past misbehaviors, most of these boxes were checked. Some of the typical limits are no unsupervised contact with minors; no use of electronic devices except for work or school; the implementation of a software program blocking any pornography; an ankle bracelet monitoring his whereabouts; and not frequenting locations where children congregate. His most salient sanction, however, was to complete a sexual offender-specific treatment program. Our Clinic is continuing a treatment program for Thomas employing aversive conditioning, satiation and cognitive restructuring techniques. Thus far, he has participated in all sessions and we believe, once he completes treatment, including one year of monthly booster sessions, there is greater than a 75% chance that he will not sexually reoffend. We cannot guarantee he will abstain from drugs or alcohol but he has completed a substance abuse program and continues to be active in AA.

Ulrich, a 19-year-old construction worker with no prior criminal history, had dated his girlfriend since he was a junior in high school and she was a freshman, 14 years of age at the time. As their relationship became more intimate and exclusive, they decided to marry once she graduated and turned 18. The girl's parents, at first approving this match, began to question whether he was the best match for her. Arguments ensued. The parents believed their only recourse was to report that Ulrich was having sexual relations with their daughter, a minor, as she was just 15 at that time. Ulrich pled guilty to *Rape in the Third Degree*, and his attorney persuaded the DA to list the crime as a misdemeanor (it could also have been, and initially was, charged as a felony.) Thomas was sentenced to three years of probation, prohibited from being in the vicinity of children unsupervised; prevented from living within 100 yards of a school; could not frequent parks or other places where children congregate, including malls; and could only use a flip phone rather than a smart one. In addition, he was prohibited from accessing porn; could not use his laptop, until he had a porn blocker installed; and he also had to complete a sexual offender-specific treatment program.

It is obvious that these are two vastly different types of sexual offenders who represent two ends on the spectrum of sexual criminality. It would appear they should require different conditions of supervision but, on paper, at least at first, their restrictions seemed almost identical. Why should Thomas be prohibited from the use of electronics? He had never used his smart phone or personal computer in any of his crimes of molestation. A point could be made that he could use his devices to lure other boys into sexual activity or to view child porn but he had no history of such. Why should Ulrich be prevented from a fast-food restaurant or a mall? Would he be a danger to anyone in such public settings? Indeed, in our report, we specifically noted no risk of ever molesting a child. In fairness, the supervising officers can modify these conditions over time as trust is built and there has been no evidence of a violation.

The standard "sexual offender package," makes little distinction among the types of offenders or of their scientifically proven level of risk. Often, a PO or a PPS officer strives to ensure community safety by checking all these boxes just to be on the safe side, but rarely considers the limitations these place on offenders and their families, with little to no justification based upon a multitude of scientific studies. Neither do they even meet the lower criterion of common sense. Many such supervisors must answer to a sexual offender corrections committee or board and do not wish to appear overly supportive to sexual offenders. Therefore, they appear to check all or most of the restriction boxes just to be safe but to also demonstrate to their own supervisors, the DAs office, the courts, the public, and to the offender himself, they are not "soft" on sexual offenders.

I must, however, take some small part of responsibility for the "sexual offender package," which can be viewed in Appendix B at the end of this text. In the early 1970s our Clinic proposed certain standard limitations which should be applied to *predatory* sexual offenders. Some of these were even more draconian than those used today. For example, I have always recommended that pedophiles, either of girls, boys or both, should have no contact with children, even supervised. Even in a room with hundreds of people, if a child is present, the pedophile could be focusing on, and fantasizing about, that youth.

However, at that time, we were treating mostly pedophiles and the restrictions made some sense. With the arrival of electronic devices and their use to entrap presumed offenders (after the fact) or to access child porn, certainly some of the electronic prohibitions are reasonable. But with many situational offenders, especially of the R&J statutory offenses, such as those of Ulrich, most of these restrictions make no sense. They impose unreasonable restrictions which have no bearing on the type of crime committed; and of greater importance, they do not take into account the research published on recidivism rates, which are close to zero in child porn-only and statutory cases.

Restrictions are also placed on most sexual offenders concerning the areas in which they can live. Most offenders are prohibited from residing within a certain distance of a school, including elementary through high schools. Similar constraints apply to parks and playgrounds as well. Prohibitions also exist against frequenting fast-food restaurants, malls or other places where children might congregate. At times these limitations appear to make sense but appearances can indeed be deceiving. In fact, few offenders against children molest strangers and even fewer do so by preying upon children they meet near a school or playground. Certain of these restrictions do make sense for the predatory offender, but, compared to men who are situational offenders, they comprise a minority of child molesters. In our series of over 27,000 men who have molested children, fewer than 27% could be classified as predatory.

Does it make sense for an R&J offender, such as Ulrich, to allow the government to restrict where he lives? What about Curtis, the man who occasionally viewed child pornography but never demonstrated arousal to prepubescent youth? Should he be prohibited from shopping at malls and eating at McDonald's (as unhealthy as that might be)? Certainly, the state has the responsibility to protect all of its citizens. But certain supervisory mandates and restrictions harm not only the offender, who may have trouble being approved for an apartment or a job once a background check is completed, the hardship may well extend to his family as well. They may be deprived of the offender's ability to provide financial assistance. Moreover, his children, who might not, nor ever could become, his victims, may be prevented from essential contact with their father during crucial phases of their development. Despite their crimes, many of these men have no tendencies or pathologies which would impair their ability to be a nurturing parent.

In the past, even more severe penalties were levied on sexual offenders returning to a neighborhood. Some were required to post a visible sign on their doors or front yards proclaiming A SEXUAL OFFENDER NOW LIVES IN THIS HOUSE (or APARTMENT). To this day, some supervisors make house calls to inform or leave notices for families in their neighborhoods that a sexual "predator" lives close by. Unfortunately, science is again ignored in these otherwise well-intentioned actions. A number of studies have demonstrated that restrictions on where a sexual offender lives, no matter how close or distant from children, bears no relationship to whether that offender will commit another sexual crime. Unfortunately, I believe that, given the noxious reputation which such offenders bear, no amount of scientific evidence will persuade lawmakers or probation or post-prison supervisors to palliate these mandates. No senator or representative, state or federal, wants to be seen as lenient on sexual offenders, despite the science, let alone common sense.

Among the many mandates listed on the standard sexual offender package is the requirement to obtain sexual offender treatment from a sexual offender-certified provider. Different states have a variety of means by which to certify who is approved to treat sexual offenders. Most require specialized training through a program of apprenticeships with an already approved provider, a somewhat circular standard. The guidelines are clear in terms of who may be considered "approved" on paper but are less so in reality.

Often, the requirements conform to those of a national organization which (I say with pride) originated with our efforts in Oregon in the early 1970s and is now known, by the cringeworthy but all-encompassing name, as the Association for the Treatment of Sexual Abusers or ATSA. It has even spawned a journal, again with a necessary but originally overburdened name of *Sexual Abuse: A Journal of Research and Treatment*, now thankfully shortened to simply *Sexual Abuse*. I served as editor of this peer-reviewed publication for a number of years.

But does every sexual offender require treatment? The majority surely do but a case could be made that some, such as those of a statutory nature (R&J type, for example) may not. Nonetheless, almost all sexual offenders will be mandated into some type of sexual offense-specific treatment program as part of their supervision. More of this, the fourth pillar of our justice system, Rehabilitation, forms the subject matter of Chapter Five.

There remains a concern that a number of sexual crimes go undetected, though that number has been lower since the beginning of the present century. Fortunately, more victims have been willing to come forward; even young children in school are learning what is "not OK touching." If a supervisor detects, through reports from offenders, their families, or through a failed polygraph, that an offender has violated the terms of his supervision, she or he can impose sanctions on the offender. Examples include additional time in community service, several days in jail, or, in egregious cases, an extension of the offender's original time incarcerated or under supervision. But a problem exists in that we can be unaware of sexual crimes which remain undetected. A 2023 study in the Sand Ridge Treatment Center in Wisconsin, employing a number of ingenious techniques, has found that a first sanction had an immediate effect over a number of months curtailing future violations and repeat offending, but later sanctions, regardless of severity, had no effect on a sexual offender reporting a subsequent offense or of authorities reporting any further sexual crimes. Their belief was that the majority of sexual offenses do not go undetected over longer periods of time.

To be fair, I am in no position to criticize sexual offender supervisors. We only hope that they take into account the specific risks of re-offense in each individual case. A broad brush often punishes not only the offender unduly but creates collateral damage to innocent bystanders. Families have been split asunder; left bankrupt and dependent on the State; children have lost contact with a parent during their crucial upbringing years; and it may be difficult for an offender to find an adequate job or decent living quarters, thereby partially eroding the opportunity to lead a more stable life, participate in work, and support his family.

It is possible that certain offenders could have contributed significant advances in their specialties at work but these restrictions rendered such potential benefits impossible.

Vincent, 37 years of age, had committed a number of forays at night into residential neighborhoods to attempt to find an unblinded window where he might capture a couple in sexual activity. Following a brief period of incarceration, he was placed with a PO who checked many of the items on the sexual offender package. Yet he had never been attracted to prepubescent children. He had functioned as a valued financial officer who had re-organized and improved a tech company's profits and hence increased its contributions to national conservation organizations. Our recommendations, seemingly more of a fit to his crime, included an ankle bracelet, a curfew of 6 PM and making certain he would call his wife after he left work so she would be aware of when he should have arrived home. She was infuriated by his peeking behavior and, we judged, strong enough to report it if he violated any of these provisions. We also suggested that, aside from travel to and from work, he always be accompanied by an adult when out and about. Yet none of these suggestions found their way into his supervisory program, which consisted of most of the prohibitions mentioned in the above cases.

The discrepancies cut both ways.

William, a 26-year-old married man who had worked in construction and had one daughter, was in the habit of surfing the internet on sites known to be populated with teenage females. He had formed a cabal of sorts with other male friends at work who had sought to entice adolescent girls into liaisons by first engaging in harmless chatter but consistently identifying their ages as "almost 18" or "around 20 or 21." The majority of these girls rebuffed their advances as teens are becoming more sophisticated about such scams but a few of the more adventurous ones continued communications, which the men would soon turn increasingly sexual. William and a friend arranged a meeting at a motel with several adolescents promising to provide them alcohol and marijuana. At the motel, the men would make sexual advances, subtle at first, but becoming eventually overtly sexual. William persisted in badgering several of the girls into sexual activity, including intercourse. On occasion, he used threats of telling their parents in order to ensure compliance with his demands. One of the females later perhaps summarized the feelings of many of these teens by stating to police that "I finally gave in because of all the pressure."

As so often occurs in such cases, the girls spoke with their friends at school about their sexual experiences, one of whom notified a school counselor. As a mandatory reporter, she notified authorities. A subsequent police investigation uncovered at least five girls 14 and 15 years of age whom William had harried and, at times, coerced into intercourse. Nonetheless, at trial, the DA decided to pursue charges only

> involving one teen; perhaps the problems of gaining testimony from many others would have proven tedious. The charges were pled down to Sexual Abuse in the Second Degree and Vincent received only a probationary sentence despite our recommendation for incarceration. We believed his behavior was predatory and might well recur. He was required to engage in treatment with another agency which did not specialize in sexual offender treatment. Just a year into probation, William again lured a 15-year-old runaway girl into a motel where he pinned her down and forced intercourse on her. He is currently awaiting trial.

We believed that, although both men committed predatory acts, Vincent was far less dangerous than William, and they differed considerably in their risk to their communities. Yet their restrictions following sentencing were much the same. These inconsistencies within sentencing and follow-up by POs (and PPSs) may be secondary to a variety of factors:

Public officers such as DAs must render decisions on an abundance of cases, the sheer number of which can be staggering, and to which only a limited period of time can be allotted. Certainly, their offices must take into account the severity of the crime and the nature of the criminal. They tend to prosecute the most heinous of crimes more promptly, including cases in which the public and the media have shown interest. This is entirely defensible but leaves many sexual offenders in the purgatory of waiting to learn their fate for months to years.

Since most sexual offender cases rarely proceed to trial, plea deals must be arranged. This process takes protracted periods of time as both the DA and the perpetrator's attorney must pore over many documents, arrange extensive meetings and conversations, and must consider the offender's history and the impact the crime(s) has/have had upon the victim(s). This is especially true in cases in which a public defender or a private attorney has been assigned by a county due to the offender's parlous financial state, rather than directly hired by the client. This can occur in counties which lack public defenders and must appoint a private attorney for the defense. Such attorneys are paid, but not as handsomely as if they were defending private clients.

Courts are perpetually besieged with too many cases to hear in a timely fashion. Delays for minor reasons occur as a matter of course. Attorneys often request postponements as they have had insufficient time to review all materials. In addition, many defense attorneys encourage delays, believing that, as the case goes cold and the prosecution tires of bargaining, they will gain some advantage.

The burdens described above pale in comparison with those of supervising officers. Many such POs and PPSs bear caseloads of hundreds of released individuals who have committed a host of crimes ranging in severity from rape and murder to DUIIs, a minor in possession of drugs, child pornography cases, or engaging in an R&J type of offense. They are required not only to meet with each offender but to conduct home visits; be aware of offenders' work or job status; field requests for their hopes of travel out of state; arrange, then review, polygraphs; receive and review progress reports from their treatment providers; and review the status of their urinalyses.

Some sexual offenders, but not most, also have a history of conduct disorder as adolescents which then mutates into a sociopathic personality disorder, in which an individual might lie as easily as they breathe. This is not the usual history nor course for most sexual offenders. However, the presence of a sexual offender with a chronicle of multitudes of crimes, especially if they include a variety of violations aside from the sexual, must be scrutinized with more supervisory intensity than the offender with but a single paraphilia or a child porn-only (CPO), R&J crime, or an entrapment offense alone. It is an error, frequently committed by POs and PPSs, that such simple sexual offenders must automatically be assumed to be sociopaths, and thus excessive time and restrictions may be placed upon such individuals, both of which are essentially unwarranted.

Supervisors are simply human beings with the same prejudices and predilections of us all. Some are more strict, some more lenient and we judge them, but shouldn't, based on our own biases. Moreover, they do not operate in isolation; most counties and federal supervisors report to a board, often a specialized one such as a supervisory sexual offender board, and thus must undergo administrative scrutiny of their decisions. We all have bosses; we doctors are no exception: our bosses are our patients.

To summarize, sexual offenders encompass a vast variety of individuals, some of whom have committed the most egregious of crimes, while others have truly misbehaved sexually but pose little to no risk to re-offend.

Yet they all will carry the stigma throughout life of being listed as, and considered as, sexual offenders. This appellation has proven more disheartening to many of our patients than any temporary restrictions and even worse than the time they spent incarcerated. There remain just two means by which a sexual offender can partially rid himself from this stigma: 1) *expungement* (the record is cleared and the crime is placed in an inactive file), and 2) having a court order that the individual can be removed from *registration* (an exceedingly rare occurrence in most sexual offender cases.)

There have been, in our experience, only exceptional cases of any sexual offense, even a minor one, being expunged. It can only be requested after ten years of crime-free living but courts have been reluctant to allow a sexual offender's record to be wiped clean. An occasional case of an offender who committed his single crime as a youngster might be expunged if he has led a crime-free life over an extended period of time, but even these are infrequent. Most folks would believe that a record, once expunged, is one no one would be able to access. Unfortunately, security companies have seemingly magical powers and often can locate even expunged records, perhaps through contacts with police departments, or liaisons within the justice system. Some of our patients have lost their jobs due to background checks revealing a past sexual crime, even after it had been expunged.

Of even more worry for many sexual offenders is the need for all such individuals to register as such. *Registration* for a sexual offender requires that, following serving whatever sentence was meted out, be it probation alone or following a jail term, or post-prison supervision subsequent to a prison sentence, the offender must register with the appropriate county official. Such an authority might be the supervising officer who last dealt with that offender but more often it is a corrections officer unfamiliar with this specific adjudicated individual. It may make little difference, however, as the requirements specify only that the offender call the corrections office (or a certain number connected to that county's justice system) within ten days each year on either side of the offender's birthday (before or after). In most counties, the system has been automated such that a computer system records the call and logs it in; no human contact is required.

However, there are additional mandates: The offender must also report to the system within ten days before a planned change of address, before acquiring a new job, or an alteration in his living arrangements, such as a new girlfriend moving in with him. The latter becomes thorny if the woman has any children below the age of 18. In that case, a corrections officer may well become involved to review the case.

> Xavior had sexually abused a 7-year-old stepdaughter from a previous marriage. The abuse occurred one time, at night, after both Xavior and his then-wife were highly intoxicated with the dangerous ingestion of a mixture of alcohol and cocaine. Yet neither were, fortunately perhaps, chronic substance abusers. Hence, they had not had the opportunity to become tolerant to the unpredictable and often uncharacteristic effects of such a potentially lethal combination. In our presentence psychosexual evaluation nonetheless, along with our typical recommendations, we advised a substance abuse program for both. DHS had taken a dim view of this situation and deemed Xavior and his ex-wife unfit by allowing the abuse while heavily intoxicated, despite no prior record of substance abuse or domestic violence for either parent. Although we argued for no incarceration, given the situational nature of the crime and the fact that Xavior had no prior criminal record, he was charged with *Sexual Abuse in the First Degree* and penalized with a five-year prison sentence. He subsequently served three years (often original sentences are reduced to time already served awaiting trial and for good behavior) and five years of PPS.

While many periods of supervision are cut in half with good behavior, such as no further crimes or violations of the conditions after release, the severity of the charge and the fact that the case was tried in Federal Court, required Xavior to serve under supervision for all five years. (The duration of Federal PPS is rarely ever reduced.) During that time, he was prevented from any contact with children under the age of 18, even though he had nieces and nephews who always participated in family gatherings. Xavior was finally allowed supervised visitations after three years of PPS, even though in reality, he posed no danger to any child as he had completed our typical cognitive and behavioral program, which has had, in similar cases, a record of 95% success in preventing any offender with this type of history from repeating a sexual crime over a 25-year period of follow-up.

More to the point of registration, however, a difficulty pertained to the nature of Xavior's employment: he had served as a senior advisor to the Governor of a Western State and his expertise in negotiating public–private investments was so highly valued that his former employer, now elevated to a US State Department Deputy Director, requested that he be allowed to change district supervision to Washington, DC; that proved no problem. An obstacle arose, however, when he was required to enter negotiations with foreign countries. Even a senator's and Director's recommendations proved fruitless as he was prohibited from obtaining a passport and his requirements to register were believed to be too onerous for the original federal supervisors to oversee; the Washington, DC supervisor believed she could not overrule the original federal requirements nor mandates and, unfortunately, Xavior lost this coveted position on the sole basis of the requirement to register as a sexual offender.

This was not a typical case. For example, most sexual offenses do not occur under a state of intoxication. Moreover, many people drink or use drugs heavily, yet do not commit sexual crimes. While a sexual offense can occur in which the offender has been habitually using drugs or alcohol, we commonly refer that individual to a substance abuse treatment program but never assume that he does not require sexual offender-specific treatment as well.

In addition, and to be fair, most corrections personnel are quite flexible in matters of changing locations and employment. Few, however, feel comfortable allowing an offender to leave the country and it may be that a receiving country might object to accepting a visitor with such a criminal record. But this highlights the troublesome difficulties of the requirement to register as a sexual offender. Such registration not only requires a call once a year; it also mandates that any individual having pled to, or found guilty of, certain serious sexual crimes, must register *for life*. Doing so automatically places the offender on the sexual offender registry list, accessible through a simple computer search.

Thus we are aware of dangerous predatory offenders being listed alongside men who wandered onto a child porn site seeking novelty or a 19-year-old boyfriend having sexual relations with his future wife when she was 16 years of age. In other words, the registry simply lists names, not the offense, or the danger an individual presents to his community.

The rationale for registration stems from several sexual offense cases which led to a triad of regulations nation-wide: Megan's Law, in which a young girl was raped and murdered in 1994 in New Jersey; the Wetterling Act in 1996, rendering Megan's Law a federal mandate; and the Lychner Act, also in 1996, requiring each state to publish information regardless of local law enforcements' assessment of risk of recidivism.

This sorry state was erroneously but indelibly encoded into federal law by one flawed edict (among many) enshrined by the Supreme Court in the 2003 case of *Smith vs Doe*. The decision to uphold federal mandates on sexual offender registration was deemed by the high court as based on three false premises:

That among all criminals, sexual offenders are the most likely to reoffend. (Their re-offense rate is among the lowest of all criminals, exceeded only by sociopathic offenders with lengthy histories of committing a variety of crimes and certain drug- and alcohol-related offenses.)

That among all criminals, they are the least likely to be cured. (Scientific studies demonstrate that the vast majority of sexual offenders who complete a treatment program will never reoffend.)

That sexual offenders prey upon the most innocent members of our society. (A minority of offenders have children as their victims; many have no victims at all, as in entrapment cases and in cases involving public urination – yes, that is considered, and treated like a sexual offense, even if it was barely noticed by a passing adult.)

Preying upon children may be true for a minority of offenders. It is surely not for the majority of sexual offenders incarcerated, under supervision, and/or in treatment today. Rather, the bulk of offenders these days have been arrested for child porn-only offenses, Romeo and Juliet types of cases, and those involving entrapment.

There has been a recent refinement of registration laws, which are now classified into Tiers.

Tier I offenders, deemed low risk, are required to register for five years, but only if they have not committed any violations of their supervision or broken any laws.

Tier II offenders are required to do so for ten years, with the same caveats mentioned for Tier I offenders. At ten years, relief from registration must be submitted to the original court; it is, in the main, granted if the offender has not committed any further crimes or violations of the conditions of his supervision. A request for relief from registration most often must be accomplished through an attorney due to the copious paperwork and the need to argue the matter in court.

Tier III offenders are required to register for life.

Only Tier I offenders are allowed to apply for relief from registration with a reasonable hope they can be eliminated from the list. Tier II offenders may apply for relief and Tier III offenders must essentially register for life, with infrequent exceptions. In certain cases, however, a Tier II offender can be lowered to a Tier I and in occasional cases, a Tier III can be lowered to a Tier II. The classification of the Tiers is left to the discretion of the local corrections' divisions and thus is prey to wide discrepancies. However, it is those very officers who often complain about the registration system. While no study has been conducted about their reactions, numerous anecdotes quote corrections officers bemoaning the burdens of supervising registries.

The consequences of being on the registry vary from one offender to the next. However, it is common to learn from actual offenders, many of the situational type alone, that collateral damage is not rare. Many men report that being on the registry has led them to shun former friends; they have lost family support; and they have had to avoid social gatherings, such as get-togethers, volunteer activities, and religious services. Some have had to obtain employment through temporary job agencies at salaries much lower than those of their former jobs; many could not move away from crime-infested neighborhoods; the majority have had to avoid family functions such as celebrations; they often lacked the courage to make new friends; younger offenders often were forced to discontinue any further education; a substantial number believed they could not pursue romantic relationships; most have been constantly anxious about what others will think of them; and the lion's share have also experienced shame, hopelessness and depression.

The toll of registration on sexual offenders can also involve harassment, the need to move, and loss of vocation and income. However, at times, the outcome can be nebulous, prejudicial and inequitable; it can even be deadly. A number of offenders on the registry have taken their lives, although honestly, we do not know if being on the registry was the sole reason. Several offenders have been killed once identified on the registry; those committing murder of sexual offenders must have held immutable hatred of them, even though they may not have been aware of the circumstances of the offenders' crimes as the registry makes no distinction between situational and predatory offenders.

There now exist almost one million individual humans on various sexual offender registries in the United States. In 2017, California spent US $140,000,000 to manage all sexual offender registries; the costs are higher at present. These burdens and costs have prompted some states (New York is prominent among them) to forego registering sexual offenders altogether; these states are being punished by the Federal DOJ by withholding certain assistance funds, even though the Federal funds are inadequate to cover the costs of maintaining registries. It makes even less sense; in the words of a state official, "The registration system is not effective...at estimating the likelihood of reducing recidivism."

At any rate, in terms of public safety, how many random people decide one day, out of the blue, to look up the sexual offender registry list? Probably barely a few. But what if you are moving into a new neighborhood? Or if you are about to rent an apartment or condominium inhabited by many families with children? Astute prospective buyers or renters might well consult this publicly available list. The stigma of being on that list becomes an offender's worst object of dread and one of the chief obstacles for any offender to find a job compatible with his former employment or to dwell in a location equal to what was available to him before adjudication. In addition, it renders it difficult, if not impossible, to live in close proximity to a potentially new job.

There is, however, a crucial difference among periods of supervision, registration, and expungement. Supervision has a definite end-point. In fact, many periods of supervision, especially those for men who have few prior criminal charges, have committed a situational type of offense, and have had no violations of the conditions of their probation, can have their period of supervision cut in half. This relieves the burden of corrections officers, who have back-breaking overloads of cases and also helps them concentrate on more serious offenders.

Expungement of a sexual offense, however, is rare. Expungement means that, supposedly, all records of an offense, including discovery materials used by the DA, attorney, and viewed by multiple experts rendering their opinions prior to sentencing, are, so to speak, cast aside. The record is, in other words, wiped clean, as if the offense never occurred. In reality however, after dealing with security companies for many years, I have come to understand that there are means by which such records can be obtained; I am not privy to such means but I know that, just as you cannot really truly delete anything on your electronic device, despite what your IT expert tells you, it can always be found – a warning to those with criminal intent or who carry out affairs. Thus a sexual offense may return to haunt the offender even after the record of its occurrence has supposedly disappeared.

Therefore, we warn all sexual offenders never to expect their sexual offense to be wiped from their history. The sole exception could be for juvenile offenders. Recent state laws in certain cases will allow the court to consider expungement if a juvenile has committed a relatively "mild" offense, such as a statutory one (see the case of Ulrich, above, as an example) or a child porn-only offense. This is, in our opinion, a fortunate development but, alas, an incomplete one. Certain one-time-only sexual offenders, such as David (Chapter One), should not, in our opinion, be marked for life for an offense that did not portend future risk to his community. From a scientific perspective, the risk of a reoffence in many such cases can be close to zero yet the stigma of your name being on a sexual offender list for the remainder of your life creates a permanent dark cloud over many of the activities other more serious offenders (think of those who commit *Murder in the Second Degree, Vehicular Manslaughter, Aggravated Assault* or repeated *Domestic Violence)* will never bear.

In summary, pseudoscience, fear and misinformation have once again triumphed over empirical facts and basic common sense. In the identical manner in which artificial intelligence is an oxymoron (it is neither artificial but, rather, human-manufactured, and it lacks emotions; if you kick a computer, it doesn't kick back) so is common sense (it is rarely universal or common and often contains unprovable nonsense). For many years, sexual offender treatment providers had perceived supervisors as more punitive than necessary while they, as therapists, held a duty to care for their clients. It has been a good sign that, more recently, both POs and PPSs have attempted to cultivate an alliance, embracing the concept of collaboration. In our experience, the majority of supervisors have accepted therapeutic suggestions while therapists have been more keen about, and aware of, the limitations the law places on those who must supervise offenders who are at large in their communities.

In a compromise, neither party achieves everything they want; it is the transparent nature of discussion and communication amongst all involved to bring about a supervisory and treatment program in which the supervisor has been informed and to which she or he agrees. It is only within such a mutual accord that true progress toward the shared goal of reduced recidivism can be accomplished.

I am hopeful this chapter will not be perceived as pejorative to those corrections officers assigned to supervise sexual offenders. Many bear the weighty burden of protecting their communities and are trained in the school of "better safe than sorry." Some have been stung with regret when a sexual offender reoffends on their watch. In addition, in most counties and all federal districts, they must report to supervisory boards which review their cases. Among such challenging careers (think divorce attorneys and disability judges), responsibility for the lives of relative strangers, let alone the safety of entire communities, is a vexing encumbrance, one in which every choice may be questioned. Our main concern, however, with this pillar of our justice system is the distance, still to be pruned, between perceptions, emotions, and science.

Chapter 5

The Fourth Pillar

Rehabilitation

In this chapter, treatment of sexual offenders will be considered as one of the measures which should be included under the general rubric of rehabilitation, although, in our opinion, it is its most important constituent. Other segments under rehabilitation, which will be more thoroughly discussed in Chapter Seven, might include vocational training and education of inmates. Treatment to prevent a sexual offender from reoffending (the legal term of course must be more complicated; it is known as recidivating) is almost always a requirement for a sexual offender. Treatment is most often begun once a charge is brought, even prior to any determination of guilt. Such referrals to treatment programs are usually initiated by attorneys, who wish their clients to appear to be cooperative and desirous of change.

Almost as frequently however, a treatment program begins after a sexual offender leaves jail or prison, or, if not incarcerated, once supervision begins. But what of the common perception that sexual offenders are beyond redemption? "Once a sexual offender, always a sexual offender" remains the received wisdom among the majority of the public's perceptions, a condition until now unchangeable and irredeemable.

Science offers a more optimistic view: I will not quote an extensive list of peer-reviewed journal articles here (see the Bibliography if interested) but anyone familiar with the literature would dispute the belief that all sexual offenders are untreatable and are doomed to repeat their crimes if provided the opportunity. This all-too-familiar sentiment makes several logical mis-steps in its assumption that sexual offending is an illness similar to diabetes or epilepsy; that is, a chronic life-long condition, perhaps similar to a personality disorder (which, despite what your psychologist tells you, is almost impossible to eliminate entirely).

Contributing to such an erroneous assumption is that all sexual offenders can be considered as a group, one no different from another. Adding to this misconception is the idea that deviant sexual desire, especially in men, is too powerful to alter, no matter the object of attraction. A third error stems from observations of men with a fetish who do not break the law but retain their affinity, at least until senility. In contradistinction, most sexual

DOI: 10.4324/9781003532590-6

offenders can be provided treatment that will greatly reduce, or even eliminate, the sexual proclivity that caused them to offend in the first place.

Perhaps a fourth source of the belief that sexual offending is a life-long malady occurs because we cannot pinpoint its source. It is believed that not knowing what causes sexual offenses prohibits their successful elimination. Were that true, woe to those who suffer from migraine headaches, a variety of cancers, and cardiac arrhythmias. The exact, micromolecular etiologic conditions which cause these ailments are, as yet, not completely manifest, although much recent work towards this goal is progressing. Nonetheless, we can treat these conditions, and many more, such that suffering is either greatly reduced or even eliminated.

It is true that we cannot pinpoint with accuracy all the causes of sexual offending. Many researchers in the field wish to pin the blame for sexual offending on dysfunctional family attachments; or being a victim of sexual abuse themselves; or social ineptitude; or on faulty early behavioral conditioning. In all honesty, however, we must admit that we have no idea why most men choose to molest a youngster or expose to a woman. Most boys subjected to these horrendous experiences do not grow up and become sexual offenders.

Nonetheless, many, but not most, sexual offenders have experienced trauma of some sort during their upbringing. Many have had parents who abused drugs or alcohol and a few are inheritors of fetal alcohol exposure. A certain group of such offenders also have undergone frequent shifts in their home locations and some of these have endured harsh institutional or foster home placements; others have endured physical, emotional and sexual abuse. Could these deprivations and traumata have caused a man to commit deviant sexual acts?

We lack a means of scientifically testing this hypothesis in a double-blind manner as isolating a cohort of abused children, then following them over the years involves too many confounding factors; moreover, it would be unethical. For example, a child might have been abused as a youngster, then placed in a welcoming, warm and stable home during adolescence. Others might have experienced trauma as an adolescent but enjoyed a nurturing upbringing. It is most certainly not true that most sexual offenders were victims of sexual abuse themselves.

Approximately 27% of sexual offenders have been victims of similar abuse in their childhood but the vast majority of victims do not proceed to become offenders themselves. Were they to do so, our offices would be overflowing with boys molested by priests alone. I might also relate an aside here: most women who suffer sexual harassment or abuse (the dispiriting statistic is between 35% to 40%) do not bear the cross of PTSD, anxiety or depression as a result. Were that inevitable, our offices instead would be teeming with such victims. Although politically incorrect, it is nonetheless a fact that most female victims are able to employ the astonishing human ability to adapt and prosper despite heinous acts perpetrated against them earlier in life.

It is true, nonetheless, that many sexual offenders have been raised in conditions in which they bear witness to physical, emotional, and even sexual abuse, either to themselves or their parents. Many are sadly aware that either one or both of their parents abuse alcohol or other mind-altering substances. Some run away or are placed in a series of foster homes of dubious quality. However, while statistics can be manipulated, bold numbers do not lie: the majority of sexual offenders grow up in homes much as yours, accompanied by the usual bickering every union endures, and sometimes in marriages in which relationships are severed. At any rate, the majority of children raised under adverse circumstances do not become sexual offenders, although they may well show other pathologies, such as conduct disorders and, as older teens, antisocial behaviors.

The rate of divorces or separations in unmarried partners in America is escalating and now stands at a dismal 60%. The fact remains that exposure to such misfortunes does not inevitably lead to a lifetime of psychological pathologies. The bulk of boys raised under abominable or reprehensible conditions do not become sexual offenders. Indeed, most children are remarkably adaptable; many thrive better in a happy divorce than in a testy marriage.

Recent scientific research has, however, surprised the long-held belief that inherited DNA holds the master hand in propelling the emotions and subsequent behaviors of all organisms. In fact, it now appears likely that early life experiences, such as parental abandonment; lack of nurturance; a paucity of positive and loving physical touch; exposure to physical and emotional abuse; and the nomadic lifestyle of youth forsaken and cast to and fro from one home to another; all can actually alter a growing child's genetic structure.

Indeed, both positive and negative life experiences may well not only modify or transform neural connections in our brains, but actually change the genetic material in our living cells. It had been a canon of neural physiology that, once formed, neurons and their connections (synapses) were immutable. It now appears that many organisms can not only alter their synaptic strength, thus enabling learning, but that new links can form or dissolve; in addition, new brain cells can, in fact, be formed, perhaps as a result of life experiences. Moreover, epigenetic alterations can occur throughout a lifetime; thus experiences can actually change our genetic code to some extent.

We are at quite some distance from an understanding of exactly how such links are produced, why new connections are created, and what external forces shape such an evolution. Therefore, it will be a lengthy period before scientists can identify, with the slightest degree of accuracy, what and how life events can either promote or accelerate our central nervous systems. It will thereafter be a protracted process to learn how certain life experiences are affected by such changes and, if adverse outcomes are to be avoided, how to alter those experiences to produce happier outcomes. At present, this is more the material for science fiction than present-day concerns.

As stated above, in many cases, delays in reaching a final judgement have led to sexual offenders obtaining treatment during the prolonged period of time between arrest and receiving a final sentence. Approximately 50% of the sexual offenders receiving treatment in our Clinic do so during this prolonged period of time. They are usually referred to us by their attorneys in the belief and hope that their clients, actively involved in a treatment program, would sway the DA and the court to view them, in terms of sentencing, in a more favorable light. This is especially true if we can provide them with positive progress reports demonstrating not only their admission of the crime, regret at its occurrence, acceptance of responsibility for it, and adherence to treatment assignments.

We prepare these reports based upon measurable progress for each offender. The acceleration of technical and scientific progress emblematic of the 21st century provides hope for the future. While every generation believes tremendous technological progress has been achieved within their own time frames, I do not believe we are blinded at present with the delusion of exponential growth. Current advances have been enabled, in my opinion, by five factors:

The entrance of over 50% of the population, namely women (in most countries), into the workforce, especially in the fields comprising scientific endeavors.

The increasing power of modern medicine to alleviate disabilities in a variety of illnesses, including "mental" diseases, thus adding talented individuals to the workforce in order to realize their full potential.

The prestige (let's be honest) of science, technology, engineering (particularly in electronics), and mathematics, spurring ever more intelligent and creative folks into such fields.

The enhanced communication amongst academia, governmental research institutions, and commercial scientists made possible by advances in electronics and the intensified trade and migration amongst countries. Almost half of all published journal articles in America are co-authored by scientists born in other countries, mainly Asian ones and those from India. In addition, 23% of all US patent holders are produced by immigrants and half of all advanced degree holders in academic and governmental research facilities were born abroad.

The acceptance of positive reinforcement, as opposed to punishment, in molding human behavior.

The increasing use of caffeine as a stimulant and memory enhancer in all manner of workplaces.

Admittedly, this last may appear unusual in relationship to the others but, compared to the offices and other workplaces of centuries past, the work environments of the 21st century are awash in coffee and its caffeinated substitutes to a far greater extent than in the past.

I have also probably omitted other factors which a reading of journals of sociology can supply. Nonetheless, I believe these six changes have contributed to an acceleration in science and in the improvements in the quality of life for most humans on our planet, especially those who live in Southeast Asia, Australia and New Zealand, Western Europe, Canada and the United States. Regardless of partisan bickering and inflation, America's Gross Domestic Production (GDP) accounted for one quarter of the increase in GDP for the entire world's countries despite its population being less than 0.4% of the remainder of all other nations.

Moreover, our country contributes 58% of the world's GDP, despite the rise of China's increasing productivity; the number of patents obtained for US companies and academic institutions over the past year alone (2023) exceeds that of the European Union and all other nations except China. Americans' mean family income, even taking into account inflation, has risen 86% since 1990.

Of even greater significance, the income of the poorest families has risen within that time frame by 74% in real terms. Unfortunately, the grimmest statistic remains static: despite being wealthier, America's poorest have suffered the greatest inequalities in income than ever before when compared to upper middle-class and upper-class citizens. Thus poverty, substance abuse and physical abuse, remain and undoubtedly contribute to a share of criminal behavior, including sexual offenses.

Nonetheless, as a result of advances in research, science has been increasingly accorded its due in the explanations of human behavior. The same cannot be said about the criminal justice system as it is applied to sexual offenders. Part of this is not due to any particular segment of the system or the individuals working within it. Rather, it can be attributed to the apparent disinterest we, as professionals and purported scientists, have shown in researching the basic causes of offending, compounded by the lack of resources to fund any studies into the etiology of such sexual misbehavior and to express our opinions and publicize our achievements.

Here, we are competing with the Department of Defense, the National Institutes of Health (where cancer, diabetes, and cardiovascular disease, for good reason, hog the budget), and academic institutions, which have shown a dismal disinterest in anything associated with the assessment and treatment of sexual offenders. True, some medical and psychology departments have funded a modicum of research into this field but it is largely focused on assessment rather than origins or treatment.

Hardly any funding into the genesis of sexual offending has been offered, and, to be honest, hardly any proposals for such exist. We are woefully ignorant in this regard, despite all the psychobabble of attachment disorders and substitution hypotheses, in which a sexual offender is supposed to be derelict in finding adequate sexual appeal in nonforceful sexual relations with adult partners. This is as false as it is lacking in the results as published in the scientific literature within the past many decades.

There are rare times when we can, with some leeway, point to some possible connection between early life experiences and sexual offending.

> As a nine-year-old boy, Yarrow, was enjoying his thrice-weekly bath when his six-year-old female cousin, visiting his household, complained in urgent fashion that she needed "to pee." There being but a single bathroom in this flat, she was allowed to use the toilet in the bathroom where Yarrow was bathing. He attempted to cover his genitals but found the experience of her using the toilet while watching her proved exciting in a manner previously foreign to him. He began to invite her brother to his home knowing she would have to accompany him. In a variety of manufactured settings, which he arranged, he would be alone with her and began to play "show me" with her. In his early adolescent years, he would masturbate to such fantasies and, as a young adult, he had accumulated a number of charges of *Public Indecency*. (*Indecent Exposure* is a different charge in some states; both terms vary but usually the latter relates to a man urinating in public while the former involves exposing as we think of it as exhibitionism.) In other respects, Yarrow was a rather successful sales representative for a nationally known corporation until his charges became known. He returned to work after serving a brief sentence and completing several additional online courses and is now an accountant.

It is difficult to attribute with 100% certainty that Yarrow's early bathing experience served as the sole cause of his later exhibitionism but it *appears* to be so. However, we cannot allow possibilities or common sense to substitute for scientific study.

Common sense (not always wrong) would place the responsibility of treating sexual offenders on the justice system itself; and the most appropriate and effective time to apply treatment would be in close proximity to when it occurred. In the real world, this is almost never the case. Treatment programs for incarcerated sexual offenders should begin while they are still in jail or prison. Yet institutional programs to treat such men are sadly lacking. As more sexual offenders were prosecuted after the middle of the 20th century, some prisons did initiate treatment programs. Jails rarely did so as the length of stay there was often too brief.

Such in-prison programs attempted to incorporate what was employed by outpatient centers. These were in the main based solely on group therapy, where, unfortunately shaming was rife. Certain groups centered on a "hot seat" approach in which a different offender each week would receive a grilling from the others.

However, more enlightened programs were eventually introduced which included techniques shown to be partially effective in outpatient programs, including cognitive therapy, in which "thinking errors" were dissected and "corrected". I have a personal distaste for these terms as they reek of authoritarian rehabilitation camps, but in all honesty, we continue to employ cognitive restructuring (a term implying less brainwashing) to examine the thoughts offenders use to justify their harmful behaviors. No institutional program consistently used conditioning techniques but many current clinics omit this as well.

Enlightened state systems made a valiant attempt to treat sexual offenders in programs lasting up to two years; others would initiate "orientation" programs within six months before release, but these were devoid of true treatment and were designed mostly to acquaint the offender with what to expect on parole. Excellent programs were managed by well-trained and ATSA-certified providers in states such as Washington, Oregon, California, and Minnesota. None survive to this day because, as you may have guessed, funding simply evaporated. By the early years of the present century, sexual offenders in prisons across the nation could receive several excellent treatment programs on substance abuse and, in a few cases, domestic violence, but none on sexual offending.

Most prisoners also signed up to generalized programs with titles such as "Building Bridges" and "Lifetime Satisfaction," which aimed at reducing antisocial behavior. We all wished such courses had a greater impact but, in a variety of studies, results were disappointing. This is not to say some general offenders gained no benefit whatsoever, but the majority of attendees demonstrated about as much change as they did in "finding religion" while incarcerated.

It has therefore been left to probation officers and post-prison supervisors to mandate sexual offender-specific treatment programs for sexual offenders once they are released into the community. In other words, although supervised, potentially some (but a minority) of dangerous offenders will be present in a community before they have received adequate treatment to render them safer to be at large.

Post-incarceration, such supervisors in most counties employ a list of accredited sexual offender-specific treatment programs to which they can refer offenders for treatment. Certification by ATSA and/or an apprenticeship at an already certified program help in making these referrals. Unfortunately, in a few well-intentioned probation and post-prison programs, even seemingly qualified therapists do, frankly in my opinion, a slipshod job of treating sexual offenders. Some use groups exclusively, even though the literature specifies individual treatment as the most effective modality to reduce recidivism, though often accompanied by therapeutic and support groups. Many such programs fail to incorporate the cognitive and behavioral treatment techniques which research has demonstrated to be most effective.

Some of these programs set their initial goal as reducing or eliminating denial as a first and necessary step in treatment. After all, if the offender says he didn't commit the crime, how are we to initiate treatment? However, study after study has demonstrated that some form of denial is not only almost ubiquitous amongst sexual offenders but that it is *not related to ultimate outcome* as measured by the most relevant statistic we can measure: rates of repeated sexual crimes.

Admitting to the commission of a sexual crime, especially against a youngster, constitutes one of the most severe assaults on one's ego. First, let us examine the most prevalent forms of denial we encounter:

Total denial: "I didn't do it;" "My wife's ex did it and the girl is confused;" "Her mom is making her say it to get back at me."

Minimizing or denying sexual intent: "I was just teaching her about sex."

Misattributing blame: "She was saying no but her body was saying yes."

Blaming the victim: "She came on to me"; "She's always jumping and hugging me." "The way she dresses, she had to have wanted sex."

Minimizing consequences: "She'd had sex before; it's no big deal"; "She's been friendly with me, even after the accusations." "She seems fine now – she's happy."

"Justifying the cause: "I only did it because I was molested as a kid"; "If my girlfriend did what I wanted, it never would have happened."

In such cases, we might begin by asking the offender to imagine someone else, perhaps a new friend, and how he would react to that person. Gradually, the conversation can be angled toward the offender taking responsibility. More typically, group therapy can often confront the denial: "We also couldn't admit it at first." The modelling effect here is most successful. In almost all cases, the offender will eventually admit to something, even if he still must hold on to some measure of self-respect. That is fine, as additional treatment techniques, briefly described below, can markedly reduce recidivism in even the most recalcitrant of offenders.

Of crucial importance however, are studies that demonstrate that initial denial is not correlated with treatment outcome or recidivism. Although counterintuitive, offenders who deny any culpability can and should be treated. Research has clearly indicated that men in denial can achieve meaningful outcomes with a marked reduction in reoffending even if they maintain denial throughout the therapy process. Most deniers will admit, at some point in treatment, that they did in fact commit something akin to what they were charged with, and even that is a significant step, marking progress in the treatment process.

Studies have shown that interventions that are consistent with the client's learning, personality styles and cognitive abilities, combined with personality characteristics and a good match with the therapist, account for a significant proportion of progress and in successful treatment outcome. Most important is the initial establishment of trust between the client and therapist. Even if the offender is initially defiant and complains of the time and expense of therapy, or even that it is unnecessary, the clinician must strive to convince the offender that she or he is not an extension of the supervisory apparatus but instead is supportive of the offender as someone who has made a mistake, as we all have. This bond will prove crucial in implementing the elements of cognitive and behavioral therapy described below.

Cognitive therapy: This text will not delve into the particulars of the variety of treatment techniques; those interested should consult the Bibliography in the back for more information. In general, cognitive distortions are confronted and alternatives provided. A few examples will suffice.

Distortion	*Countervailing positive cognition*
"If she doesn't put up a fight, then it's OK."	"It's never OK without obvious consent."
"It's OK because she needs to learn about sex."	"Children never need to learn about sex in that way."
"I can get away with it; she'll never tell."	"It always comes out sooner or later."
"I can't control my sexual needs."	"There's a difference between needs and wants."
"I would never hurt anyone."	"Non-consenting sex always hurts the victim."
"It won't hurt if I just masturbate to fantasies."	"Deviant fantasies augment deviant behavior."
"I gain power when I rape a woman."	"I surrender power when I have to use force."
"I truly love her."	"What you did wasn't love; it was lust."

An initial period of treatment consists of reviewing the offender's history. This is followed by explanations of the variety of treatment techniques the therapist is proposing. This helps the offender know ahead of time what he will be asked to do in participating in treatment. In our experience, the vast majority of offenders are accepting of the need for treatment; however, many may be providing lip service to assuage the therapist as they have been mandated into treatment. Nonetheless, once involved we have been gratified at how compliant offenders have been in carrying out assignments and in tolerating even the most unpleasant of approaches.

Cognitive therapy also involves examining how to obtain common human goods without harming others. Such goods might include a sense of purpose, becoming involved in a community, obtaining inner peace, and improving happiness. Certain programs employ the "Good Lives Model" to encourage offenders to create meaning and purpose in their lives as they become increasingly regarded as positive contributors to society. Attending a support group, such as the 12-step Sexual Addicts Anonymous, volunteering at a charity, returning to college, or helping a neighbor move, are just a few examples of re-inserting purpose and challenge in an offender's life and may well prove incompatible with sexual offending.

To assist with this approach, a workbook is employed with homework assigned. At present, we employ the workbook, *The Road to Freedom*, published by Safer Society Press at safersocietypress.org. Each chapter deals with an area of the offender's life and asks the client to write his own story and his approaches to counter a life involving sexual abuse. In-office sessions then review the content and further discussions proceed about the reality of the plans and the sincerity of the offender's admissions of his sexual history and especially of his offending.

Preemptive steps incompatible with an offender's former lifestyle are emphasized, then assigned in the offender's ongoing life. It has been helpful to encourage the participation of a spouse, girlfriend or other significant person in the offender's life to obtain their perspectives. Of importance, the workbook (there are several for different types of offenders) structures treatment and we can more accurately measure the offender's progress to ensure concepts are not only assimilated but actualized in real life.

We also examine the chain of behaviors leading to a sexual crime. Often, opportunity, proximity to a victim, and high sexual drive all combine to create a scenario in which it becomes increasingly difficult for an offender to resist. This is especially true in young males; sexual crimes peak between the ages of 18 and 25. The full maturation of the male human brain does not occur until reaching that age (females mature earlier, with which most educators and parents agree). We attempt to help the offender predict what situations might increase the likelihood of a crime and how to avoid those situations, such as never being alone with a youth under the age of 18, never putting hands on a woman he does not know well, or never being alone with a woman who is intoxicated. The issue of consent is of vital importance these days and is extensively discussed with offenders. No matter her age, a woman who is intellectually disabled or intoxicated may not be able to provide consent, even though she may not put up a fight or even if she is your girlfriend or wife. Not saying "no" is not a defense.

In addition, despite being politically incorrect, men and women do differ in the degree to which sexual activity is of importance. This is no mere observational or anecdotal point of view. Both physiological studies employing the penile plethysmograph, which measures men's level of penile erection, or the female equivalent, a device measuring female lubrication (a Geer Gauge), show more immediate and greater arousal when viewing pornography or when listening to sexually based story-lines. Thus we must recognize how important sex is to men, though of course the intensity of this drive differs across individuals. Many sexual offenders, however, do have a high sexual drive, although this is not accompanied by higher-than-normal levels of testosterone. It might be related to the sensitivity of testosterone receptors in the brain but we cannot examine this yet; progress toward that goal, however, is being made.

Therefore, simply talking rarely eliminates paraphilic urges. For those who hold attractions to children or to aggressive unwanted sexual activity, a therapist must get up out of her or his comfortable chair and actually *do* something. In the case of sexual offenders, that will often mean some form of conditioning. Recent studies have gauged sexual preoccupation, though admittedly via questionnaires, which can always be somewhat suspect from an objective point of view. Nonetheless, a definite increase in "sexual preoccupation" was found in men compared to women. Unfortunately, the same academic institution studied "compassion," again a somewhat muddled concept. It will come as no surprise that women beat men handily on such measures.

The most common form of conditioning employed for pedophiles, rapists and exhibitionists is aversive conditioning, using a foul odor in association with story-lines, composed by the offender himself, though edited by the therapist. The offender is taught relaxation and imagery techniques, then presented with a number of stories of what he actually did, such as molesting a young child. At a certain point in the scenario, a negative element is introduced along with the foul odor. This element might be being discovered by a wife, being apprehended by the police, or encountering a nauseating image, a foul-smelling odor on a child's genitals. A variety of such scenes with negative consequences, and even actual putrid odors, are utilized to prevent habituation.

Homework is assigned by recording these scenes and providing a flask of the vile odor; the client is asked to tape record how he employs this technique at home three times each week so as to ensure compliance. Should we suspect resistance, the client is asked to perform the procedure in private but at the Clinic. The frequency of sessions is reduced as arousal to the deviant stimulus is achieved. The foul odor produces nausea (though vomiting is fortunately rare); this is crucial since, in the brain, nausea acts to eliminate arousal. It is difficult to be aroused when close to throwing up.

In consultation with the Monell Chemical Senses Center in Philadelphia, we have experimented with, and used, a variety of chemical and organic odors best described as putrid. We have varied these smells with each patient to prevent habituation. I will spare the reader the exact composition of the nauseating odors we use. It is simpler to merely ask you to imagine rotting chicken and cheese combined with dog feces as one example.

An additional technique employs the penile plethysmograph as a biofeedback device. If the offender can see, on a screen, his erectile response to deviant subjects, sometimes paired with stories matching his offenses, such as a young boy or girl, or to a scene and story of rape or exposing, he can learn to control that arousal with competing images in his mind or read to him, such as being apprehended. We might also introduce the foul odor at points of arousal to deviant stimuli. For example, an exhibitionist might begin exposing to a young woman from behind her only to find, as she turns around, it's his own daughter. The offender's progress is recorded and profusely reinforced to encourage continued progress toward the goal of reducing or eliminating an attraction to a subject who may be harmed by his actions.

Aversive behavioral rehearsal is an additional approach. The offender is asked to replicate what he has done in committing the offense. We use realistic boy and girl dolls for the offender to demonstrate to his therapist how he grooms youths, then offends against them. Yes, this is shaming and creates anxiety and embarrassment, which associates the deviant act with those negative emotions. Nonetheless it is highly effective. The offender is rewarded for his courage in re-enacting these scenes and much support is offered during these sessions. Some might believe that such an anxiety-provoking practice is cruel and even tantamount to torture. However, in the pursuit of public safety, we believe it is warranted. We have yet to note any long-lasting side effects from utilizing such techniques.

Masturbation is a powerful reinforcer of deviant desires and behaviors. Therefore, we ask the offender to masturbate at home to deviant fantasies involving activity with a potential or actual victim to stop just before the point of ejaculatory inevitability and then use imagery of a consenting adult. Then, we ask him to stop masturbation at some midpoint to change to normal sexual scenes, then earlier and earlier in masturbation until he is masturbating to normal sexual activity 100% of the time. To ensure compliance we ask the offender to occasionally record these in-home sessions out loud. Why use normal fantasies? Because we want to not only encourage normal arousal, but the crucial point of this technique is impulse control.

Imagine a man entering a relationship with a woman who has a 14-year-old daughter; or a male high school teacher confronted with a class containing attractive 16- and 17-year-old females. If he did not raise those girls from birth, there is no hard-wired CNS taboo against arousal. How many such men might be tempted? Possibly a few; more likely, many. How many would act on it? The majority would exert self-control and not allow fantasies or, if they had them, would not act upon them. Thus impulse control features in our treatment programs, such as the masturbatory technique mentioned above.

Other examples need not be sexual at all but would still ask the offender to practice the habits which restrain the self-harmful behaviors many of us cultivate. Examples include: instigating an exercise program; creating healthy eating habits; parking as far from the store instead of searching for the closest spot; taking the stairs instead of the elevator; and speaking softer and more slowly when disagreeing with a partner. Role-play in office sessions is helpful in this latter example.

Empathy training is stressed in the workbooks mentioned above but can also be achieved through an assignment to write a letter to the victim(s) owning full responsibility; acknowledging (but not assuming) harm the offender may have caused; stress that he is the only one responsible for his misdeeds and that the victim was never at fault; and, perhaps most vital, explaining that the offender is in treatment so that the victim and others in the community will never be traumatized again in a similar manner. Discussions in office sessions can review the letter(s) and make suggestions for change if necessary. These are letters to write but not to be actually sent as that might re-expose a victim to her or his original trauma. Through this process the offender can reverse roles, acknowledge the harm he may have caused, and take full responsibility for his actions. Apologies are inappropriate; the two weakest words in the English language are "I'm sorry."

There are cases in which the victim and his or her family actually want to reunite with the offender after the punishment phase and treatment have sufficiently progressed. For example, a stepchild might desire the offender, a father figure, back home even after being molested; a mother may wish him back to help for financial support; or placement back home might render the offender even less likely to reoffend when returned to a family setting which can offer support.

In such situations, delicate negotiations must occur with family members, the victim(s) and, of course, approval must be obtained from the supervising officer, a family's and/or victim's therapists, and the sexual offender's own therapist as well. A number of clarification sessions involving all parties are necessary, along with trial placements of a temporary nature. These should all precede such placements prior to any permanent arrangement. In our experience, only the most minor of offenders who have fully disclosed their crime(s) and largely completed treatment in a successful manner would be considered for such a homecoming.

Thus far, we have discussed treatment as an individual process, in which the therapist meets singly with the offender, usually on a weekly basis, for a number of months. But group therapy cannot be ignored. There exist several types of groups depending on purpose and conduct of the therapist, but in reality, there may be wide differences within the two broad categories of treatment vs. support groups.

In treatment groups, individuals may be singled out and asked about their histories, level of denial if any, and then provided with additional assignments for the following session. Often, all members are asked to contribute their ideas, not only about the individual being discussed, but also their concerns and suggestions in general. Wide variations exist in how such groups are conducted but, in some clinics, group therapy may be the sole mode of treatment offered.

We are opposed to group-only programs as so many dissimilarities occur amongst offenders. In addition, research indicates that groups composed of predatory offenders (such as serial rapists and pedophiles) combined with situational offenders (as for example child pornography-only offenders or those who have offended against a household member just once) are less effective than ones composed of offenders with comparable crimes.

Support groups, on the other hand, can be invaluable in breaking through denial and providing a step-like program of self-examination, succor and aid in undergoing what is probably among the worst of times for most offenders. In addition, a mentor or sponsor can be called upon not only for support but for advice as well. In our clinic, we conduct support groups along with individual therapy but outside 12-step programs such as Sexaholics Anonymous, Sex Addicts Anonymous, or Celebrate Recovery are encouraged as they can reinforce treatment progress.

How lengthy should treatment be? Many would opt for a lifetime but that is not only frightfully expensive, but binds the offender to a schedule which might interfere with his job or place of residence. In fact, for a situational offender, about one year of treatment is typical, usually conducted once each week for a number of months depending upon the type of offense, and the client's history and application to assignments. This is followed by a tapering schedule of every-other-week visits, then monthly follow-up "booster" sessions, typically extended throughout the better part of the second year.

However, predatory offenders may require several years of active individual sessions and follow-up to ensure complete treatment success. How success is defined, of course, can vary. In many cases, we believe that situational offenders such as men with a single familiar victim or men who are caught watching child pornography but have no record of ever molesting a child nor of arousal to prepubescent youth, can be expected, after completing an adequate course of *evidence-based* treatment, never to commit another sexual crime. In our series, this has proven true in over 95% of such cases, according to our follow-ups in coordination with the Oregon Department of Justice (which also receives criminal records from other states).

For predatory offenders, the record of recidivism is, as expected, higher but not by orders of magnitude. Approximately 85% of heterosexual pedophiles (men who repeatedly offend against female children) who have completed treatment have not reoffended over a period of 35 years. These figures are lower, unfortunately, for homosexual pedophiles, but not as low as you may think: about 70% of such men never reoffend. Among serial rapists, however, this figure drops to about 65%.

We clearly have more work to do in devising effective treatments for such habitual sexual aggressors. Unfortunately, some of these men may require extended periods of incarceration until they reach advanced ages where improving impulse control combined with treatment and disabilities prevent further such horrendous and traumatizing crimes.

Most recently, the Good Lives and Self-Regulation Model (GL/SRM) of treatment is proposed and has gained traction as it is easy to apply and coincides with the best workbooks for sexual offenders. However, it also makes the unproven, and unprovable, assumption that substituting positive behaviors – such as honest self-examination, correcting cognitive distortions, and making lifestyle changes (such as abstaining from illegal substance abuse, attending church, maintaining employment, and volunteering in the community) – for negative ones (offending) will promote the achievement of goals which improve the quality of life for offenders and thereby automatically reduce recidivism.

Such substitution theories have been disproven in general psychiatry and, by themselves, do little to tackle the offending behavior itself. There is no question that following the GL/SRM program achieves positive lifestyle changes as it promotes beneficial activities which are meant to block repeat offending while encouraging cognitive self-examination, both of which prove beneficial to offenders in general, but, by themselves, are insufficient to reduce or eliminate sexual offending.

However, combined with the behavioral techniques described in brief above, this model can achieve marked improvement in deviant lifestyles which enhance behavioral and cognitive methods in encouraging skill acquisition, especially when combined with role-playing and experiential learning.

Relapse prevention, in which we review the offender's initial steps toward an offence, then construct how to intervene at the earliest points, can be of enormous assistance. Once very close to committing an offence, it may prove almost impossible to thwart it; therefore, the earlier the prevention, the better the chance an offense can be prevented. It is the combination of techniques, honed to each individual's strengths and deficiencies, which prove most dependable in generalizing what is gained in therapy into one's actual day-by-day life.

The description of many of the techniques utilized in the treatment of sexual offenders raises interesting questions of governmental coercion and disregard of the fundamental constitutional rights of all citizens, including released sexual offenders. After all, their liberty had been erased for some period of time and they have suffered financial hardships, family discords, restrictions imposed by supervision, and marked at times for life by the stigma inherent in the label of being a sexual offender. Should additional incumbrances be imposed by treatment that is mandated by the state and consists of distasteful methods as mentioned above? Fortunately, most offenders, contrary to how it may appear, do not reject the need for change.

Yes, a few, perhaps ten percent, rebel; but most can establish trust in their therapist and the majority actually carry out their assignments, are cooperative, supportive of therapeutic efforts, and appreciative of the support they receive, especially in group therapy. Would they be so accommodating if not mandated into treatment by their conditions upon release? It is impossible to know now as that study would be difficult to undertake, and ethically impossible.

We do know that men who complete treatment may not enjoy every aspect of it but they are, in the main, appreciative of our efforts, especially as they gain benefits in terms of a lessening of supervisory restrictions as they progress in treatment and finally graduate. In fact, with the onslaught of supervision cases each corrections officer must handle, many minor offenders are offered time off their period of supervision upon treatment graduation, up to cutting their period of parole or post-prison supervision time in half for many. In treating sexual offenders, we try to build as much trust and hope as possible to men who are undergoing what, for most, will be the most distressing time of their lives. We encourage them to remember that behind every shadow, there must be a light.

Admittedly, "treatment" of all sexual offenders can be an amorphous concept. The types of cognitive and behavioral methods described above, while generally accepted, are rarely incorporated into most programs. Each treatment clinic has its own set of standards and I would be remiss in insisting that our clinic (The Sexual Abuse Clinic in Portland, OR) contains the most powerfully beneficial ingredients available. Further research will continue to define and inform therapeutic techniques. Nonetheless, treatment, and thereby rehabilitation, must remain a crucial component within the criminal justice system. Without it, criminal anarchy would, I fear, persist.

There also exist several types of sexual offenders who never receive any semblance of modern-day treatment. One group are men whose supervision ends and they drop out of a treatment program without consequence. Others are placed in clinics which do not specialize in treating sexual offenders and receive a panoply of generic psychological "talk therapy" without the benefit of scientifically proven efficacy. We cannot know the numbers of a different population of sexual offenders who are never identified or apprehended but we do know that many victims are hesitant to come forward.

Pessimism about the efficacy of treatment for sexual offenders ("Once an offender, always an offender") may stem from the notion that all sexual offenders are antisocial or have psychopathic personality disorders. Nothing could be further from the truth. Yes, a few men or male teens who have committed a sexual offense have histories of general criminality. We must admit that, despite reams of research into the causes of antisocial personality disorder, some therapists claim that either individual, or more likely group therapy, can alleviate a pattern of vehemence and rageful behavior. In real-life practice, and across a broad range of large post-treatment studies, no such beneficial effect for those with an antisocial (or psychopathic) personality disorder has been demonstrated.

Especially worrisome are those sexual offenders who have histories of physical aggression, whether associated with their sexual offending or manifested in nonsexual crimes such as domestic violence. We remain most concerned about those sexual offenders who use force or threats of aggression to gain compliance, as well as men who coerce their victims not to disclose abuse lest their target will get into trouble, not be believed, or that disclosure will disrupt the family structure. Other offenders may compel nondisclosure by portraying themselves as victims, threatening that if the real victim tells, he himself will go to prison, again disrupting the family, and perhaps depriving them of financial survival.

This is not to deny that certain individuals can be rescued from a lifestyle typified by aggression but, in the main, most such offenders will slowly improve with age and maturation. Indeed, the majority of aggressive or forceful sexual crimes are committed by men from the ages of 18 through 30. It is of more than passing interest that male brains do not reach full maturation until about the age of 25.

Anger management therapy (which we would recommend be accomplished by a specialized program) may be helpful in selected cases but, despite the fact that the majority of such belligerent or combative offenders are more difficult to treat in terms of reducing hostility, their deviant sexual interests can be addressed employing the methods described above.

In a similar fashion, we see and treat a number of sexual offenders who also have issues of substance abuse. Of particular concern are men who combine a stimulant such as cocaine or methamphetamine with alcohol. Popular these days are amphetamine substitutes such as MDMA (I will spare the reader its chemical name), also known as "Molly" (believed to be derived from the word "molecule"). If habitual use is documented, whether related to the sexual crime or not, referral to a specialized substance abuse program is also recommended. Clinics that combine all such specialized therapeutics, I believe, are diluted in each area and do not produce the desired levels of reduced recidivism as more sexual offender-based-programs-only can achieve.

We can only imagine what unprincipled chemists can concoct in the future but I am certain we will encounter novel chemicals on the streets and, unfortunately, schools near your neighborhoods in due time. By the way, a sexual offender who claims that alcohol "made" him commit the crime may be referred to a substance abuse clinic but intoxication is never the sole reason a sexual offense took place: many men drink but just a handful of them commit sexual crimes when intoxicated. At times, the alcoholic sexual offender will claim he committed his crime in an alcohol-induced blackout, thus reducing or eliminating responsibility. Studies, conducted both in a forensic laboratory and in a hospital setting by our group, demonstrate that sexual activity, even in the muddle of a blacked-out condition, is not so easily erased from memory.

I have omitted certain special cases of sexual offenders, many of which will be discussed in Chapter Six. These will include the rare female offender, juvenile offenders, "Romeo and Juliet" (R&J) cases (I hate that term but it is convenient), child pornography-only offenders (CPO), hypersexuality, and the offenders who commit internet-only sexual crimes.

Unfortunately, little heed has been paid to the *prevention* of sexual abuse. Education in public schools should incorporate protective approaches, especially for young females, but should also include advice to teen males about the repercussions of statutory offenses, such as R&J cases, and the laws relevant to providing consent.

There may be some who realize they have sexual interests that are illegal and harmful but who actually view their affliction with distress and would volunteer for treatment but for the fear of imprisonment. A recent study from the United Kingdom discovered a number of men with sexually deviant urges never acted upon them. These men fear imprisonment or at least social rejection, loss of employment and even loss of family. Therefore they never acknowledged to others their sexual desires, nor had they dared to seek treatment.

A recent program originated in Germany offers help to men who openly admit an attraction to prepubescent youth. This proactive approach involves the voluntary admission to an outpatient program with a guarantee of anonymity and with no mandated reporting to authorities. Treatment is provided, along with support not only for the purported offender (who may or may not have committed any crime) and their families as well. Trained clinicians employ techniques which exceed those of a 12-step program and include the well-recognized cognitive and behavioral methods described above in addition to medication to lower sexual drive, if indicated.

Of interest, however, is that, as of the most recent reports, men graduating from the German voluntary program have an exceedingly low rate of recidivism, around 0.9%, but the numbers as yet are too few to render definitive conclusions. The rate of sexual offending in Germany, however, is approximately one-tenth that in America. Thus this program (see the Bibliography) has enjoyed initial success but its follow-up period is too brief to award credits thus far. Moreover, it must be repeated and tested outside of its originators' laboratories to achieve world-wide acclaim.

A different type of offender than those noted above is only rarely encountered in this country. We have treated only a handful of men who have not been reported to authorities but who wish treatment for an attraction to youth. We are obligated by statute to report these willing offenders to authorities for judicial management. Unfortunately, we are hardly as advanced as many European countries; anyone committing a sexual crime would be unlikely in our country to self-report, given the harsh punitive consequences that are unavoidable, given the mandated reporting system all therapists must follow.

Forty years ago, an eminent Yale Professor of criminology, Dr. Francis Allen, suggested that, "Critique of the rehabilitative ideal rests on scientific ignorance; the [most] appropriate response is not the abandonment of such programs, but rather, the production through research of new knowledge." It is vital to recognize that treatment of sexual offenders is not merely putting on a bandaid to cover the problem underneath. Scientifically proven evidence-based treatment can eliminate the risk of re-offense in the vast majority of cases. Criminal justice systems which pay no heed to scientific advances in the assessment and treatment of sexual offenders will not be judged kindly by future historians of criminology and the administration of justice. Nor should they be.

Chapter 6

Special Cases of Sexual Offenders – Their Disposition and Treatment

Female Sexual Offenders

Female offenders are seldom encountered in clinical practice, though some studies claim a ratio of male to female sexual offenders as between 18:1 to 25:1, or between 5% to 3%. This ratio differs by study as some research articles remain anecdotal in nature while others are based upon undersized populations. To add to this dilemma, some cases involving an adult woman are never registered as such in cases in which a man is also involved (see Category 1, below).

In our Clinic, for reasons which remain obscure, out of approximately 35,000 sexual offenders treated, the number of women offenders we have encountered remains about 45, or less than 1%. None of these have been girls under the age of 18. I am unaware of any substantial treatment program for female sexual offenders only. This undoubtedly stems from their rarity; thus they are provided treatment in programs established in the main for male offenders. Unfortunately, to date no risk assessment for female sexual offenders in any of the typologies noted below has proven, in a double-blinded study, predictive of recidivism, though it is rare in the first two categories listed.

As with male offenders, there exist a number of types of female culprits. Although several authors have more recently divided female sexual offenders into a variety of more highly nuanced groups, I believe that a simpler tripartite grouping, employed for many years, is more appropriate for this summary. There remain essentially three subtypes of sexual offenders who are girls (quite unusual) or (more typically) adult women. They can by categorized as:

Male-associated female offenders

Mentor/neophyte offenders

Adult female offenders of minors

- a Against boys
- b Against girls

DOI: 10.4324/9781003532590-7

Category 1 consists of women associated with partners, whether random, boyfriend or husband, who invite or coerce their participation in their own molestation of children. This group comprises the majority of female sexual offenders. Although percentages are difficult to derive because of the paucity of recorded cases, in our Clinic the most common type of female sexual offender is the woman who commits a crime in association with a male companion.

When Zoe married Troy, she believed that the commitment of marriage would help him reduce or eliminate his drinking, as would the additional responsibility of caring for her 13-year-old daughter, Sienna. Unfortunately, she could not have been more mistaken. Troy soon found the developing adolescent as, or more, attractive than his wife. Zoe had been raised in an alcoholic family herself and a combination of low self-esteem and sub-assertion led to a passivity not restricted just to typical domestic affairs but to the bedroom itself. She first suspected that Troy was becoming more openly attentive to Sierra as he would attempt to isolate the girl with him on routine trips and chores. Soon he was hugging and kissing her as well as slapping her buttocks, all in Zoe's presence. During one heated sexual encounter with his wife, Troy suggested they invite Sierra to join them, "for sexual education," though Zoe demurred. Troy was nothing if not persistent, however, and she finally relented.

The couple began to routinely invite Sienna to join them in sexual trysts. At first, the girl expressed reluctance, telling her mother it was "gross." It became, however, a ritual and Sienna at times, in all honesty, appeared to enjoy parts of this *ménage à trois* to the point where she bragged about it to friends at school. Needless to say, her friends, alarmed at this activity, spoke to the school's counselor, a mandatory reporter. At court, Troy accepted a plea arrangement with several charges of *Rape in the Second Degree* (force was not used; otherwise, the charges could have been in the *First Degree*). He received a prison sentence of five years followed by five years of supervision.

Of interest is that Zoe was treated in a more lenient fashion, though with identical charges: she was placed on five years of probation only. Part of the difference might have been her lack of any criminal history while Troy had multiple drug, burglary and driving infractions. However, it is difficult to escape the conclusion that her considerably more lenient sentence was highly influenced by twin factors: she was aggressively impelled into these actions involving her daughter and she was a female.

In fact, a retrospective comparison of sentences meted out to female offenders in our Clinic concluded that punishment of female offenders was generally more moderate than male offenders with similar charges. This area begs for more qualified research, larger samples and double-blinded studies in which the gender of the culprit is unknown to the finders of fact.

This example, while not atypical, should not be taken to exclude a number of cases in which prepubescent children of both genders are involved. Men who either coerced or persuaded their female partners to involve children, usually not ones they have raised from birth, are increasingly reported. On rare occasions, the child involved was a boy. In such matters, society and the justice system deem these crimes as more horrendous and sentences of between 10 to 20 years in prison have been imposed.

The second type of female offender, in terms of prevalence, is our Category 2, the mentor/youth, in which a female adult is in some position of authority over a youth under the age of 18. One such case, that of Olivia, was described in Chapter Three; that case is somewhat atypical (though not rare) as it involved a single female offender and a male teen. A different case will be instructive.

> Ann had been a youth pastor for just six months when she became attracted to one of the girls in her study group, Charity, 14 years of age. Though married, and seemingly in a happy union with her wife, a frequent volunteer at the church, Ann began to ask Charity to stay after class a bit, at first so she could "explain" biblical concepts in a more accurate and contemporary manner. Thereafter, lunchtime provided a convenient excuse for her to accompany Charity to a local diner. She soon began to buy her gifts, nothing extravagant at first, but sufficient to arouse her wife's suspicions. Of interest, and not unusual in such cases, Anne's parents, quite religious themselves, were delighted that such a pious person, a junior church counselor such as Ann, would take an interest in their daughter, who appeared to them as straying from the church in the past, as so often occurs with teens.
>
> However, they became concerned when, on a camp retreat, Ann assigned the sleeping arrangements so that she and Charity were alone in the special counselor's tent. Her subsequent "cuddling" with the girl made Charity feel uncomfortable. Over the next several days, Ann began to probe Charity's sexual history, asking about prior boyfriends and her sexual feelings and behaviors. The following evening, Charity asked for their sleeping arrangements to be changed. Nonetheless, Ann continued to shower more attention on her and, over the next several weeks, when alone with the girl, would put her arm around her, then on her thigh and eventually progress toward her genital area. As so often occurs in such cases, Charity could not confront her youth pastor, Ann, directly out of fear of retribution and disbelief; of course, her parents were the last to learn of her discomfort. Instead, Charity began to talk with other girls at the camp, who convinced her this was not right and encouraged her to report it to the head minister.

> Following disclosure, Department of Human Services/Child Welfare (DHS) and police were alerted, and charges of *Sexual Abuse in the Second Degree* were levelled against Ann. Since no actual skin-to-skin touching had occurred, Ann was fortunate (and had hired an experienced attorney) and pled guilty to a misdemeanor of *Sexual Harassment*. She received three years of probation with mandated treatment.

Was Ann a pedophile? Many, unfamiliar with this area would categorize her thus. In clinics, however, any paraphilia must be manifested by a repetitive attraction, whether acted upon or not, to an object, person or group of people considered "unusual" (hardly helpful) or who cannot provide consent. We did not consider Ann to be a pedophile; most men find female teens attractive as they have secondary sexual characteristics; the same might be said about Ann, who was gay, about her attraction to Charity. Unfortunately, in some countries, this alone would have justified forced marriages between middle-aged to almost senile men and girls as young as 12. We hope these practices are beginning to be shamed by most civilized societies.

However, by dint of her age, Charity could not provide knowledgeable consent; she would be considered in all US states to be too young. Some states reserve the right to provide consent to youths 16 and older with parental permission while others adhere to the stricter standard of 18. Consent is crucial in such cases. Examples include a person too intoxicated or incapacitated (such as an intellectually challenged individual) to knowingly consent to participation in sexual activity.

Most would agree that 14 is too young an age to be afforded the privilege of knowing whether they "should" have sexual relations; but there are vast differences in the maturity of many 14-year-old girls. Arguments going back and forth as in a tennis match have been offered about the age of consent. The state is forced to designate an age but there will be an eternal dispute in this area. Many "Romeo and Juliet" cases, described more fully later in this chapter, hinge on this distinction.

Yet as teenagers become more overwhelmingly connected to the outside world, the concept of the government making arbitrary decisions about what age an individual is capable of saying "yes", whether in words or behavior, can be a nondefinitive conundrum. The state cannot examine the ability of every 14-, 15-, or 16-year-old girl to determine whether each girl is sufficiently mature to provide consent. If governments decided to undertake that onerous task, what criteria would they use for such a finding? Therefore, establishing a minimum age of ability to consent to sexual activity is, at present, inescapable.

In the case of the victim, Charity, most would agree that Ann's behavior constitutes deviant activity, potentially harmful to the victim. But what if Charity complains to authorities and her parents that she enjoyed not only the attention of Ann but her sexual advances as well? In fact, in this particular example, she was mortified that she got her youth pastor in trouble and continues to experiences guilt in playing a role in having done so. We would counsel her with support and try to convince her that it is not *her decision* to prosecute Ann. Even if she refused to testify, the DA could still (and did) bring such a case to court. It is the State that is prosecuting Ann and that is why all indictments begin with "The state of [state name] vs. Ann [last name]."

The third category of female offenders are true pedophiles. These cases are uncommon but not unknown.

> Brianna, 37 years of age, had been married for three years but DHS had snatched her two children away and gave custody to her mother following allegations of neglect and abuse. She was a regular user of street drugs, chiefly methamphetamine mixed with alcohol, and had been unable to maintain her apartment in a healthy manner; she had also left the children alone on many nights when she was too intoxicated to return home. She maintained visitations with her children as she attempted to successfully complete a substance abuse program.
>
> After completing that program, she was asked to live for six months in a halfway house setting, absent any drug use. Brianna adhered to the program, attended follow-up support groups, and became employed in warehouse work. She made friends with ease and through group met another ex-alcoholic, Fred, whom she dated for several months. They abruptly began living together in an apartment where Fred was the sole parent of Josh, a boy seven years of age.
>
> At first, Brianna was quite taken by Josh but soon she began to become a bit too close. She took him to school each day and to the park on weekends, while Fred was at work. She began to "help" him dress and undress and, in doing so, also began to fondle his penis. She later explained she was "trying to see if I could get him to have an erection." DHS was still following her case as she wanted custody back for her own children. They had no prior reason to make a cross-report to police when her children were removed from her as no crimes had been committed. Had DHS investigated her prior criminal history, they would have discovered that Brianna had two prior arrests and convictions for *Sexual Abuse* when she had molested two sons of a neighbor.
>
> Almost immediately, Josh told his father what was happening and, now with a third charge of *Sexual Abuse in the First Degree* against her, Brianna was facing ten years of prison time. With good behavior and with time served prior to sentencing, she may be released during the coming year. While she received no treatment for her pedophilia, she did learn to be a seamstress, gained computer skills, and became adept as a cook. Now, she may be employable in situations where contact with individuals under the age of 18 would be unlikely.

Brianna's case constitutes the least common of the three main types of female offenders we see in clinical practice. Her gender would not alter our therapeutic cognitive and experiential (behavioral) treatment approaches. However, she cannot participate in plethysmographic feedback, although a device purporting to measure the amount of vaginal secretions, called the Geer Gauge, has been used in such females. Results have been plagued by false negatives, as have those from the plethysmograph itself. Due to the infrequency of encountering such female pedophiles, we have not attempted to use this Gauge in our clinic.

Discussions of female offenders brings up an issue about whether the gender of the therapist plays any role in successfully treating mostly male sexual offenders. A number of studies have shown no significant difference in outcome – that is recidivism – between female and male therapists. In my anecdotal observations, females have shown greater empathy and support for offenders. Since building trust between offender and therapist is a crucial early step toward a successful treatment outcome, female therapists may have an advantage; men these days are quite willing to discuss their previously covert fantasies and desires regardless of therapist gender. Of interest is that male offenders also do not object to a female therapist employing the penile plethysmograph with them.

Mentor/Pupil Relationships

We have encountered a number of egregious cases in which the perpetrator is male and the victim is a prepubescent female; the opposite, in which the perpetrator is a female, are rare. Therefore, it should be of greater interest to first examine the more typical case of a male teacher and a female teen.

> Cedric, age 52, taught science in high school and had a stellar record as a teacher; he was beloved by most of his students and fellow teachers and had received several "Teacher of the Year" Awards. Married, with three children, he coached Little League and volunteered at his church. In his freshman class one year he couldn't help but notice an attractive blonde, 14-year-old Madison, but actually he had known her since she was a toddler. That was when her parents moved into a house in his neighborhood. He and his family were friends with this girl's family and had enjoyed a number of social events together. However, Cedric had never paid much attention to her before becoming one of her teachers. Seeing her develop breasts and hips, thus becoming a more mature female, he found it at first annoying that he couldn't keep his eyes off of her but soon he acted on an impulse to invite her to stay after class for some "individual tutoring."
>
> This led to Cedric asking his wife to try to arrange several social outings with Madison's entire family. Outings, barbeques and campouts followed. It was on several of these that Cedric managed to take

Madison on a hike to a "special place" he had visited in the past. It was mildly windy so Cedric snuggled against her as they took in the view. But then Cedric, unable to restrain himself, moved his hand toward her breast. On subsequent occasions, after class, he would pretend to help her with her science homework alone in his classroom. On those occasions he would fondle her breasts over her clothing and eventually rub her vagina, also over her clothes.

At first, Madison was confused and never mentioned this to her parents. She actually was fond of Cedric but she knew the sexual touching was wrong. She rationalized that it was infrequent and it would stop anyway once the semester ended as she was to proceed to a more advanced science class. However, even after she completed the semester, Brad would visit Madison at home to "help" her with her studies and then asked her parents if she could accompany him out of town for a science fair. Cedric's wife and Madison's family became increasingly suspicious but, in actuality, the girl partly enjoyed the attention; she was fond of Cedric, and at first could not bear the thought of him getting into trouble with the law. She also realized that her grade of A+ might not have been an accurate assessment about the quality of her work. Eventually her older sister convinced her that, to protect other girls in Cedric's future classes, she needed to report the sexual activity.

Madison was caught between some devotion to Cedric and the embarrassment of disclosure, in addition to the potential risks he might cause to others. In the event, she told another trusted teacher and the legal process proceeded from there. With charges of *Sexual Abuse in the Second Degree*, Cedric accepted a plea deal of three years in prison followed by five years of post-prison supervision. Despite his stellar record, Cedric realized that he could never teach again, at least in grades K through senior in high school. Of interest in this particular case, Cedric, now in the midst of five years of his post-prison supervision, is participating well in a treatment program and remains in his marriage. He has unsupervised contact with his children (two are over 18-years-old); is being allowed by his supervisor to teach adults, as in English-as-a-Second-Language courses; and has been allowed to provide tutoring to Community College students in basic sciences, although only online.

Unfortunately, the victim in this case, Madison, suffered guilt and was blamed on social media for ruining a favored teacher's life. Thus, victimized twice, she ran away and the last we knew, was living in a shelter for wayward teens.

It appears that similar incidents, involving both female and male perpetrators can create widespread strife for victims, offenders and both of their families.

We have witnessed more severe penalties in cases involving those in authority over children, such as teachers, leaders of boys' and girls' clubs, coaches (now sensationalized in the media as more athletes become sufficiently courageous to tell their potentially embarrassing stories), fitness coaches and physicians employed by sports teams, youth pastors, and even day-care providers. Although typically the perpetrator is a male, individual cases of a female engaging in sexual activity with a young male are not unknown; indeed, an example has already been offered in Chapter Two. Another example, this time of a female offender, provides some contrast.

> In a recent case, a middle-aged woman, Darlene, operating a day care facility in her home, became attached to a boy, 12 at the time. She subsequently carried on an affair with him over a period of six years. She had clearly initiated the sexual activity but he appeared receptive to it. She later claimed she "fell in love" with this boy. This activity took place mostly after her other day-care children had left for the day but it also occurred during the day as well. Because his relationship with his own family was fraught with both substance and physical abuse, he eventually moved in with Darlene and it was "normal" for them to sleep together each night.
>
> As the boy grew older, however, he became increasingly rebellious and arguments between the two became both more frequent and aggressive. He eventually moved out on his own at the age of 17 and became involved with a group of friends who used street drugs. He sought therapy and disclosed his relationship with Darlene. He also claimed he was suffering symptoms of PTSD, although observers had seen him being apparently quite happy in his new home and with his new girlfriend. Nonetheless, Darlene was charged with multiple counts of *Rape* and *Sexual Abuse in the First Degree*, and was sentenced to a twenty-year term in prison followed by ten years of post-prison supervision.
>
> To add to her misery, the boy and his family filed a civil suit against her, though she had no money or insurance to cover any damages and, although his family won, they recovered no recompense due to Darlene's impecunious state.
>
> We were asked by her attorney to accept her into our treatment program and we had about four months with her before she was sent away. She proved resistant to the idea that she had done anything wrong and we failed to help her in any meaningful manner. Her self-absorbed demeanor did not placate the DA or the judge and she was sentenced to twenty years in prison with ten years of post-prison supervision. As do many of our clients, she wrote to us from prison but even then, she appeared to show no remorse and presented herself as the victim in this sordid affair.

The courts, DAs and juries do not look kindly on those entrusted to care for our children who then proceed to sexually abuse them. A similar example of a female teacher (Isabel) engaging in sex with a teen male was cited in Chapter Two but the outcome in that example proved more fortuitous, demonstrating the considerable variance in how justice is meted out in such unusual cases.

Internet Sexual Crimes

Most people are familiar with TV shows about so-called predators who are charged with a sexual crime after communicating over the internet with a "minor" who is actually a police decoy pretending at first to be above the legal age in a particular state. When a meeting is arranged, the decoy suddenly admits she was lying and that she is just 16. Not knowing the truth about her age, the male undertakes the drive to a site designated by the decoy. Upon arriving, he is arrested by police on the assumption he traveled there to have some type of sexual activity with the "underage girl or boy."

> Earnest, a 54-year-old divorced father of three boys, began searching for female companionship on a site known for facilitating sexual liaisons. He began communicating with a female who claimed at first she was 16 but later corrected that to 18. Their texts back and forth became increasingly sexual and finally the female admitted that, in fact, she was actually 16 after all. Nonetheless, Earnest agreed to meet her at her house as she told him her parents were away for the weekend. He brought some beer and condoms with him as he drove to her residence, where he was promptly met by police officers, who searched his car and electronics and arrested him for *Luring* and *Contributing to the Sexual Delinquency of a Minor*; both or either can be used, though the latter is more common. Both were Class B felonies, although a plea agreement lowered both to Class C felonies.
>
> Earnest had no criminal history nor any of substance abuse; he had been steadily employed, and volunteered in his community as a firefighter. He eventually accepted a plea deal specifying 11½ months in jail and a five-year probation. Following his incarceration, his Probation Officer (PO), placed him on the usual package of conditions (see Appendix B) and also included, at first, the prevention of his use of any electronics, including a smart phone along with the usual prohibitions against being anywhere children might congregate. This led to his losing his IT consulting job and visitations with his two sons who were under the age of majority, 18 in his state. He will have to re-register as a sexual offender for the remainder of his life, although he will be eligible to have his registration cancelled after ten years if he has had no probation violations and commits no other crimes of any nature. It is unlikely he will ever be able to have his record expunged.

Another example demonstrates how such internet crimes are pursued.

> Shy and afraid of rejection, Evan, 21 years of age, had turned to the internet to meet women. He struck up an electronic relationship on Snapchat with Hannah, a girl who told him she was 16. Their communication turned increasingly sexual in nature and they agreed to meet in a park. No sexual activity occurred at first but they began dating and Hannah even introduced him to her parents, who appeared to accept their relationship, despite knowing Evan's age. Their relationship became more exclusive and continued for approximately two years. They planned to marry after Hannah turned 18.
>
> Both were raised in strict religious families and agreed to abstain from intercourse until after marriage. However, they did engage in sexual foreplay, which eventually led to intercourse. Authorities became aware of their connection through their internet texts as these contained their ages, sexual activities, and several semi-nude photographs. A number of quasi-official organizations, one called SAFE, automatically inform police and sheriff offices when they suspect a sexual crime has occurred.
>
> Because Hannah lived in a contiguous state, the FBI was notified in this case and, following an investigation, Evan was arrested on charges of *Rape* and *Sexual Abuse*, both in the First Degree and *Contributing to the Sexual Delinquency of a Minor*. That latter charge was pled down to a Class B felony and the *Rape* charge was dropped; had it not been, Evan stood the possibility of ten years in prison.
>
> Against our advice, and believing Hannah's parents would vouch for him, as they indeed did, he took the case to trial, was found guilty on all charges and sentenced to five years in a Federal Penitentiary. He was not immediately taken into custody as he posted bail and there were the usual problems with overcrowding. He was told that he would be sent to a facility in Colorado, quite distant from his home and family. Unfortunately, Evan committed suicide before he was incarcerated.

These two cases are quite different. Earnest was, to all appearances, intent on having sexual intercourse with a female who was underage, at least in her state. After all, she told him twice she was 16, although she did vacillate. Moreover, he brought alcohol and condoms to their first liaison. However, he never had hands-on sexual activity with anyone and only interacted with an adult female police officer. In such a case, there was no actual victim. Evan's case was a statutory offense as he knew, or should have known, that he was having intimate sexual conversations with a minor. Even if Evan and Hannah had never met in person, he would still have been guilty of *Contributing to the Sexual Delinquency of a Minor*. Different jurisdictions may use different wording to describe such "crimes", such as *Luring a Minor for Immoral*

Purposes, although that phrase has fallen out of favor among DAs, except for entrapment cases.

Both cases share one important aspect, however, which can be addressed by an examination of the criminal justice system: who is the victim in each case? Earnest never had any sexual activity with anyone and only communicated with an adult female police officer. Do we know for certain that he would have proceeded with a sexual encounter if an actual 16-year-old girl met him? Can we attribute with scientific accuracy that he *intended* to act if the girl looked and acted like a 16-year-old? Was she just playing a game by varying her age in their prior communications? Intent is assumed by the presence of condoms but it was not proven beyond a reasonable doubt. In fact, in such cases it can be employed with success by prosecutors without reasonable doubt because of the *assumption of intent*.

In Earnest's case, there again was no actual victim. No one was harmed by his actions. Indeed, in certain states, such entrapment is prohibited. Yet common sense would appear to indicate he had an obvious intention to commit a crime. In addition, common sense would have most of us believing that bringing condoms and alcohol to what he thought was an underage female's house is evidence of a pure intention to commit a crime. However, common sense, while common, can be at times, be senseless. If I announce to a police officer that I intend to enter a bank, then rob it, but then proceed into the bank and make a withdrawal from my own account, have I committed a crime? A citation and a warning to Earnest, as described in more detail in Chapter Seven, would have surely prevented him from engaging in such behavior in the future.

Another general problem, not limited solely to Earnest's case, is his freedom to live in the community until space could be provided for him at an institution. This is not unusual, even in cases in which more aggressive crimes have been committed. If Earnest was a rapist, why was he not immediately jailed? We know of even more egregious examples of sexual offenders who are permitted to await incarceration due to overcrowding.

The solution to overcrowding should probably not be the expensive construction of yet more jails and prisons but rather a home arrest situation, monitored by an ankle bracelet with GPS capabilities. Indeed, many modern systems do monitor offenders by such means. However, they also place nonviolent offenders and those most likely to not reoffend, such as in Earnest's and Evan's cases, on such systems as well, and often, the offender must pay for the monitoring process, a not inconsiderable expense which can amount to US$40 per day, and run into the thousands of dollars.

Most people, including me, would think that it was clear that Earnest intended to have sexual relations with a 16-year-old girl but do we know for certain? No individual was actually harmed in his case (except for himself). Was Hannah harmed by Evan's sexual activity with her? She expressed both guilt and horror at what happened to a man she hoped would be her future husband. His suicide led her to require therapy for a number of years. A case could be made that, later in life, she might look back upon her relationship with Evan as one in which she had been exploited. But that is, at best, speculative.

Even more appalling entrapment cases are not rare.

> Gavin, a 25-year-old male, was just beginning a relationship with a new girlfriend after realizing that his present partner and he were not compatible. Gavin suffered from a lifelong history of anxiety and some depression and was taking antidepressant medication at the time. Between relationships, feeling lonely and seeking adult companionship, and actually just someone to talk with, he entered an adult website, MeetMe, expressly limited to adults. He noted a profile of a woman, age 22, and initiated a dialogue with her on that site. In reality, the "22-year-old female" was actually an undercover, or decoy, female police officer seeking to root out men targeting minor females.
>
> As their conversations began, the decoy initiated sexual talk with Gavin, such as "I'm up to try new things. I'm not experienced, just looking for fun." She subsequently sent a photo to him in which her face was "obscured" and "dark." However, the photo, which we subsequently examined, clearly showed a blonde adult female. We presented this photo to a random group of women and men, all of whom confirmed that the photo appeared to be of a woman in her early-to mid-twenties. The decoy repeated at first that she was indeed 22, and continued to lead Fred into a sexually tinged conversation with comments such as, "I've only been eaten out once."
>
> Gavin sent her his photo, which showed only his face and was absent any nudity. The decoy officer replied, "So are we having sex tonight?". The decoy also suggested she would like to drink. Gavin subsequently agreed to meet her at a place she designated, but, on the drive to their agreed-upon location, only then did the decoy tell him, with a phone call, that her true age was 16. Uncertain what her actual age was and wondering if she was enacting a fantasy, Gavin arrived at the destination, where police immediately arrested him. He made bail the next day and is now facing charges of *Online Corruption of a Minor* and *Luring a Minor.*
>
> Gavin is now awaiting his next court hearing and has obtained an attorney. No one is certain that he would have actually followed through with sexual activity if he had found a girl who was in reality a 16-year-old teen. This most egregious case of entrapment is one of the handful of cases in which we are recommending that Gavin and his attorney take these charges to trial.

Should the government determine with whom a person can associate or whom to admire or even with whom an individual might fall in love? Yet most would argue that some age of minority must be established. Had Gavin lived in Washington or Massachusetts, he would not have been considered a sexual offender as the age of majority in those states is 16. Had he lived in many such states, he could not have been prosecuted as his case would also fall under the rubric of entrapment, outlawed in many of these jurisdictions such as in California. Should there be a federal law specifying the age of ability to consent? We are living in the United States, supposedly a single country. Yet a troubled tapestry of statutes exists across individual states leaving us with an automatous kaleidoscope to such a degree that laws regarding essential rights, such as possession of guns, ages of consent, and abortion, are criminalized in states even adjoining one another. Such major inconsistencies are rare in other Western democracies and even in autocracies across the world.

Should a crime require a victim? Should a person actually be hurt in order for an individual to be prosecuted? Intention is difficult to prove, although in Earnest's case, most would agree he intended to commit a crime. But he never *acted* against anyone. I believe that absent a victim, there is no crime. I realize that most would disagree.

There could exist a middle ground without changing states' rights, one in which a person is issued a citation and warning but not yet labelled a sexual offender. In Chapter Seven I propose alterations in laws that would, if not eliminate, at least markedly reduce the emotional turmoil and expense of entering the formal criminal justice system. This would thereby eliminate either the need for a plea deal or a trial and subsequent incarceration. Had Earnest been cited in that manner, it is highly unlikely he would ever have repeated his mistake.

Such an approach would not only save taxpayer dollars, but it would ease the burden placed upon overworked and understaffed police and sheriffs' offices, corrections officers and our tardy court systems. It would also spare the stress and hardships placed upon the families of potential sexual offenders. It is these latter relatives who are the forgotten human beings harmed by a seemingly uncaring system which punishes an offender without regard for the impacts such penalties impose upon these innocent families and, in many cases, the absence of an actual victim.

Consumers of Child Pornography

The vast majority of men, single or in a relationship, will watch pornography (porn). Surveys are hazardous in arriving at definitive statistics, but it appears that over 90% of men and 50% of women watch and enjoy adult porn. Child pornography (CP) is a different matter. In fact, the only sexual crimes which have increased in incidence over the past decade are CP and entrapment cases, both enabled by our increasingly electronic world.

While the term for a child pornography offence has been, at times, referred to as "child sexual exploitation material" (CSEM), this term is not employed universally and it conflates sexually soliciting pre- and post-pubescent minors online, a quite distinct population from men who either wander onto CP sites out of curiosity or those who prefer CP or are sexually attracted to children. I will use the abbreviation of CP as more explicit, succinct and descriptive of both types of men who watch CP.

It is crucial to distinguish two types of men who watch child pornography:

1 Men attracted to prepubescent children, either girls, boys, or both, who watch child pornography and are aroused by prepubescent children and either act on these desires by molesting children or masturbate preferentially to such images (child porn-pedophilic or CPP).
2 Men who wander onto CP sites but are not sexually attracted to children (CP-only cases or CPO).

An example of Type 1, or a CPP offender is described here.

> A 57-year-old widower, Herbert, had retired from the postal service several years ago. He had been attracted to prepubescent boys for many years even though he had married and had several grown children. It is not uncommon for men attracted to very young children to also have arousal to adult women. We subsequently learned that, for a number of years, Herb had first groomed boys as a volunteer at a Boys and Girls Club (*Don't they do background checks?*), paying special attention to them, taking them on camping trips, and buying them presents. About ten years earlier, after parents and personnel at the Club suspected him of molesting boys, Herb faced a trial. However, witnesses refused to testify and various other technicalities resulted in a mistrial.
>
> Herb moved to a different state and changed his name. He began watching CP almost immediately and soon joined an internet cohort with similar tendencies toward boys. They downloaded videos and paid for the best of them. In addition, Herb actually met several of these men locally and invited them to his house for "porn parties." Federal authorities were alerted as cross-state activities were involved. Upon a raid by the FBI during one such gathering, officers not only confiscated all electronics but found a ten-year-old boy on the premises who later testified he was offered money to engage in group sexual activity.
>
> Because of his past activities (there is no statute of limitations in certain sexual abuse cases) and the scores of child porn discovered on Herb's devices, the best his defense attorney could arrange with the DA was a 20-year sentence in Federal Prison, where he remains today.

This case is an example of a pedophile attracted to prepubescent boys. Of all the cases of CP brought against men who view and download CP, the CPP population represents about just 15% of cases referred for treatment. These men, whether attracted to boys, girls, or both, watch CP because of that attraction; they are aroused by youngsters who have smooth skin and no secondary sexual characteristics. Many marry and may also be aroused by adult females and, more rarely, adult males. If they are aroused to prepubescent boys, they form a particularly dangerous and difficult to treat population.

Compared to all sexual offenders successfully completing a sexual-offender approved treatment program, over 80% of either type will not commit another sexual crime. However, many of these are men who commit situational crimes or are CPO offenders. Pedophiles who prefer boys yet who complete such treatment have about a 70% success rate but 30% may well go on to commit another similar sexual crime. This is unacceptable and awaits further refinement in our treatment techniques.

As noted above, among all sexual crimes committed in the US, the sole crime which has increased in occurrence over the past decade is child pornography. Approximately 85% of men arrested for CP fall into the second broad group of CPO offenders.

> Ian, a 19-year-old college student, was in the habit of watching porn three to four times a week. However, bored with the usual videos, he experimented, searching for ever more exotic forms of porn and stumbled upon the dark web, where he clicked on and watched minors, both boys and girls, engage in sexual acts either between themselves or under the direction or participation of an adult, almost always a man.
>
> The National Center for Exploited and Missing Children (NCEMC) notified state police of Ian's smart phone and computer activity and a warrant was issued for his arrest and seizure of all his electronic devices, standard procedure in such cases. Of all the porn Ian had watched, less than 1% was comprised of child porn; indeed, he had spent about five minutes watching it and had downloaded just a single photo, then tried to delete it. As most IT experts know, everything you watch, type, or manipulate on any electronic device can be retrieved, even if you attempt to destroy that piece of equipment.

Ian was sentenced to three years of probation only, as he had no criminal record, sexual or otherwise. However, he was forced to drop out of most of his classes as they required computer assignments yet his supervising probation officer (PO) ordered that he could not be in possession of any electronic devices. While some POs will grant students and workers the ability to access computers for school or work, they will typically do so only after a period of at least three months of no computer access. Ian had to drop out of college for that semester, then return to class the following term with the

PO's proviso that he be monitored by an approved supervisor whenever he used the library's computer for academic assignments, quite an embarrassing circumstance as everyone thereby knew what had occurred.

Moreover, Ian was prohibited for two years from any contact with children (defined as anyone younger than 18 and of any gender). This included his 15-year-old brother and 12-year-old sister. At first this prohibition precluded his attendance at any family event, such as birthdays and holiday gatherings. After two years, he was allowed to attend such events as long as he was always in the company of an adult. This led to further contrived and embarrassing tales he tried to manufacture in order to explain these situations to distant family and friends.

Ian had no prior history of trouble with the law. Moreover, repeated testing and polygraphs demonstrated no sexual interest in prepubescent children. His goal was to take pre-law classes in college, then apply to law school, a career path now denied him due to his sexual offense. He is still on the sexual offender registry, which makes no distinction between a CPO case and a serial rapist. Were he to attempt to enter any professional field, such as law, medicine or nursing, similar prohibitions would apply. In other words, his entire life course was shattered by five minutes of simply exploring the web for something more exciting or erotic than typical porn. A citation and warning, as described above and in Chapter Seven in more detail, would have guaranteed that Ian never would access CP again.

Ian's case is not an outlier, although most POs are also not as stringent or austere as his. More typically, CPOs are placed on probation for three years and allowed electronic access with monitoring, especially for work or school. Programs can be implanted on devices to restrict any porn and to notify another person, such as a PO, if porn is being watched. Also, POs have the ability to cut periods of probation in half if the offender has no violations.

Yet Ian must remain on the sex offender registry for at least ten years before he can apply for removal. It is still uncertain if he can ever have his record expunged; only a handful of sexual offenders have succeeded in obtaining their record being wiped clean. Even those are not entirely in the clear. My communications with background-check companies tell me they can always discover expunged criminal records, although they stopped short of letting me know how.

If a teen driving while intoxicated is stopped by police, his car is impounded, he is fined and may temporarily lose his license. He probably will have to undertake a substance abuse program. Yet, in fact, such a youth, with the potential of accidently hitting and seriously injuring another individual, is actually punished in a less draconian manner than a CPO offender, who has never directly harmed anyone, even though, in theory, he might have contributed in a minor way to the creation of additional CP. It is a similar matter with cases involving entrapment. Who is the more dangerous? Yet who is treated in the most restrictive manner? I believe there is a vast increase in the potential of harm in the case of the drunk driver than in the entrapment or CPO offender.

Egregious cases are not rare for CPOs. Consider the following.

> A 43-year-old single man on disability for manic-depressive disorder, Jesse was reported to authorities for accessing and downloading child porn. His explanation at first appeared to be contrived. He explained that, in a manic state, he thought he could eliminate such material from the internet through a series of "maneuvers." His access to CP was minimal but occurred when he had discontinued his medication and was accompanied by a flurry of bizarre and atypical activities, including unprovoked anger outbursts against his parents, ordering a new car though he lacked the funds even for a down payment, and entering a marathon run even though he hadn't exercised for years. In other words, he was displaying typical signs of a manic episode.
>
> Jesse's parents confirmed that he was in a manic state at the time and a pharmacy check showed he hadn't picked up his medications for at least a month prior to the incident. Psychiatric defenses rarely play well in court so Jesse accepted a three-year probation but his PO insisted he could no longer remain in his parents' home, where he had been living since birth. He was forced to use his disability check to pay for a room in a halfway house which accepted sexual offenders (few do) and, due to the flu pandemic, his case was delayed even coming to arraignment for over two years. By three years he finally received his sentence of a three-year term of probation but was barred from shopping for food by himself and was denied access except to just a single store and that was only if he was accompanied by his parents. His PO refused to accept our recommendations for more flexibility in his living and shopping arrangements.
>
> After 2½ years of such restraints, Jesse was finally allowed to live with his parents but was still denied access to any but a select group of shops and stores. Now free of supervision, one good thing that evolved from his ordeal is that Jesse now takes his bipolar medicines on a regular basis.

Neither Ian nor Jesse posed any threat of sexual harm to their communities. Neither had even been in trouble with the law in the past. Yet both were severely hampered in the basic rights of all citizens and Herb lost precious opportunities. Since the vast majority of CP offenders are CPO and they consist of mostly law-abiding individuals who pose no risk, should the government be spending tax dollars pursuing them, then punishing them in such a caustic manner? Should police and corrections officers spend so much time and financial resources on individuals who were prompted by curiosity rather than deviant sexual gratifications and who pose no threat to be at large?

Yet recently, an aspirant for the attorney general of a northeastern state, formerly a DA, boasted, in a campaign ad that, "I have put away more child porn criminals than ever before; these child predators are now off the street." This statement reeks not only of prejudicial ambition but of ignorance of science as well.

Some might think that what you do on your own computer or phone is your own business, but most others believe that the government has some right to tease out dangerous individuals and groups for our own safety. Yet in over 52 studies of over 2,000 CPO offenders from Croatia, Canada, Denmark, Germany, Finland, Hong Kong, Singapore, Shanghai, Sweden, the UK, and the US, the recidivism rate for a CPO offender has varied from 0.7% to 0%. In our more limited experience with over 500 such CPO offenders over a 20-year follow-up, we have yet to encounter a second sexual offence. A recent study noted that "CPO offenders form a distinct group of individuals...whose motivation for CP differs from those who physically are likely to sexually assault minors" (Seto & Hanson 2011).

A second recent study, after an extensive review of the available literature, found that, "A number of men appear to use CP because it is more convenient, unharmful [they believe] and undangerous" (Seto, Hanson & Babchishin 2011). Moreover, a study by Ward, Finkelhor and Motchell published in 2011 in *Sexual Abuse: A Journal of Research and Treatment* found that, among men who watched CP, "No one in the study sample who had no history of sexual crimes was [subsequently] convicted of a hands-on sexual offense." The single study attempting to show that many men arrested for CP had actually molested children in the past was deeply flawed as it stemmed from a base of all sexual offenders and the researchers were aware of their crimes before assessment, thus rendering the results biased. Moreover, a re-calculation of the raw data showed significant deficiencies in the statistics employed.

Yes, there do exist a few cases of men first arrested for CPO who go on to show actual arousal to children, but these are so rare that they make good fodder for journal studies. There exists a better way to manage such CPO cases, as described in Chapter Seven on potential solutions.

Hypersexuality

Although women may show a high sexual drive in rare cases, I will focus on men as these are the largest group requiring, and sometimes requesting, treatment for hypersexuality. Men who are hypersexual can present with the following problems, which affect their lives and often the lives of those who are closest to them.

- Frequent use of pornography, often to the point of "addiction." (True addiction to porn is not equivalent to that associated with substances, where the absence of a substance is followed by a period of withdrawal with physical symptoms; "obsession" would be a more useful noun.) Such use may affect their ability to accomplish the functions of their employment, demonstrate responsible behavior, and enjoy satisfying relationships. These problems can lead to physical symptoms of impotence or premature ejaculation as well.

- Inappropriate use of sexual language and jokes in mixed gender settings.
- Rushed and impetuous sexual approaches to women, rendering them uncomfortable; this also includes sexual harassment.
- Frequent affairs, divorces and separations.
- Repetitious solicitations of prostitutes.
- Frequent masturbation, which renders the person dysfunctional at work or in relationships.
- Incessant thoughts or fantasies of sexual behavior.
- Unwanted physical contact with women which is not consensual.

Counterintuitively, many such men rarely commit rape. However, they are bedeviled with almost constant thoughts and fantasies about sex and in many such men, these are unwanted, foreign, and interfere with their livelihoods and relationships. We treat such men, of course, if they have committed a crime, such as inappropriate touching, harassment or rape, employing the usual complement of behavioral and cognitive techniques described above.

However, a surprising number of such cases are voluntary; they enter treatment absent any police charges but with the realization that they have come close to breaking the law. They are also painfully aware that they are fracturing relationships and failing to realize their potential in advancing their employment opportunities. By doing so, these men are prevented from sharing new ideas and hampering their potential creativity at work and in their communities.

Such hypersexual men respond reasonably well to standard treatment techniques but, in a number of them, we also recommend the use of an antiandrogen to lower their testosterone almost to prepubertal levels. Depo-Provera, an injectable long-acting medication, has been the subject of the most studies in such cases; it is sometimes described as "chemical castration." Lupron, a similar injectable, has also been thus employed. Side effects are rare, except for reduction in sexual drive. While on these medications, these men can still maintain an erection to have intercourse with a wife or girlfriend, but they only rarely initiate it. The more common antidepressant, Prozac, has occasionally been used for hypersexuality but it has too mild an effect to be of much benefit for these men.

As an aside, testosterone levels are not generally higher in any type of sexual offender, even in those with hypersexuality. It may be, however, that the testosterone receptors in their brains are either more prodigious or more sensitive than normal. One feature in such men, however, is quite common:

early exposure to pornography. A child's brain is just developing sexual awareness beginning at age of seven and progressing into the early teenage years. Perhaps too much sexual excitation at just the right (or wrong) moment might predispose them to a heightened sexual drive as these children develop into a more mature sexual state.

It is not as surprising as you may imagine that a number of such men enter therapy on a voluntary basis, distressed by their condition and desperately wanting to be freed from a preoccupation with sex. For a few such men, we prescribe oral Provera as they would be compliant in taking their medication on a regular basis. However, predatory offenders, now involved with the justice system, are a different matter They will require the injectable form as they either would reject the notion of a lowered libido or have a troubling history of repeating sexual crimes yet have served their sentences and are now at large in their communities.

Supervising officers should think of utilizing such medical approaches for dangerous offenders such as men who have repeatedly molested boys, committed multiple rapes, or have either refused treatment or failed to successfully complete a certified sexual offender treatment program. Mandating a medication on an involuntary basis is a tenuous approach from a legal perspective but it must be weighed against the very real risk these offenders pose to their communities. The medication can be discontinued in such offenders should they successfully graduate from a certified program; its effects are reversible but in many voluntary hypersexual men, they choose to continue it.

> Kenneth is a 32-year-old chef with a troubled history of addiction to methamphetamine and alcohol. He had been successful in discontinuing both substances through treatment programs and AA. Now sober for a number of years and serving as a sponsor for many others, he entered our Clinic asking for help with his constant use of porn and frequent intrusions of sexual fantasies. Moreover, his relationship with a girlfriend of two years was in jeopardy due to his obsession with porn. Kenneth desperately wanted to be free of these thoughts. Aside from a number of cognitive and experiential (behavioral) approaches, we prescribed oral Provera, 50 mg each day. He subsequently has noted no intrusive sexual fantasies, has been totally abstinent from watching any porn and refuses a trial of discontinuing the drug. He married his girlfriend recently, enjoys intimate relations with her and is now a successful chef at a high-end restaurant in a major metropolitan area.

Some readers will question the use of a medication for a behavioral problem but it can be conceived as similar to Methadone or Buspirone for a narcotics addict. While not a perfectly matching analogy, the results justify, in my mind, the use of any non-harmful medication to promote not only community safety but individual benefits as well.

Many would scoff at providing sexual offenders with any type of treatment, despite overwhelming evidence of its efficacy. As with similar conditions, such as epilepsy and diabetes, the sole contraindication to treatment for a sexual offender is the absence of a patient. For those interested further in any of these treatment approaches, an annotated Bibliography is attached at the end of this text, though I would warn the reader that some of these publications can be as dry as the Atacama Desert but others might prove as fruitful as a tropical forest.

Chapter 7

Potential Solutions to Provide Informed Justice for Sexual Offenders

In this chapter, I have employed the terms of rehabilitation and the rehabilitative ideal as broad concepts limited in the main to sexual offenders. Thus any efforts to prevent recidivism are included, many of which pertain to practices outside of a clinical setting. Examples might include programs initiated not only for sexual offenders while still incarcerated and not usually considered as treatment. These might encompass in-prison attempts to provide job training and, following incarceration, endeavors by probation officers (POs) or post-prison supervisors (PPSs) which might ease the offender back into society in a more civilized and humane manner. Thus clinical treatment is considered under the broader rubric of rehabilitation as all such efforts, I believe, have the potential to reduce the likelihood that an offender will commit another sexual crime.

I am not an expert in criminal justice nor an attorney. Nonetheless, over the course of 50 years in assessing and treating over 35,000 sexual offenders, certain changes, largely informed by the scientific research in this field, prompt me to offer suggestions which I believe would unclog the justice system, provide enhanced community security, and save taxpayer funds.

I offer these suggestions with the realization that many would oppose them as either too lenient or costly and overly controversial, although they would reduce taxpayer burdens by billions of dollars over a single decade. Yet it is the very nature of dispute and the back and forth of debate, that fuels the fire of scientific innovation and advances the course of most human endeavors. We should be especially cautious when everyone agrees. Moreover, I realize that, even were all these suggestions enacted, they would not yield a perfect criminal justice system. I may be optimistic, but certainly not naïve.

Create a Sexual Offender Court

The first such suggestion is the formation of a court exclusively dealing with sexual offenders, perhaps under the auspices of, or modelled after, the already successful mental health and substance abuse courts now established

DOI: 10.4324/9781003532590-8

in many counties and states. A leading jurist, now retired, James Gray, first proposed substance abuse and mental health courts in the 1990s. His follow-up research demonstrated how such specialized courts, which provided halfway houses and treatment programs, reduced recidivism in such offenders by 40% to 50%.

These courts are part of many states' judicial systems these days and operate under a similar code of conduct, including indictments brought forward based upon police investigations; a finding (or not) of guilt whether through some sort of plea arrangement or a trial (rare in such cases); and a sentencing. Sexual offender courts could operate as an extension of a mental health court or be completely separate entities, informed by specialists in the area of assessment and treatment of these specific offenders.

It is in the sentencing phase that crucial differences abide. In a case involving alcohol or illegal substance abuse, the judge (along with a prior agreement from the DA's office) may remand the guilty party not to incarceration or impose supervision alone but offer the option of sending the offender to a halfway house (Oxford Houses are commonly employed in the West), where his freedoms are curtailed but not as restricted as they would be with incarceration. For example, the offender might be required to get, or retain, a job or enter an educational program such as a community college to learn an employable skill. He could be monitored with a GPS-enabled ankle bracelet so his movements could be monitored. He would also be required to enter and successfully complete a substance abuse program sanctioned by the court. The following examples could be considered, the first for a substance abuse court.

> Larry, 27 years of age, had accumulated two *DUII*s before his third arrest, this for fighting in a bar while intoxicated. However, he had no other criminal history, was in a stable relationship with a supportive wife and had retained the same job over a ten-year period. Prior attempts at a 12-step AA Program had proved ineffective. The initial criminal court judge sent him to a substance abuse court, from where he entered a structured setting in a halfway house. At first his movements were constricted. Within that setting, he was required to participate in twice-weekly individual and group therapy sessions. Following three months of confinement, Larry was allowed to seek work through a temporary contracting firm. He also continued his treatment sessions and began attending outside AA sessions as well. After two years in the halfway house, and under the supervision of a PO, he was allowed to return home.
>
> Larry found full-time employment at one of his temporary jobs and remains abstinent to the present day, as confirmed through random unannounced urinalyses. He now has a son, for whom he provides an excellent role model. He also serves as a sponsor for several new individuals in his AA Group. In addition, he has been placed in charge of organizing semi-annual state gatherings for AA.

Of course, not all such cases are as neatly resolved. But in Larry's case, the state's analysis of the actual dollar amount saved through such a program was US$2,300. This should be compared with the usual process within our present criminal justice system, including an indictment, followed by the typical extended plea deal negotiation, a 30-day jail sentence, then three years of probation services (the average for such cases). Such a typical course would have cost taxpayers approximately $130,000. Not very much for one such individual, I admit, but considering the number of such cases with which each state must contend, the savings amounts to millions of dollars each year. Nation-wide, that figure expands into the billions.

A recent re-analysis of the costs of incarceration from the US Department of Justice (DOJ) found that the annual cost of imprisoning sexual offenders amounts to 5.4 billion dollars. This did not include, however, the costs associated with such offenders first being held in county jails nor did it take into account costs prior to incarceration, such as court fees or expenses related to supervision and registration thereafter. The authors wisely emphasize the value of early sexual education and prevention strategies aimed at helping children to be safe from sexual abuse.

The routine use of buprenorphine or methadone clinics, or of monitored Antabuse Programs, could also be seen as part of the follow-up such courts could consider. New research, including DNA identification and molecular biology, may well hold out promising new treatments in the future for afflicted individuals. Enlightened justice systems are only now beginning to realize the merits of treatment with precautions as not only a more humane manner of resolving such cases. It serves also as a means of saving jail and prison space along with the money required to house the millions living therein, many unnecessarily. It might also provide a model for a more civilized and science-based manner of demonstrating to our children that we all make mistakes and it is of importance to judge the act but not the actor:

> A 67-year-old fruit farmer, Morris, had a history of anger outbursts against his employees and family members. Though he had no prior criminal history, he recently entered into an argument in which several of his employees were involved. He took the side of one and, at one point, retrieved a rifle from his farmhouse and pointed it at the other man, then fired it in the air. By doing so, he was actually guilty of *Reckless Endangerment*, although thankfully no one was injured. However, Morris also had a history of paranoid schizophrenia and was taking his medication on an irregular basis.
>
> He was referred to a local court in a rural part of the state, which recognized that Morris needed restraint, was of potential danger to others, but was also likely mentally ill. A review of his psychiatric history revealed that his temper outbursts occurred when he was acutely ill.

> He was referred to an urban-located Mental Health Court, which placed him into a state psychiatric hospital, where he received treatment for several months. He was released to a halfway house in a small town close to his farm but was still under the supervision of a PO who ensured he attended all therapy sessions and that his blood level of medication was assured by bi-weekly injections of an antipsychotic medication. Following a year of supervised living, Morris is back tending to his fruit trees and abiding by the restrictions of his probation.

There are but a few individuals with mental illness who are dangerous to be at large. The most common type of such a person has bipolar disorder and is in a manic state. Those with schizophrenia rarely commit person-to-person crimes, or, for that matter, any crimes at all, despite public opinion. Mental health courts can avoid imprisoning those who suffer a psychiatric illness and commit a crime *as a direct result of that illness*, and may not belong in jail or prison, where they are unlikely to obtain treatment to match in quality that which is available in hospitals and mental health outpatient clinics. Such confinement may actually worsen their conditions.

Could there be an analogue for the sexual offender? Certainly not for the men who prey upon children, rape repeatedly or commit multiple sexual crimes. Also ineligible would be the minority of men who have committed a sexual crime but in addition have an antisocial personality disorder, rendering them likely to have committed nonsexual crimes as well. Other exclusionary factors might include men who have failed to complete an approved sexual offender treatment program or who have violated the terms of their supervisory mandates.

But what about several of the examples of situational offenders cited in previous chapters? There exists a populous cohort of men who have committed but a single sexual crime, and that under circumstances that may never recur if appropriate action is taken. A sexual offender court is a possible solution for those who have committed a situational offense or a crime which has no actual in-person or hands-on victim.

Eligibility criteria for a hearing in such a court might include:

- Clear evidence of a statutory rather than a predatory offence
- No prior criminal history
- No serious history of drug or alcohol abuse
- Relative stability in employment or education
- No use of threats, intimidation, force or any other aggressive behavior in the commission of the crime
- The absence of any immediate actual victim
- The sole sexual crime was committed under the influence of drugs or alcohol
- Passing a full-disclosure polygraph to rule out the possibility of prior crimes. (I do not believe the polygraph is a scientifically proven lie detector but justice system officials may be reassured by its results.)

Serious problems with the interpretation of these criteria exist as there are scientific studies which can reveal level of risk but they are not foolproof. Nonetheless, if the criminal justice system elects to embrace the facts of science, each case can be evaluated and the safety of treatment without incarceration should be considered. This is especially true in several types of sexual crimes:

- Statutory offenses – Sometimes these are referred to as "Romeo and Juliet" (R&J) crimes (although I don't think Shakespeare gave exact ages for those protagonists). For example, a 15-year-old female sophomore is dating a male senior who just turned 18. Should they engage in intercourse, the 18-year-old is technically guilty of *Rape in the Second* or *Third Degree*. However, would he pose a sexual risk to remain at large, provided he had a restraining order against any contact with the girl, at least until she turns 18? As an aside, according to the US Health Department statistics, by grade 10, 37% of high school males and 32% of similar females have experienced sexual intercourse. By grade 12, those figures climbed to about 89% for males and 76% for female teens. Studies have demonstrated no relationship between age of first intercourse and any future psychological impairment thereafter.

Placing this hypothetical 18-year-old in jail would not only interrupt his education but cost him and his family significant expense. It would also brand him as a sexual offender with the need to register as such, at least for ten years if not for the remainder of his lifetime. He might be able to have his record expunged but that task would prove expensive and formidable.

Moreover, he may have difficulty in being accepted into a college of his choice, may never be allowed to obtain most professional degrees, and may even find an apartment difficult to obtain in close proximity to whatever school or job site he might prefer.

- Child pornography only cases (CPO) – A minority of those arrested for child pornography (CP) are truly aroused by prepubescent females or males. In our clinic, approximately 90% of all those arrested for accessing CP are neither attracted to either such group of youngsters but become bored with typical pornography and wander onto such sites promising more exotic sexual fare. Men frequently search out specific types of porn, such as S & M or facial ejaculations. Many sites are labelled "Barely Legal" or "Just 18". By making a number of leading clicks, they can eventually arrive at a CP site.

Our Clinic has treated many hundreds of CPO cases; their prevalence has been increasing rapidly while more severe sexual offender cases are declining. The reason for this explosion of CPO offenders is the enhanced surveillance now available to not only official police and FBI agents but to quasi-official agencies such as the NCMEC. These organizations are valuable resources and help officials identify possibly abused or exploited children across the country, yet sites containing CP continue to expand.

Some believe such sites can only be accessed on the "Dark Web" but it is possible to access CP on the regular web as well. Although many of our CPO cases insist they "wandered onto" such sites in error, it takes a dedicated search, by and large, to uncover explicit photos and (more commonly) videos displaying sexual activity between children, often accompanied by adults. The children can appear to be enjoying the sexual activity at times but more often, they appear stoic or disinterested. Only a few appear to be physically forced; many seem to be actively prodded and, in a number of such videos, it appears as if the staging is in a home and perhaps within a family. Most individuals viewing CP falsely believe that by doing so they cannot be detected if they delete such access after viewing it.

No matter how skilled you believe you are in information technology (IT) and no matter what you are told by your IT technician, NOTHING, in the vast majority of cases, can ever be truly deleted that you do electronically on your smart phone, laptop or desktop computer. It is mostly encoded in the ubiquitous "cloud." Authorities schooled and skilled in forensic IT analysis can ALMOST ALWAYS find anything you have typed, clicked, sent, messaged or viewed. Throw your device into the ocean or batter it all you will, forensic analysis experts will discover it and will be able, in most cases, to recover its contents. I know many will disagree but they have not read through the endless pages of forensic analysis reports from seemingly destroyed devices to be able to access contents that were "deleted". More criminals (not just sexual) have been captured through electronic traces, it seems, than there is water in all the oceans.

But why is viewing and, especially downloading CP a crime? Is there a victim? In this case, despite the fact that the children used in this manner have already been abused, the DA has a legitimate obligation to charge those who access CP in the main not because they are child molesters but because they are promoting it. The producers of CP are certainly the more culpable criminals here but they are also aware of every click on their sites and of the potential that someone, even if a small percentage of those viewing it, will pay for more, or at least the promise of even more explicit and exciting videos. The DA's opinion, not substantiated by any research findings, is that a click on a CP site prompts its producer to manufacture more of the same.

In our Clinic we have followed CPO cases after completing our treatment program in coordination with our State's Department of Justice. Follow-up times range from a few months to 15 years. To the best extent of our follow-up records, we have found *none* of these men have repeated a CP offense. In the most recent follow-up research in over 50 journal studies published to date, the recidivism rate of CPO offenders has ranged from zero to 2%; the average rate is 0.7%. (See the Bibliography for a sample.) Yet law enforcement agencies have spent millions of hours and dollars pursuing these cases.

Most CPO cases are accused with charges that are vague and do not reflect what the offender actually did. Such charges are usually *Possession and/or Distribution of Child Pornography*, the latter in cases (quite a few) in which the accused shared a common website with others, even though he had no intent to distribute, deliver, or profit from the CP itself.

The older charge of *Contributing to the Sexual Delinquency of a Minor* is less popular, although both carry similar sentences, usually from 30 to 364 days in jail (to avoid prison, which would be mandated by any sentence exceeding one year), followed by three years of probation. Often, these men are released earlier than most due to overcrowding along with the realization that a CPO offender poses little risk of committing another sexual crime.

Many CP material is produced overseas. The FBI cooperates with Interpol in investigating and, in some cases, prosecuting the more dangerous producers of these materials but so often international probes are thorny and tedious, requiring the cooperation of a multitude of agencies, sometimes in countries rife with corruption. Scrutiny, however, must continue, especially because some, perhaps many, of the children involved in manufacturing CP are the victims of extortion rings or have essentially been sold by poor families to criminal enterprises involved in blackmail, coercion and graft.

As you can imagine, conditions of supervision for CP offenders, including those identified as CPO, are heavily weighted toward restrictions on the use of electronics. Most CPOs are no longer permitted to use a smart phone but must be content with the embarrassment of an old-fashioned flip phone. Their use of computers may at first be prohibited entirely, but eventually they are generally allowed to employ computers solely for the purposes of either work or school study. Porn-blocking programs are mandated, such as *Covenant Eyes* or *Ever Accountable*. In both, the supervisor can always check on her or his office computer what the parolee is or has been accessing.

If we compare a CPO offender with a teen cited for a DUI, who is the more dangerous? Surely the latter, especially if the driver has multiple traffic convictions in the past. Yes, he may lose his license for a limited period of time, be required to take a drivers' education class, and pass another driving test. He may also be required to complete a substance abuse program or attend AA. Yet the retributions for a CPO offender most often greatly exceed these in scope. In addition, they also affect not only the individual convicted of accessing CP to a far greater extreme but alter the course of his family life; they can indeed often extend over a lifetime.

These penalties are therefore galling and incommensurate with the gravity, both actual and potential, of the crime itself. For example, despite the research demonstrating that recidivism in the CPO group of men is close to zero, and that they have never offended before nor can they be demonstrated to have any sexual interest or arousal to prepubescent children, or even to young teens, restrictions that are of dubious purpose are standard and include the entire slate of prohibitions against contact with "children" below the age of 18.

These include not only restraints on the use of any electronics, but prohibitions against contact with members of their own families, despite the fact that, if raised together, brothers are hardly likely to molest a sister, due to the incest taboo inbred to prevent fetal abnormalities. Families are thus fragmented, often against the will of the majority of their members.

Better coordination amongst international police agencies (see p. 00) might also help to stem the tide of CP and indict the people most responsible for it: those who control extortion rings and thus actually produce CP in the first place. These international agencies are promising to expand their efforts. The pace of such efforts now appears glacial.

Bypass Grand Jury Proceedings in Sexual Offender Cases

Despite many critics of the grand jury system, it had originally been established to make certain that local DAs do not bring extraneous, frivolous, or poorly argued charges against any individual or corporation. The criterion to find that a charge is reasonable is *probable cause*, not *beyond a reasonable doubt*, as in an actual trial. The major objection has most recently been that it excludes any member of a defense team to speak for the alleged defendant.

Yet the purpose cited above would not logically require a defense at all; it is merely a constraint on the DA's otherwise unchecked power to bring forth charges regardless of their merit. Defense attorneys would add little at that point in the proceedings as, since prior to the hearings, there have been no charges to warrant a defense. In addition, enlarging the proceedings by expanding them to include a defense team would only bring additional bureaucratic complexity, add expenses and time, and alter the purpose of a grand jury hearing itself.

From the point of view of a sexual offender treatment provider, however, a grand jury hearing is a major obstacle to proceeding because of justice delayed. This is because over 99% (yes, that's no typo) of such hearings for sexual offenders are decided in favor of preferring the exact charges the DA has offered. In other words, the hearing itself is superfluous; bypassing this phase may be against judicial law but such statutes were never meant to be immutable.

Moreover, by delaying such adjudications, the treatment for many situational sexual offenders can only begin long after the crime itself. Studies demonstrate that treatment delayed is also less effective in preventing recidivism.

In my opinion, charges determined by the DA should go directly to court, with discovery materials rapidly dispensed to the prosecution and defense so that either a trial or a plea arrangement can be offered within a reasonable time frame. While the grand jury proceeding is not the sole major hindrance to the more rapid delivery of justice and treatment, it is one step unnecessary and wasteful of time for the jury members, the DA, and the offender himself.

Disentangle and Simplify the Plea Deal Process

About 99% of sexual offenders accept a plea arrangement, often following a prolonged, expensive, and anxiety-inducing phase which can last for many months to years. During these negotiations the DA pushes for the most harsh of charges with the knowledge that the attorney will reply with a gentler option. Over countless hours of haggling, the life of the offender hangs in the balance but he is rarely privy to these deliberations. Even those in complete denial give pause in attempting to convince a judge or jury that they are innocent in the face of a victim's testimony.

To accelerate this cumbersome process, would it be possible to eliminate this arbitration? While each individual who stands accused of a crime deserves to be heard in court, few ever are. Instead, back-room deals substitute for a trial, and not incidentally, enlarge the bank accounts of defense attorneys at the expense of victims and, of particular and cruel effect, their families as well. Could this policy be dramatically simplified, based upon what we know, both through our experience with sexual offenders and the science concerning their assessment and treatment? We are now able to pinpoint, with great accuracy, which offenders are dangerous and which are harmless.

I would suggest that the DA forego any grand jury hearings. (See later in this Chapter as well.) Approximately 99% of these for sexual offenders find the charges justified, making a grand jury hearing superfluous and unnecessarily expensive of time and money. An offender could meet with an attorney the DA, and a judge as soon as possible after charges are brought. This single meeting would have to await the discovery process, which entails both parties reviewing all available information, including police reports, interviews, and psychosexual evaluations. Our therapists have access to all these materials within at most a month after an arraignment, when charges are announced.

At such a *single meeting*, plea negotiations could ensue and a determination made, at that time, of an equitable penalty, approved by the judge. In rare cases, the victim(s), if appropriate, could also be included. If my first suggestion of a special sexual offender court becomes involved, this process could proceed with dispatch. Certainly, defense attorneys might regard this as abrogating the adversarial process to which any offender is entitled. Thus, the decision to accept this route must be made by all parties involved, including the defendant himself. However, this suggestion would not only save time and money, but reduce the period of time during which the anxiety of both victim and offender must endure. It should be noted that numerous studies demonstrate that punishment, while rarely effective in reducing recidivism by itself, is especially feckless when administered long after the actual behavior has taken place:

> Owen, an 18-year-old student, was discovered by the NCMEC to have been accessing child porn for a period of one year. He had recently moved from his birthplace in a distant state to a new state and new school. Shy, and socially fearful of rejection, he could think of just one way to make new friends: the internet. There, the friends he happened across introduced him to porn and, eventually, to child porn.
>
> It took authorities one year to compile interviews and associated materials, employing a high-priced forensics expert who took months to compile everything internet-connected to his account, before the case was even ready to be assigned to an attorney. Legal fees, including several court appearances and a review of all discovery materials, at a charge of $30,000, it took many weeks for an expert in the assessment of sexual offenders to interview Owen and complete a 27-page report to the attorney, at the additional cost to his family of $5,000. It then took an additional year for the attorney and DA to reach a plea deal. The attorney's charge of between $30,000 and $50,000 should also be added to these staggering sums.
>
> His case, now exceeding two years, is still awaiting resolution, which may occur within the next six months. The total cost of such unnecessary shenanigans in a simple case could have been cut to one-tenth of the total in terms of money wasted and time preoccupied if the process were simplified. In the event, Owen lost an opportunity to attend college and now may never attain his full academic and employment potential, merely for following the urging of a few misguided "internet friends" and clicking on what amounted to a few child porn photos. He had no criminal history nor was he ever, nor would he ever be, sexually attracted to children.

I realize this is a drastic suggestion, overturning tradition and legal necessities. But there are no absolute statutory obstructions to such a plan; only the intelligence and perseveration to pursue it. Drastic changes are necessary when individuals suffer unduly. It is not only the offender who would benefit, but his family, his victim and her family as well. Reducing the period of time such cases hang in abeyance would relieve distress to all involved, except perhaps the defense attorney. Moreover, officials would save time and taxpayers would save money, reasons sufficient to consider radical change.

Standardize Federal Regulations about Sexual Offending

It is of interest to review the history of the establishment of states' rights. As the Constitution was being formulated, certain southern states became fearful that the more populated northern states could, by forceful means, impose their will upon them, particularly about the abolition of slavery. In addition, in the late 18th century, southern states voiced a concern that northern states would not lend military aid were a foreign attack to occur in the south; this worry occurred because the north abhorred slavery. Such an issue is moot in the present day, yet a wide array of confusing laws still exists in states simply defined by borders established by terrain (rivers, for example) or by longitude and latitude.

Thus, the Second Amendment, among others, specified that each state had a right to form its own militia. For the absence of a comma, that Amendment is now mistaken to mean any citizen had the right to own any type of weapon.

Since that time, each state has rights to legislate areas concerned with manners of voting, local taxation, and building construction. This makes sense as conditions vary in those areas based upon local factors such as weather, size of certain areas, and financial needs of the state. Nonetheless, states surrendered the statutory power of control in important areas of human rights, including equality of gender, equal access for those suffering with disabilities, and the right for each of-age individual to vote in local and federal elections.

It is difficult to fathom how and why location would influence basic human rights. Yet the federal government has ceded control over important areas, such as abortion, the age of consent, and the requirements for warrants to search and seize. Blinded by local politics, this slapdash system is worse than haphazard, which implies a lack of intent; rather, it is erratic, which implies the consideration of what is right or wrong. Political considerations often fail to examine jails and prisons with a scientist's critical eye. Thus, the lack of legislative oversight by a Federal Bureau of Prisons has created cacophony in place of the harmony and consistency such a matter as incarceration requires. As an example of such incongruity, one area of particular concern in sexual offending pertains to the age of consent to sexual activity.

> Pete, a 19-year-old senior just graduating from high school, was charged with *Sexual Abuse in the Second Degree* in Oregon for engaging in a sexual relationship with his long-term girlfriend, a sophomore, 16 years of age. He had no other history of committing any crimes. However, the charges stemmed from several dates the two undertook while away from their homes in Vancouver, WA visiting friends in Portland, OR. Had they never visited Portland, there would have been no charge as, in Washington, the age of consent is 16 whereas in Oregon it is 18.

Is Pete a felon because he lives five miles across a river? Surely, some coordination across state lines should be covered in federal statutes instead of the kaleidoscope of state regulations now in place. In setting a national standard of age of consent, present-day data should be taken into account. By the age of 16, over 50% of American youth of each gender have engaged in sexual intercourse (CDC data for 2023). There is no evidence that the age of first sexual intercourse bears any relationship to sexual offending, PTSD or any other adverse outcome in either gender. Several well-controlled studies have documented the lack of any dire result of engaging in mutually consenting sexual activity amongst teenagers.

A similarly galling example of unequal laws is the case of Evan, in Chapter Six. I doubt that teens in Texas are any more or less rebellious than those in Maine, or that a woman who has been traumatized by rape in Massachusetts suffers in any vastly different fashion than one raped in New Mexico. A complex of differing laws across states defies the concept of a single country, called the *United* States of America.

Other state regulations regarding penalties for a variety of sexual crimes differ by large degrees across state borders. Whether too lenient or too harsh, it is doubtful that a teen in Texas differs from one in Massachusetts to the degree that warrants differing penalties. The same may be said for all sexual offenders. The rapist in Oregon should expect the same judicial fate as one in New York. The federal government should standardize the range of penalties such that equal justice prevails across all state borders. There is a reason the states combined into a single country; it is not solely for the purpose of national defense but should also be true for the equally crucial goal of a humane civilization and hence a common manner in which criminals are judged, penalized and sanctioned.

At present, states are now isolated fiefdoms ruled by governor-kings, especially if they share a larger proportion of political party affiliations in state legislatures. Such law-makers are often ill-informed about the science of sexual offending. It is these federal and state legislators who have thrown a wrench into the rachet of progress in building a set of scientifically based and common-sense proposals for advances in the field of justice for sexual offenders.

Differing laws create a fragmented system of justice which promotes extremists to positions of power and fuels the flames of discord in what we call a democracy but is, in actuality a duopoly of red and blue. Were New York to be attacked by a foreign power, should South Carolina refuse to send troops in its defense? Local distinctions in land use, mineral extractions and zoning may make some sense; a nation with splintered laws, however, only leads to a concocted fury combined with inconsistencies, making an offense in one state a lawful action in its neighbor.

Certainly, each family should be free to offer guidance to their own children. But artificially creating differing, and inappropriately older ages of consent runs counter to science and common sense. If a parent wishes to punish a child for sexual activity, that is their right; it should not be within the government's purview to bestow penalties for consensual sexual activity beyond a reasonable age, in my opinion 15 (although many would disagree). That is not the issue. A standardized age of consent is a necessity and might reduce unnecessary costly legal battles without jeopardizing community safety.

Differences across international borders matter as well. A recent study in Great Britain (reported in *The Economist*, November 10, 2023) found that punishments for offenders were often "contradictory" and emphasized that overcrowding in jails and prisons wastes valuable resources in financial terms and in other areas. It calls for shorter sentences for those who have committed minor crimes absent any violence. It has also documented that briefer incarcerations result in lower re-offending rates. It raises concerns that the number of offenders not on remand (free in the community until sentencing) has created a backlog of cases and delayed resolution of each case. Yet recent budget cuts have resulted in fewer courts and judges, hence longer delays in resolving sentencing.

Longer sentences have been demonstrated to result in poor outcomes in terms of recidivism, employment opportunities and yet greater costs to taxpayers. Moreover, prisoners must endure harsh prison environments while lacking opportunities to advance their education, gain job skills and not be exposed to criminals who may have committed high degrees of violence, both in the outside world and while incarcerated. It recommends consideration of both community-based strong community supervision along with halfway house-like residential placement for the majority of sexual offenders who pose little to no risk to the community. Such placements should provide encouragement for completing education and job skills as well as assistance in finding placement in the community once the sentence allows. Quite often, the major complaint we hear from ex-prisoners is the difficulty in locating housing after release.

Certain areas of the law may differ across state and international borders, such as population and regional differences in penal institutions and community attitudes. But human rights should not differ based upon the state or county. We are left with a "Mr. Potato Head" panoply of patchworked state-level regulations based on the composition of state legislatures, which can change from year to year. Over half of US states have a lower age of consent than 18. In America today, it is more likely than not that families will move to a different state. They should be able to do so with the assurance that the law does not also shift with them.

Change Funding Priorities in the Criminal Justice System

America is a shockingly violent country when compared not only to other rich-world nations, but even to those we deem high in savagery. Our murder rate is six times that of most European nations and 20 times that of Japan.

Violence, in the main perpetrated by those wielding guns, cuts short the lives of some 24,000 people each year. Estimates put the annual cost of murders at $400 billion. Yet we keep building more prisons to house more inmates than does the entirety of Europe.

America spends about one-tenth of that sum and a lower proportion of its GDP on police training and hiring than comparable wealthy nations. For example, the US spends more on prisons yet devotes 20% less as a share of its GDP on policing than any other rich country. Although a recent bill now passed in Congress portions out $37 billion to reduce crime, that sum, divided by the number of police departments to receive it, is insufficient to implement the hiring of more officers or to improve the training they will receive. Thus, a victory here and there does not equal a triumph.

Studies do document that police presence in a community can reduce crime. It is doubtful, however, that the abundance of police on the streets can accomplish much in minimizing sexual offences. Some of those funds however could be employed in training officers to become specialized in investigating sexual crimes.

Such training could also include familiarity of the research literature for field supervisors in community corrections. They would be best employed to utilize the most appropriate restrictions on those whom they supervise, For example, more dangerous offenders can be more closely tracked while fewer resources would thereby be diverted to manage and regulate situational offenders, who pose little risk to the public.

Increase Funding for Sexual Offending Research

No sub-sub-specialty in the sciences has ever requested of the NIH, NIMH, or an academic institution, *less* funding for research. Never have I encountered a scientific research article which did not end with an entreaty for more research into whatever the authors were studying. That is the nature of science. Each finding opens additional areas of inquiry and, at any rate, requires replication.

However, the scientific literature on the assessment and treatment of sexual offenders is particularly sparse. Much of it concerns minutiae of the validity and reliability of various testing instruments; studies on the success of various treatment techniques is practically missing. Equally absent is research into the origins of sexual offending. Genetic factors touching on impulse control combined with the epigenetic neural effects of a troubled upbringing go begging for extended study. It is unlikely a child is born a sexual offender. While some such offenders have relatives who also have offended sexually in the past, these are rare.

Moreover, the commonly accepted notion that a sexual offender must have been himself a victim of similar abuse as a child is not borne out by the evidence: Fewer than 25% of SOs were victims of being thus abused as children.

Those of us treating sexual offenders owe part of our practice to clinical research. I am afraid that most of us appear unconcerned about how effective our ministrations are, as studies documenting long-term recidivism following treatment are almost unique in our field (see the Bibliography for the few that do exist). Treating such offenders is not the easiest way to a highly secure financial future. Insurance payments are sparse or absent, and the majority of sexual offenders are only rarely wealthy, especially after paying legal fees. Therefore, clinicians in this area have precious little time to devote to clinical research and may have to reserve the majority of their time to work that is rewarded in a financial manner.

Our subspecialty is among those least likely to afford a luxurious lifestyle during our active years or in retirement. To bolster that argument, one need only recognize the absence of psychiatrists in this field. As of the first decade of the present century, there were just two MD psychiatrists in America treating sexual offenders. As of the second and the beginning of the third decades, there is but a single one.

It remains a compliment to the integrity of the women (mostly) and men who undertake what is a difficult and unpopular specialty of treating sexual offenders. They do so with the certainty they will make less money than their peers in other subspecialties. They should be congratulated, though most often they are hardly recognized.

The formation of the specialty organization, ATSA, awkwardly-named the Association for the Treatment of Sexual Abusers, has helped to at least recognize our existence and the legitimacy of our work by setting standards of quality in accepted practices in this field. It has accomplished but a bare minimum, however, in helping to secure funding for such research.

There has been progress, especially in persuading academic institutions to support work in this field. Especially encouraging are recent advances in genomics, neuro-biochemistry, and computation. It would be of immense interest to have recordings from implanted electrodes in nonhuman primates' brains, particularly in the limbic, hypothalamic and amygdalar regions of both female and male animals, then record synaptic firing when a female is in heat, when a male has an erection, or makes attempts at penetration. Of equal interest, we need to learn which stimuli precipitated sexual arousal.

I am uncertain if such research could be helpful in learning more about sexual offending but none of the 20 or so primate research centers in this country and abroad have ever approached this area, so ripe for exploration. With some chagrin, I must admit that here in Oregon, I have been unable to interest one of the leading primate research centers in the country, located nearby, to undertake such examinations.

This deficiency represents a gaping hole in research that appears to be decades away at this time. Congress has recently approved $370 billion on green energy research (much needed), and passed the Chips and Science Act, which provides $52 billion to enrich the semiconductor industry, in the hope of outcompeting China in AI (an uncertain but necessary endeavor). The Advanced Research Projects Agency, a part of DARPA, the research arm of the Defense Department, has recently allotted $6 billion for biomedical research, up from $4 billion for 2022. America spends $800 billion on weaponry and wartime projects, equivalent to 3.8% of its GDP; none of those dollars is earmarked for basic mental health studies except as they address military applications. Neither does any current government or academic funding pertain to studies designed to *prevent* sexual abuse.

Private investment has doubled from 1% of GDP in 1979 to 2.3% of GDP in 2022; of that amount, the sum to be spent on mental health is 0.01% and of that, zero is earmarked for research on sexual offending. Assistance from pharmaceutical companies and academia is as likely as an untreated patient with paranoid personality trusting his therapist. Although medications can be helpful for a minority of obsessively driven pedophiles, rapists, and men with hypersexuality, this is an unprofitable avenue for pharmaceutical firms anxious to introduce medications afflicting a broader swath of the population.

Nevertheless, The Research Unit of the *Economist Magazine* has estimated that the financial returns to research are at least ten times the value of the original investment.

I must end, as usual, in a plea for governmental cooperation and coordination in such fields, thus helping further the study of the efficacy of treatment for sexual offenders of all types. Less recidivism, fewer sexual crimes, and fewer victims, should surely be a goal not only worthwhile but hardly controversial. Unfortunately, given the present political environment, increased funding in these areas in about as likely as your teenage daughter putting down her phone during dinner.

Increase Funding for Research on the *Prevention* of Sexual Crimes

An ounce of prevention is...well, you know. Yet studies about the origins of sexual offending and how to prevent it are not only sparse but practically nonexistent, especially the hypothesis that such crimes *can* be prevented. There exists a plurality of journal articles about early childhood trauma and theories, some impossible to prove, others emphasizing early childhood abuse and lack of satisfying attachments as significant to later development. However, the vast majority of those who have suffered physical and sexual abuse, exposure to domestic violence, experienced parental abandonment, and bore witness to substance abuse, do not, in general, commit criminal behaviors nor even sexual crimes.

Yet sufficient evidence exists that many, if not most, sexual offenders encounter and endure such traumata. Nevertheless, it is just these unfortunate youngsters, shunted from neglectful homes to foster placements to institutions, who receive only brief and often interrupted mental health treatment, if any. They also have borne the brunt of harsh punishments for their impulsive and often oppositional behaviors. Mental health clinicians, facilities, and institutions need to be mindful of these youngsters' needs for affirmation, attachment, and positive reinforcement for impulse control and respect for a rules-based society. Such youth crave respect and positive models yet are most often placed into settings which emphasize punishment; indeed, the most attention they will receive is when they break the rules.

One concrete suggestion would be to forgo, short of overtly harmful behavior toward people or property, punishment. Indeed, the worst form of a negative response to oppositional behavior is most often nonresponse. Why reward breaking the rules with so much attention associated with punishment? For most humans, regardless of age, the most severe reaction to negative and hostile behaviors is neglect. It would be worth studying the effects of such a penalty in concert with rewards for unobtrusive and compliant behaviors.

This should not be restricted to troubled youngsters or institutional placements but can begin at any home. How many parents pay attention to their children when they are quietly studying or completing their homework? How many say "Thanks, I appreciate it when you help out." Many adults believe their offsprings' duties should not require any response but I believe that is an error. Paying attention to kids when they display good behavior should be more common than punishing them for bad.

In 60 years of treating general psychiatric patients of all types, the most concrete and functional statement I ever heard came from a 17-year-old teen who had lost her mother in an automobile accident. She had worked through the grief process well when she made the following comment: "For 17 years my mother cooked dinner for me but I never said 'thank you'." She carried that guilt, mild as it might become over the years, for the remainder of her life. We share with most primate species many emotions, such as anger and even grief. Guilt is not among them; it is uniquely human. Hence empathy training has become a routine part of sexual offender therapy.

Another area of concern in preventing sexual crimes is the limited availability of mental health services for youth who are obviously going astray. Temper outbursts, lack of advancement in school, limitations in communication initiated by children, and lack of wholesome relationships can all be signs of depression, anxiety or an adjustment disorder. All these are treatable conditions. Early counselling and, if indicated, medications, can all be helpful in preventing further decline.

It has been estimated that over 50% of prison inmates suffer some form of mental health condition. While among these, substance abuse might constitute many of their disabilities, other potentially treatable psychiatric and psychological conditions are common aside from antisocial personality disorder. These include depression, ADHD, PTSD, and anxiety disorders. Yet the status of mental health services in correctional facilities is woefully inadequate. This is not the fault of providers; rather it is an observation of the lack of sufficient funding for all health services so emblematic of prison facilities.

Yet providing appropriate and comprehensive mental health treatment to those who might become offenders in the future, and to those who have already broken the law, might well achieve a reduction in all crimes overall, and particularly for sexual offenders, who are amenable to treatment, even if it is mandated.

This is more than a sad commentary on the limited availability of ample mental health services in prisons; it represents a national embarrassment when compared with similar rich countries which do provide such benefits and hence achieve much lower rates of all criminal behaviors. Once again, our legislators appear to place politics and profit above scientifically determined policy.

Abolish Entrapment by Federal and State Police Agencies

In some countries, secret police carry out clandestine practices and encourage citizens to report anyone expressing an opinion disparaging their governments or which they find objectional. Once identified, those making these statements are subject to a variety of retributions, including imprisonment, often without a proper trial or ability to be represented in a dependable and trustworthy court of law. Some might immediately think this would occur in a dystopian and authoritarian world as embodied in China or Afghanistan but, in truth, such a country lies closer to home. It is called America.

> Quinton, at 21, was a shy individual who had been diagnosed in early life with autistic disorder, although several professionals had offered differing opinions. Though he had graduated from high school and was attempting to obtain a trade through a local community college, he had been bullied through his early school years and had never dated nor engaged in any sexual or romantic relationships. He had never been in trouble with the law nor had he ever engaged in any type of substance abuse. Through the internet, however, he had been attempting to establish some connections that, at least at first, did not involve a face-to-face meeting.
>
> Using iMessenger, then Snapchat, he had met several women but, frightened of rejection, he had hesitated to initiate any request to meet them in person. He had posted a photo of himself along with some biographical information when he received a response from a woman who appeared interested in him. She told him she was 22 and she was as lonely as he felt he had been.

The following is an actual recording of their communications, largely through texting with the common abbreviations and misspellings used these days in electronic messaging:

FEMALE: U seem so nice; what do U like to do?
QUINTON: I'm not very good at this.
FEMALE: No probs. Neither am I.
QUINTON: I play games. How old r u?
FEMALE: Me 21. I like the ones where u can see guys w great abs & girls who r sexy.
QUINTON: can u send me a photo? How old r u?
FEMALE: Im 22 but some peebl think im younger. Here's the photo hope u dont judge

(Photo sent of an attractive adult female, fully clothed, face partly obscured.)

QUINTON: Wow – u r beautiful! (accompanied by a smiling emoji)
FEMALE: I've had bad trubl w boyfriends...mostly in bed
QUINTON: What kind?
FEMALE: guys just like it rough, u know?
QUITON: I would never do that. I'm not into that stuff.
FEMALE: C an we meet up? U seem so nice! (multiple positive emoji's)
QUINTON: YES YES YES I'm shy but may be we can get along?
FEMALE: If u r up for it, we could do sum exploring. Im into most anything, physical, sexual whatever.
QUINTON: Where can we meet and when?
FEMALE: St Joe's parking lot 7 tonite cuz its hard to find my house so ill lead u. Know where it is?
QUINTON: Yep
FEMALE: Bring condoms just in case.
QUINTON: I like that!

On the way to the parking lot, Quinton received a text:

FEMALE: *Wnt to b honest w u; um I'm 17 but turning 18 in one month OK?*
QUINTON: *If u are almost 18, I guess itd b OK.*

As Quinton turned into the parking lot, he was apprehended by multiple police with guns drawn and hustled into a police car. He was told he had committed a crime: *Communicating with a Minor for Immoral Purposes*. (In more recent cases and different jurisdictions the charges are often changed.) *Encouraging Child Sexual Abuse* and *Luring* are but several of many, including awful-sounding ones bearing no relationship to what actually occurred, including *Sexual Abuse in the Second Degree* and *Rape of a Child*!). Quinton's public defender urged him to accept a plea deal with the DA for 364 days in County Jail, dismissed, then three years of probation. No one bothered to look but it was telling that Quinton had no condoms in his car.

> This offense occurred three years ago. He is still not allowed to be in places where children might congregate, such as fast-food restaurants, malls and parks. His PO has finally allowed him internet access through a program, *Covenant Eyes*, in which the PO can monitor all his electronic activity. Quinton is not allowed to have a smart phone. He works as a custodian in a downtown office building but can only be on the job at night. He could not attend his cousin's funeral, must register as a sexual offender, and his family were forced to move due to the stigma associated with that label. In short, although he will soon be out from under supervision, he is sentenced to a lifetime of shame without the possibility of parole.

Those who watch popular TV programs are aware that such men are labeled "predators" despite the fact that they have neither sought out nor had any sexual activity with minors. Charges are most often the poorly worded *Online Sexual Corruption of a Minor*, or the more indefinite *Luring*, although the exact words can vary by district.

Who was the victim in Quinton's case? There was none. Yet his guilt was predetermined by the very act of driving to a parking lot. If he had seen an actual 17-year-old female, would he have engaged in sexual behavior with her? We do not know, nor do the authorities who arrested him.

Most females at 17 certainly look mature. Yet there could be no defense; he was guilty of driving to a designated location where he *might* have met a mature female and *might* or *might not* have engaged in some sort of sexual activity. An expensive trial would be pointless. Indeed, in an actual count of entrapment trials in such cases in Washington and Oregon over the past ten years, the verdict was guilty in 99% of cases. Nonetheless, we are aware of one trial in which a man was attempting to meet a girl claiming to be 15 but he was acquitted on technical grounds. Dissatisfied, local police set up another sting operation but this proved unsuccessful.

Some background in the origin of such cases proves instructive. In the past decade, online predator cases have mushroomed. State patrols have used a variety of unofficial and quasi-legal entities to detect the presence of child porn on anyone's computer or smart phone. They have also collected suspected cases from child protection programs justifiably established to detect and hopefully deter child exploitation operations.

Another worthwhile organization has been helpful in monitoring internet activity for such purposes, The Internet Crimes Against Children Task Force. An additional such group, often helpful in extortion cases, is the National Center for Missing and Exploited Children (NCMEC). While these groups' main goal was to expose criminal gangs associated with child exploitation, they have also frequently notified state authorities when they detect any male either interacting electronically for sexual purposes with young women or accessing child porn. State legislatures have certified such cases under "Community Protection Acts."

When a man is identified as communicating with *anyone* for a sexual liaison, adult or not, he is fair game for further intrusive investigation and a "sting" operation in which such individuals are first tricked into conversations with a young female officer posing as a teen, then only later admitting she is "just underage". Some tricksters use the age as 17 but others use lower ages as well. Never do they lie to the extent of pretending to be an immature girl or boy who is sexually undeveloped, such as an age of five through 11. Any communication suggesting sexual activity proves sufficient evidence for further investigation, even if the suspect believed he was initially communicating with an actual adult. Regardless, he has already committed a crime.

We have encountered even more egregious cases. In the past several months, individuals have been charged with *Luring* and *Communicating with a Minor for Immoral Purposes*. (Who was the minor?) Yet these particular men, all without any prior record of criminal behavior or substance abuse, never actually go to the pre-arranged site. They may either be aware it is a "sting" or may be too shy to meet a real female face-to-face. Despite never acting on the decoy's suggestions, they decide to not meet her. Yet, in the clouded eyes of the law, they have already indicated sexually tinged conversations with a "minor", despite the fact that no minor was ever involved and despite the fact that, often, the decoy initiated the sexual nature of their conversations.

It appears the sole beneficiaries of such deceits are the DAs, who may proclaim they have "won" a case and made a community's streets safer. They also benefit financially. Moreover, the police thereby take credit as well. Many DAs and some sheriffs are elected officials whose tough stance against sexual offenders can be employed as political fodder in contested elections. In such cases, the DA may derive satisfaction (and additional funding) with a guilty judgement or a plea arrangement, but in all honesty, it is worse than claiming victory; it is simply that the DAs and the criminal justice system simply do not care.

State detectives have eagerly participated in such scams; indeed, certain officers have established a supposedly nonprofit organization, OUR organized by a group of former detectives as a nonprofit charity. In reality, OUR, which stands for Operation Underground Railroad is a well-established enterprise first created to help black slaves escape over a century or more ago. More recently however, it has joined the pursuit of ending child exploitation, a laudable goal. This group has indeed been somewhat successful in exposing gangs devoted to ensnaring children for sexual exploitation.

More recently, a group of former police officers has co-opted these deceptive exploits to form a linked, but actually separate, nonprofit to identify computer users who might be attempting to identify those they believe are attempting to arrange a sexual liaison with underage youth. One of its founders claimed that "God told me to find the lost children." Under the auspices of OUR, this subgroup has actively solicited funds "to protect children from predators." They have associated their logo alongside state police emblems and OUR and have obtained contributions exceeding half a million dollars. Yet state agencies have been unable to determine where that money went. Investigations into this appendage of a legitimate organization, OUR, are ongoing.

Nonetheless, it is apparent that we live in a nation supposedly dedicated to privacy when no such privilege exists in the internet age. Authorities have been enabled to track your location, hear what you have said on your smart phone, and see what you have typed on your laptop or texted on your phone and with whom you have interacted, even if you believe you've deleted it. Traces can always be detected by police forensics experts. Once a suspicion has been raised that a man might be attempting to arrange a sexual liaison, there is no restraint or legal impediment to prevent authorities from establishing a "sting" operation to determine if a man is willing to engage in a sexual act with a minor.

This system is abetted now by artificial intelligence (AI, an oxymoron) and Chatbot or OpenAI. Should I, as a physician and researcher, conduct a Google search for scientific papers on child pornography, I would be reported by some of the agencies noted above to police authorities simply by using "Child Pornography" in the search engine. I might be visited by officers with a warrant to search my electronic devices or be called by a "young woman" in a sting operation. Unlike some, I am not opposed to law enforcement listening to anything I have to say or communicate electronically and am glad they can apprehend and possibly prevent threats to our safety. I am concerned, nonetheless, that the algorithms used cannot react to the specific circumstances and contexts of many communications.

By the way, I have tested supposed AI and chatbot-AI applications and, most often, in response to a query, I receive back utter nonsense. I realize that smart tech engineers are refining these programs, but I still fear that no machine will be able to discern the context and intent of actual human dialogues.

There are three means by which all animals learn: modelling, strengthening neural connections when an action achieves a desired effect, and through pain or happiness. When you kick an AI machine, it doesn't kick you back (unless it was programmed to do so – unlikely). Until a machine can be constructed with a cerebral cortex, hypothalamus, limbic system and an amygdala, it will never experience the emotions associated with rewards and punishments. Another limiting factor is that the need for strengthening connections is necessarily based upon human-derived algorithms which are limited to what has already occurred. Yes, AI can predict the future but only upon learning what has happened in the past. True innovation is, at present, improbable. Organizations employing automated systems to determine the likelihood of criminal activity will probably be necessary; one hopes they will always be overseen by actual human beings.

There is no question that predatory offenders against children should be identified and prevented from continuing such activity. The national groups dedicated to detecting such offenders deserve our full support. Indeed, a recent FBI sting uncovered a nefarious organization attempting to use ransomware by posing as an undercover operative. Millions of dollars were saved by their covert actions.

But arresting a man and thereafter labelling him for life as a sexual offender because he was tricked into arranging a meeting with an adolescent can be an unconstitutional intrusion into a private life. The majority of such men have no criminal history, are not attracted to children, and should not become the target of a pre-arranged encounter in which police carry out a deceitful engagement to trap them into a victimless crime.

Most adult men are attracted to postpubescent females; the decoy never assumes the identity of a 7–10-year-old girl. Yet such police actions have never come under public scrutiny nor judgmental challenge. To allow a governmental agency such as state police or the FBI (some such interactions occur across state boundaries) to carry out duplicity may eventually diminish the reputation of law enforcement in many areas. Deceit serves as a poor example for our children who may well learn from the examples set by the workings of the criminal justice system.

Moreover, the majority of men caught in such stings are between the ages of 17 and 25, a period in which the male CNS is particularly prone to impulsive actions. They are often similar to Red, a case cited above, in that they are reluctant to meet females in public at first and feel more comfortable arranging an encounter online. Many carry on such communications for months before agreeing to meet. Yet they are communicating with a female police officer (or sometimes even a male should the communications be conducted absent any phone contacts).

The female officer is chosen carefully; she is often the most junior of the staff and the photos she sends are rarely of her but of attractive females, all of whom are adults or are of ambiguous age, and most purposely obscure facial features. They may ask the male for photos of a sexual nature and at times the men send photos of their genitalia, thereby strengthening the case against them as this constitutes *Communicating with a Minor for Immoral Purposes*. Yet who is the minor? There simply is not one.

In addition, like Brian, most such men have no history of accessing child pornography, no criminal histories, nor of substance abuse. Their sole mistake was exchanging information with a female police officer usually originally claiming to be of age, then suddenly informing the men she is under the age of majority. It is as likely that if the men originally knew the spurious female was underage, they may never have continued their chats. It is also more probable than not that if a man met a real teen, perhaps 13 to 15 years of age, they never would have proceeded to actually engage in any sexual activity. The term "jail bait" is widely understood.

The police also fail to take into consideration that the most sophisticated men who actually prefer sexual activity with a teen, male or female, are well-aware of the decoy operations. They can, with ease, decipher a police decoy's stock phrases in an ad or in text chats because such communications employ the standard "come-ons", abbreviations, phrases and patter which have been popular over the last several decades with many teens.

In addition, when the decoy, who initially introduced herself as a 20-year-old, suddenly says she is really 16, any potential offender who has been through such exchanges will automatically identify this as a sting operation and, in haste, terminate the exchange. It is thus only the unexperienced, naive and artless individual, rather than a habitual sexual offender, who is entrapped. Such "offenders" with few, if any, history of communications with a decoy or a teen, are the ones who are trapped in such operations.

In other words, the authorities, in the majority of cases, are arresting men who are not specifically targeting teens nor preferentially attracted to them. Instead, the police are focusing on men who, most often, are too shy to arrange a first meeting with a person in real life, but prefer to initiate conversations online. The real predators of adolescents are rarely caught in such stings, while the police continue to search for, and arrest, unseasoned men who pose little to no threat of harm to anyone. These stings thus waste valuable time and money in a pointless endeavor which almost never reduces the risk of sexual assaults. In our as-yet-unpublished series of over 100 men caught in such deceptions, 95% have had no criminal record, let alone any history of sexual crimes.

It is these men who are arrested, charged and convicted of a crime which never took place. They are thus stigmatized for life because of an event which never harmed anyone but themselves. Do such men have a greater potential of abusing teen females? No evidence, in multiple studies, document the opposite as they have no criminal record. Instead, they are presumed to be guilty because of an *intent* to have sexual relations with a minor, relations that never occurred in real life. It is difficult to prove intent or lack of it but in these cases it is assumed. It is as if a man speaks of a desire to rob a bank but never does, yet is arrested because of his stated intent, which might as well have been a joke or a wish never to be realized in real life. I may wish someone would fall off a cliff but I would never be arrested for expressing that desire. Another example might prove instructive.

> Russell (Russ) was 19 when he began trolling the net after breaking up with his girlfriend. A chemistry major at a local university, he had planned to work in the tech industry, where chem majors are needed but rare. He visited sites known for arranging sexual liaisons but one which prominently displayed the usual warnings, never enforced, that anyone using the site had to be 18 years of age or older. He entered into an online relationship with a mature-sounding voice but a sexually

obvious w4m post (woman looking for a man) with a hashtag of "htpnts,". For the sake of brevity, I will edit their texts and calls.

RUSS: Saw yur pic looked hot.
FEMALE POLICE OFFICER PRETENDING TO BE HTPNTS: That's what all the guys say.
RUSS: No man; I really mean it! (emoji added with tongue sticking out)
FEMALE: if ur serious, text me tmrw at (xxx-xxx-xxxx).
RUSS: Will do!

(Next day)

FEMALE: Still interested?
RUSS: not gonna stop.
FEMALE: What r u into?
RUSS: Anything that gets you wet.
FEMALE: I'm already 1/2way there.

Both communicate via text and phone for about one month, during which Russell receives a photo of a woman clearly in her twenties and tries to determine her true age.

RUSS: I loved you pic-dont go south on me.
FEMALE: Never but uv got to show up & stop talking.
RUSS: Jus say place & tim.
FEMALE GIVES A HOUSE ADDRESS AND TIME BUT THEN SAYS: Bring beer & pro; I'm really 15 but my folks are gone on vac so no prob.
RUSS: 15? R U kidding me. Ur pic looked like 25.
FEMALE: Yeah, I get that a lot.
RUSS: U R JOKIN.
FEMALE: Only 1 way to find out.

Russell drives to the house, where he is charged with *Sexual Abuse in the Second Degree* (for reasons that are unclear) and *Engaging a Child for Immoral Purposes*. He receives a sentence of five years in state prison followed by five years of post-prison supervision. He will have to register as a sexual offender, perhaps for life.

Russell soon learns that even after release, which might be curtailed after three years for good behavior, he will not be allowed any contact with his sister, then 15, thus he could not live at home. He could not walk his dog in a park, access the internet without monitoring, shop in a mall, would not be allowed to attend family functions nor travel to the university he had been attending. The authorities, as usual, set an arrest date months ahead due to prison overcrowding. Russel could only say that he thought she was playing a "mind game" on him to test him; he told the judge he would never have had sexual relations of any kind with a girl if an actual 15-year-old teen appeared. Wasted words; cynics would say these were mere rationalizations.

It is true that some dastardly threats have been uncovered through falsifying information. Years ago, a 19-year-old college student of Iranian descent was enticed by the FBI to join Al Qaeda after they saw vague thoughts in an email he sent to his parents in Iran, expressing dissatisfaction with Western ways. Over a period of summer and autumn months, the agents, themselves of Arabian ancestry, prompted the student to plan what they described as the most volatile event against America which would garner the entire world's attention: to explode a bomb in the midst of a heavily attended large city's Christmas Tree lighting event. He pushed the button that would have killed thousands of innocent bystanders. Of course, the bomb was as fake as the FBI operatives' true intentions. He now resides within the walls of a federal prison from which he will never escape. He has one hour five days a week to experience outdoor air and to see the sky, sun and clouds.

Most Americans are glad he was apprehended but, in reality, would he have ever considered such an explosion had he never been coached and even cajoled? We will never know for certain but he had no record of prior Islamic Fundamentalist attachments or actions, nor had he even attended a mosque.

Do we want a country where the police are dishonest? They often are so in questioning individual cohorts who committed a crime together, urging each to benefit by tattling on the others. This can produce necessary testimonies and capture criminals who might never had been identified by any other means.

In such cases, deals, often involving immunity, may be necessary. However, do we want a model for our children that teaches them that the only way to stay safe is to lie? Our law-makers lack the courage to defend honesty and defame deceit when it involves potential criminal activity, especially of the sexual sort. In fact, most of us do so as well. It will remain a foul stench for future generations in which science and reason prevail and our habit of ceding the right to lie to governmental authorities would be considered abhorrent at best and at worst, a crime itself.

Would Russel have actually had sexual relations with a 15-year old female? We will never know. A day before he was scheduled to begin incarceration, Russell committed suicide. A life was taken for a lie born on a deceit based upon the presumption of an intent, for an event that never took place, all for a victim who was a figment of someone's imagination. We have entrusted an infinity of power to the state, at times to prevent crime. But on too many occasions, such trust has also been built on faulty foundations, its mortar pulverized, resulting in the ruins of lives and, on occasions, the blood of the innocents. Shame, shame.

Provide Judicial and Professional Discretion in Sexual Offender Sentencing

Significant discretion in sentencing lies within the province of three individuals: The DA, the defense attorney and the judge. Few would ever face a jury in a trial in which they would, in all likelihood lose, and then suffer even more severe punishment. None of the three officials mentioned above have studied the scientific literature concerning sexual offending nor have they had any experience in assessing or treating such offenders. In certain jurisdictions, sentencing is mandated, particularly in the more egregious sexual crimes. Mandatory minimum sentences leave little to the discretion of the court. A rigid sentencing structure may breed novel inequalities of its own. Yet in this particular area there appears to be a sign on legislators' doors reading "Do Not Disturb."

Yet each case is different, not only in its extent and frequency but in ameliorating factors, such as family support, level of coercion used, criminal history, amenability to supervision and treatment, and unique personality features, all of which should be taken into account in sentencing. Why tie the hands of the three individuals, especially the judge, in imposing a sentence which takes scant account of all these factors and, in addition, fails to add the sexual offender treatment provider's findings of level of risk?

A national system of sentencing which includes the recommendations of the professionals who actually can assess and treat the offender would make penalties more equitable yet also allow for the idiosyncrasies of each case. These would not necessarily be too lenient on sexual offenders but would provide some uniformity yet allow discretion based upon the unique features surrounding sexual crimes. Most DAs and judges do not wish to be viewed as "soft" on sexual offenders, but discrepancies across districts are at times difficult to reconcile:

> Sam, a 32-year-old restaurant worker, had been molesting prepubescent girls (mostly 6–10 years of age) over a period of years. He would befriend them, ply them with gifts, provide drugs and alcohol for them, then gain sufficient trust to seclude them in his home, where he would sexually molest them. At sentencing, despite the gravity and chronicity of his crimes, he was sentenced to five years in prison, followed by five years of post-prison supervision.
>
> A different offender, Trent, 20 years of age, had viewed child porn on a number of occasions but had no other criminal history. He was enrolled in a university studying archeology and received ample support from his family. We determined that he had no sexual arousal to children. His sentence was five years in prison followed by five years of post-prison supervision.

These are extreme, but true examples of equal penalties imposed in actual cases with vastly differing histories and extremely dissimilar potentials to reoffend. The differences arose because Nathan and Howard, while dwelling in the same state, lived in different, though adjoining, jurisdictions. Neither example included opinions of specialists familiar with the assessment of risk of the offender nor his amenability to treatment. A federal but flexible guideline for all sexual crimes, allowing for judicial discretion and including a clinician's input, would allow not only uniformity but provide impartiality informed by scientific findings.

> Uri, a 24-year-old married man who was in love with his wife of four years; but she was prepared to engage in sexual activity less frequently than he preferred (3 days each week on average). He began trolling the internet and received a note on iMessenger from a coworker, just one month shy of her 18th birthday. She had been attracted to him but, up to that moment, he had ignored her flirtatious behavior. He began to reply to her via texts and, for about two months their internet communications became increasingly sexual, although not overtly so. In fact, the first hint of sexuality came from her when she sent, unsolicited, a nude photograph of herself. Uri then began to show admiration for her body and she sent several more photos and a video, all while she was either partially or fully naked. However, he had immediately deleted the images from his phone as he knew she was not yet 18. The girl's father found her phone, however, and lodged a complaint with the local sheriff's office.
>
> Following an investigation, including forensic analysis, Uri, who had never been in trouble with the law, did not use drugs or alcohol, and had worked and supported his family for years, was charged by the local DA of 34 counts, including *Using a Child in a Display of Sexually Explicit Conduct* and *Encouraging Child Sexual Abuse*. He now faces over 30 years in prison although we believe many of these charges will be dropped in a subsequent plea negotiation.

This is clear case of over-prosecution. The girl initiated the sexual part of their communications and they never had any sexual contact. Yet it appears in some, but not the majority of cases, prosecutors are inappropriately zealous in bringing the harshest of charges possible. They may win the minds of those who believe a sexual offender is beyond redemption, but hubris plays some role in this as well. No DA wants to appear tolerant of any sexual crime, regardless of its severity and the offender's risk of repeating it.

Institute Financial Penalties for Sexual Offenders

Sexual offenders may have to pay compensation to victims but, in the main, many are impecunious enough that the court rarely makes an attempt to provide for these. There are court and supervision fees (in some jurisdictions), the former amounting to a few hundred dollars, the latter approximately $40–$50 per month. If placed on supervision, the offender must pay those fees for many months, which could amount to thousands of dollars in some cases.

In addition, if the offender meets certain financial criteria, he may be eligible for a public defender; if not, he and his family will need to hire a private attorney. Should a plea deal be arranged, the lawyer's fee these days is at least between $30,000 to $50,000. Many such families have had to take out second mortgages to sell their homes to help their accused relative. Should a rare case proceed to trial, the attorney may insist on an additional $100,000.

My suggestions above might alleviate these financial burdens, particularly if the plea negotiation is streamlined, but this will not happen soon. However, added to these burdens may well be the after-effects of incarceration, including lost wages during jail or prison, and temporary unemployment, followed by a job paying well below what the offender was earning before being imprisoned.

I would suggest alternatives to incarceration in certain cases of low risk sexual crimes, such as statutory R&J or CPO offenses and those involving entrapment. Rather than crowding these offenders into cages, the government could substitute an ongoing fine – garnishing wages, say of 10% of the offender's total salary each month for a certain period of time befitting the serious nature of the crime and the offender's criminal history.

An example of the impact financial penalties may have can be found in the recent innovation of vehicle charging zones in large metropolitan areas, such as London, Milan and Stockholm. In these megalopolises, drivers must pay a fee to enter into their congested inner cities. As a result, all three cities have managed to curtail traffic because of such a financial penalty.

I believe this type of punishment would not only benefit the taxpayer, reduce the prison population, and prevent the risk to the offender of a potentially hazardous sentence, it would have a greater negative impact on the offender. The garnishing of wages would be one which could last longer than most jail and prison sentences. Overcrowding in jails and prisons remains a serious impediment to effective jurisprudence. At present, only El Salvador leads the list of prison populations per 100,000 inhabitants; the US is second, even behind autocracies such as China and Afghanistan.

It is quite plausible that such a financial penalty might even exert a preventive effect on potential sexual offenders, many of whom receive brief jail sentences or probation, both of which are typically cut in half if the offender does not create problematic behavior while incarcerated or violate any terms of his probationary supervision. It could be the equivalent of corporal punishment such as whipping (considered barbaric) minus any injury to the offender's body. I truly believe more offenders would be affected to a greater degree by losing a portion of their monthly income than spending a few months in jail.

Issue Warnings, Citations and Fines, not Arrests

What if, instead of costly and pointless incarceration, supervision and family fragmentation, at the initial discovery of a CPO offense or a first entrapment offense, a police detective or, better yet, an FBI officer appeared at the door of the offender with a message such as:

> We are aware you have been viewing CP [or have engaged in an R&J statutory crime, or an entrapment case] and if you continue, we will know and you may well be sent to jail or prison and lose most of your access to electronics for at least one and possibly three years. You will have to undergo random polygraph examinations, for which you must bear the cost. You will also have to register as a sexual offender and the registry will become available online to anyone choosing to access it. As a result, you may have difficulty finding a decent-paying job or apartment and may not be able to pursue many educational programs. In addition, the court may impose financial penalties on you, such as garnishing 10% of your future income for a period no shorter than ten years.

How many CPO offenders receiving that warning (and perhaps a citation along with a fine) would return to watching CP? Of all the CPO offenders we have treated, all have replied they would never have repeated their mistake if so warned, but that is an anecdotal and uncontrolled result; a formal study would be difficult as the question is obviously biased on its own; a control would be ethically challenging if not impossible; and the question itself is almost rhetorical.

Still, I believe this approach would save time, money and family suffering while relieving the DA's office, the courts, and supervising corrections officers, of the necessity of dealing with a group of CPO offenders who are the very least likely to pose any sexual threat to anyone at any time among the vast majority of sexual offenders.

Such a warning, or citation, could be re-worded to affect R&J and entrapment cases as well. Both these and CPO offenses pose almost no risk of harm to anyone in their communities.

Refine Police Involvement

There is little need for a horde of police or federal officers to conduct an arrest of a nonviolent offender in the same manner as they would a drug dealer with a known weapon or a man suspected of serial murders. Yet, surprisingly, the approach of arresting a sexual offender, whether he is a man who has committed a situational offense (such as molesting a step-daughter or viewing CP) or an exhibitionist, is conducted in the same fashion. Ablaze with assault rifles, five or more officers will commonly approach the residence of such an offender in the early morning hours (to make sure he's home and usually in somewhat of a daze).

In fact, police now have the availability of increasingly scientific forensic evidence in investigations of sexual crimes. While victim recognitions in line-ups have proven often, but not always, unreliable, it does put a strain on those who must provide testimony. Better to have computer-assisted finger-print, fluids and DNA evidence, along with CCTV cameras, now seemingly in every conceivable business, street, garden, many rooms in most homes, and on most urban corners. All to the good. Even more promising, recent studies document that an individual's DNA is not only deposited on items he touched; it resides in the air he exhaled in any room or house he entered, and may remain detectable for over 24 hours after he left.

This is not only wasteful of time and money but highly disturbing to family and neighbors, who may now believe an extremely dangerous individual was living among them. It also antagonizes the offender, and quite often his family, such that further compliance is diminished. Most offenders want to comply with the police and, despite what every attorney will tell them, which is, "Don't say a word", their first instinct is to cooperate, admit something, and hence attempt to placate the authorities with the sometimes-mistaken notion this will ameliorate whatever punishment will eventually be administered.

In contradiction to all the lawyers I know, I must admit that in most cases this compliance, while based on a desire to cooperate and prove that arrested sexual offenders are not terrible people, is instinctive and usually does not make much of a difference in ultimate sentencing distinctions in such cases. It would be more honorable and lawful if the police informed the offender of his Miranda Rights before taking statements but things progress so swiftly and in haste that this often does not occur.

An alternative was recently implemented in Denver: titled The STAR Program – Support Team Assisted Response, it employs specially trained officers, absent police uniforms, to respond to minor crimes. These personnel are authorized to issue citations and fines, followed by a hearing, without an attorney or a DA, in which the judge assigns a sentence, usually comprising brief incarceration, if any, but also specifying community service, amount of fines, and conditions of supervision.

This muted response may not please those who believe all sexual offenders should be subjected to harsh treatment but would appear to satisfy the justice system, especially in cases of CPO, extortion, and R&J offenders. Since this particular program has been implemented in Denver, there has been a 34% decrease in reports of such crimes over a five-year period of follow-up. The cost for such an apprehension and hearing has been reduced from $600 to around $150. In total over a year's period of time, this has resulted in savings of $35,000 in individual cases and millions of dollars during each year of its implementation. Savings nationally could well amount to trillions over a ten-year period.

Of greater concern are the police reports themselves. I have great admiration for local and federal officers. In fact, a greater police presence on the streets of high-risk neighborhoods has most recently resulted in a reduction in criminal activity in several large American cities. However, after interviewing offenders after adjudication, their families, employers, witnesses, and even victims, I must reluctantly conclude that police reports taken at the time of arrest and in subsequent interviews have proven to tend toward a predetermined assumption of not only guilt, but an exaggeration of the severity of the crimes being investigated. Certain cases are egregious: One example is given in the case of Aaron, in Chapter One. Not only did this man never commit a sexual crime, the police report contained lies and exaggerations later proven to be false.

Most police officers are honest and well-meaning individuals but there abides an overriding presumption of guilt and even evil intent in sexual abuse cases. These can often influence an officer when conducting an interview and thereafter, bias her or his investigation. These can include leading questions and outright suggestions when taking statements from victims, witnesses and the offenders themselves. Allow me to provide an additional example.

> A 21-year-old medical student, Victor, was arrested when his roommates discovered a hidden camera in one of their bedrooms. Charged with a variety of crimes, the police report suggested that Victor was actually a voyeur who had been stalking the university's campus. There had been such a stalker, but he had been arrested weeks earlier after admitting to his crimes. The claim against Victor however remained in his official report and was never corrected, despite his attorney's frequent requests.

A different problem occurs when the police fail to interview the victim. Quite often, the victim is referred to a specialized facility, usually connected to a medical institution such as a hospital. These children's centers are staffed by well-trained psychologists, social workers and the like, to interview youngsters who have undergone trauma. They serve a most beneficial service as staff therein are experts in how to make a child feel comfortable and believe they are never under scrutiny nor judged.

The problem occurs in that these centers do such an outstanding job in collecting information about the crime from the victim's perspective that the police themselves often use these reports in lieu of conducting their own interviews. While minimizing trauma to the victim by obtaining just one source of the criminal event(s) in question, are they fulfilling their duty under the Equal Amendment Clause to hear directly from the victim herself? Moreover, the offender is often interviewed at first apprehension. At that moment, he is alarmed and distressed; thus he may not be able to provide his own perception of what has actually occurred.

I am not advocating for doubling the trauma to the victim of re-living what occurred. However, when we do review both the police's interview of the victim, when they complete one, then compare that with the children's center reports, we have noted a number of disturbing discrepancies. I would suggest that the victim interview has not been demonstrated to add trauma in any permanent way and may even prove therapeutic, should both the children's center and police interviews of the victim be completed so as to compare and recognize any discrepancies.

I would also suggest that both sources of information include interviews of witnesses and families; often the police track down multiple witnesses who are crucial to their investigation. The children's centers rarely do so. Yes, it would take more time but a man's life is at stake.

It is crucial here to distinguish between truth and fact. An anecdote does not suffice as a scientific study but in this case, it may prove illustrative: prior to undertaking a climbing trip to the Himalaya, I invited a climber from Fairbanks, AK, and another climber to join us who lives in Needles, CA. I had set my home's temperature at 72 degrees. The Alaska chap complained of being annoyed with how hot the room was; the fellow from CA grumbled that it was too chilly. Was either lying? The scientific fact was that the temperature of the room was 72 degrees. But each individual's perception based upon their own level of comfort differed. *Points of view can be the result of inherent biases but should never affect decisions informed by scientific fact, rather than by what any individual believes to be the truth.*

Nothing in the above should be mistaken to imply victims lie. Studies demonstrate conclusively that victims, particularly children, do not concoct embarrassing stories which may disrupt their families.

Almost all sexual offenders either deny outright what the victim claims ("Her mother made her do it to get even with me") or minimize what actually occurred. ("I was only giving her a bath"; "I was just cuddling with her but my hand slipped".)

Children and adult victims have little motivation to invent or fabricate such sexual stories, which may only bring them additional trauma associated with family disruptions, fear they will not be believed, interviews, court testimonies, etc. Studies of offenders in treatment have demonstrated that only about 1% of their victims' accounts are invalid.

On the other hand, offenders have a multitude of motivations to minimize, justify or dissemble the narrative. Aside from the obvious fear of punishment, sexual offenders in particular also dread the notion they would commit this particular type of crime because of the iniquity imposed upon a sexual offender, especially the havoc this knowledge would create to their often-fragile self-esteem.

In summary, both police and children's centers could take a bit more time and patience in collecting, then accurately recording all statements and strive to be objective while withholding any personal contempt they may assume toward the alleged offender or his particular offense.

Assign More Female Police and Interviewers in Sexual Offender Cases

Most sexual offenders appear to open up to a greater degree about their sexual habits and fantasies to women than to men. In fact, they not only tell us so but, in a review of the details of thousands of interviews, when we can determine the gender of the person conducting it, this also appears to be the case. This also confounds a paradox: women speak about 7,000 words per day whereas men utter about 2,000. Yet it is often the active listening of women, along with delayed latencies of utterance and thus the tolerance of brief periods of silence, which encourage patients to reveal more about themselves.

At any rate, many men find it easier to talk with their female friends than those who are male. This may be attributed to any number of poorly researched findings and suppositions, such as that women are more sympathetic, less judgmental, and can share emotions more easily than their male counterparts. It could also stem from our evolutionary past, where men required silence to successfully hunt whereas women needed to communicate better to locate favorable foraging sites and to help each other find their way home. (Unfortunately, this premise is based upon the hunter/gatherer hypothesis but recent findings indicate women actively participated in many hunts, even against large game.) Of peripheral interest, agoraphobia stems from a fear of being far from a familiar place and is much more common in women, although such attributions about the origins of phobias, while they make sense, are not researchable utilizing present-day methods.

Women also seem more at ease at chatter among friends and at parties. Whether any of these traits would enhance sexual offender disclosures is scientifically unexplored but would make an interesting series of studies. In our experience, we often prefer that women be considered as the primary choice for interviews of sexual offenders. In addition, such offenders do not bristle against a female therapist performing a penile plethysmograph, an area one would have thought would be more facile for a male.

In our Clinic, we have also found that the gender of the professional treating the sexual offender makes no difference in rates of reoffending.

Improve Coordination Among International Policing Agencies

Much of the exploitation of sex workers and children originates in foreign countries. We don't know how much, however, because geographic and political barriers have prevented closer working ties amongst the multiple policing agencies tasked with such investigations and these are disbursed across the globe. While many American attorneys general and prosecutors believe such exploitation originates in Eastern Europe, others point to Indo-Pacific countries such as Cambodia and The Philippines as major culprits.

Interpol is considered the major policing authority responsible for investigating such exploitation and bringing the perpetrators to justice. This is no easy task. Certain countries, at times even including America and its Western European allies, are not keen to hand over jurisdiction to an international agency which consists of 181 countries, many of which may be the sources of such exploitation; moreover, other signatories have brittle relationships with the United States. Although Interpol expressively prohibits political interference and military operations, there is sufficient ambiguity in its originating documents such that even the FBI and CIA have been reluctant to fully cooperate with this international agency, at least according to international legal critics.

Unfortunately, in real practice, Interpol utilizes most of its resources concerning sexually abused children in collecting data rather than acting upon it. For example, it has identified over 23,000 child victims and holds more than 20 million images of missing youngsters. Of those, this agency identifies over 60% as prepubescent girls. Interpol shares these images with a large variety of governmental law enforcement agencies and NGOs but its own investigative arm is, at best, a paper tiger when compared with the sophisticated factories churning out child porn. Such porn is produced and protected by well-paid and ingenious electronic wizards who utilize the dark web, and even the regular web, to entice men to watch children engaged in sexual activities.

Interpol does share these images and corresponding information with local policing agencies in many countries, including Europol and Ameripol, but what officials do with that information depends upon funding the resources and finding the zeal, or lack of it, to investigate, then prosecute producers of CP. Similar problems bedevil the United Nations High Commission for Refugees (UNHCR) which is tasked with the protection of children. This arm of the UN's Refugee Program struggles with the well-publicized travails of over nine billion displaced individuals world-wide. It employs 19,000 personnel and partners with over 900 nongovernmental organizations dedicated to locating and rehabilitating missing and exploited children; again, it lacks the manpower to thoroughly investigate, then enforce and prosecute the propagators of CP itself.

A similar international agency, Unitas, functions in North and South America and Europe, and focuses especially on Eastern Europe. It specializes in training and education, producing YouTube videos, teaching tools and publications for schools, police agencies, and clinical specialists. However, it lacks a robust investigative arm. Its streaming documentary *The Lost Girls* is a stomach-churning film but, as with most such NGOs, actual data on detection and prosecution of CP producers are absent.

Several other agencies, such as The National Center for Missing and Exploited Children, provide a hotline, Amber Alerts and a cyber-tipline. The American Society for the Positive Care of Children, provides information about lost children and conveys access to professionals and police task forces. In the United States, these agencies perform an admirable, though of necessity incomplete, job of tracking and arresting consumers of CP. What they lack, however, are the ability and resources to investigate its producers and then share that information with the FBI.

The National Center and the American Society have mainly been successful, however, in enhancing training for teachers and parents about signs of sexual abuse in youngsters. Nonetheless, these nonprofits cannot afford to fund robust investigative and enforcement functions. For example, America's budget for Interpol, combined with support for the NGOs mentioned above, constitutes nine billion dollars per year, a sum which appears impressive, especially when compared with contributions from other countries. Yet this figure comprises less than 1% of America's GDP; it pales in comparison to the 18% of GDP allotted to our military budget.

While it appears impossible to bridge over these difficulties, it may still be possible for agencies devoted to eliminating sexual exploitation to share information in a more cooperative, less nationalistic manner. Studies of these institutions have identified not only low funding priorities as one problem but found that this was compounded with difficulties accessing information with partner agencies and lack of education within such agencies about the extent of sexual abuse and exploitation. One means to accomplish the main objective of the justice system's apprehension and prevention of the *production* of CP would be an increased sense of urgency by America and its allies at the United Nations. We could contribute not only enhanced funding but increased vigor in making the case for an expansion of the United Nation's Unitas to prompt more robust investigative and prosecutorial functions.

Moreover, as a major funding resource for Interpol, we could also press for better coordination amongst the various and widely dispersed NGOs to coordinate their activities and establish an international task force in coordination with policing agencies of participating countries and with our own states' attorneys general to identify, pursue, and prosecute producers of CP within and outside of our own borders. CP is not only generated abroad in Eastern Europe and Southeastern Asia; its origins may also be found in areas as diverse, yet as close, as Florida and California as well.

While international efforts to improve coordination amongst such agencies are said to be underway, those involved might be not only taking an afternoon nap, this has turned into what appears to be a hibernation.

Freedom of the press is a vital foundation of a democratic society. The problem lies in the emphasis placed on how deplorable this offender must be; it appears that the nature of the sexual crime is not apparent in the accompanying story.

We are primed for disasters in the news, not for events which go fairly well. Better to sleep in the trees than on the ground, where snakes and lions roam at night. When the wind creates swaying in the tall savannah grass, better to believe it's a lion than just a brief gust. Many people read only the headlines and inevitably conclude, in their own perspectives, that the sexual offender featured must be a loathsome person in general. Such generalizations do not conform to the facts and may taint not only the offender himself but his family as well. Even sexual offenders should be defined by who they are now, not by what act they have committed in the past.

Improve the Adverse Conditions within County, State and Federal Jails and Prisons

As noted above, few Americans would tolerate the temperature, ventilation and furnishings inherent in the majority of institutions housing sexual offenders. Nor should such offenders expect to serve their terms of incarceration mirroring the norms of even lower-earning Americans. If punishment is necessary, the comforts of home should not be expected to provide the cushioned ambience of even a poverty-stricken domicile. Yet there remain individual reports from unbiased visitors of intolerable heat, cold, odors, rats, insects (some carrying potentially transmissible diseases), pools of urine and feces left uncleaned on the floors of such institutions.

The American taxpayer would bridle at the cost of providing modern comfort to those who have committed heinous crimes. Nonetheless, modest sums could remedy much of the appalling conditions documented in the observations of even the most heart-hardened outsiders once personally encountered. It is not only the comfort of prisoners to be considered: the University of California has documented results that even an increase in temperature of just one standard deviation can yield an uptick of almost 15% in temper outbursts within a number of institutions, including jails and prisons.

Even fairly modern houses of correction often lack any means of heating, air conditioning (even in our southern states), ventilation, adequate plumbing systems, with furnishings barely comfortable to tolerate for even brief periods of time. Even at rest, asleep and at night, interns are left alone to face yet many more hours of darkness.

It may be enough to remove the freedom of movement for those imprisoned; to add the burdens of inadequate temperature control and only a modicum of proper toileting represents a doubling of the penalties already incurred by any person regardless of their past mistakes. A person is still a member of our species lest we lose all respect for our commonality of humanity. Moreover, although as yet unstudied in controlled studies, these abominable conditions have been linked to an increase in criminal recidivism. The longer a person lives in a jail or prison, the more the likelihood he will commit another crime increases. Of course, this is confounded by the severity of the initial crime – the worse the crime, the longer the sentence.

However, several studies (see the Bibliography) in sexual offenders, regardless of type of sexual crime, show that improving these horrid conditions lowers the probability of recidivism. For example, brighter lighting conditions, improved accessibility to the outdoors and sunshine, more comfortable furnishings, and placement of prisoners in proximity of their relatives, have all been shown to reduce the incidence of a repeat crime and the revolving door of recidivism.

Several studies have even demonstrated that having family visit often is another factor that reduces repeat criminal behavior. A related factor is that research shows that granting prisoners access to friends and family not only through visits but even via Zoom-type calls (while somewhat soulless) can also be helpful in the same manner: proof enough that the conditions of a crowded, unkempt and unhealthy environment, combined with exposure to other criminals, absent any attempt at treatment, increases the risk any sexual offender poses upon release. This constitutes reason sufficient to improve in any way feasible, the toxic atmosphere which imprisoned sexual offenders endure.

Improve the Conditions of Employment for Supervisors, Guards and Prison Administrators

Overcrowded prisons and jails create difficult conditions not only for inmates but for guards, supervisors and corrections administrative personnel. Overcrowding places additional pressure on supervisors who already labor under an overwhelming case load. According to state and DOJ officials, this problem will only worsen. The DOJ anticipates a 10% increase in prison populations within the next decade. Yet wages for such employees have not kept pace with inflation. It is no wonder that applications for each of these positions have declined in recent years.

For example, better conditions and a competitive salary for corrections employees could be shown to not only increase the number and quality of such workers but reduce recidivism. This supposition bears further scientific scrutiny.

No taxpayer wants to increase funding for departments of corrections nor would any politician sponsor such a bill. Yet if the general population were made aware of the dire and wretched conditions within these institutions, combined with the correlation with higher rates of recidivism, they might consider such progressive steps offered throughout this chapter. It has been estimated that a reduction in sexual offender recidivism could not only spare more potential victims but save millions of dollars each year in government expenses; lower rates of offending result in reduced costs for courts and supervisors.

Establish Positive Supervision

All sexual offenders are followed by supervisors following either incarceration, probation in minor cases, or prison in more serious crimes. If the individual is sentenced to probation only, with one year or less of jail time, he will be supervised by what is called a probation officer (PO). If he is sentenced to a crime demanding over one year of incarceration, he will be followed by a post-prison supervisor (PPS; formerly known as a parole officer).

At present, the standard list of prohibitions for all sexual offenders, regardless of the type of crime they have committed, is replete with what the offender *cannot* do. I have attached this list in Appendix B. Some examples include:

- Prohibition against contact with a person under the age of 18. This comprises any relative, such as a biological daughter or son and to all nonrelatives as well.
- Prohibitions against being present at a school, day care center, park, playground, library, or other areas where children congregate. (Does this include shopping malls? Supervisors vary on this issue.)
- Sexual offender treatment; the offender must pay for this treatment.
- No contact with the victim(s).
- Prohibition against viewing, listening to, owning or possessing any sexually stimulating material.
- Consent to a random unannounced search of the offender's residence or vehicle.
- Application of a curfew established by the supervisor.
- Report to a supervisor any change of residence or place of employment.
- Prohibition against residing within 100 yards of a school, park, or playground.
- Restrictions against leaving the state or country without approval of the PO or PPS.
- Prohibition against owning or using any electronic device, including computers or smart phones. (This restraint is used mainly for CP and entrapment cases but it is also frequently employed in many child abuse cases as well; exceptions are left to the supervisor but, over time, may permit the use of computers for work or education; these must be monitored by the supervisor however.) A flip phone is permitted.
- Disallowing consumption of alcohol or the use any illegal substances. (Medical marijuana is sometimes permitted with a physician's prescription.)
- The requirement to either find a job or enroll in an educational institution.

What if these prohibitions, which make sense in certain cases, were formulated in a positive manner, detailing what the offender is *allowed* to do?

- You may visit your son if an approved adult is present, although you may not have any physical contact with him.
- Here are the locations where you may live: (followed by examples, such as a halfway house or an area away from children).
- Here are some of the restaurants and stores you are allowed to visit.

- You can use a computer for work or school but it must contain a porn blocker.
- You can travel outside the state if you receive approval from your supervisor.
- Here are the hours you can be out of your home.
- You can have one alcoholic drink and use marijuana (if you are over 21) but cannot use these substances to excess; depending on the nature of the offense, urinalyses and, on rare occasions, blood tests (for marijuana or alcohol) will be performed on a random and unannounced basis.

Restrictions are only rarely tailored to the offender by some POs and PPSs based upon the nature of their crime. For example, a statutory offender (e.g., R&J and CPO cases) will contain restrictions against child contact, which appears irrelevant, either from a common sense or scientific point of view. They will, in all probability, not be restricted to location of his residence except if it close to the "victim" in a particular case.

However, if you scrutinize the restrictions in Appendix B, it would appear that all sexual offenders must adhere to many requirements which bear no relationship to the crime they committed. Does it enhance public safety for a child molester to not live near a school? It might seem so but study after study reveals no relationship to where an offender lives and whether he repeats a sexual crime. Indeed, most sexual crimes against children are committed at great distances from the offender's place of residence, such as at a home of a relative or at the offender's own home, which he is already automatically barred from inhabiting.

Have random searches (with consent) of a sexual offender's vehicle or residence enhanced community safety? No study has ever discovered any connection. Why would a prohibition against accessing a computer prevent further crimes of an exhibitionist? Certainly, the offender should have no contact with a victim but why prohibit contact with biological children? This restriction prevents the most mild of offenders from even attending family gatherings such as birthdays, reunions and holidays, where many adults are present. In fairness, certain supervisors, especially POs, work with treatment personnel to craft safety plans for attending such celebrations, always including the stipulation that an adult must be present if any children are in attendance.

In a 2023 study conducted at the Sand Ridge Evaluation and Research Center in Madison, Wisconsin, scientists tackled the difficulty in determining the rate of undetected sexual offenses in sexual offenders once released from incarceration into the community. Amongst other findings, the authors determined that a first sanction for a violation of a restriction, generally consists of extra community service or extra time in jail.

There is virtually no danger to a child the offender raised from birth becoming a victim of his sexual abuse; this is again proven by science because of the incest taboo, an evolutionary precaution promoting survival of our species. Yes, fathers have been known, rarely, to molest their own offspring, but not only is this exceedingly uncommon, it almost only occurs when that father was not involved with the child continuously from birth. Nonetheless, biologic fathers are most often restricted from any contact with their own children.

Electronic restrictions have resulted in egregious and onerous handicaps for employees and students. The latter have been forced to drop out of college while the former have lost their jobs. Yet this type of restriction has been applied to men who have no history of electronic crimes. In fact, we are aware of not a few men who, because of this unscientific restriction, have been doubly or triply punished: not only have they at first lost some measure of their freedom, they have suffered financially as well. All the while their families may have lost income generated by the offender and thus have borne burdens foisted upon them for committing no crime whatsoever.

I must admit that a number of current restrictions make eminent sense. No victim should have to be re-traumatized by contact with their offender. No actual child molester should have access to a computer which has the capability of accessing CP. A PO or PPS should know where his offender is and should rightfully possess the obligation to supervise his travel.

Yet the impact of always hearing "you cannot..." rather than "here's what you *can* do..." can improve compliance, induce better adherence to restrictions, and establish an enhanced and cooperative relationship with a supervisor; such relationships have been correlated, in a variety of scientific studies, to a reduction in sexual offense recidivism.

I would suggest a specific application of restrictions, voiced in a more positive manner and based upon what the offender actually did, rather than the present one-size-fits-all standardized list. The manner in which all sexual offenders are lumped together not only deprives them and their families of privations that have nothing to do with community safety but also perpetuate the received, yet flawed, conception among the general public that all sexual offenders are equally dangerous, untreatable, and are reprehensible individuals. This misperception not only punishes the offender in multiple ways, it insults the science of the administration of justice.

Abolish the Sexual Offender Registry

No study has ever demonstrated that a sexual offender being placed on a publicly available data base through a computerized list, by and large, has reduced the chance that he will re-offend. All studies, and there have been many, demonstrate that presence on a registry has exerted no effect in preventing a repeat of a sexual crime. Countries with no such lists all have lower levels of sexual crimes than does the US.

Being on the registry makes the offender's name known to anyone who accesses it, though honestly, most citizens rarely bother to search for it. Its main use is for the benefit of private background companies employed by large real estate firms which own blocks of rental properties; it is also utilized by a number of employers, especially those who have authority over children, such as school districts and youth organizations, such as the Boy Scouts and Girl Scouts. In both cases, this would be appear to be a legitimate use of this tool. However, the same information could be available to such groups by simply calling local or national authorities, such as the FBI. Issues of confidentiality would not present a challenge in the face of the need for public safety.

When asked, sexual offenders state that their major fear of being labelled a sexual offender has often been being placed on the Sexual Offender Registry. It can be, and has been, abused throughout its existence: men cannot rent an apartment, even one without children residing within; others are automatically prevented from obtaining a job, despite their training and experience, and despite any employment which would entail no interaction with children.

Does it make any sense for an 18-year-old man with a 15-year-old girlfriend to be blacklisted in such a fashion? Would such an R&J offender pose any risk to anyone, regardless of where he lived or where he worked? Should a PhD psychologist be prevented from continuing to practice, once penalties have been levied, if his sole crime was accessing CP and he has no history of any hands-on crime, nor any arousal to children? He could be allowed to practice but never counsel anyone under 18 years of age. A teacher who has an affair with a 17-year-old female student could be allowed to teach at an all-boys' school, teach only on-line, or only in adult classes: so much potential is now wasted.

The Sexual Offender Registry has achieved only additional stigma and hardships on the offender far beyond his initial penalties, and these can extend to his family as well, even though they are innocent of anything other than being related to an offender. All this can occur while not providing any additional safety for the community. I suggest a limited list available only from police agencies upon a request made reasonable by its direct relationship to a residence or a place of employment.

Moreover, no other offenders are required to submit their names to such a degrading and opprobrious roster. You can commit murder, vehicular homicide, and domestic assault without such an embarrassing publicly available roll-call. Once again, emotion overrides common sense combined with science: a triumph of technique over purpose, emblematic of our criminal justice system.

Eliminate Neighborhood Notifications

In past years, POs and PPSs would routinely warn all neighbors in person if a sexual offender was about to move into their area. The problems with such an approach are several and varied:

- Pedophiles rarely molest neighborhood children.
- Rapists commit their crimes at a distance from where they live.
- Situational offenders, such as CPOs, R&J offenders, and entrapment cases do not hardly ever re-offend regardless of where they live; their crimes are not location-specific.
- The situational child molester with a single victim has almost always offended against a child living within his home or one he might have visited at a distance, such as within an uncle/niece relationship. Neighborhood warnings accomplish nothing in such a case.
- The stigma imposed upon many SOs can become unbearable. Many of these men and their families have been harassed, both in person and online; some have had to move on multiple occasions. An unfortunate few have been the victims of physical assaults or even murder. The label of "sexual offender" is often a perception which obscures reality.
- Of greatest importance, no study has ever documented that such warnings protect the community or reduce repeat sexual offending.

More recently, this shaming process has abated, perhaps as corrections personnel realize it as a misuse of their time; however, it remains in several jurisdictions. It is a waste of time and money, and unfairly stigmatizes the SO. It can also be considered double punishment, cruel and unusual. Yet no such warnings are required in more violent and contemptible crimes. Why not notify the neighbors that a man who has committed murder has just moved in? This practice antagonizes the purpose of rehabilitation, and makes it more difficult for a sexual offender to find a living situation and job, opportunities, all of which could reduce the risk of recidivism.

Encourage Companies and Institutions to Act with More Vigor in Cases of Sexual Harassment

It is becoming increasingly clear that many women employed in companies or involved in higher education have been adversely affected by unwanted sexual comments, jokes or even physical approaches. It has only been within the last decade that this problem has been brought to light, extensively studied, and changes have been attempted. Yet there remain many examples in which women are subjected to harassment but their voices have not been heard. Afraid of retaliation and even losing their jobs, women have, have been silent for too long. Unfortunately, even today, the typical response from the victims of attempting to work in a toxic environment is muted and the perpetrators of such odious behavior go unchallenged.

It may not be against the law to make a sexual comment or utter a sexually oriented joke, but too many female employees and students have been reluctant to lodge complaints, especially if the perpetrator is in a position "above" them, such as a professor or a supervisor. One woman was courageous enough to initiate an Instagram account asking other women to share their stories of being sexually harassed at work. In a mere two days, the account had registered 10,000 followers; after another month, it had over 100,000.

Although well-known Hollywood types and entrepreneurs have been charged and convicted of multiple crimes perpetrated against women working with them, lesser instances of sexually harmful behaviors still go unmentioned. A recent study found that, when asked in anonymous fashion, 55% of women agreed that they had suffered in silence about being the target of sexual harassment. While such cases rarely rise to the level of criminal activity, they have caused untold apprehension of, or even job changes for the women who felt demeaned and objectified. Most recently, orientation sessions for new and established employees have stressed what constitutes harassment but we are unaware of how such courses have thus far altered objectional male behavior.

The criminal justice system could have an impact, however, if such obnoxious behavior were part of a company's or a university's culture. Perhaps such sessions could be conducted by *police officials* or *even members of the District Attorney's office.* This would serve to emphasize that males engaging in harassment are walking a thin line and that some behaviors (examples could be provided) could be considered criminal in nature.

Improve Education of Children about Sexual Offending Before they Reach the Age of Puberty

There are several layers within the educational process, beginning in elementary school and even extending into PhD programs, during which some information about sexuality in general and sexual offending should take place.

However, we live in a country in which many well-meaning parents are afraid of their children, even in their adolescence, hearing or reading anything that remotely alludes to any subject which broaches sexuality. School Boards are now actively banning any such literature from K-12th grades, and scouring school libraries to make certain their brood never has to bear the horrors of learning about normal sexual behavior. The Nazi book burnings come to mind although I realize that is not an exact analogy. Still, the state-supervised Sex Police do come to mind.

Are they aware of the scientific studies in this area? Wouldn't they rather talk to their children about sex? They rarely do. They appear to be satisfied that the vast majority of kids learn about sex from their friends and occasionally from coming across their dad's porn collection. Are they unaware of other countries' sexuality classes beginning in first or second grade? In such nations, the incidence of sexual crimes is one-tenth that of America's.

There has never been any research study to document harm of any sort from teaching young children about normal sexual relations, no matter how old that child is. In fact, the incidence of teen pregnancy and sexually transmitted diseases (STDs) is far lower in such enlightened countries, including Denmark, The Netherlands, Sweden, Norway and Finland. In a recently published list of sexual crime statistics, teen pregnancies, and STDs, the US is an abysmal 23rd, ranking below almost all European nations, including the Eastern Block, even below Ecuador and Uruguay, according to several lists produced by the US Department of Health and Services, and by the GLAAD (Gay and Lesbian Alliance Against Defamation Foundation) along with the United Nations World Health Organization and its Office on Drugs and Crime.

It is important to recognize that by the age of 13, more than 70% of both boys and girls not only have some rudimentary idea about sex but have engaged in "petting" activities. The Centers for Disease Control and Prevention provides figures for the frequency of sexual activity by age. They found that, by the 9th grade, 20.1% of females and 25.7% of males had engaged in intercourse. Those figures rose to 39.1% and 47.1% by the tenth grade respectively, and to 57.2% and 63.1% by the eleventh grade. The figures for seniors differ slightly as they are sourced from separate surveys but are definitely higher. One anonymous survey revealed that among graduating high school seniors, the percentage of females having had intercourse was 72%; that of similar males was 92%.

It makes little sense for states or local school officials to dictate what and when sexual education should begin. Were sexuality to be explained to students at the beginning of their seventh grade, would that prove harmful? Every study conducted on the early introduction of actual sexual education, the basic physiognomy and practice of all sexual activity, including intercourse, has demonstrated improvements in the prevention of teen pregnancies, less social media stigmatization, and the normalization of sexual reproduction.

One fairly recent example stands out in the manner in which sexual activity is tainted by shame and made to appear abnormal and taboo, especially concerning youth. This occurred several years ago: during the Superbowl, a well-known vocalist in a halftime show "mistakenly" revealed her breasts. (We don't really know if she simply wanted to burnish her declining popularity by an outrageous act.) An outpouring of rage ensued as there were children watching and the network was fined.

How would a 13-year-old boy, seeing what a female's breasts looked like, be harmed? Would he become overly sexualized (whatever that means)? Would he be scarred for life and denied a "normal" sexual life? Such censorship not only makes it appear to a youth that sex is somehow wrong, dirty and taboo. It is more likely, in our experience, that sexual offending can occur in households which refuse to openly discuss reproduction and its anatomy. We have experimental proof in international research that early sexual education can be helpful, but in addition, anecdotal evidence is at least as informative and conclusive.

In contrast, there is no study of which I am aware, that demonstrates psychological harm to children from learning about, and viewing naked male or female bodies. Harm may accrue, however, to youth so restricted that they are never exposed to nudity. They may well be naturally curious, and learn about the anatomy of bodies from gossip among friends, often inaccurate, or from early exposure to porn, even worse. Do children suffer in some manner from school visits to museums, where they are exposed to nude sculptures? If so, this must be a rare phenomenon as there is no literature documenting adverse effects. It could be argued that sculptures are in stone or marble and inanimate; thus they may present no intimations of sexuality. I would argue that hiding the notions of sexuality from children than if they were taught about these matters from a certified education specialist; far better than innuendo from the streets.

This speaks to the general taboo about sexuality in our country. Indeed, we rarely utter the word "sex" in descriptions of intercourse, almost as if it is unmentionable, a toxic topic relegated to euphemisms: instead of simply saying, "We had sex that night," we shy away from naming it directly. We might use more genteel phrases, such as "We slept together," or "We made love," or "We went to bed together." We refer to intercourse as "one-night stands", or "We cheated", or "We had an affair." Most folks know exactly what each of these statements means but dressing them up without saying the dreaded word is commonplace. I also believe that "sex" should be a noun depicting an act; gender is an identity.

The two things *homo sapiens* (and most other species) must do to perpetuate our species is to eat and have sexual relations. Why can't we simply acknowledge that sexual activity is pleasurable, yet we dare not speak of it, at least in most public settings? Do we deny that a good dinner can be a source of public conversation, which can be openly discussed? Yet the topic of sexual activity is shrouded in an air of toxicity and must not be, in most situations a topic of conversation. Indeed, we eat in public but have sex in (mostly) private settings.

Part of the privacy of sexual activity may have to do with the fact that participants are baring their bodies, but I believe a larger part is that, at the moments of sexual pleasure, we exhibit our most vulnerable emotions. Few would like to share with friends, family, or the world, that they are more passionate when making love than when they are discussing a filet mignon or an ice cream sundae. There has been a move towards enabling the discussion of sex more openly of late, in my mind this is a vector in a positive direction. It will, however, take enormous periods of time before such conversations become as routine or even habitual as almost any other topic.

Early sex education, well-informed by science, can lower the temperature, now red-hot, of discussions about sex. Such early enlightenment has been proven to reduce teen pregnancies in a variety of studies in the US and abroad. In Sweden, youngsters are shown pictures of what intercourse is all about, beginning at the age of six. Their rate of sexual offending is 14% that of America's. Although a correlation does not prove causation, nonetheless, these observations are crucial in our society, in which traces of religion and a prurient sense of sexuality remain, thereby hindering knowledge about which youngsters probably already have some knowledge.

Better to allow professionals to teach this course, including adequate protection against pregnancy, than for young teens to pick up notions conveyed from friends and social media. It is equally vital that they receive this knowledge not solely from their parents. Though the majority of adults would likely disagree, household discussions about sex cannot be accomplished in an objective, non-pejorative and non-embarrassing manner as opposed to those conveyed by professional educators. Parents are more likely to convey, in their discussions about sexuality, that the topic is somehow morally indecent or at the very least, an embarrassing subject. Moreover, they would, in all likelihood, delay such discussions until their children have already gained some notion about sexuality and are in their teenage years – too late to stress the importance of safe sex.

There are several additional advantages to early sexual education. Teachers should strongly emphasize to boys what consent entails. While a formal signed document is impractical, they need to be made aware that any signal that a female is reluctant to engage in sexual activity automatically means "no." Examples could be used with role-play to demonstrate to students how a female might indicate not only outright refusal but, more realistically, hesitance, doubt, or ambivalence. Any hint of such must be considered non-consent. I realize that a female teen or young adult may often be in shock or fear if an assault were about to occur. Therefore, girls must also be encouraged to forcefully refuse and make their intentions as clear as a glass of water.

At an early age (I believe in elementary school), young girls should be acquainted with the issues surrounding sexual abuse, what constitutes it, and, of crucial import, that no matter what any threats of harm to a victim or to her family are made, it is *always* important to tell an adult what has happened without fear of retribution, embarrassment, or disbelief.

Girls may notice a sibling who is uncomfortable about someone who has abused them. They may hear about sexual abuse from a friend. In such cases, such youths must feel safe in making disclosures of sexual abuse. Moreover, friends should be encouraged to report any suspicions they have to a teacher, a counselor, or an adult member of their own family.

It is so rare as to be almost inconceivable that an offender's threat of harm to a victim, should they disclose, be actually carried out. Some victims, and even their mothers, may harbor fears of financial loss if the abuser is identified and loses his liberty. In my opinion, financial loss does not outweigh the burden on a victim to conceal sexual abuse; indeed, keeping silent may only encourage further abuse. An adult ignoring a child's sexual victimization is as guilty as the offender himself.

In addition, boys (and actually all men) should be informed about definitive guidelines in social settings, such as:

- Never put your hands on a girl you do not know well.
- Hugs only if the female is a well-known friend or relative.
- Never be in a room, home or apartment alone with a female you do not know well.
- Never be alone with a female who is under the influence of drugs or alcohol.
- Never drive an unknown female home, especially if she is intoxicated.
- If you are going to have any type of casual sexual interactions with a female, protect yourself and her with condoms, or other forms of birth control.

Note: Scientists are working towards a birth control pill for males. A survey in India in 2021 found that 78% of young men had unprotected intercourse with their last partner. Amongst those females, 34% got pregnant unwillingly.

Girls should also strive to make their intentions clear:

- Never flirt with a male in an isolated setting, especially if he is a relative stranger, unless you desire sexual activity with him.
- Never be in a room alone with a male who is under the influence of drugs or alcohol.
- If you are not interested in sexual activity, make that abundantly clear, not only to the male, but to others present.
- Never initiate sexual activity such as kissing or foreplay with a male with whom you do not want to participate in intercourse; teasing could get both of you in trouble and you may assume a male can control his impulses; you would be wrong much of the time; quite often young males lack requisite control.
- If you do not want to engage in intercourse, do not assume the male doesn't. Let's be honest: most males, especially in their younger years (teens and twenties), set their highest priority in social settings (usually parties) on having sexual relations.
- Never be alone in a room with a male who is intoxicated.
- If a male forces unwanted sexual touching, yell and fight back.
- If you are going to have any kind of sexual interaction with a male, protect yourself with birth control measures.

I realize this is a reaction with which many would disagree. In our experience, when the female screams, punches, kicks yells and bites, the male's ardor will wane. But most females are frankly in shock, do not know what to do, and are afraid that any physical resistance will generate the male's force in return. I have no desire to see girls hurt but, in many retrospective reviews, when the male is forcefully spurned, he will desist. Girls should yell loudly enough to be heard if others are within a reasonable distance. The female should also let the male know that if he persists, she will report him and he will go to prison.

Of course, this advice caries some degree of danger. It is given only in circumstances in which the male perpetrator is unarmed and is not a complete stranger. If you are in bed alone in your apartment and an unknown man enters and threatens you with a weapon, forget about all the above; it is not worth physical harm. But the majority of forceful sexual assaults (in our series, about 79%) are perpetrated by a known assailant and over half of these involved drugs and alcohol. Women and girls are not only the first line of defense, but sometimes they may be the only means of preventing sexual abuse.

None of this implies that the female is responsible by not defending herself. No one has the right to determine to what extent a female places herself in danger. You do not need to take a course in self-defense or carry a taser or pepper spray (though that might not be a bad idea). But you have the power to defend yourself, especially if the situation is within a social setting where others are nearby; even if you are afraid of retaliation, studies show that the majority of men who would have sexually assaulted a woman are dissuaded when met with determined outright physical resistance.

Along these same lines, it would be of help to teach teens about the general workings of the criminal justice system, perhaps as a small portion of a civics course. School systems have fled the notion of what used to be called "social studies": the manner in which the three branches of our system of government works, the virtues and perils of our type of democracy, and how justice is administered. These are all areas of importance of which every American should be aware. Unfortunately, recent surveys demonstrate a shocking lack of information in the general public about the most basic of ground rules about how our government operates, and thereby, most citizens have limited notions at best about how our criminal justice system functions (Annenberg Center for Public Policy, University of Pennsylvania's year end report of 2022). For example, many US citizens are unaware of who their state reprsentative is, nor are they aware of the names of all Federal Departments, The State Department, Department of Justice, etc.

Improve Public Education About Sexual Offending

The common notion that a sexual offender is immune from treatment and can never be trusted is equivalent to thinking that an infection can never be eliminated. The received wisdom that all such offenders are wicked is based upon misinformation. While we cannot excuse the common citizen of prejudgment without further education, those operating within the Criminal Justice System could work harder to inform the public about the fact that some such offenders are not totally evil.

While "cured" is a dirty word in much of medicine, so many other conditions, from juvenile diabetes and epilepsy to bipolar disorder and schizophrenia, really cannot be exterminated, even allowing for all the progress medical science has made. These will, unfortunately, be life-long conditions for quite a while into a distant, better-informed future. For the present, they will require life-long care to prevent the return of symptoms. Sexual offenders, however, can be treated and, in a majority of cases specific to the actual crime, many, if not most, if properly treated, will never offend again.

Some of the origins of sexual offending may stem partially from genetic conditions but our DNA code is complex. Sexual offending is not solely an inherited condition. Ancestry may contribute to such behaviors by exposing sons to intrafamilial drinking and drug abuse, bearing the scars of physical abuse, being the victims of such abuse, or other factors we as yet cannot fathom. It will require sleuthing out which codons of which genes, and the results of epi-genetics, which turn codons on and off during a lifetime, to understand the origins of such offending.

Sexual offending should be thought of as more like a serious infection. It is not irreversible and scars may persist but scientifically validated treatments exist which can be brought to bear upon it so as to markedly reduce the likelihood of it ever recurring. For many situational offenders and quite a few predatory ones as well, treatment can eliminate the offending behavior in its entirety. This is especially true of offenders who have committed crimes of the "Romeo and Juliet" type, child porn-only offenders, entrapment cases, and also many other types of situational offenders.

I am hardly a marketing expert and I doubt any corporation would wish to mount a public education campaign à *la* child exploitation or sexual offending in general. Nonetheless, the medical profession could better inform the public about which sexual offenders are dangerous and those who are never likely to re-offend. Physicians, mainly psychiatrists, psychologists, and clinical social workers could help prevent the stigma associated with such offenders, as could many of the changes recommended above and below.

Public and social media could play a role as well, by underscoring the difference between the minor situational offender and the true pedophile. Not every case of a man with no criminal record who wanders onto a child porn site out of curiosity is a lecher poised to terrorize a community. Such individuals hardly pose such a danger as to be afforded front-page headlines in local newspapers.

It could help as well if some attention were paid to education about the different types of sexual offenders which exist and the efficacy of treatment for the majority of them. Courses in the administration of justice, law schools, psychology classes, and medical schools would surely help those professionals in correcting the received wisdom about the futility of success in treating the majority of sexual offenders; they will, in all likelihood, confront such cases in their future careers.

In a similar fashion, it would be of interest to see if any science magazine for the lay public, such as *Scientific American* or *Science News* would publish an abstract or full-length article about sexual offending. Would any producer or network be so brave as to feature a documentary discussing sexual offending from a scientific perspective? Unlikely. One wonders whether any Hollywood confection could possibly produce a film depicting sexual offenders as normally fragile individuals, although with a terrible flaw. Public education can only go so far in altering long-held misperceptions; the "war on drugs" is a good example. Nonetheless, medical and psychological societies could make a case for such a production. We are now hoping to convince National Public Radio producers of the value such public education might bring in de-stigmatizing all SOs without distinction as to type and amenability to treatment.

Prohibit Local Newspapers from Prominently Headlining Situational SO Crimes

It would be unusual for the *New York Times* or *Washington Post* to blaze a front-page headline that a man living in their communities has committed any sexual crime. However, local, small-town, and rural news outlets often display front-page, large font-size headlines, along with photographs, of a man arrested because he complied with a police sting operation and visited a home in which he thought there might have been a potential underage victim. The same is true for child porn only offenders and the age difference inherent in mutually consenting sexual activity between a high school senior and his sophomore girlfriend (R&J cases).

No one entity can or should censor how news is reported, nor should any government entity dictate the manner in which news is communicated. I do believe, however, that news editors should at least be requested by the authorities to differentiate between news-worthy sexual offenses which pose future risk and those which carry an insignificant threat to anyone living in their communities. Even then, a headline in a newspaper or on TV or social media is unlikely to prevent a repeat of any sexual crime. It is therefore pointless but it is definitely deflating, demeaning, uninformative, and ineffective in preventing future sexual crimes as well. Spoken words can evaporate in the atmosphere of time and memory but written words remain.

Work to Eliminate Sexual Biases

Although this text does not directly address cultural and political issues outside of how sexual offenders are managed within the criminal justice system, some comment about attitudes and behaviors designed to attribute abnormality, and even blasphemy, towards gay and transexual individuals is required. Enough has been written already about these contentious ideas and, fortunately, younger folks these days are beginning to at least tolerate, if not totally accept people within the LGBTQ communities. They are unaware of the recent progress made in CNS studies which demonstrate that many such individuals are born with these predilections. One would hardly choose an LGBTQ lifestyle simply for personal gain.

Having treated hundreds of transexual (TS) patients (I use "patients" as a category, not to imply they are "ill") two physicians now must certify that the person represents a bonafide transexual. Moreover, to qualify for treatment, including medications and counselling, the patient and treating clinician must then adhere to the international standards from the World Health Organization of the UN. These now require living in the preferred gender entirely for one year under the supervision of the clinician, at the same time undergoing voice and bearing training. If they then qualify, the individual must then be approved for surgery (if they can afford it). This extensive process combined with PET studies has convinced me that gender identity dysphoria is a biological condition. We require the following criteria in considering a candidate for gender reassignment:

- Having a documented history of preferring feminine behaviors, such as playing with dolls, putting on makeup, choosing women's clothes and avoiding rough-and tumble sports.
- Persisting in feminine preferences throughout the teen years.
- Having no other psychiatric diagnosis with the exception of dysphoria (sadness) because of the TS condition.
- Being the age of majority in the state involved.
- Choosing a female name.
- After several sessions with a clinician, agreeing to a one-year period of presenting as a female, using a female name, wearing female clothing, and verification of such from family, friends and employers or co-workers.
- Legally changing name from male to female, if indicated.
- Taking, when the clinician deems appropriate, female hormones, then submitting to hormonal blood tests, including liver function tests as, in rare cases, the liver might be affected by a change in hormones
- Undergoing voice and posture training.

If all the above are satisfied, two clinicians must certify that the case is a bona fide male-to-female transexual before any approval for surgery can be recommended. Many TS individuals lack the financial resources to pay for such surgery while others travel to another country, generally in Southeastern Asia where the operation is less costly. Too many, unfortunately, will never afford surgery to effect a complete transformation, though eventually the majority do.

At present there is a great debate about whether male-to-female TS clients should be given hormones before adolescence. This is based upon the terrible feeling of being ripped apart by a gender mis-allocation, especially in the teenage years. However, hormones in both male-to-female and female-to male individuals can produce irreversible changes, including fertility and muscle strength. Against the current grain, however, I do not believe male-to-female individuals should be allowed to compete in girls' and women's' sports. Debate rages on but only scientific studies can be the deciding factor and these are, as yet, too limited in numbers of subjects and length of time to draw firm conclusions.

I am convinced that conditions such as gender dysphoria and homosexuality are biological in origin in the vast majority of cases. PET scans from Johns Hopkins University have noticed female patterns in male-to-female TS patients' brains, Moreover, maternal immunosuppression has been linked to males who have an excess of older brothers. With each succeeding male birth, male hormonal sensitivities might be compromised in women pregnant with yet another male fetus. This effect does not correlate with the number of older sisters in these individuals.

This cannot explain all gay men as a number of them have no siblings, but it can explain some gay males. Similar studies have not been undertaken with gay females. The single study we have generated was with men attracted to young boys. Among such pedophiles we also found they often have a number of older brothers but the effect did not reach significance.

It will prove difficult for many, especially older and firmly religious folks, to accept those in the LGBTQ community, but I am optimistic that we are witnessing a shift toward understanding and accepting these individuals, particularly by our own children and grandchildren. The future appears brighter than the past in such matters.

Let Teachers Teach

The male teacher who forms a sexual relationship with a pre- (rare) or post- (more common) pubescent youth should be prosecuted, hopefully with an eye toward what damage he has caused. It is normal for an adult male to be attracted to a teen female, though we would hope he would not act upon that desire. The choreographer Balanchine is rumored to have said, "The history of man over 40 is *Lolita*."

Many adolescent relationships with teachers do not result in the victim suffering anything more severe than temporary embarrassment and guilt. Certainly, the offender should be prohibited from teaching youth following any judicial sentence, along with supervision and the successful completion of a certified sexual offender treatment program.

However, such a teacher has certain skills that could be useful in other educational settings without exposure to youth:

- Such teachers could lead adult education classes, such as ESL, citizenship classes or computer use for the elderly.
- He might even be able to teach college-age students via virtual education only.
- Such a teacher might also serve as a tutor for adult males having problems with literacy or mathematics.
- He could also prove to be a useful tutor for male college or postgraduate students.
- Taking into account his experience, he might be allowed to return to postgraduate study, then serve as an instructor for males in courses in a teacher's college or other vocational training courses; such instruction can often be confined to virtual computer-assisted study only.

It is doubtful such positions would pose a hazard for any repeat of a sexual crime and would provide the added benefit of actually utilizing the offender's skills for useful purposes. Unfortunately, in the present climate of judgmental attitudes against sexual offenders, such proposals are about as unlikely as your barber telling you that you don't need a haircut.

Allow Catholic Priests to Marry or Have Intimate Relationships

In the earliest years of Catholicism, the rule that priests remain celibate evolved for financial reasons: priests without offspring would be more likely to leave their assets to the Church. Although the Church has attempted to address and correct the problem of priests molesting youths, it has a long road ahead. It has opened up a door but the cathedral is clothed in concealment and camouflage. The Church, to its credit, is just now in most cases facing a lengthy path to transparency and the law. The abuse of prepubescent and adolescent children has been familiar to most by now but the cover-up within the priesthood still occasionally continues, although to its credit, the Church has attempted to become increasingly open to criticism.

Investigations are ongoing but will surely still underestimate the true extent of the problem, especially in poorer countries where there remain over 9,000 Catholic residential institutions. The number of victims in France alone was estimated to be 216,000 in the past 70 years. An institution which hushes up allegations, then shuttles suspects to alternative locations, cannot be expected to yield numbers of those affected in an accurate manner.

We cannot say, with scientific certainty, that priests molest children because they are denied intimate relationships with adults. It could also be that priests enter the seminary in order to be close to, and trusted by, children as they already have a sexual attraction to them. It may also be true that such an attraction develops as close and trusting relationships are built through the years.

There also remains the possibility that men entering the seminary do so with a hope that a spiritual environment and adequate devotion to morality will help them avoid these dark desires. Regardless, they are in an authoritarian position over children and, at least until the past several decades, would never have been suspected of sexually molesting children, most of whom, by the way, are boys.

> Xilai (born into a Chinese family who emigrated, as Catholics to America) had developed claustrophobia as a young teen. He had experienced discipline at the hands of his priest between the ages of 7 and 11, in which he would be forced to strip naked and be whipped on his buttocks while the holy man fondled his genitals. This all happened in a small closet with a locked door. He subsequently developed claustrophobia, and, at the age of 12, an attraction to young boys. He entered the priesthood believing his devotion to the Catholic Church could cure him of these afflictions, but he continued to isolate, then sexually abuse a number of prepubescent choirboys over a ten-year period. Rumors of his attention to these boys led to suspicions by his supervising Bishop, who subsequently urged Xilai to concentrate on prayer and transferred him to a parish distant from his original placement.

Researchers believe that the prevalence of sexual interest in children is held by 6% to 9% of Catholic priests but, quite honestly, it is difficult to pin down accurate numbers as cases may never be reported and some priests who have pedophilic interests may curb those and never molest a child.

There have been attempts by sectors of the Church to break free from celibacy. Early in 2022, a German group began to campaign for women to become ordained, an effort promptly squashed by Rome. More recently, certain European synods endorsed a proposal to allow lay personnel to select their bishops. Australia's Royal Commission into institutional sexual abuse of children concluded that celibacy was a major etiologic factor in child sexual abuse.

In America the share of Catholics attending mass weekly declined from 31% in 2000 to 15% in 2023. Moreover, the Church is, at present, woefully short of priests. But the official orders from Rome remain steadfast in insisting on a life devoted to God and not distracted by any other close relationship. There is also a hint of the thought that sexual activity is somehow irreligious, and even a sin. This perpetuates the unfortunate aura of evil and depravity associated with normal sexual activity. It was the serpent who tempted Eve. Evolution has primed us for being afraid of serpents (witness the dragons in Chinese mythology and in popular media as villainous) as well as large apes.

Popular opinion is shifting: approximately 59% of North American Catholics favor allowing priests to marry; majorities in Latin America and Europe agree. There is a growing realization that denying priests the very human need for intimacy is itself a crime against humanity.

We do know that other denominations, which allow marriage and intimate relationships, do not have the sheer numbers of their clergy accused of sexually molesting children. There have been limited Catholic churches who have allowed priests to marry but we lack data on their propensity to commit sexual crimes.

One study (see Dressing et al. 2021), cited by the Church, claimed that priests had only a "minor" number of abusers compared with other Protestant congregations . Unfortunately, this study was flawed statistically and of equal concern, it was funded by The Institute of Anthropology of the Gregorian University, an arm of the Vatican. Unbiased studies have shown the opposite, with a major disparity implicating priests offending more often than leaders of other denominations.

It would be of interest to follow such rebel congregations which do not enforce celibacy to determine if they also suffer similar rates of child molestations over a lengthy period as compared with those that prohibit marriage. Such studies would prove of value but it may take more than science to convince a hardened and hidebound hierarchy of the value of empiricism.

However, the Church cannot, and should not, be allowed to forego the treatments proven to be effective for offending clergy. It appears that this 2,000-year-old institution would prefer to keep even treatment in-house. Mandating approved sexual offender treatment in addition to whatever the Church itself prescribes as therapy, including prayer, is surely a necessary requirement once such a case is identified. The failure to do so, such as a reassignment to another parish, is a Cardinal sin, equivalent to not wearing a belt nor suspenders; men would prefer to make certain they are not found to have let their pants down.

In summary, priests who molest children should be treated by the criminal justice system as any other offender, rather than handled in-house through church interventions alone. If immediately upon awareness, or even suspicion of sexual abuse of minors, priests should be brought to justice with greater alacrity, monitored more closely, and be required to undergo effective treatment. They should also be barred from positions of authority over children and closely monitored by non-Church-affiliated personnel. Such changes are more than a necessity; they would indeed be a blessing.

Encourage Post-graduate Study

At present, no medical school, internship or residency program in psychiatry or psychology of which I am aware has ever offered a course on the assessment of risk sexual offenders pose or the treatment of such offenders themselves. I have personally been a failure in even trying to introduce such a course in the residency program at the medical school in which I have taught. We have, however, trained a number of post-graduate psychologists and MD residents in psychiatry in our Clinic through shadowing, then practicing under tutelage this knowledge and these skills. Nonetheless, this occurs at the discretion of the university's appropriate curriculum department and remains the choice of the post-graduate fellow. It has been the rare such trainee to select a sexual offender program in which to undertake such an apprenticeship.

I believe it is unconscionable to omit this important topic, at least as part of a general forensic program at the doctoral level. Of course, there are many topics of crucial import for such trainees, including genetics and the effects of early childhood trauma. Some fraction of time should, however, be allotted to these aspiring professionals who may be asked to consult on sexual abuse cases or who have never undertaken any prior generalized training in sexual offending.

Curriculum committees are an easy target of blame yet they have much to consider, especially in light of exiting new findings on the workings of the CNS and the impact of epigenetics in children raised within turbulent family surroundings. Yet it is just such youth who are at increased risk of becoming antisocial or of committing sexual crimes. It is up to us therefore, the professionals in this subspecialized field, to more forcefully make our case for the inclusion of such course-work. We have a long road ahead to accomplish this vital task.

Yet another area of study should also include much more of the scientific findings applicable to sexual offending: courses in The Administration of Justice. Future employees who will work in the many fields associated with the criminal justice system seldom receive any training specific to sexual offending. A few such individuals do enroll in internships or apprentices in sexual offender programs, but these unfortunately constitute just a few who will, in the future, need to deal in some manner with sexual offenders.

Investigate College Rapes as Jurisdictional rather than Academic Crimes

It is all too common: at a frat party, a college male engages in intercourse with an inebriated female who would not have consented had she been of clear mind. These days, it is fortunate that the woman is most often believed as, in our experience combined with scientific studies, the charge is usually correct and justified. The issue here, of course is consent, or lack of the ability to obtain it. As part of college orientation, the discussion of consent should occur for all freshman. It should include examples, warnings and consequences for the perpetrator. Further, classes on sexuality should be mandatory for all college students. While this might, in part, duplicate what was taught in high school, repetition is no bad thing.

While there may exist cases in which it appeared that the woman agreed, if she is even moderately intoxicated or verbally pressured or coerced, it is rape. Although there now exists a backlash in favor of the male perpetrator, and perhaps there exist cases in which an angry co-ed wishes to punish an ex-boyfriend or the like, these are exceedingly rare. To prove consent, it would prove awkward for a formal hard-copy signature to be required. But college courses should emphasize that any female under the influence of drugs or alcohol is incapable of providing informed consent. However, ambiguous cases do occur:

> Yoon, a Vietnamese immigrant, had recently planned a party at a family reunion, as most of them had also emigrated to the US. However, this family was no stranger to alcohol. After most attendees fell asleep, or were in an alcohol-induced blackout, Yoon's like-aged female cousin began flirting with him and they subsequently undertook intercourse. Upon returning home in another state, she claimed he raped her. However, his smartphone recorded videos of her not only initiating flirtatious behavior and sexual talk, but beginning to kiss and hug him as well, all the while laughing and seemingly aware of what each was doing. Although Yoon was also in a partially blacked-out condition, he believed her actions and words not only implied, but agreed to the sexual activity.
>
> The case, after two years, is still pending and it is rumored, Yoon's cousin is foregoing the complaint. However, the episode does emphasize how fraught such situations can be – a valuable case study for any college student to consider and perhaps debate.

The lack of such sexual abuse coursework may put in jeopardy both men and women from considering their actions before undertaking them. At the height of sexual drive, the college-age student may well place a higher and more immediate priority on sexual pleasure than consideration of its ramifications to be faced over time; all the more reason that issues of sexuality and consent should be part of the curriculum.

Jurisdiction of such cases has, until recently, been seen as best handled by college authorities, thus kept in-house to avoid adverse publicity. Many universities would prefer that public knowledge of a crime of such nature be withheld so that the institution not be tarnished. A parallel can be found in the same manner of Catholic priests being treated only by the Church. Thus college personnel are allowed to dispense their idea of justice in allegations of nonconsensual sexual activity, yet they are not aware, by and large, of the criminal justice system nor of recent research about sexual offending.

Yet a crime on campus remains a crime and should, in my opinion, be immediately reported to local police authorities, who should undertake the investigation. The land boundaries for a campus should not delimit the nature of criminal activity nor should they determine that a rape should be adjudicated in any different fashion because it occurred within the borders of an educational institution.

When a high school student is sexually assaulted, the principal is not the authority determining guilt or innocence. When in a public park, the investigation of a sexual assault therein is not allowed to be undertaken by the city's Bureau of Parks and Recreation. Official police departments are more experienced, have the trained personnel, and can manage scrutiny, examination, and analysis in a more unbiased manner than school and university administrators. They can also refer a victim to programs either within the community or on campus who are experienced in providing adequate support for her.

Prohibit Nondisclosure Agreements from Including Incidents of Sexual Harassment and Abuse

Many workers across a multitude of industries require employees to sign a nondisclosure agreement (NDA). This makes sense as companies have a right to guard propriety information crucial to their profitability. These agreements may, for example, prevent employees, both present and past, from disclosing procedures, components of electronic equipment, software essential to a business and the like. Should there be a dispute, these agreements include a clause that the matter be resolved through arbitration rather than in a court of law.

Unfortunately, these NDAs have been taken to include issues of sexual harassment and frank sexual abuse. Men making sexual jokes and comments appear relatively harmless but can render a workplace toxic to female employees if they occur on a regular basis. Men's comments to a specific female employee are especially pernicious. Unwanted touching, even if it is momentary, can be construed as sexual abuse. Just as a person in authority, such as a preacher or counselor, is the person committing such abuse, a boss, manager or supervisor in a workplace is in a position of power and influence over many female employees. Therefore, acceptable behavior requires abstinence from sexually tinged comments and outright sexual acts.

We should understand that this places a burden on those in supervisory positions to take precautions against unwelcome sexual behavior that, in the past might have been considered harmless. Some women may be thought to be overly sensitive to such behavior but that is no justification for harassment or abuse. At present, just 13 states in our country have laws demanding that such matters be settled utilizing the justice system rather than arbitration.

However, at the present, a federal law compelling harassment and abuse to be reported and not to be precluded by an NDA is being debated in the House of Representatives. In my opinion, we need uniformity in such a sensitive matter and perhaps such an overarching federal law will be enacted, although that depends upon the blue/red distribution of Congress. In the meantime, state legislatures should review their own laws regarding NDAs and ensure that harassment and abuse are well-defined and constitute a matter to be determined in a court of law rather than by an arbitrator chosen by the employer.

A related issue is workplace affairs. It should not be within the purview of employers or governments to arbitrate with whom you can engage in consensual sexual activity nor determine with whom you can fall in love. However, it is certainly their right and duty to ensure that such liaisons do not interfere with the duties of any employee.

Can a boss invite a female employee to lunch? Does a hello or goodbye hug constitute harassment? These are complicated issues determined by circumstance and familiarity. It is not within my expertise to comment further about employment law. I merely wish to emphasize that sexual harassment and abuse are against the law, can create a poisoned work atmosphere and should never be precluded from the scrutiny of the criminal justice system nor should any NDA include language suggesting otherwise. Yet this quietly consequential change lies pending, it appears indefinitely, within many institutions.

Legalize Sex Work

While police these days focus on citing the male "John" and compelling classwork while rarely arresting prostitutes, "sweeps" for both genders on *Solicitation* charges are conducted on a routine basis by many urban task forces and sometimes include the arrests of sex workers, though they are often cited, fined, and quickly released. However, even the DA knows such use of enforcement time is ineffective, especially when prostitution is another "crime" such as entrapment, which has no victim as long as child exploitation is not involved. In countries, mostly western European, in which sex work is legalized, it has proven safer in terms of very little physical harm to sex workers; it is also of financial benefit to the state through taxation, and is much more free of exploitation and criminal activity, including sexual crimes. The same has occurred in the several counties in Nevada in which such work has been legalized and monitored.

It is undoubtedly too early for a federal statute making sex work legal despite its obvious benefits. This has to do with legislators, mostly aged men and women of a former generation. I am hopeful of a more enlightened future, distant though it may be, in which sexual activity outside of marriage can be proven to be of benefit to the state and not of harm to the individuals involved.

Many conservatives may shudder in horror at the idea that it might be permissible, let alone preferable, for a husband or wife should want to "break" the bonds of marriage. Yet, increasingly, couples, especially, though not uniformly, young adults prefer to live together rather than officially marry. This constitutes a practical means of ensuring to some extent that compatibility is achievable; dating is not the equal of inhabiting the same living space in a constant manner.

It is as if we recoil at the notion that sexual foreplay and intercourse are pleasurable. Some in the psychologic and psychiatric community posit "reasons" why people might turn to affairs. Certainly, if couples are having difficulties within their unions, or in addition, not engaging in, or enjoying, sexual relations, turning to alternative sources is understandable. The problem is too often that such extra-partner sexual activity is hidden from a partner, who almost always learns of it eventually, and often, such secretes beget a legitimate lack of trust and may trigger either a series of events or by itself fracture the relationship.

Most infatuations and sexual attractions end at some point during all monogamies. In the US, separations and divorces occur in over 60% of relationships. In marriages, the most frequent times of divorce are at three, then seven years into the union. These are the times during which a couple must protect a first, then a second, child. Evolution has lessons for us all.

Moreover, while it is difficult to extract unbiased data on affairs outside of marriage or steady relationships, it appears that a majority of men and a large minority of women have extramarital affairs. Unfortunately, these data are biased by the participants' honesty, even in anonymized surveys. Many answer such questionnaires in a manner in which they prefer to picture themselves or with the suspicion that they might later be recognized.

We cannot say, with scientific rigor, that legalizing prostitution would reduce sexual criminality. The data are, however, convincing in those countries which have taken that step, although confounding factors, such as uniformity within a population (think Finland) or small populations (Iceland) may not be comparable to the United States. These countries boast a markedly lower prevalence of all sexual crimes. Regardless, legalization would have definite benefits in terms of reducing certain crimes and enhancing tax revenues. Unfortunately, US legislators are not close to shedding the "sex is dirty" notion, combined with the fear of losing the votes of a horde of the religious and those of a morally conservative population. I apologize for characterizing a large swath of Americans as backwards, but the truth can only be found within scientific research rather than in any hold-over notions of sexual activity being within the province of marriage alone.

In Nevada, the state allows houses of prostitution in counties adjacent to large cities. Governmental regulation and oversight ensure that the sex workers are free of sexually transmitted diseases (STDs) and are of age. Each is required to undergo physical examinations and blood tests on a weekly basis. Moreover, care is taken by state officials that only women over the age of 18 are thus employed.

Nevada is a state with just two large metropolitan areas. Nonetheless, with county and state governments imposing oversight (and collecting taxes), the incidence of sexual crimes or STDs is within the lower range compared to most other states. Nevada may not be a model for other states, however, only in that it is tourists who mainly use the "ranches", rather than local inhabitants.

The major benefit in legalizing prostitution would be, I believe, a reduction in the incidence of sexual crimes and an increase in revenue, both of which could take place as the evidence shows, from the countries mentioned above.

Some states could at least test this theory on a temporary basis. As with the legalization of marijuana, police resources would have less need to engage with petty crimes which have no actual victims and thus devote more resources to monitor and pursue more harmful ones, such as the exploitation of children and young women from being forced into prostitution. Unregulated prostitution is inevitable; why not allow it to come under the supervision of state authorities? State oversight could follow Nevada's example and test whether such a mitigation could occur.

In summary, federal legalization of prostitution would:

- Eliminate the "middle men", (pimps).
- Ensure sex workers are well taken care of.
- Ensure sex workers do not have any STDs.
- Enhance the safety of sex workers by getting them off the streets and into sanctioned brothels.
- Make certain the government, whether state or federal, has an oversight mandate, with weekly inspections.
- Eliminate the criminal element in prostitution.
- Recognize and destigmatize sexual activity outside of committed relationships, thereby bringing the level of jealousy and secrecy down to match the reality of sexual relations.
- Reduce the unrealistic stigma about sex as a taboo topic.
- Assist sex workers in saving money to proceed on to other careers, should they wish, as they age out of prostitution.
- Liberate local police forces to focus on crimes which have actual victims.
- Enhance coordination among international police agencies in locating and preventing extortion of minors in the sex trade.
- Provide much-needed tax revenue, whether at the county, state, or federal level.

Nothing in this recommendation should be construed as encouraging child sexual abuse nor does it apply to the horrendous crime of exploitation of children or women by criminal gangs. Indeed, with legalization, such crimes might become both less numerous and the perpetrators more visible to international policing organizations.

Federally Legalize Abortion

By recently overturning the 1973 nation-wide ruling making abortions legal and returning to the states the right to determine its regulation, the Supreme Court has ignored human rights in this country by removing a prerogative for individual citizens guaranteed by the Constitution. It has thereby not only created grievous harm to 51% of the American population, it has also committed an illegal action as specified in the United Nations Human Rights Declaration, to which America is a signatory.

But what does the currently heated debate around abortion have to do with sexual offending? Quite a lot, as we will demonstrate. The Court's ruling is certainly in error from a medical perspective. When the Supreme Court legitimized abortion in 1973, it based its decision on the Fourth Amendment, which states that US citizens have a right to be secure in their persons; and on the Fourteenth Amendment, which guaranties equality of rights which shall not be abridged based on gender.

Writings and comments about abortion usually begin with, "While I am not an attorney…" You do not need to graduate from law school to consider how overturning *Roe vs Wade* has treated women, physicians, and the general public with distain. While it does not eliminate abortion, it awards each state the prerogative to establish its own laws concerning a medical procedure. Many of these have rendered it impossible for a woman residing therein to obtain an abortion without undue expense and effort; in some states it essentially eliminates abortions altogether as, for example, limiting these procedures to a pregnancy lasting no longer than six weeks; at that point, many women cannot know they are pregnant.

To add insult to women in addition to actual injury, these rulings have also prohibited travel to a state with more progressive rules about abortion, a questionable restraint which violates the US Constitution. Certain states also make it a crime to abet such travel and may punish the woman and whomever aided her upon return to her native state. Such states also render severe penalties upon such actions and encourage family members, friends or strangers to report, Gestapo-style, such activities to state authorities. They may also prohibit access to an FDA- approved drug regimen which would prevent implantation of a fertilized, or *even an unfertilized egg* in a woman's uterus. This impediment is not only illogical, but assumes that every egg, fertilized or not, represents an actual human being.

I have read the full recent ruling overturning Roe; it has nothing to do with the specific guarantee of abortion and only makes the case that the Constitution doesn't mention a right to this medical or surgical procedure. Neither does it grant computer companies the ability to spy on citizens, or mention that gay people have the right not to be murdered, nor does it even create a Supreme Court. In fact, the original writings 250 years ago about a "constitutional court" never mentions such a Court in the original drafts of what would become our Constitution. There are many common sense, scientific and medical reasons why this recent ruling is plainly wrong-headed and likely political in nature, thereby subverting the separation of powers guaranteed by our Constitution.

- In many states, the ban would begin between four to six weeks after fertilization. That is two weeks after a missed period in many cases, allowing precious little time for a woman to even realize she is pregnant.
- Many women experience irregular menstrual cycles; therefore, using an early and arbitrarily determined time period is unjustified.
- Fertilization does not automatically occur by a sperm entering an egg cell nor does a pregnancy automatically result even if it did. Well over half of fertilized human eggs fail to implant in a woman's uterus; many never make it down the Fallopian Tube.
- Even if a fertilized egg does implant in the uterus itself, this egg is a growing ball of cells which requires just the perfect combination of chemical conditions to implant and grow once it attaches to the uterine wall. Many fail to do so.
- Should a fertilized egg make the error of implanting in the Fallopian Tube, an ectopic pregnancy would occur, severely endangering the life of the mother. Nothing short of recognizing the symptoms and ending this ectopic pregnancy (technically an abortion), will prevent the mother from a certain cruel and often fatal outcome. Nonetheless, under some current state laws, a physician could be imprisoned if she operated to relieve its cause, thereby performing an "abortion" and thus committing a criminal act. At the same time she would have had to allow the affected mother to die: an inhumane conundrum defying not only human rights but sowing disdain upon human life itself. In addition, that physician, should she fail to do so, would also lose her medical license by not operating to save a human life.
- Certain states believe that once a heartbeat is detected, the fetus deserves to have the same rights as a born human being. Unfortunately, the "heartbeat" heard on an echo-sonogram is not the result of an actual heart beating and moving blood throughout the fetus. It merely represents the electrical fluttering of immature heart cells detected by the test; such a "beat" could never produce blood flow, as it would much later in pregnancy. It is the ultrasound itself which is, in part, producing the "heartbeat."
- Other states are considering the viability of a fetus as a point in time at which the fetus can perceive pain. These states believe a fetus may feel pain as early as the eleventh week of pregnancy. Since we cannot ask the fetus about such perceptions, this presumption flies in the face of science. In order to experience pain, the brain needs to have developed connections in a variety of areas, chiefly in its thalamus and limbic

sections. Those areas and the connections between them are not functional until about week 29 of pregnancy.

- There actually is no evidence of viability for any particular fetus; we do know that very early births, even at 125 to 200 days, can survive, but many would not. Some can be saved through advances in neonatal care but others will perish. In their 2023/24 Summary Report the American College of Obstetricians and Gynecologists calls the notion of viability "a complicated concept" about which, "blanket statements cannot be made."
- The same organization has stated that "Abortion regulation is based on flawed medical and scientific premises."
- Over 50 research articles, comparing women who have had an abortion to those who requested one but were turned away, resulted in the latter group suffering worse outcomes in terms of physical and mental health, as well as being more likely to live below the US poverty line and to be unemployed.
- If a fetus, even at the point of conception or at 20 weeks has the same standing as a viable infant at birth, then, throughout pregnancy, implausible effects should be considered. The pregnant mother might claim the fetus as a dependent on her tax forms, drive alone in a carpool lane, and demand child support from the father if they are divorced.
- Too many of the unborn can be detected as having a serious abnormality or deformity that could not be corrected. Between 21–24 weeks of pregnancy, physicians term these fetuses as "periviable;" they are often the size of a russet potato. If born at that time, they would have less than a 40% chance of surviving. It is true that with modern neonatal care, some of these infants might survive, though for a brief time, but *all* such babies would develop severe disabilities and the majority would live a brief and painful few years before their demise. The obstetrician, at the point of detecting such fetuses would, under many state laws, not be allowed to perform an abortion lest she or he lose their medical license and they might even be fined and imprisoned. At birth of such infants, the doctor would be forced to attempt resuscitation, even with the inevitability of, eventually, a fatal outcome. Such a cruel restriction would not only be punishment for the physician. The unfortunate family would be forced to raise such a child even with the knowledge they would soon be attending a funeral featuring a tiny casket. A well-known neonatologist was quoted in *The Economist* (Jan. 18, 2019) expressing her horror at such legislation, which would "Force me to do something that would not in the best interests of the patient or the parents. In my ethical, moral understanding of the situation – I just couldn't do it." Hippocratic Oath indeed.
- The number of children a woman bears is directly correlated with the level of poverty that family suffers. The fewer children in a family increases the economic level of that family over a ten-year period of

time. A woman forced to bear an unwanted child significantly reduces her, and her family's, economic stability.

- The fewer children in a family increases the chances that each of those children will achieve a higher level of education and, thereby, greater financial security and productivity over each child's lifetime.
- According to statistics from the DOJ, an unwanted child is about 50 times more likely to commit a sexual offense than one the mother chooses to keep.
- Falling fertility rates have demonstrated that, should child-bearing be limited to two children within a family but never exceeding that number, each such child receives better nutrition, achieves higher education levels, attains better-paying employment, and is less likely to commit any type of crime than in families of three or more offspring.
- Moreover, the fewer children a woman bears, the more likely it is that she herself will achieve higher levels of education and employment. A recent study in Nigeria showed that lowering the fertility rate by one child per woman would double the income per person in that country within the next 35 years.
- Studies demonstrate that a child born which a woman did not wish to bear has a greater than 75% chance of failing to graduate from high school and a 67% likelihood of engaging in criminal activity as a teenager and as an adult. It is therefore highly unlikely that a child born by a woman delivering an unwanted child would result in a productive, intelligent, and creative individual. We cannot be certain of this but we must acknowledge the research in this area.
- Pregnancy by itself is more dangerous than an abortion. The US already holds the dubious distinction of having higher pregnancy mortality rates than most of the rich countries of the world; scientists estimate that a national ban on abortion would increase those death rates by 21%. The Supreme Court's legally flawed and inhumane recent decision leaves the country with a hodgepodge of differing regulations and forces women to travel to a more permissive state, something women lacking the financial means may be unable to accomplish. Even more recently, some states are rendering such travel itself illegal, a questionable stance as this would negate federal statutes which prohibit laws making interstate travel illegitimate.
- A gruesome but necessary thought experiment underscores the ignorance (beyond the sheer and shameful politics of it) of allowing the states to regulate a medical procedure: if the umbilical cord is cut just before birth but still within the womb, the fetus would die, regardless of its viability once delivered. The fetus is completely reliant on the mother for its nourishment. It is the *delivery*, whether vaginal or by Caesarian Section, which confers personhood upon the now-born child.

- While it is true that the murder of a pregnant woman is counted as a double homicide, this is based upon the *potential* viability of the fetus and does not automatically confer full personhood on the fetus regardless of its period of gestation. In addition, murder is a crime and forms an imperfect analogy to abortion.
- Of interest, the First Testament elucidates how the unborn should be regarded. One parable states that if a pregnant woman suffers a non-fatal accident resulting in a miscarriage, the offender must pay a fine; should she perish because of the assault, he must be sentenced to death for her demise; no mention of how the death of the fetus should be taken into account is offered.
- It thus appears that the present Supreme Court has not only broken international law, interfered with the rights of individuals practising at least the Jewish Religion and, more likely, all of Christianity in exercising their Religion (already deemed untouchable by the Supreme Court) and ignored the Fourth and Fourteenth Amendments, but it has also committed an illegal act within this country: practicing medicine without a license.

What does all this have to do with sexual offending? I fear that, as controversial as the abortion issue may be, my next argument, though based on solid evidence, may appear prejudicial; it certainly cannot be based upon controlled scientific studies. However, sometimes the facts speak louder than religious beliefs and moral values. Since the *Roe vs Wade* decision and before the Hobbs decision to overturn it, abortions had markedly increased, concurrent with a reduction in all crimes, especially sexual offenses. Bearing an unwanted child often creates conditions which have proven to increase sexual offending, including the child's exposure to abuse, both through substance use and emotional, physical and sexual trauma, forming the nexus for future criminal behavior.

Children, at the height of brain plasticity, may not be destined by their DNA to become criminals, but the mere fact that their mother did not want them makes it more likely they will be the object of abuse. They may already at birth be burdened by genetic alterations in their DNA to render them more likely to have low impulse control, ADHD, conduct disorders and antisocial personalities.

Moreover, recent research has demonstrated that epigenetic changes can occur after birth in children who experience a chaotic upbringing, frequent relocations of placements, and the variety of abuses noted above based upon these adverse life experiences. I realize that many unwanted children not only survive but thrive and have the potential to contribute value to society. It is simply much less likely if they were born against their mother's wishes.

Proponents of laws prohibiting abortion hold that their views are not personally directed at women who are pregnant; they are in error – it does not get any more personal than this.

The facts are indisputable; controlled studies are difficult for political reasons, but they are not impossible. However, there is some value in common sense, in which correlation plays some part in causation. Fewer unwanted children may help society in terms of reducing over-population, and also in terms of avoiding financial burdens upon those least likely to afford them.

But it may also have helped in the reduction of many sexual crimes, especially rape. Is this controversial? I hope so; knowledge advances within the atmosphere of healthy and respectful debate. In other words, I could be wrong. More intelligent scientists in the future may be able to conduct tests, possibly including impulse control, comparing children born to mothers or families that were forced to bear them with those born to willing parents. Research grants await.

Hire Foreign Experts and Students Interested in the Field of Sexual Offenders

For many years the United States has offered over one million immigrants HB1 visas for talented and skilled workers to enter our country. These have traditionally been awarded to individuals with specialized talents in the sciences, particularly physics, chemistry and engineering and mathematics. Such workers often enter into high-tech firms or academia. In certain cases, these immigrants may choose to remain in America for an extended period or they may wish to return to their country of origin.

In addition, via a foreign student visa, F1, students can request study in an American university, usually limited to one year but often extended indefinitely if immigration officials believe their continued stay in the US would benefit our country. Because America contains the world's most prestigious universities, these are eagerly sought out by foreign students. The allure to such students extends to their home countries if they return, as possessing an American degree confers upon them an exalted status in boosting their potential future careers, not to mention the financial benefits they would accrue.

Among the HB1 and F1 visas granted each year, none has been awarded to sexual abuse experts in other countries, a dismal statement about how our country perceives the insignificance and triviality of our field. Efforts must be made to consider the assessment and treatment of sexual offenders, and of even more crucial importance, the field of *prevention* of such abuse. Locating such talent should not be difficult; among a host of nations contributing to our field, Sweden, Switzerland, Australia and New Zealand come first to mind. Their contributions to the literature have recently been bounteous and beneficial; they would be a welcome addition to local talent.

Change School Hours and Terms

Most parents recognize and endure the perpetual tussle of trying to get teenagers up in the morning and to school on time. Physiological studies have consistently demonstrated that this is not entirely due to laziness. The actual circadian rhythms of adolescents cater to a late-to-bed, trouble-getting-up-early pattern, which is in the main, universal. The need for a change suggest appears both sensible and feasible. Some forward-looking school districts have responded by slightly delaying morning school hours by half an hour for teens, but this still is such a minor change, it is uncertain if this helps attendance, tardiness, and, most importantly, academic performance; studies are ongoing.

I believe a more radical change might help in reducing the possibility of teens courting trouble, such as sexting or actual offending, by spacing the school term in a somewhat different manner. Several European countries have re-imagined what would happen if our sacred summer vacation was shortened and the academic year broken into perhaps three sections; as an example, from September through November, then January through March, then May through to July.

This would provide breaks of one month each. Studies demonstrate that the longer summer break contributes to extensive forgetting and thus requires much make-up time. It is doubtful that students, teachers, parents and probably everybody else would react with horror if such a schedule were put into place in our country but, besides better academic performance, nations such as Denmark have found a reduction in teenage crime rates by eliminating vacation in at least one hot summer month. US studies have shown that teen sexual offending, which can, of course, occur regardless of season, does increase as the temperature rises. An increase in ambient temperature also correlates with a surge in aggressive behavior as well.

With two months free of school, especially in the heat of summer, teens might get bored and stray into illegal activities, including sexting and using messaging to embarrass a foe. Better to be preoccupied with homework and school attendance for part of the summer. But what of summer camp? And of extended family vacations? Probably these could readily shift to a more fragmented but a more academically efficient schedule if at least one summer month free of school responsibilities were at least put under the research microscope. Limited pilot projects might help to determine whether crime rates, and particularly those of aggressive sexual crimes, would respond in a favorable manner to such a transition. It should be of note that the American Academy of Pediatrics now recommends that middle and high schools begin no earlier than 8:30 AM. I would offer 9 AM as an even better hour.

While all this is well-known among academics and public-school authorities, change, especially within legislative bodies, is dilatory. Yet it remains a paradox, in this age of flexible work hours which many of these officials enjoy, that they have recused themselves by engaging in other issues while ignoring this crucial factor and ignoring these issues..

Enhance treatment, academic and skills-based programs for incarcerated sexual offenders and facilitate housing following release:

With good behavior, it would be prudent for the incarcerated sexual offender to begin the acquisition of job skills before release into the community. A number of such programs existed decades ago but funding these has proven a challenge. Some who hold punitive opinions might chafe at the idea of taxpayer funds being employed to teach skills such as construction, plumbing, welding, HVAC, or IT knowledge for potential occupations to sexual offenders. Such job training, perhaps in coordination with private companies and community colleges, could better prepare inmates for a life in the community. This is especially apt if accompanied by both temporary contract employment services and coordination with private industries, perhaps as apprenticeships. Studies demonstrate a reduction in recidivism for ex-convicts when work is secured immediately upon release or at least soon thereafter.

A recent study indicated that more than 70% of inmates have the literacy skills of a fourth-grader, that is, a nine-year-old child. New programs in a few institutions have provided electronic tablets to certain prisoners and provided tutoring in literacy skills. The same report from the RAND Thinktank predicted that $1 invested in prison education reduced the rate of re-offense by 40%. Sexual offenders were included in this review but not isolated as a separate group. The $1 invested in prisoner education was estimated to yield $4–$5 in taxpayer savings in the three years following release, largely due to a reduction in re-arrest.

Prisoners who obtain an associate's degree have a re-offense rate well below the rate of all released inmates, which now stands at about 40%. A bachelor's degree reduces that rate to 5.6%. Unfortunately, although sexual offenders were included in these reviews, they were not separated out by type of crime. (Sexual offenders overall have a recidivism rate of 13.4% but, separated by groups, as explained in former chapters, those rates can vary between 0% to 30%.) Such statistics are worth the attention of authorities, especially legislators. However, these retrospective studies are confounded by a combination of variables not yet taken into account, including the type of inmate who would agree to be involved in such educational programs and the type of crime they committed.

As an example, selected maximum-security facilities in California prisoners received dozens of desktop computers in a pilot program funded by a private tech company. Teachers were selected to deliver lessons to inmates on USB drives employing a program called "Canvass." In a similar arrangement in Maine, prisoners were allowed to enroll in a new curriculum to receive laptops monitored by prison officials. It is too soon to learn whether these programs will also reduce recidivism but the trend from the results of similar educational programs is promising. Politicians will always be reluctant to spend taxpayer dollars to enhance a criminal's life after incarceration. They may rue the day when such results are more broadly publicized.

Another example of a slightly different sort was initiated in a Saskatchewan prison. Canadian Corrections authorities allowed Rockwood Psychological Services to initiate, then maintain a program of a CBT/Risk-Needs-Responsibility sexual offender treatment program from 1991 until 2013, when the re-allocation of a number of participants were transferred to a different facility. Nonetheless, an impressive number of sexual offenders were offered the program, and 579 inmates eventually completed its course. Results on follow-up, reported in 2020, demonstrated that the treatment groups displayed lower rates of sexual offending than a control group of sexual offender inmates who were not enrolled. That group was equivalent to the treatment group in that they did not refuse the program but could not be accommodated due to limitations on the number of therapists available. The authors concluded that, "The results demonstrate that prison-based sex-offense specific treatment can be effective."

More world-wide examples exist. A pilot program in Japanese prisons demonstrated a reduction in repeat offending when social workers and job placement professionals were included in prison programs beginning at least one year prior to anticipated release. Several European countries have devised a scheme to train convicts in small-scale farming, then offering them part of a small plot of land upon which they could begin organic gardening and thereafter sell their produce at local restaurants and grocery stores.

In fact, Japan has recently expanded this program to include disadvantaged individuals, although not all were sexual offenders. Just prior to release they were provided a small plot of land, taught sustainable farming practices and were supplied with the basics to accomplish this. Preliminary results demonstrated a low incidence of repeated criminal activity in those selected. Besides many advantages of such a program in terms of exposure to light and outdoor air, the individuals thus chosen were not mandated to return to their former neighborhoods, often the strongholds of much criminal activity.

In our country, a number of restaurants and bakeries have held jobs open specifically for sexual offenders. They are usually happy to employ these men, who have stellar attendance records given that their supervisors have mandated work as part of their post-release requirements. Another innovative plan was initiated by Dominick Crispino, a former attorney and former inmate as well. Mr. Crispino now works with the Rikers Debate Project, a group of volunteers with debating talents, to teach prisoners at Rikers Island Penitentiary such skills, thereby imparting a sense of logic as well as literacy competence through weekly debating classes. Several former prisoners have been encouraged sufficiently to go on to obtain college and even master's degrees.

Social workers have also been brought aboard to assist those leaving prison to help in locating appropriate housing. Several European countries have followed this approach; although it is too soon to generalize their results more broadly, first analyses indicate that the most relevant correlations between a sexual offender relapsing or staying free from repeating a new crime, have been a stable home, steady employment, and entering into a treatment program specific for sexual offenders.

Provide Better Mental Health Facilities and Professionals to Assess and Treat Psychiatric Disorders and Drug and Alcohol Abuse for Inmates

Accurate figures are difficult to find to identify the number of sexual offenders now incarcerated who have mental health issues. Sexual offenders as a group do not possess any single psychologic or psychiatric disorder which generated their offending. Nonetheless, many have suffered early lifetime traumas, including broken homes, parental discord, single-parent upbringing, violence during their formative years, and multiple placements. A recent study concluded that as many as 60% of inmates have a history of mental illness. We are imprisoning a heap of broken humanity and the most significant failures in this regard are the lack of recognition of these problems and the lack of adequate treatment for them.

While we cannot attribute sexual offending with any degree of scientific rigor to early childhood trauma, mental health counselling might shine some light into the depths of despair which accompany such an offender's public reputation, their subsequent low self-esteem and the fears of returning to a community which now regards them with shame. (Released offenders are mandated to return to wherever their crime occurred.) Such counselling could better prepare the offender to deal with the crushing realties, of life after prison, including dealing with robots on the phone and spending countless hours utilizing computer and phone screens to hassle with most details of their lives.

We are unaware of the exact number of sexual crimes committed under the influence of drugs or alcohol. No studies have yet been published addressing this issue although in our experience, that number would be around 15% to 20%. Certainly, that figure would be higher in cases of spontaneous rape, such as during college parties. Moreover, we do see a number of men who use domestic violence against a female partner which culminates in forcible sexual relations. While alcohol can lower a man's ability to attain, then maintain, an erection, this has been a minor impediment in most such cases as drinking also reduces impulse control.

Even were sexual abuse to occur by an offender under the influence of drugs or alcohol, it must be borne in mind that, while many men drink or use drugs, the vast majority do not commit sexual crimes under the influence of illegal substances or alcohol. In other words, it is the rare case in which substance abuse can be solely attributed to the offender's use of alcohol or illegal drugs. As stated above, substance abuse can be the major contributor in cases in which, at a party a college-age male forces sexual activity upon a female (who may also be inebriated). Other cases can occur with the pernicious combination of a stimulant, primarily methamphetamine, with alcohol. These combinations can elevate anger to rage, but, in our experience, only a slim minority of sexual abuse cases can be attributed to such combinations. Also, in such cases, additional factors may well play a role, including the absence of impulse control.

In most prison settings today, substance abuse classes are available, although participation remains on a voluntary basis; 12-step programs, such as AA are offered to inmates in many prison settings as well. We have known a number of substance abuse inmates who never attend such programs, believing they can navigate their freedom after release without returning to substance abuse. In an outpatient setting, we will always refer such individuals to appropriate substance abuse and/or domestic violence programs.

While a minority of sexual crimes occur which might have been prevented had the perpetrator been sober, most such misdeeds are planned by a sober and clear mind, seeking the cover of privacy, isolating a vulnerable victim, and weighing the odds of not being accused or apprehended. Such planning, especially if it represents a repetitive pattern, is inconsistent with the acute or chronic use of alcohol or illegal drugs.

Nonetheless, effective substance abuse treatment programs exist, both on an outpatient basis and in institutions. However, they may fail to address mental health issues which could have contributed to sexual offending, such as mania and antisocial personality disorders. Yet counselling programs in prisons have been seriously curtailed in recent years due to budgetary restraints – a false economy as studies demonstrate that such programs have reduced sexual re-offending and thereby saved millions of taxpayer dollars. Moreover, in the few instances in which sexual offender-specific treatment was offered in prisons, that cohort of men had a demonstrably lower risk of re-offense than offenders who did not receive such treatment.

Public education about sexual offending would be of help in stressing that not all, nor even the majority of sexual offenders are monsters to be socially avoided at all costs. Such enlightenment could bring some pressure on corrections departments to reconsider the implementation of mental health and substance abuse counselling as necessary services to inmates. These may be as valuable in many cases as providing medical assistance to the ill, or religious services to the faithful. Several studies have recently demonstrated a higher risk of recidivism in offenders with much psychological baggage upon discharge. It would be money well spent to facilitate their release by providing housing, employment, and sexual offender-specific treatment. This would undoubtedly help them assimilate into their general communities.

Unfortunately, funding is a matter most often determined by legislation. It is the rare legislator who would embrace policies their constituents believe favor any additional funding for either research or treatment for sexual offenders. Many lawmakers at local, state, and national levels may talk about rehabilitation for those who have committed crimes but those sentiments are akin to Civil War surgeons discussing saving the leg of a wounded soldier while knowing full well that amputation will be the only cure.

No local or national organization, such as the National Health Service, or political body such as a state legislature or Federal Congress, has ever proposed a bill specifically aimed at assessment or treatment of sexual offenders, a sad commentary on placing a higher priority on getting re-elected than helping those who might benefit from rehabilitation. Cowardice is personified by such neglect.

Consider the Release of Elderly, Disabled or Terminally Ill Sexual Offenders

All studies investigating the incidence of sexual crimes show that advancing age reduces the incidence of any such crime recurring. We have treated offenders who have committed molestations such as exhibitionism and frottage in their seventies and eighties, but their numbers are exceedingly low. While senility can occasionally retard the ability to control impulses, sexual activity is as low in such individuals as in a population of boys under the age of six.

With the crowding in penal institutions an ever-increasing problem, release on humanitarian grounds could be considered among such inmates. We know, from the scientific literature, that there comes a time in almost all men's lives where the probability of committing another sexual crime is so slight as to be practically nonexistent. This is also true of those terminally ill, suffering from a debilitating disease, or wheelchair-bound. If sufficient rehabilitative or supportive and supervised living situations can be found, it is both more humane and less costly to transfer such individuals to alternative placements. Not a few men die in prison of illnesses, some, but not all, associated with aging. Others might suffer currently incurable and debilitating illnesses which render their capability to reoffend non-existent. They already live within a gray world, then are faced with eight hours of total darkness during many sleepless nights. Are we committed to allow them, after living such a hidden life, to finally rest in unvisited tombs?

Improve the Diet of Inmates

The food served to inmates is rarely a topic of discussion. It is not, as imagined, and sometimes exaggerated by ex-prisoners, as "glop." Nonetheless, Aramak, a giant global distributer of meals for schools and prisons has been taken to task for providing "mystery meat" and cholesterol-laden meals for prisoners. A study at Harvard has shown direct links between diet and a healthy body. This study has been extended to demonstrate that a nutritious diet improves mental health as well. Several reviews have noted that, compared to the general population, prisoners in federal penitentiaries, in aggregate, have a higher Body Mass Index (BMI) than those who have committed crimes for which they had not been incarcerated.

While lack of exercise may contribute to a higher rate of obesity in prisoners than in the general public, we honestly have no studies linking remaining in prison and gaining weight thereby. Nonetheless, meaningful guidance from professional nutritionists could have a beneficial effect on the physical and mental conditions of inmates. Of even greater benefit would be some general education for prisoners on adequate dietary habits post-release. Based on our experience, the offenders who show the greatest concern about remaining healthy after release are those least likely to re-offend.

Provide Prisoners Opportunities to Volunteer

Work crews are commonly used by prison authorities to accomplish necessary societal tasks, such as road and park clean-ups. This is often helpful as prisoners have some access to the outdoors. Studies have shown proven mental health benefits from exposure to outdoor air when compared with atmospheres within offices, homes or other confined settings. Unfortunately, such work is only rarely reimbursed; if so, the going rate is $1.00/hour.

Allowing good-behavior inmates to volunteer at nursing homes and libraries (without exposure to children at certain hours), participate in beach clean-ups, or even volunteer as participants in sociological studies could provide benefits of enhanced self-esteem and a feeling of being part of a community. The use of prisoners in potentially harmful medication trials or stressful psychological studies has been rightfully outlawed in most states. I know of no controlled studies demonstrating positive effects on reducing recidivism based on the use of inmates in volunteer activities; however, anecdotal stories from prisoners now released lead me to believe in the therapeutic effect such volunteerism can bring to bear.

Several studies, have, however, documented the hesitance of citizens in accepting sexual offenders into volunteer and nonprofit organizations. However, what appears to be common sense is often at odds with the experiences of most such offenders. One report noted that the general public showed some appreciation and less negative judgement of sexual offenders who helped in their communities. This effect may have occurred by emphasizing that these offenders are individuals who are paying for their crime(s), have families (having children was found to be the most crucial element in acceptance), may attend church, and intend to work on a regular basis. Volunteer coordinators had enhanced acceptance when they referred to the offenders as "people who have problems with sexual behaviors" Separating an individual offender from their specific crime acknowledges their humanity and capacity to change.

Allow Inmates Better Access to the Outdoors

Most of us these days live our lives on screens. The value of getting outside is greater than just the exercise, though that is important. There exists a number of differences in the quality of indoor and outdoor air. Aside from greater opportunities to exercise, the ionization of outdoor air and exposure to sunshine have, as stated above, not only improved mental health, but have been shown to enhance the performance not only of athletic achievements but of gains in the productivity in industries we commonly consider to be indoor vocations, such as office and factory work.

Unfortunately, I know of no study conducted in prison populations, let alone sexual offenders, demonstrating a correlation between exposure to the outdoors and the rate of recidivism, but such research would be of more than passing interest.

I do believe, though only from anecdotal narratives, that prisoners denied the outdoors except for limited time periods, such as those in solidarity confinement (and thus who may need it the most), instead endure the toxic darkness of almost perpetual stagnation. Research studies, again to repeat the common refrain, would surely be of interest.

Allow Individuals with Felonies to Vote

Should a man who committed a murder be allowed to vote in local or federal elections? Most would say no without a thought. What of a sexual offender? Again, no. Yet what are the scientific bases for such discrimination? There are no studies indicating that offenders of any crime are too misinformed to make a knowledgeable decision about whom to vote for or what measures, local or federal, to favor? Removing the right to vote for felons constitutes just one of multiple penalties for a crime, usually a single one. A felon already has had his liberty curtailed, his comfort removed, his finances dissolved, his health jeopardized, and his future made bleak. There appears to be no logical reason to also remove his vote as he is a citizen who will likely be released one day and will experience the consequences of a vote.

It is of interest that, in the United States, there are several million adults who cannot vote because they are felons. However, in certain states, felons who are not incarcerated are allowed to vote. Those who cannot include 1.5 million inmates in prisons, or approximately 2.2% of America's population. More egregious still, this includes 5.2% of our African American population, who are barred from thus participating in their country's elections.

That figure is fully 2% of the Hispanic population as well. Such discrimination would appear to be in violation of the Fourth Amendment but court battles have been unsuccessful in gaining voting rights for the majority of felons in America. Yet felons can read the news on the web and in newspapers and magazines and view it on TV and online, and would appear to be as well-informed or better than many with no criminal histories.

We do not bar the mentally ill from voting, nor do we, nor should we, eliminate from the voting rolls those who have expressed extreme and even violent views. In many states, felons can vote once they have proved to be sufficiently responsible to have reimbursed the state or federal government for all legal fees, such as court and supervisory costs and restitution. But these may also include therapy for the victim(s). Unfortunately, most sexual offenders are rarely in a position to have paid full restitution as they will, in all likelihood, not be able to regain former higher-paying employment due to the nature of their crimes.

One example, that of Florida, is emblematic of many state regulations for voting rights of felons. Amendment Four of the State Constitution deals with eligibility; after paying all fees, a felon out of prison may vote with two exceptions – having committed a murder or a sexual offense, further undefined. Thus a man wandering onto a CP website out of curiosity or an 18-year-old senior in high school who engages in sexual activity with his 15-year-old girlfriend, can never vote in any state or federal election. It would seem as if federal law should assist in an overall delineation of what crimes prohibit voting in federal elections, but it is currently left to the states to make that determination.

What of the right for those still incarcerated for a felony to be able to vote? Just two states, Maine and Vermont, allow prisoners to vote. Twenty states prohibit felons from voting while in prison and on supervision until all fees are paid; seventeen inhibit voting to those in prison but allow the vote to felons who are on supervision but have paid all fees. There exist eleven states which forbid voting to any individual who has ever been convicted of a felony, regardless of its type, whether under supervision or having completed it, or even after all fees have been paid.

It is a pity that even liberal states such as California, Oregon and Washington, continue to deny the constitutional right to vote to felons who exist somewhere within the criminal justice system. Yet there is no evidence such individuals are unfit to render an opinion on matters which will impact them in the future. There is simply no research to support the rules that felons, punished in multiple ways, do not deserve a voice in rights guaranteed by our Constitution. Indeed, the Constitution makes no mention of such prohibitions. Felons may have harmed others; so have most of us. That, by itself, is an inadequate reason to suppress their voices in one of our most cherished prerogatives.

Explore Racial Disparities Among Sexual Offenders

It is often thought that all crimes are more commonly committed by minority populations. Certainly, the numbers of men in jails and prisons in our country are disproportionally African American or Latino. The sole exception is among sexual offenders. Just one-half to one-third of all sexual offense arrests are committed by members of minority groups. In other words, Caucasian males constitute almost 70% of all such arrests (including rape).

Studies indicate that, not only have prison sentences for sexual offenders at the federal level increased in duration and severity over the past decade, that is particularly true amongst African-American and Latino men. This finding is mirrored when nonsexual crimes are included in these analyses as well.

In our Clinic, while Latino men constitute about 35% of all patients, this is a skewed figure as many individuals who live in this area emigrate from Latin American countries to perform manual farm labor. Just 2% of all patients we have treated over a period approaching 50 years have been African American. The belief, promulgated by many on the conservative spectrum, posits that allowing immigrants into our country put native-born Americans at higher risk of becoming the victims of crime. Statistics belie this notion, According to the American Migration Institute, rates for all crimes, including sexual offenses, are lower amongst our immigrant population than amongst native-born Americans. This held true both when the numbers of crimes committed by Latino immigrants were examined apart from migrants from all other countries and when sexual crimes were isolated from other types of offenses.

Many causes of racial disparities have been proposed but none appear wholly satisfactory. Perhaps African American males more frequently receive longer prison sentences but over our studies, exceeding 50 years, that would be unlikely. It is possible that African American offenders are less likely to attend treatment (although they are mandated to do so), their victims may be less likely to report sexual crimes, or that such offenders are more likely to have received treatment in religious settings. Victims or witnesses are less likely to communicate with police if they live in high-crime areas. Again, the statistics are too lopsided for such explanations to prove definitive.

Thus, a variety of reasons may exist; although difficult, studies on this counter-intuitive finding beg for at least a doctoral study, let alone a professional inquiry. If we only knew why African American males appear to be the least likely group to be identified as sexual offenders (if that is truly borne out in further studies), we might be able to discern the reasons why and apply these to public health measures.

Reduce dependence on the polygraph

There has been no controlled study documenting that the polygraph can distinguish whether or not a person is telling the truth or falsifying an answer. Some uncontrolled articles have claimed such but these have not been controlled for external factors. In addition they have almost always been published by polygraphers themselves, suggesting self-interest. Such proof of invalidity and lack of scientifically based research have led the courts nation-wide to exclude results from the polygraph in trials determining guilt or innocence.

Despite this decree, POs and PPSs continue to rely on the polygraph when supervising offenders begin their dominion after offenders have left jail or prison. In fact, failure on a polygraph can be grounds for a supervisory violation and might even result in re-incarceration in rare circumstances, though commonly for short periods of time.

There are two types of polygraphs usually administered to sexual offenders: One is a specific-issue test. This consists of a few general questions amid requests for information about the crime supposedly committed or about the likelihood of similar crimes having been committed before which had never come to light. A full-disclosure polygraph includes a variety of questions, in the main centering on any type of crime committed in the past, especially sexual crimes and includes not only overt acts but fantasies about acting on these as well.

A specific-issue test is sometimes employed by defense attorneys in an attempt to intimidate (they would use the term "inform") the DA to either dismiss or reduce some of the charges against their client or supposedly demonstrate that the offender didn't commit the crime at all. This rarely achieves much of a result. The full-disclosure test is employed by supervisors to ascertain whether they have garnered a complete history of any crimes of which they were unaware. Again, the results are most often desultory, rendering the test of questionable value.

Major problems with polygraphs lie in the lack of scientific rigor which should be proven before making assumptions about its results. In the polygraph, an individual is connected to a variety of monitors which measure cardiac rate, rate of respirations, and electrical skin resistance. None of these tests, alone or in aggregate, have ever been linked to lying or telling the truth. False negatives are common as these measurements are resistant to rapid changes. Yet false positives, which may result in calamitous penalties, may occur because normal fluctuations in these parameters can be due to anxiety or simply because the human machine is unsteady, irregular and unpredictable regardless of the questions asked.

To confound these difficulties with the interpretation of the polygraph's results, these tests are administered with no control over time of day, when a person last ate, whether an illness such as an anxiety or a cardiac disorder is present, or whether the person is taking medications. All of these conditions can alter the polygraph's results but both supervisors and polygraphers refuse to recognize the impact these factors may have, even when they are informed about them beforehand.

A maintenance polygraph adds between $250 and $400 to the balance sheet of the polygrapher. A full-disclosure one will set the offender back

$500, although in rare cases, a county supervisor may request governmental assistance for those clearly lacking funds. To add to this burden, supervisors recommend or require maintenance polygraphs six months following the initiation of supervision and every six months thereafter, during which their sexual offender is under probation or parole. Should the offender fail this test, they must undergo another such polygraph within 30 days after the failure. Despite the ample financial rewards the polygrapher acquires, any result from such a flawed test, reinforced by all courts' decision to disallow it in testimony, leaves one wondering about the financial burden and the awful penalties to sexual offenders should they fail, even on one crucial question, which can result from such a wayward assessment instrument.

Emphasize Individual Rather than Group Therapy

Many sexual offender clinics feature group therapy as the most appropriate approach to treating sexual offenders. Indeed, not just a few hold twice-weekly group sessions while limiting individual sessions to weekly, less frequently, or none at all. Group therapy has been of help for many offenders in confronting denial, obtaining feedback on cognitive distortions, and providing support. In fact, our Sexual Abuse Clinic offers three groups each week. These are aimed at two separate populations: predatory and situational offenders. Many professionals suggest that sexual offenders require group therapy alone. The scientific data for altering this preconception proves otherwise.

One specific inadequacy of group therapy is that clinics usually lack the numbers of clients with similar crimes and needs, such that dissimilar cohorts are combined; the R&J and CPO offenders, who have committed minor crimes with an extremely low (if any) risk of reoffending, may be paired with men who have preyed upon young boys or who have committed multiple rapes. A number of studies have demonstrated that such heterogeneous groupings are less effective in preventing recidivism than groups composed of men who have committed similar types of sexual crimes.

A different and crucial problem with a focus on group therapy is that it ignores relatively individual factors unique to each offender. It cannot focus exclusively on a single individual as that would deprive the remainder of participants of sufficient time to address their own issues. Techniques directly vital to individual offenders, such as aversive conditioning, sexual impulse control, thought stopping, and relapse prevention, prove formidable in a group setting as opposed to utilizing such procedures in one-to-one therapy.

In addition, methods to improve the quality of life cannot be directly addressed for every participant equally in groups, even over lengthy time frames. Such personal objectives, include the application of the Good Lives/Self-regulation Model (GL/SRM), which emphasizes that the offender should aim to obtain common human goods, such as sexual pleasure, self-esteem, and the maintenance of satisfactory relationships. These have proven to be inimical to sexual offending yet need to be personalized in a manner difficult to achieve in a group format.

Some sexual offenders will inevitably believe they were neglected if a group therapist chooses to focus on a single individual in that particular session. Neither can such treatment techniques be delivered in a virtual format or a telephone chat. Hands-on treatment will require more effort from the therapist but is of crucial importance in treating sexual offenders: no Zoom meetings please.

A number of support groups, such as Sexaholics Anonymous, Celebrate Recovery, and Sex Addicts Anonymous, all have been helpful adjuncts in providing support in a nonjudgmental atmosphere. Moreover, in such groups, sexual offenders can, and should, obtain a sponsor – a person experienced in helping others and one upon whom the offender can rely in potentially dangerous situations. While some object to a 12-step model which is forceful in promoting religious idealism, actually working the steps minus any focus on a "higher power" is acceptable these days in most such gatherings.

I am afraid that time and money are sometimes involved in clinics requiring attendance at groups (ours are offered free). In a group of eight offenders charged $50 per group session, the clinicians can make treatment more affordable for each offender while also reaping the majority of their income by simply sitting and talking.

But research has shown that it requires a much more active role in directly addressing each individual's set of unique circumstances, manner of committing a crime(s), type of crime, and specific needs to effectively treat the offender. Individual therapy is more expensive than group but may require less total time in treatment. Insurance coverage for sexual offender treatment would appear to be a public safety and mental health issue and increasingly, partial coverage is provided by certain insurers. Surely such treatment, from a public safety perspective, is as vital as, for example, substance abuse therapy, which is partially covered by most health insurance programs. I cannot think of any such reimbursement needed in a more urgent fashion.

Use Medications for a Certain Set of Sexual Offenders

I have mentioned the use of injectable long-acting medications such as depo-Provera or Lupron to diminish libido in certain sexual offenders. A cohort of predatory offenders may be released from prison having served their sentences. Therefore, there is a period of time, not inconsiderable, during which such offenders may be at large in the community but have not yet received any behavioral or cognitive treatment in certified sexual offender treatment programs. Moreover, a cohort of such potentially dangerous men may have served out their entire period not only of incarceration but also of PPS supervision. These men are unlikely to enter a treatment program on a voluntary basis. It would make more sense to release all such potential offenders while they still have sufficient time to be ordered under their parole into a sexual offender-specific treatment program.

Some supervisors have mandated the use of medications in such highly dangerous cases, even against the client's will. State laws must balance the Fourth Amendment rights of all individuals against unreasonable force or bodily intrusion when considering potential recidivism. This issue should be adjudicated within the adversarial process through the court system. A difficult choice must be made between an individual's freedoms and safety to the community.

As treatment providers, we favor the latter but civil rights groups may bristle at the thought of forcing medications onto an unwilling recipient. Both points of view are valid and need to be determined by higher courts. If mandated, the medication should be discontinued once there is proof that cognitive and behavioral methods appear to have markedly reduced the offender's tendency to relapse.

Some men on hormone-reducing medications to reduce sexual drive have been known to ingest, or even inject, testosterone supplements if they can obtain them. However, these can be detected by random unannounced blood tests.

A less intrusive approach would be for the client to submit to taking antidepressants, such as Prozac or similar (Zoloft, Paxil). Such drugs usually reduce men's sexual drive, though to a lesser extent and more erratically, than hormonal medications. Blood levels for such serotonin reuptake inhibitors and for testosterone would (and can) be checked on a random basis to assess their efficacy and check an offender's compliance.

There may arrive a day when we are more certain about epigenetics and whether neurological connections can be scrutinized and directly targeted for sexual offending. That day, I'm afraid, will be a long time coming: there are over a trillion connections (synapses) among central nervous cells in any individual – more than there are stars in our galaxy and more than all the countable galaxies in our universe. But progress in this direction is ongoing, with innocuous insertions of electrodes thinner than a human hair into brain areas and functional imaging of nervous system cellular activity. Whether these types of findings will lead to any progress in assessing sexual arousal and enhancing the harmless sort while reducing the deviant variety is for future generations to determine.

Examine Satisfaction by Victims and their Families with the Penalties Meted Out to Sexual Offenders

One premise of the criminal justice system is to allow the victims and their families some emotional recompense when a sexual offender is finally sentenced. We have treated victims and their families; most are not only dissatisfied with the penalties but disheartened by the time it took to reach a punitive decision. In many cases, girls molested in their prepubescent years only learn what their abuser received in terms of retribution by the time they are in college. It is not unusual that such cases creep along at a snail's pace for years before a final decision is reached.

Some of the suggested solutions mentioned above might speed up this process but I am not sufficiently naïve to believe that any of these will be achieved in the short term. At any rate, it is the rare victim or family which is satisfied with the result. Years have drifted by and victims may well have moved on while others may still be suffering PTSD-like symptoms. These latter often require years of therapy. Others often frequently do not want to re-live the trauma the abuse has caused and would prefer to try to forget: the unforgivable can morph into the nebulous forgettable.

I am not advocating for milder penalties here; just quicker ones. Human emotions such as the quest for revenge might not be admirable but, in sexual abuse cases, it is unfortunately inevitable. We cannot, as scientists, ignore such a basic human emotion. However, in most such cases where we have access to a victim and their family, whatever price their offender paid appears to be never enough.

Really consider what you would feel if your son or daughter were sexually abused. What would you consider adequate recompense? Castration is a common answer though the least likely in practice. Surgeons are understandably averse to removing healthy organs and the procedure is irreversible; hormonal treatment is the better alternative in cases in which a still-dangerous offender is at large. I believe there is no penalty in reality which would satisfy those who have been thus abused. Yet the justice system must somehow strive to at least partially sate this quest for revenge.

It has attempted to do so by fixing in place arbitrary sentences for certain crimes. Yet this only ties the hands of judges and DAs in considering the idiosyncrasies of many such cases. Mollifying factors, such as lack of a criminal history, stability of employment and relationships, and the situational nature of a crime should all be taken into account. No judge or DA, let alone a legislator, wants to be seen as being lenient with sexual offenders. Yet many lives can hang in the balance from these decisions, including those of innocent families and employers.

It should be understood that the majority of sexual offenders suffer multiple penalties aside from their loss of freedom, including monetary loss (many have lost their life savings); familial discord, including denial of seeing their children during their formative years, and even divorce; difficulty finding housing after release if they were incarcerated; the inability to return to their chosen professions; losing friends; being on a registration list; in many cases, avoiding places where children might be found; lack of medical and psychologic and psychiatric care barely equivalent to what would be provided on an outpatient basis; and the stigma they will always carry of being labelled a sexual offender, regardless of the type of crime they have committed. For those imprisoned, these represent multiple punishments.

Since no penalty will likely satisfy the abused, I would plead for judicial discretion and the elimination of fixed penalties, such as Oregon's Measure 11 and the Nation-wide Annie's Law, which increases maximum sentences for offenders, especially for repeat offenders, thus eliminating judicial discretion; requires in-person requests for changes in address, workplace or appeals to travel out of state. It also establishes the basis for community notification. In combination with Meghan's Law, which demands local community notifications, such as to neighbors, this trio of nation-wide rulings stamps a sexual offender label onto a sexual offender, often for a lifetime, regardless of the severity of the crime he committed or the risk of him repeating a sexual crime once released.

Unfortunately, these laws do not take into account crucial variables, such as how an offender who is a student will be impacted for the remainder of his lifetime should he be deprived of furthering his studies, or an offender's opportunities for a decent job or living situation. One other major factor should also be taken into consideration: the distinction between a situational offender as opposed to a predatory one. The science of risk assessment should be regarded and applied in a much more intelligent and flexible manner. The idiosyncrasies of each case merit consideration, as should the long-term impact draconian penalties may impose.

Revenge may be a black-hearted emotion but an indelible, ubiquitous one within us all. Forgetting a sexual offense is, and should be, impossible. Forgiving one is even more onerous. But while forgiveness cannot change the past, it might help to alter the future. The past holds many regrets for most of us; the future might, in some ways, keep alive promises more brightly kept. I would hope that we can look forward rather than back.

Investigate Financial Benefits of, and Liaisons Between, the Criminal Justice System and For-profit Organizations

A number of sheriff's offices, prosecutors and courts benefit substantially from administering justice. Almost hidden from public scrutiny and oversight, through Title IV-E funds, sheriffs and courts are entitled to retain a portion of seized property beyond the usual fines and court costs borne by offenders. For juvenile offenders, judges will remand youth to detention facilities owned and managed by private corporations. Often, these are not nonprofit organizations but large corporate entities whose main interest lies in profiting from retaining youth over extended periods of time and maximizing the number of youths (or more) who can fit into any one facility.

In adult cases, offenders are often fined, their possessions sold with the proceeds accruing to the courts and sheriffs' offices, and even to DAs' offices as well. These are no small amounts. In a single county in Ohio, the court received almost $900,000 through federal reimbursement funding. Another county in Florida collected over $56 million through subsidies, fines and auctions of re-possessed property in 2023.

It is reasonable for private companies to expect to profit from their contractual associations with the criminal justice system. Such companies are not lightweights in the corporate world: the Ohio and Texas courts have contracted with JBI and GBO, two national for-profit companies; no small sums are involved. Arcadia and Bain Capital have acquired similar companies so as to benefit from their contracts with all segments of the criminal justice system.

In Texas the annual contract with the court system, termed an "interagency cooperation agreement" netted $10,500,000 just for the juvenile court system alone. Numerous official and internal documents in many states note similar gains from both the juvenile and adult offender systems. The Minnesota Department of Human Services, surveying as part of an oversight operation, sent an email praising the amounts collected and shoveled into both the courts' and sheriffs' offices. One reply featured a salivating emoji with large dollar signs for eyes and urging other recipients within the system to "get more money."

The Attorneys General Offices also seek to profit from outsourcing bids for juvenile and adult correction contracts not only for prisons but for halfway houses following incarceration. In addition, civil forfeitures from seized property are allowed to flow into the coffers of individual police and sheriffs' offices. Such funds derive not only from seized electronics but from more expensive items such as automobiles and re-possessed homes following an eviction.

Such practices have been challenged, almost always successfully in most cases, but that has not halted these contractual arrangements. Even two rulings by the Supreme Court, identifying the conflict of interest inherent in such contracts, one in the 1980s, then the 1990s and most recently a ruling in 2015, have emphasized the dangers in outsourcing government services to private companies. Yet these rulings have done little to discourage such arrangements. Indeed, the DOJ's Inspecter General urged the Federal Government's reliance on such contracts with for-profit companies to be "phased out" in its annual reports of 2021 and 2022. Such rulings and directives have shown the urgency of a camel train crossing the Mongolian Desert.

In a capitalist society, it may appear to be expedient to contract with a private company to provide such services as imprisonment, collection of fines, court and supervision costs. Nothing could be further from the truth. The problem resides in the unsatisfying muddle of companies' responsibilities and their goal of maximizing profits.

There exists an inherent conflict between the goals of providing adequate facilities and generating income. The tussle has resulted in murky confusion, aggravated by these arrangements largely being opaque and rarely known to even government officials let alone the average citizen. Private prisons, as stated above, are in dire condition with little heed paid to humane conditions. Things are worse in the use of private companies' handling of detention facilities, day-care centers, and juvenile and adult correctional half-way houses, such as those for substance abusers and sexual offenders.

Conditions in such placements are well below the standard of those managed wholly by the government. It is an error to assume private companies will always be more efficient than the ones under the control of state and federal governments.

Egregious examples are common-place: inmates crowded into facilities which were constructed for half their present occupancy rates; regular beatings of inmates by guards and other meals denied as punishment; inmates being forced to lie in their own excrement; youths being forced to use a toothbrush to clean a filthy toilet, then forced to use that same toothbrush on their teeth; prisoners without guards' awareness; work crews forced to labor in temperatures exceeding 100 degrees; others working in prisons or detention centers for $1 a day; even worse, inmates denied appropriate medical and mental health care; and inmates actually dying from malnutrition, heat stroke, or an aggravation of pre-existing conditions.

The US Governmental Accountability Office in a Testimony to Congress on January 23, 2024 said "We have identified cases of abuse and death at such [private] facilities." I would suggest more continuous and localized oversight of the offices of state AG's, DA's, police and sheriffs' departments, jail and prison facilities, and aftercare placements such as day-care living centers. Such scrutiny must be untethered from the criminal justice systems to prevent conflicts of interest. It would also save precious governmental funds, thus lightening the tax load on ordinary citizens. Until prosecutors, AGs, DAs courts, and jails, prisons and aftercare facilities can be observed by unbiased oversight, especially in private placements, the criminal justice system's use of such facilities will remain suspect and in defiance of Supreme Court dictates.

Eliminate Private Prisons

Studies leave no question that privately run prisons display more abuse and inhumane treatment of inmates than those administered by governmental departments of justice. Stories of unheated quarters in winter combined with no air conditioning in desert locations in summer have been verified. We do know that hotter temperatures beget hotter tempers. Research has also demonstrated the increased incidence of violence as the ambient temperature rises.

Since more profit can be made by increasing the numbers of prisoners, men are sandwiched together in unhealthy crowded conditions. The private corporations administering such institutions are beholden to the finances of their chief executives and their shareholders. Their incentives deprive inmates of basic human dignity regardless of the nature of their crimes. In short, these are wretched industries with aims not to prevent future crime but perhaps to actually increase it.

An interesting analogy can be found within the Veteran's Affairs (VA) Health System. It was well-known that veterans did not receive care equivalent to that of private and other government medical services for many years. Yet these were the individuals who dedicated parts of their lives to protect our country. VA health care for a number of years was partially contracted out to a variety of health care conglomerates in the private sector. But care did not improve: a veteran might have to wait over 100 days simply to see a physician or a nurse-practitioner. Moreover, visits were brief, care providers at times seemed uninvested, and groups were the standard therapy offered to those suffering from PTSD whereas many of these patients have been demonstrated to gain benefits not only from group therapy but from individualized care as well.

Bureaucrats have an ill-deserved reputation, but they are simply human beings. Thus it took the VA's health bureaucracy to investigate these delays and shortcomings, then regain control for the government instead of ceding it to private firms. New, and easier-to-navigate websites and continuous surveys and consultations, plus on-site visits from federal health authorities, have regained trust in the VA system, as documented by questionnaires to patients and by interviews with many of them. These veterans now can gain access to excellent health care and can do so in a much more rapid manner. This is not to say all VA problems have been eliminated but "bureaucracy" should not be a dirty word.

Prisons cannot be managed as a business. The federal government is impervious to market changes, profits and losses, and does not operate solely with an eye to the bottom line. Government agencies, including Inspector Generals, are staffed by people who do not have to change every four years. They exist to serve citizens as best as they are able. Even in a capitalist society, basic human rights ought not to be disregarded. The lack of federal and congressional oversight has created a patchwork of often conflicting and confusing statutes. These have only encouraged inhumane treatment which is intolerable in a civilized society. I believe governmental supervision and inspection will prove necessary to correct these wrong-doings.

Certain tasks are better administered by an institution not beholden to the primary goal of enhancing financial gain. Solely in government can we hope to challenge and improve such huge systems as that of criminal justice. Taking away one's right to liberty is squarely within the province of the Departments of Justice. That is what is in their name and that is what they were designed to accomplish – the administration of justice. No corporation, regardless of its flowery promises and humanitarian expressions can provide what each human being deserves: a chance to live under decent conditions so as not to be doubly or triply punished, and to not be considered merely a sum figure on a corporate spreadsheet.

We must fund Departments of Justice in an adequate manner to abolish such heinous treatment of our fellow humans, which only encourages hopelessness. At present, the privatization of correctional institutions resembles an economic casino – a lottery in which prisoners, and at times the personnel working to guard them and ensure their safety, always lose and the house always wins. The science is too vital, robust and indisputable to be left to the conceit for the urge of the bottom line. By improving basic living conditions in our institutions of incarceration, we may be encouraging better people upon their release as well.

Chapter 8

Summary

The pace of scientific information involving the criminal justice system is accelerating while advances and innovations in the rehabilitative aspects of this system are glacial and desultory at best. They represent a mindset which could be emblematic of the blind conviction of the flat earth society. I realize that many, if not most, of my suggestions for change in Chapter Seven will be considered too radical, naïve and too biased in favor of the sexual offender to be enacted soon. But the rehabilitative ideal should not be abandoned lest we continue the stench of sexual abuse at its current unacceptable rate. This system is not at the brink of a cliff where one either jumps or withdraws; it is sliding down a treacherous slope where both the system and its principal actors know not where the bottom lies.

The key components for prevention of future sexual abuse are to identify, mainly in teen males, tendencies toward sexual aggression and general delinquency. Only a minority of such youth will proceed to sexual offending but, at present, both individual and group therapy are feckless in altering the inevitable antisocial behavior of many such youth as they mature into their adult years. This lack of efficacy in addressing the problems these juveniles present, such as minor crimes, general disobedience and rebelliousness, has unfortunately led to the overall conclusion that such individuals will always present problems to society.

While it may be true that an antisocial personality disorder represents a severe challenge to any therapist, we must differentiate youth with a conduct disorder and antisocial tendencies from those who commit only sexual crimes. Most sexual offenders do not have an antisocial personality nor a record of general criminality. It is therefore crucial to tease out those whose sole transgression is sexual in nature and regard them in a different manner than the delinquent youth who will go on to commit a variety of crimes.

We expect a certain amount of rebellious behavior in most teens; it is a sign of moving away from parental control and establishing an independent personality. It is important to recognize that the adolescent brain is primed for such autonomy. A variety of studies demonstrate that it is only when most younger males reach the age of about 25 that full maturation occurs.

DOI: 10.4324/9781003532590-9

Thus we expect impulsive behavior of adolescents and individuals in their early twenties, accompanied by some recklessness, occasionally bordering on the criminal.

However, it is vital to distinguish those who harbor generally criminal traits from the teens and young men who commit only sexual crimes. In our Clinic, men with a history of criminal versatility comprise just 10% of our clients. While they will require sexual offender-specific treatment, we make it clear to their supervisors that we wield no special powers to alter their personalities. Such men may prove a challenge to treat in terms of attendance and compliance with assignments and the like but, in terms of reducing the risk of committing another sexual crime, they are as likely to benefit from sexual offender-specific treatment as those without antisocial traits. Clinical studies prove such counterintuitive results.

Nonetheless, the criminal justice system and the youth authorities in each state appear to equate and manage these two distinct populations in similar fashions. A boy who commits a sexual offense but has no other criminal history is often comingled with youths with a variety of nonsexual crimes. Thus he may be launched into a boys' home or prison, and forced to associate with a host of youth with conduct disorders well on their way toward sociopathy. He may be discriminated against as, often, the sexual offender is not of the criminal mind, and is often sub-assertive, even passive, in his attempts to associate with the general population.

This well-intentioned but scientifically flawed approach has intensified in the latter part of the 20th century and the earliest years of the present one, during which the population of institutionalized youth aged 14 to 18 has doubled. The justice system dealing with adolescents has thus been overburdened as funding to provide for such an increase in numbers has not kept pace with the cohort of youth who have committed only sexual crimes. Hence the "one-size-fits-all" approach survives in the face of a burgeoning population of youthful sexual offenders.

In considering the rehabilitative stance we would prefer for such youth, we believe their cases should be processed apart from the general population of young delinquent males. True, some may come from ruined homes, replete with substance abuse, sexual violence and domestic abuse. But these are in the minority. Some might be considered for foster care, but just a few. We find their biological families to generally be supportive of their sons and of treatment as well. Offenders who have committed only sexual crimes are a distinct subgroup within the criminal justice system, one which is amenable to treatment and with excellent opportunities, once graduating from a specialized program, to live thereafter without re-committing any sexual crime.

The same can be considered for adults whose sole crimes are sexual in nature. While the number of such crimes has declined during the present century (except for cases of CP only and electronic entrapment), population growth has continued, though at a reduced rate. Nonetheless, the criminal justice system has experienced an increasing burden of such cases and is woefully behind in rendering efficient resolution of cases. Unfortunately, we have witnessed, over the past 50 years, a continuing departure from the idea that sexual offenders can be successfully treated. Yet we who assess and treat sexual offenders continue to believe that the primary purpose of the penal system regarding them should be rehabilitation through effective treatment.

Indeed, the rehabilitative ideal is strongest in societies where a pervasive belief in the ability of individuals to change exists. One needs only to compare the frequencies of sexual crimes to appreciate these differences. The incidence of such crimes is far below those in the more progressive northern European countries, such as Belgium, Denmark, Norway, Sweden and The Netherlands. Their numbers are even higher in our country compared with those in more punitive nations such as China, Russia, and those imbued with religion as the overriding governmental authority, such as countries in the Middle East.

The degree of confidence a society can muster in the capability of its therapeutic institutions to create change varies considerably; the notion that any and all criminal tendencies are immutable is a characteristic of the latter list of nations, sadly including our own. It is particularly prominent in countries led by an authoritarian despot. Yet this should not be true of America. Nonetheless, our criminal justice system exhibits an enduring pessimism about the ability for therapeutic institutions to effect change.

These sentiments stem from a hold-over notion based upon the abject failures of the earliest attempts to enact change through psychoanalysis and psychological therapies alone. Fortunately, modern psychological and psychiatric treatments have advanced a great distance from such attempts in the 20th century. Nevertheless, our criminal justice system remains in stasis, or worse, it resembles a river, swirling at first in torrents down rocky terrain, but then inching slowly as it meets flattened plains in lazy curves rendering faster flow impossible. Unfortunately, a river always runs downhill.

Nonetheless, a multitude of studies have demonstrated that we now have the tools to accurately predict which offender is likely to benefit from treatment and thereafter never re-commit another sexual crime. Moreover, an increasing series of research publications have demonstrated the efficacy of treatment methods for reducing, and in many cases, eliminating, the chance a sexual offender will recidivate. Nonetheless, in the face of such evidence, the justice system continues to conduct its processes very much as it did a century ago. It will require changes of Solomonic proportions for an immense immutable system to enact such transformations. But being difficult does not automatically mean being impossible.

Instead of taking advantage of scientific findings, political power and the authority of the state appear to disregard research findings in a cavalier manner. Thus little distinction is made between sexual offenders who have paraphilias and pose a danger to be at large as opposed to situational offenders such as CPO or R&J cases. All appear to be held in equal contempt, not only by the criminal justice system but by the public at large, as such attitudes bleed into society from the system itself. It appears that political science is an oxymoron.

A civilized society which metes out justice in concert with not only the severity of the crime but with an eye toward attributes of the individual committing it, would save time and money. There can be little justification for placing many sexual offenders in cages who pose little, if any, threat to their communities. There are dangerous sexual offenders but we know not only who they are, but how to render them much less of a risk. The present system of punishment only gives the appearance of reducing community concerns about safety. In fact, some of the most dangerous of offenders live among us while harmless humans remain impounded, their liberty denied on baseless evidence due to discrepancies in how justice is meted out.

The treatment of sexual offenders reflects views about the nature of human beings and, unfortunately, the politics of the moment. These issues transcend sexual offending itself and speak to what kind of society we desire as an example to our children. Is it one of punishment and pessimism or one which acknowledges that individuals are capable of altering their behavior for the benefit of not only themselves but of civilization itself?

Do we want our children to experience a society in which no distinction is made between the riskiest of individuals and those with the lowest chance of repeating a crime? Should we provide a model to our heirs that the seeming brutality of the crime should be matched by the brutality of the offender? In a civilized society offenders who are in treatment and are attempting to change should not be tossed into cages nor forced to wait many months, if not years, to learn their fate.

Criminality was thought, up until the middle years of the last century, to be borne of moral depravity, an aberration and a product of weakness of character. Fortunately, we have come to realize that genetic inheritance (especially of impulse control) combined with a traumatic upbringing (which itself can cause genetic changes through adverse experiences) can render certain people prone to commit sexual crimes. They are not blameless: no court would hear a defense in which the offender implies that his brain made him do it. Nonetheless, we are coming to the realization that sexual offending is not an indelible mark of an immoral and immutable condition.

But we have quite a long road ahead. I am no prophet but it could be likely that future, more progressive societies may look back upon the manner in which we treat criminals as we shudder now at the history of Roman prisoners forced to fight to the death as the penalty of committing a crime. I am hopeful that future texts on this subject will not be as judgmental as those of the past. We are also fortunate to not follow the politics of authoritarian societies which imprison those who express discontent with their leadership or their prevailing religion.

Nonetheless, our criminal justice system is still rooted in punishment and revenge. It remains dismissive of therapeutic-induced change. Such an outlook also makes it difficult for the general public to understand that change and rehabilitation are possible. There remains no question that the conditions of incarceration debase inmates and may contribute to further crime. Concepts of human dignity and freedom hang by fragile threads when we imprison those who pose no harm to their communities. Moreover, the dismissive attitude of many in the criminal justice system toward rehabilitation can be seen as an affront to modern science. Absent a devoted and exhaustive re-configuration of the manner in which sexual offenders are offered rehabilitation, the criminal justice system is a defeat foretold.

Compassionate penal reform would require political changes unlikely in the near future. Legislators are frightened to champion rehabilitation as they risk being seen as "soft" or lenient on sexual offenders as this stance generates few votes. They may be afraid to ask the difficult questions this text raises, fearful of not the answers as much as the consequences. Indeed, many of the proposed solutions noted in Chapter Seven are about as likely as the Pope conferring sainthood on Martin Luther.

Unfortunately, it is not within the capability of the current bipartisan legislative divide that many of these proposals can be achieved. Administrative officials and legislatures appear unable to effect change and, worse, equally unwilling to do so. The criminal justice system fails to differentiate one type of criminal from another, mistakes revenge for justice, and is entirely unsystematic in its application of punishments. It appears that in some cases, this system is beholden to the ignorance and brutality built up over centuries of bias and misunderstanding combined with a blind eye to scientific advances made over the past several decades.

Legislators in particular are moribund when faced with issues surrounding sexual offenders. Justice reforms are ignored with the fear of political self-harm. They appear to prefer the status quo, with its injustices and chaos so apparent to those who experience the results of our present-day criminal justice system: the offenders who suffer its inequities, and their families as well.

In the future, swamped by the prevalence of cases, the entire system may sink if it does not learn to swim in new waters. At present, I fear that this system is too content with itself to invest the energy necessary to change, lazy in its dormancy and lacking the energy to employ science to effect change for the better; it is too complacent and satisfied to nap rather than snap.

Of even greater importance, such a system is doomed to fail in preventing crime because it ignores rehabilitation; indeed, of all aspects of the system, the least amount of funding has been devoted to treatments which could prevent sexual crimes. Yet treatment, proven to be effective in recognized scientific studies, could provide the fuel to accelerate not only a more benign justice system, but a more effective one as well.

This would reverse justice's decline at present exemplified by coercing human beings into unnecessary confinement. The principles manifested by the dearth of funding for sexual offending research has warped the principles of justice in space and time, much akin to a black hole ripping away the foundations upon which a science-based system might succeed if given a chance. I am hopeful that historians of the future do not have to write texts about our justice system as repressive, barbaric, and even worse, ineffective.

Indeed, the DOJ Corrections Division in 2024 stated the need for a more humane approach to reintegration into the community. Unfortunately, this probably represents a tragedy of politically correct bureaucratic hyperbole distilled in the prose of governmental propaganda as anodyne as it is meaningless, as useful as a fork is to eat soup. Such announcements throw a camouflaged net over the System's very real day-to-day operations. Even today, most citizens, and unfortunately many officials within the criminal justice system, consider all sexual offenders to inhabit a human petri dish of deeply infested individuals incapable of reform.

Nonetheless, I am optimistic that a more enlightened and progressive, though gradual, change is in the air. I have interacted with the youth of today's generation, especially its teenagers; therein lies the hope that compassion, understanding, and a more civilized and proportionate justice system will evolve. This would consist of a system more attuned to the rehabilitative ideal. Such a system could apply not only to sexual offenders but also would be commensurate with advances in treatment techniques scientifically proven to reduce recidivism amongst many additional types of offenders, such as those who have committed a single situational or minor nonviolent crime.

Such an enlightened and sophisticated system would be mindful of the humane treatment and fundamental decency of all human beings. It would not abjure incarceration but would neither use it to conceal prisoners out of sight but instead, attempt to learn about their lives, the beneficial and harmful effects they have had upon others (not so dissimilar to ones they and we all have committed), and minimize the limitations on their freedom based on the scientific assessment of their risk to be at large.

If we use the word "Corrections" as an integral part of this System, I would urge courts, DAs and supervisors to think about *correcting* illegal behavior as much, or more, than punishing it. It would employ halfway houses with electronic monitoring such that convicts could pursue their jobs or schooling and ensure that, while incarcerated or in such placements, scientifically proven treatment programs would be made available which can reduce risk. Such a system would enhance the opportunity of all prisoners to benefit from programs of self-improvement, including in-house job training as required. It would also impose upon those in charge of imprisoning others rules of conduct based upon ethical behavior toward individuals under their charge.

Should the criminal justice system continue on its current course, it may find itself behind the arc of history as advances in scientific discovery will persist, flourish, and progress with an improved understanding of the origins of sexual offending. It will hopefully help us learn more about its prevention. The system, as it now stands, is like an exhausted runner quitting halfway in a marathon, not just defeated but staggering and embarrassed. In few other governmental endeavors has the criminal justice system failed to reveal the human drama behind scientific fact. Years of legal jostling have created an atmosphere of stasis and ennui, leaving prisoners to endure the status quo and its ill effects.

Of crucial import, such a system would be based upon the latest proven heuristic research to provide not only punishment but treatment to prevent sexual crimes from reoccurring. We have an obligation to our children and our children's children to show that the rehabilitation of many offenders, but especially low-impact, nonviolent sexual offenders, can be a hallmark of a civilized society.

I obviously lack all, or many, answers to the present deprivations inherent in our criminal justice system, but I hope that some of the solutions proposed here prove helpful. I don't have all the answers but at least I have a purpose. I hold no divine provenance in the Bible, although it is a superbly written text. Those within the criminal justice system should at least bear in mind some of its most prophetic and powerful truths:

> "Judgement is mine sayeth the Lord."
> "Judge not lest ye be judged."
> "Let ye without sin cast the first stone."

In my experience, those who judge sexual offenders the harshest are also those who have the most to hide. The iconic figure of Justice is depicted blind so as to weigh the evidence with impartiality. It should also be a lesson to us that should the criminal justice system be blinded to science it will erode the confidence of its citizens and diminish its potential to fully fulfil its major mission: to reduce the incidence of criminal behavior for the benefit of all society's citizens. Of utmost importance, no criminal justice system can succeed based on punishment alone.

Epilogue

The Long Arm of the Law Does not Reach its Grasp

The criminal justice system does not exist in a vacuum. It is a reflection of the society which informs and enforces it. But we might benefit from viewing it through the lens of evolution, particularly when we focus on the crimes of sexual offenders. Sexual abuse is not unknown in our species' closest relatives:

> Koko, a female ape, at first appears amused by Mbara's approach. This shameless silverback stares at her before exposing his erect penis, while his human scientist cousins take notes at a furious pace; it is not every day observers are privileged to witness such emotionally charged ape behavior. Perhaps their note-taking distracts Mbara as Koko lumbers off into the brush.
>
> Across the continent, Nambuko, a male bonobo, is chased off by several dominant males when he tries to mount Antemba, a young and immature offspring of another male. Later, in the same troop, Antemba is clearly unwilling to allow another male, Ngogo, sexual access; she tries to flee, then attempts, in vain, to fight off the aggressor. She shrieks and tries to push him off but he is too strong. The commotion alerts others in the troop and soon, Antemba's mother, her aunt, and several other female bonobos rush in to push Mbara off the youngster, thus protecting her. (Perhaps a lesson from which humans might learn.) Mbara sulks off into the bush.
>
> Toto, a female chimp, has lost her fetus, who was born with multiple defects. She pokes and probes the infant as if in an attempt to return it to life. A group of other females, including not only her kin but others unrelated to her, approach her. After it becomes clear the infant cannot be resuscitated, the group stays close to the bereaved mother for a number of days to offer support. Yes, this is anthropizing, but it is suspiciously close to how humans would behave under similar circumstances. Could nonhuman primates be capable of rape and sexual abuse? Could they also have the capacity for compassion? We may never know for certain.

DOI: 10.4324/9781003532590-10

What do these African observations have to do with sexual offending? Possibly little; perhaps much. They seem to support a scientific understanding that males in many species, by guile and force, commit sexual crimes. It is doubtful that Ngogo and Nambuko will face what we consider criminal justice. However, they might well be shunned by members of their group or even lose whatever status they once held. Will Antemba suffer from PTSD symptoms? We hope not, but we will probably never know for certain.

The well-springs of sexual offending stem partially from a genetic template, but one gone awry. In addition to this inherited input, adverse experiences in early life may combine in a psychosexual way to reduce impulse control and increase the potential to offend sexually. Moreover, a possible future sexual offender's after-birth traumas can actually alter his DNA. This can produce epigenetic changes which augment a reduction in impulsivity, potential increase in aggression, and a heightened sexual drive. At present, we can only guess. It is only through science that we have any hope of determining the genesis and persistence of much of human behavior. It is also only through scientific experimentation that we have any chance of improving the criminal justice system, thereby reducing recidivism, what I believe should be its main objective.

Evolution can explain, in part, many "illnesses" we psychiatrists attempt to treat (often quite successfully, sometimes less so). Perhaps these disorders originate in very normal fears designed by evolution to keep us safe but are exaggerated by a combination of genetics and circumstance. Thus it is in our best interests to steer clear of snakes and insects which might bring disease (phobias). Women who forage for greens and berries need to be assured they can find their way home; straying too far from the unknown can induce worry in anybody. If certain receptors in the brain are particularly sensitive, some present-day women may even be afraid to leave a safe place (agoraphobia).

To keep free of disease, we clean ourselves and our environments and keep things in good and predictable order; but some who may be extra sensitive, can overreact and fail to keep in check those impulses, even though they realize what they do is unnecessary (OCD). From an evolutionary perspective, panic disorder may stem from barely perceptible breathing rate changes, building up too much CO^2 in the blood stream, thereby causing a panic disorder in those with highly sensitive brain centers monitoring such levels; these alert us (falsely) that we must struggle to breathe.

We are also more sensitive to negative probabilities than positive outcomes: Today, we watch the news to hear about wars rather than to learn of peace; in our distant past, better to believe that it's a lion when the tall savannah waves, rather than the wind.

Such explanations are compelling in the light of new ways of studying not only CNS cellular activity at large but, in a more granular manner, the more than trillion synapses firing within our most complicated and entangled organ. This latter subspecialty in science is called the connectosome. Our brains function through the relatively slow mechanism of electrochemical transmission when compared to a computer, whose transmissions are purely electronic, and hence many millions of times faster than we can manage.

This is but one reason why artificial intelligence is an oxymoron. Computers learn through strengthening correct patterns; while humans do so as well, we also learn, in the main, through modelling and reward and punishment. Lacking a limbic system and a hypothalamus, a computing machine is just that: it cannot experience the emotions associated with pleasure and pain. It also relies largely on what humans believe it should review, essentially limiting AI to what has already occurred. Yet innovation, while often building on former advances, also requires a creative mind unburdened by historical events when appropriate. We can learn much about physics and mathematics and, indeed, all the sciences, through AI, but we cannot, at present, duplicate the emotions which underpin and motivate the vast majority of our actions.

Therefore, we might gain increasing knowledge from observations and experimentation with our closest relatives, the primates; after all, we share over 98% of our DNA with chimps. Animal activists have an interest in protecting these close relatives; I can only argue that we have an obligation, indeed a necessity, to preserve our own species, and can do so without harming others if ethical treatment of experimental subjects is practiced.

It is also instructive to examine the sexual differences between us and our closest relatives. Human males have relatively large penises and less body hair than other primates. Females have mammoth breasts yet this mass is not needed for milk production. Human females also differ sexually from other primates in being able to ignore time – at least when premenopausal – as they are not tied to a menstrual phase but are receptive to, and enjoy, sexual activity throughout any days of the month.

These differences have resulted in elevating visual attraction in humans as opposed to olfactory or biochemical signals in most other species. Thus, at least for a period of early human development, men and women displayed frontal sexual organs (perhaps at least before Adam and Eve), including pubic hair and figural changes, to signal fertility. This may have led to the elimination of the need for chemical signals for sexual arousal. Thereby, sex became an everyday prospect.

Unfortunately, sexual activity is held to be a private and even, in many religious eyes, an evil-intentioned interaction lest Adam lose his fig leaf and Eve refuse to conceal her sexual features. Thus sexual offenses are often considered more notorious in severity than other crimes. Indeed, because sex is regarded as a covert event, concealed from the general population, even from friends and family members, it is a silent, unmentionable, and furtive pursuit with a tinge of immorality and even a slightly sinful aura.

This is most evident in Middle Eastern countries, in which women are commanded to veil any gender-revealing parts of their bodies by wearing coverings, like the Hijab. Even feminine characteristics, such as long hair, must be masked lest they create arousal amongst males. The origin of such dictates, not often considered, lies in the fear that men and boys cannot control their lust and that women must not flaunt their sexuality. In point of fact, the Quran only mentions that both men and women simply dress "in a moderate fashion."

Many of the differences between male and female mating strategies can be understood within an evolutionary framework. Females are limited in producing offspring by gestational period, pregnancy and menopause; males would be more interested in partner variety in order to spread their genes more widely. Males would therefore be less invested in a long-term relationship and more prone to jealousy while females would bring more commitment to a union and would be more particular in choosing a mate based upon his ability to provide and protect their offspring. It is of interest that the peak times of relationships dissolving are at three and seven years. In prehistoric times, it took three years to raise a single child to the point at which two parents were no longer a necessity. With two children, that period extended to seven years.

Can such paleopsychology inform us about anything related to sexual offending? Perhaps. All male nonhuman primates display erections before attempting to mount a female; exhibitionism is among the most common of human sexual crimes. While pedophilia is rare among chimps and apes, it is seen in nondominant males who lose competitions to stronger males. Sexual aggression is common in apes, though it is rarely successful. Among humans, juveniles may be sexually attractive to some male adults (who did not raise them from birth) due to the phenomenon of stimulus generalization, especially as girls attain the beginnings of secondary sexual characteristics.

Although politically fraught with labelling, it also makes sense that males are more aggressive and women more passive during sexual activity. This is never universal as roles can often change. Such topics are rarely discussed and are even less likely to be the subject of research. It's a pity that we shun discussions and research about sexuality as so much more could be learned. Indeed, biological factors combined with life experiences are within the capacity of scientific experimentation. Such complex behaviors are assuredly multidetermined and demand a host of studies across a wide variety of scientific domains. Unfortunately, politics and religion render funding such studies dormant.

Descending from leafy branches to a world of savannahs may have shaped our physiognomy and enhanced our brain power, but could not erase all genetic forces shaping our behavior. Those ancient and aggressive elements of masculine sexuality, especially in their darker and forceful shades, persist today but, because we have evolved the ability to remember the past and predict the likely outcome of our actions, and aided by a greater ability for impulse control, most of us have been able to resist sexual temptations, especially those which we realize may have harmful and legal consequences. It is nonetheless of more than casual interest to recognize that the forerunners of misaligned passions reside in phylogenetic templates for male aggression in the service of sexual access. Attempting to unhook all our links to our progenitors in the animal kingdom would constitute a costly deceit.

Paraphilias are loveless. At times, this may occur because the offender wishes to avoid interaction and intimacy. Therefore, child molestation can be seen as a misplaced passion. It is possible, but unknowable at present, whether many men harbor some tendencies toward mild exhibitionism, though well-checked. Certainly, many men moving into cohabitation with teenage girls they did not raise from birth might well entertain sexual fantasies about them. It is encouraging that most would not act upon such impulses. In this quest, we cannot shrink from inquiry, even if the answers are not especially tasteful. It is likely that most men harbor idiosyncratic fantasies others might find disturbing or bizarre. Were we privy to every man's (and woman's) innermost fantasies, some of which might be actually illegal then it is propitious that most would never actualize them in real life.

Our actions are not completely controlled by our genes. Our behavior is not predicted by our DNA in isolation as genetics are rarely imperative when determining complex behavior; we have the capacity to create and enforce rules of conduct. Even if biologic factors figure into the etiologic equation, no human behavior is based solely upon a relative's genotype; none is excusable because of a biologic predisposition. Other primates lack a criminal justice system; we do not. Yet ours is almost as primitive as mankind's earliest attempts at enacting justice. A civilized society would show empathy and compassion toward even those at the lowest rung on the ladder of social acceptability.

Spokesmen for our criminal justice system make grand pronouncements about progress in the treatment of those who have broken the law: words spoken as a masquerade, a camouflage of what occurs in real life. Politicians and administrators tout progress within the system and point to new facilities, an increase in the numbers of police in communities, and the technological advances in policing techniques. Nonetheless, legislators' silence in matters of sexual offense regulation bespeaks cowardice combined with blindness to the advances achieved in the science of assessing and treating sexual offenders. They have allowed prejudice to trump prudence and prefer ritual over reality.

These proudly announced plans often morph into vanity projects, although enhanced policing along with more police involved in their communities is to be welcomed and has probably reduced certain types of crime, though not sexual offending. Such offending remains largely unchanged over the past decade while other types of crimes have been curtailed. This represents a national disgrace, especially when compared with other countries which boast much lower rates of sexual offending. Such "advances" have a long, rough and bumpy road ahead; unhappily, at the end of such roads most often lies a mirror, reflecting back what has gone before: the past lack of progress in enacting the rehabilitative process is promised but it rarely is delivered.

Spend time actually experiencing the system specifically related to sexual crimes, however, to grasp and realize the system's iniquities and inequalities. Correcting these will require attention to the science of criminal behavior, and adaptation to its findings. Placing greater emphasis on rehabilitation in a more civilized and future society depends on the insights which only science can provide. The famous scientist, Louis Pasteur, spoke most eloquently in writing, "Science and peace will triumph over ignorance...to build a future that will belong to those who have done the most for suffering humanity." We should and can go a step beyond our primate progenitors: change, humility, benevolence, compassion, choice and control are not distinctly human traits; they just should be more so.

Appendix A

A List of Common Abbreviations

AA	Alcoholics Anonymous
ADHD	attention deficit hyperactivity disorder
ATSA	The Association for the Treatment of Sexual Abusers
CNS	central nervous system (the brain)
CP	child pornography
CPO	child pornography-only offender
DA	district attorney
DHS	Department of Human Services, Child Welfare Division
DOJ	Department of Justice
EEG	electroencephalograph
EMDR	eye movement desensitization and reprocessing therapy
ERP	event-related potentials in certain brain areas
NCMEC	National Center for Missing and Exploited Children
OCD	obsessive-compulsive disorder
OUR	Operation Underground Railroad
PO	parole officer or probation officer. "Parole officer" is an older term for a supervisor for offenders following release from prison, now referred to as a PPS.
PPS	post-prison supervisor
PTSD	post-traumatic stress disorder
R&J	"Romeo and Juliet" offenses (those involving a male, usually under the age of 25, engaging in sexual activity with an underage teen female)
SO	sexual offender (occasionally used when repeatedly referenced, such as in Chapter Seven; but, for easier readability, the full term is often written out completely)

Appendix B

Common Restrictions Placed on Sexual Offenders Following a Plea Arrangement, Sentencing or Release from Incarceration: An Abbreviated List

Notes: "Supervisor" herein refers to the offender's PO or PPS. Grammar is as listed on the actual form.

1 Curfew established by the PO or PPS
2 No contact with anyone under the age of 18 (biological children included) absent supervisor's permission and a safety plan in place
3 Prohibited from presence at any location where children might congregate
4 Prohibited against being in a place intended for children, including a school, daycare center, park or playground
5 Prohibited from working in or attending a school at which children might be present
6 Entry into and successful graduation from a sexual offender treatment program approved by the supervising officer; the offender is responsible for all costs of such, including polygraphs and a variety of other tests.
7 Prohibited with direct or indirect contact with the victim except if approved by the victim, therapist, and supervisor
8 Prohibited from viewing, listening to, owning or possessing sexually stimulating visual or auditory materials relevant to the person's deviant behavior, except as required by treatment
9 Consent to a search of the person, vehicle or residence if the supervisor believes a violation has occurred
10 Participation in random polygraph examinations; the offender is required to pay for all such examinations.
11 Prohibition of driving a vehicle alone and maintenance of a driving log if permission is granted by a supervising officer
12 Prohibition of using a post office box
13 Prohibition against living in a dwelling in which another sexual offender resides
14 No access to computing devices, smart phones, tablets or smart TVs; random unannounced examinations of such devices are within the province of the supervising officer.

General conditions of all offenders, sexual or otherwise, also apply:

1 Pay all court fees, fines, restitution and other fees ordered by the court
2 No use or possession of controlled substances unless ordered by a physician
3 Submit to testing for controlled substances or alcohol use
4 Participate in substance abuse counselling, if directed by the supervising officer
5 Remain in the State of Oregon until written permission is granted by the supervising officer to leave
6 Find and maintain gainful employment, approved schooling, or a combination of both
7 No change of employment or residence without prior permission of the supervisor
8 Permit the supervising officer to visit the offender at his residence and workplace and complete a walk-through of same
9 Consent to a search of person, vehicle or residence should the supervisor have grounds to believe that evidence of a violation might be found
10 Submit to fingerprinting when requested by the supervising officer
11 Obey all laws, municipal, county, state and federal
12 Promptly and truthfully answer all reasonable inquiries by corrections officials
13 No possession of weapons, firearms or dangerous animals
14 Report to the supervisor as directed
15 Submit to a risk and needs assessment as directed by the supervising officer and follow all reasonable recommendations resulting from the assessment
16 Remain under the supervision of the Department of Corrections and its representatives
17 Be under the supervision of the Department of Corrections and abide by their directions and counsel

To be fair, many of these directives are modified by a supervising officer to fit the individual differences of each offender. In addition, while in reality the supervising officer is responsible for ensuring compliance with these directives, the rules commonly mention The Department of Corrections and "the Board" (the supervising officer's board overseeing her or his work) as also responsible. In practice, it is almost always the offender's supervisory officer who is in charge of making certain these restrictions are followed.

Moreover, as written, these directives appear more restrictive and harsher than they eventually turn out to be. Most supervisors tailor restrictions to the specific crime committed. As trust is built up between the offender and the officer, he may be permitted supervised visits with biological children. In other cases, an offender may be permitted to use an electronic device for school, although it must be monitored through customized porn-blocking programs and be accessible to the officer.

As time progresses and the offender has established a reasonable relationship with his supervising officer, he may be permitted the use of electronics, usually with monitoring. He may also be allowed to attend more family gatherings and, with permission, to travel out of state. In a few cases, family reconciliation can occur with family meetings approved by the supervisor, members of the family, the client's therapist and the victim's therapist.

Bibliography

Child Pornography and Other Internet Sexual Crimes

Adler, A. (2001). The perverse law of child pornography. *Columbia Law Review*, 209, 1–101. *Comments:* A review of how men are attracted to child porn (CP) and the difference between those who are attracted to children and those who were merely curious – CP only offenders (CPO).

Aslan, D., & Edelmann, R. (2014). Demographic and offender characteristics: A comparison of sex offenders convicted of possessing indecent images of children, committing contact sex offences, or both offences. *The Journal of Forensic Psychiatry and Psychology*, 25, 121–134. *Comments:* Increased rate of arrests for CP yet decrease in sexual offending overall. Contact offenders had an increase in sexual and physical abuse as children and often required mental health treatment.

Baartz, D. (2018). *Australians, the internet and technology enabled child sex abuse: Its statistical profile.* Canberra, Australia: Australian Federal Police. *Comments:* CPO offenders in a follow-up study revealed a 2% rate of recidivism – among the highest ever recorded. A problem was the inclusion of several men who had anti-social histories and a number who had a history of hands-on offenses.

Babschishin, K.M., Hanson, R.K., & VanZuylen, H. (2015). Online child pornography offenders are different: A meta-analysis of the characteristics of online and offline sex offenders against children. *Archives of Sexual Behavior*, 44, 45–66. *Comments:* Recidivism risk of 2.6%, but in a mixed group of offenders with and without prior sexual offenses. A review of the raw data indicates a 0.1% re-offense rate in CPO offenders.

Beech, A., Elliott, J.A., Birgden, A., & Findlater, D. (2008). The Internet and child sexual offending: A criminological review. *Aggression and Violent Behavior*, 13, 216–228. *Comments:* CPO offenders may have acted out of curiosity. Re-offense rates low but data could not be analyzed for CPO offenders as a separate group. Resources are stretched for law enforcement personnel.

Bergen, E., Ahto, A., Schultz, A., Imhoff, R., Antfolk, J., Schumann, P., & Amelung, T. (2015). Adult–adult and adult–child/adolescent online sexual interactions: An exploratory self-report study on the role of situational factors. *The Journal of Sex Research*, 52, 1006–1016. *Comments:* "The internet may serve as a facilitator of social relationships or a means of emotional regulation…amplifying positive emotions while alleviating negative emotions." Treatment was helpful in the community on mental health issues which could have increased the risk of recidivism if left unaddressed.

Buschman, J., & Bogaerts, S. (2009). Polygraph testing internet offenders. In D. Wilcox (Ed.) *The use of the polygraph in assessing, treating, and supervising sexual offenders: A practitioner's guide* (pp. 111–126). Chichester, England: Wiley-Blackwell. *Comments:* CPO offenders had 0% recidivism.

Caple, T. (2008). *A comparison of the characteristics and motivations of abusing and non-abusing child pornography offenders.* (Doctoral dissertation). James Cook University, Townsville, Queensland, Australia. *Comments:* Zero recidivism in non-abusing CPO offenders with no priors.

Clevenger, S.L., Navarro, J.N., & Jasinski, J.L. (2016). A matter of low self-control? Exploring differences between child pornography possessors and child pornography producers/distributors using self-control theory. *Sexual Abuse: A Journal of Research and Treatment*, 28, 555–574. *Comments:* Few similarities between CP possessors and CP producers/distributors. The latter had reduced self-control, increased substance abuse, and an increased history of violence. Possessors had greater marital problems, but greater job stability. "Merely consuming CP alone was not a risk factor for engaging in a contact offense."

Dazelon, E. (2013). Passive pedophiles: Are CP viewers less dangerous than we thought? *Slate Magazine*. Retrieved from: http://www.slate.com. *Comments:* Child pornography viewers are not likely to reoffend except by revisiting child porn sites. CP offenders not broken down into CP vs CPO offenders.

Diamond, M., Jozifkovia, E., & Weiss, (2019). Pornography and sex crimes in the Czech Republic. *Archives of Sexual Behavior*, 40, 1037–1043. *Comments:* Internet sexual crimes are increasing while non-sexual offending crime rates are decreasing.

Eke, A.W., & Seto, M.C. (2009). Ontario Sex Offender Registry Sample independent of police case samples. Unpublished raw data. Google Scholar. *Comments:* Zero percent recidivism in CPO offenders.

Elliott, I.A., Beech, A.R., & Mandeville-Norden, R. (2012). Psychological profiles of internet, contact, and mixed internet/contact sex offenders. *Sexual Abuse: A Journal of Research and Treatment*, 25, 3–10. *Comments:* Zero risk for CPO offenders. ["There were] too few instances of targeted sexual offending for any reliable statistical analysis…." Correctional treatment programs are unlikely to achieve [any further] reduction in recidivism…"

Elliott, I.A., Beech, A.R., & Mandeville-Norden, R. (2009). Psychological profiles of internet sexual offenders: Comparisons with contact sexual offenders. *Sexual Abuse: A Journal of Research and Treatment*, 21, 76–92. *Comments:* All internet offenders were better educated and more stable, but with anxiety and depression compared to contact offenders. One problem was that the study did not isolate men who committed CPO crimes from those who had committed other sexual internet infractions.

Endrass, J., Urbaniok, F., Hammermeister, L.C., Benz, C., Elbert, T, Laubacher, A., & Rosseger, A. (2009). The consumption of internet child pornography, violence and sex offending. *British Medical Journal, Psychiatry*, 9, Article 43. *Comments:* Data from 2,598 state, county, and local law enforcement agencies with over 2,000 cases specifically reviewed. Combined recidivism of 2.9% for a group of mixed offenders. CPO offenders had a lower incidence of sexual abuse as children, achieved greater job and relationship stability, and demonstrated increased self-control. Recidivism rate of CPO offenders was 0.9%, but this included some who had committed nonsexual crimes.

Faust, E., Bickart, W., Renaud, C., & Camp, S. (2015). Child pornography possessors and child contact sex offenders: A multilevel comparison of demographic characteristics and rates of recidivism. *Sexual Abuse: A Journal of Research and Treatment*, 15, 460–478. *Comments:* Mixed group (N=638); 428 CPO offenders were older than child contact offenders; were almost always employed; fewer were married; the vast majority had less substance abuse; had achieved higher education; and were less frequently abused as children. Recidivism rate for CPO offenders was 0.9%. Treatment should address intimacy skills. Some entered treatment voluntarily.

Gillespie, S.M., Bailey, A., Squire, T., Carey, M.L., Eldridge, H.J., & Beech, J.R. (2018). An evaluation of a community-based psycho-educational program for users of child sexual exploitation materials. *Sexual Abuse: A Journal of Research and Treatment*, 30, 169–191. *Comments:* N=192. "Child sexual exploitation material users are amenable to treatment in the community. There exists a distinct subgroup of online-only sexual offenders who pose a relatively low risk of contact sexual offending." CPO offenders showed lower self-esteem, greater depression, increased interpersonal problems, and decreased cognitive distortions. "The majority of online-only offenders pose a low risk of committing any new offense, or a new sexual offense in particular." Treatment led to a decrease in depression and anxiety, improved social competency, enhanced self-esteem, an increase in cognitive control, and an improvement in social skills. Follow-up in a group of 92 participants over a 12-week period showed that positive results were maintained. Authors noted that anxiety and stress might have been due to the police investigation and consequent legal difficulties. CPO offenders may have been trying to "alleviate negative emotions." Breaking down the raw data showed a zero re-offense rate for CPO offenders.

Henshaw, M., Ogloff, J.R.P., & Clough, J.A. (2017). Looking beyond the screen: A critical review of the literature on the online child pornography offender. *Sexual Abuse: A Journal of Research and Treatment*, 29, 416–445. *Comments:* CPO offenders were more "prosocial," higher functioning, and had more affective problems. Present tools proved not to be appropriate to assess risk. CPO offenders present "too low a risk to measure. CPO offenders' motivation was primarily curiosity." Results showed that they had a decreased history of sexual and physical abuse, less substance abuse, and less criminal history. They suffered emotional loneliness, under-assertiveness, and passivity. They also had lower self-esteem. "CPO offenders may represent a distinct group of offenders who differ from traditional contact sexual offenders. They are higher functioning and successful in life...though less successful in relationships." "Engaging in CPO offending does not inevitably lead to the direct sexual victimization of children." Over a four-year follow-up, CPO offenders had a zero per cent re-offense rate. "CPO offenders are not likely to require extensive intervention...[they are more] likely to require targeted interventions to increase victim awareness." Education for empathy and exploitation are recommended.

Howitt, D., & Shelton, K. (2007). The role of cognitive distortions in pedophilic offending: Internet and contact offenders compared. *Psychology, Crime, and Law*, 13, 469–486. *Comments:* Significantly more cognitive distortions were detected in contact offenders.

Jung, S., & Stein, S. (2012). An examination of judicial sentencing decisions in child pornography and child molestation cases in Canada. *Journal of Criminal Psychology*, 2, 38–50. *Comments:* Prison sentences were uncommon for CP possession but often given if distribution was included.

Kloess, J.A., Woodhams, H.W., Grant, T., & Hamilton-Giachritsis, C.E. (2019). The challenges of identifying and classifying child abuse material. *Sexual Abuse*, 31, 173–196. *Comments:* This article demonstrates that even among law enforcement officers, uncertainty exists and debates were frequent about what actually constitutes child pornography. Photos and videos of so-called "child pornography" showed individuals whose ages were ambiguous. In reality, many were adults and not children.

Krone, T. (2004). *A typology of online child pornography offending*. Canberra, Australia: Australian Institute of Criminology. *Comments:* Reduced risk was noted in CPO cases; probability of re-offense could only be estimated at less than 1%.

Krone, T. (2004). Typology of online child pornography offending: Trends and issues. *Crime and Criminal Justice*, 279, 1–6. *Comments:* CPO offenders had low rates of recidivism, but the exact rate was unspecified.

Long, M.L., Alison, L.A., & McManus, M.A. (2013). Child pornography and likelihood of contact abuse: A comparison between contact sexual offenders and non-contact offenders. *Sexual Abuse: A Journal of Research and Treatment*, 25, 370–395. *Comments:* N=120, 60 of each type. CPO offenders had a history of less criminality, less access to children, but an increased number of CP images. Dual offenders with a history of sexual attraction to children and CP had increased access to children, lived with women who had children, had an increase in criminal convictions for nonsexual offenses, mostly viewed female children, had increased cognitive distortions, befriended children in the neighborhood, had an increased number of stranger victims, showed grooming behavior, and were more predatory. CPO offenders showed more time spent viewing pornography. "Prolonged engagement [in all forms of pornography] leads to satiation and habituation." CPOs may have an increase in curiosity rather than a desire to actually molest a child. No recidivism data included.

Meridan, H.L., Curtis, C., Thakker, J., Wilson, N., & Boer, D.P. (2013). The three dimensions of child online pornography offending. *Journal of Sexual Aggression*, 19, 121–132. *Comments:* Clear distinction between CPO offenders and hands-on sexual offenders. Recidivism rate for CPO offenders was 0%. CPOs were older, which might have reduced risk by itself.

Mitchell, K.J., Jones, L.M., Finkelhor, D., & Wolak, J. (2011). Internet-facilitated sexual exploitation of children from a nationally representative sample of law enforcement agencies in the United States. *Sexual Abuse: A Journal of Research and Treatment*, 23, 43–71. *Comments:* Survey of 2,598 local, county, and state law enforcement agencies. Those who only purchased CP with no sexual priors and no history of violence numbered 1,051 cases. They showed greater stability in relationships, higher levels of educational attainment, and fewer prior nonsexual arrests (11%). Among the mixed sample, 9% of possessors were registered sexual offenders at the time of the CP offense; 4% had a history of violence; and 13% had a history of substance abuse. No breakdown of CP vs CPO subtypes was offered.

Nunes, K.L., Babchishin, K.M., & Cortoni, F. (2011). Measuring treatment change in sexual offenders: Clinical and statistical significance. *Criminal Justice and Behavior*, 38, 157–173. *Comments:* Community-based treatment was effective in child pornography cases. CPO offenders showed 0% recidivism in a one-year follow-up.

Oliver, M.E., Kingston, D.A., Nicholaichuk, T.P., & Wong, S.C. (2014). A psychometric examination of treatment change in a multiple sample of treated Canadian Federal sexual offenders. *Law and Human Behavior*, 38, 544–559. *Comments:*

Community-based treatment was effective in reducing recidivism to 0% over the long-term for CPO offenders.

Osborn, J., Elliott, I.A., Middleton, D., & Beech, A.R. (2010). The use of actuarial risk assessment measures with United Kingdom internet child pornography offenders. *The Journal of Sexual Aggression, Conflict, and Peace Research*, 2, 16–24. *Comments:* CPO offenders were older and showed greater job and relationship stability. Standard tests were of some help in distinguishing CPO offenders, who had zero recidivism.

Quale, E., & Taylor, M. (2022). Child pornography and the internet: Perpetuating the cycle of abuse. *Deviant Behavior*, 23, 331–362. *Comments:* This study involved a large number of mixed sexual offenders in Switzerland but found that only a few CPO offenders proceeded to commit an actual sexual offense of any type. They also noted that CPO offenders comprise "a different group" of individuals who are better educated and hold higher-salary positions in their employment, although they also note such CPO men also had a higher incidence of watching porn involving animals and violence.

Ray, J.V., Kimonis, E.R., & Seto, M. (2014). Correlates and moderators of child pornography consumption in a community sample. *Sexual Abuse: A Journal of Research and Treatment*, 26, 523–545. *Comments:* N=297. Online anonymous survey targeting Sex Addicts Anonymous and pedophile forums about problematic porn use. CPO offenders engaged mainly "out of curiosity." "Viewing child pornography is not a strong risk factor for recidivism." "Difficulty achieving intimacy with consenting adults may lead some individuals to child pornography consumption."

Riegel, D.L. (2014). Effects on boy-attracted pedosexual males of viewing boy erotica. *Archives of Sexual Behavior*, 321–323. A different sample, composed of homosexual pedophiles, was asked whether watching CP increased their desire to molest boys. Of surprise, 84.5% of the sample replied "rarely or never."

Savoie, V., Quayle, E., Flynn, E., & O'Rourke, S. (2022). Predicting risk of reoffending in persons with child sexual exploitation material offense histories: The use of the Child Pornography Offender Risk Tool in a Scottish population. *Sexual Abuse*, 34, 568–596. *Comments:* The CPORT test validated the CPO offenders' reoffense rate of 0.25%.

Sentencing Advisory Panel (2002). The panel's advice to the Court of Appeals on offences involving child pornography. (Crown copyright). Retrieved from http://www.sentencing-guidleines. The panel's advice to the Court of Appeals on offenses involving child pornography. (Crown copyright). Comments: Draconian penalties are being imposed on CPO offenders without regard to risk of recidivism.

Seto, M.C., & Hanson, R.K. (2011). Introduction to the special issue on internet-facilitated sexual offending. *Sexual Abuse: A Journal of Research and Treatment*, 23, 3–6. *Comments:* Comments about a review of the CP literature. A meta-analysis found 4.6% recidivism in a mixed group of CP offenders. "The same laws have also captured relatively low-risk individuals who may never have overtly expressed their interest in children or sexual coercion." "There appears to be a subset of individuals convicted of internet child pornography offenses who have few other indicators of criminal behavior and who show low to zero rates of sexual or general recidivism."

Seto, M.C., Hanson, R.K., & Babchishin, K.M. (2011). Contact sexual offending by men with online sexual offenses. *Sexual Abuse: A Journal of Research and*

Treatment, 23, 124–145. *Comments:* Re-offense rate of the mixed group was 3.6% but many had prior sexual crimes. Six years follow-up showed re-offense rate of CP possessors was 2%, but several had committed a prior contact sexual offense. "There may be a distinct subgroup of online-only offenders who pose a relatively low risk of committing contact sexual offenses in the future."

Smid, W., Schepers, K., Kamphuis, J.H., van Linden, S., & Bartling, S. (2015). Prioritizing child pornography notification: Predicting direct victimization. *Sexual Abuse: A Journal of Research and Treatment*, 27, 398–413. *Comments:* N=150 police files in the Netherlands. "Child pornography notification creates capacity problems for police forces." CPO offenders had no prior criminal histories. Governments invested heavily in the need to conduct thorough and exhaustive electronic searches. Dual offenders with priors showed a greater re-offense rate than CPO offenders. A separate study within the same report involved 485 sexual offender subjects. Only three re-offended and all were repeat CPs. There were no hands-on repeat offenses. The re-offense rate for CPO offenders was 0.007%. Dual or mixed offenders showed unstable work histories, increased antisocial behavior, greater impulsivity, and more prior sexual offenses. In a second evaluation of mixed offenders, the re-offense rate was 0.05%. The best indicator of recidivism was a history of a past sexual offense. This accounted for 90% of the variance. CPO offenders had "no indication of greater antisociality/impulsivity." "CP-only offenders might be more voyeuristically interested in pornographic images involving children...and may be unlikely to seek out sexual contact with children in real life."

Soldino, V., Carbonell-Vaya, E.J., & Seigfried-Spellar, K.C. (2021). Spanish validation of the Child Pornography Offender Risk Tool. *Sexual Abuse*, 33, 503–528. *Comments:* Calibration analysis in this five-year study noted recidivism rates were much lower than expected in this Spanish sample of CP users. CPO offenders had a re-offense rate of zero as opposed to a 2% rate among other offenders. "None of the 255 CPO offenders were re-arrested" or even charged with any further contact sexual offense nor any other type of sexual or criminal offense.

United States Sentencing Commission (2009). The history of child pornography guidelines. Retrieved from:http://www.1b9.uscourts.gov/websites/11documents/Henderson_History.pdf. *Comments*: A number of lengthy prison sentences were handed down to CPO offenders.

Victoria Police (2014). Offenses recorded by offense code 2004/05–2013/14 [data file]. Retrieved from http://www.police.vic.gov.au/content.asp?a=internetbridging. Page & Media ID=72209. *Comments*: Sexual offending rates are decreasing overall, yet CP charges have increased.

Wakeling, H.C., Howard, P., & Barnett, G. (2011). Comparing the validity of RM 2000 scales and OGRS3 for predicting recidivism by internet sexual offenders. *Sexual Abuse: A Journal of Research and Treatment*, 23, 146–168. *Comments:* (N=1,326). "The majority of online CPO offenders posed a low risk of committing any new sexual offense." Re-offense rates were very low among the entire sample. Three quarters of sexual reoffending were internet-related offenses. All assessment tools had moderate to very good predictive accuracy. This was a mixed group and the authors believed standard assessment tools could predict who would re-offend. "The very low rate of internet specialists made statistical comparisons difficult. In a mixed group of 690 cases, 11 (1.6%) re-offended and those re-offenses were internet-related only.

Webb, L., Craissati, J., & Keen, S. (2007). Characteristics of internet child pornography offenders: A comparison with child molesters. *Sexual Abuse: A Journal of Research and Treatment*, 19, 449–465. *Comments:* Recidivism rate of 2–3%, but some CP offenders had priors. A re-examination of the data revealed that if no priors were separated out from the general population, a re-offense rate would have been less than 2%. CPO offenders were older and had greater job and relationship stability.

Wells, M., Finkelhor, D., Wolak, J., & Mitchell, K.J. (2007). Defining child pornography: Law enforcement dilemmas in investigations of internet child pornography possession. *Police Practice and Research*, 8, 269–282. *Comments:* Resources for varying definitions of CP offenders are increasing, with large amounts allotted to CPO offenders.

Winerip, M. (2020). Convicted of sex crimes, but with no victims. *New York Times Sunday Magazine*, 36. www.nytimes.com/2020//magazine-net-nanny.html. *Comments:* This article offers a number of case studies and legal arguments against entrapment cases.

Wolak, J., Finkelhor, D., & Mitchell, K.J. (2005a). Child pornography possessors arrested in internet-related crimes: Findings from the National Juvenile Online Victimization Study (NCJ No. 210701). Retrieved from http://www.missingkids.com/en_US/publications. *Comments*: Juveniles viewing child pornography had a very low rate of recidivism for sexual crimes – approximately 0.03%.

Wolak, J., Finkelhor, D., & Mitchell, K.J. (2011). Child pornography possessors: Trends in offender and case characteristics. *Sexual Abuse: A Journal of Research and Treatment*, 23, 22–42. *Comments:* N=1,034 mixed CP offenders; 69% went to prison and 83% are on the registry. "Few are known to have committed previous sex crimes." Especially low risk were those who were not using peer-to-peer networks. "More offenders were sentenced to incarceration and were serving longer sentences than in 2000." One in six (9%) of CP cases had molested children before. "There has not been a spike in the rate of child sexual abuse that corresponds with the apparent expansion of online CP."

Wollert, R., Waggoner, J., & Smith, J. (2009). Child pornography offenders do not have florid offense histories and are unlikely to recidivate. Paper presented at the Paper presented at the 28th Annual Conference of The Association for the Treatment for Sexual Abusers. Dallas, TX. *Comments*: N = 72. Zero percent recidivism amongst CPO offenders.

Wood, J.M., Seto, M.C., Flynn, S, Wilson-Cotton, S., & Dedmon, P. (2009). "Is it 'just' pictures?" The use of polygraphs with internet offenders who deny abusive sexual contact. Paper presented at the 28th Annual Conference of The Association for the Treatment of Sexual Abusers, Dallas, TX. Comments: Zero percent recidivism for CPO offenders.

Wortele, S.K., Simons, D.A., & Moreno, T. (2014). Sexual interest in children among an online sample of men and women: Prevalence and correlates. *Sexual Abuse: A Journal of Research and Treatment*, 26, 546–568. *Comments:* N=262 women and 173 men. Nine percent of men and 3 percent of women "indicated some likelihood" of viewing child pornography. Authors believed that some of the observers might have been viewing teens.

Age of Consent Laws

Beck, V.S., & Boys, S. (2012). Romeo and Juliette: Star crossed lovers or sex offenders? *Criminal Justice Policy Review*, 24, 655–675. *Comments:* "The majority of citizens polled in California and Wisconsin do not support the age of consent laws...where two teenagers have engaged in consensual sexual behavior."

Bierie, D.M. (2018). Statutory rape. *World Research On-Line. Comments*: As age differences increase there is an increasing chance for future sexual crimes. Age differences of three to six years lead to no future sexual crimes.

Bierie, D.M., & Budd, K.M. (2018). Romeo, Juliette, and statutory rape. *Sexual Abuse*, 30, 296–321. *Comments:* Review of 6,000 police departments over 20 years; statutory rape cases were rare: Romeo and Juliette cases even more so. Exact figures unavailable.

Carpentier, M., Silovski, J.F., & Chaffin, M. (2006). Randomized trial for children with sexual behavior problems: Ten-year follow-up. *Journal of Consulting and Clinical Psychology*, 74, 482–488. *Comments:* Just 2% of juvenile sexual offenders in Romeo and Juliette cases reoffended sexually or otherwise.

Chert, R., Braslow, L., & Srinivasa, V. (2005). Statutory rape laws are too strictly enforced. Taubman Center for Public Policy, Brown University, December 7, 2005, 8–15. *Comments:* "Statutory rape laws may criminalize young love."

Henry, M.D.& Cunningham, S. (2010). Do statutory rape laws work? *Proceedings of the CELS 2009 Fourth Annual Conference on Empirical Legal Studies*, paper available at www.business.baylor.edu/scott_cummingham/research_files/statrape10.pdf. *Comments:* "Current laws make outcasts of these low-risk offenders. Despite these laws teen pregnancies are declining."

James, S. (2009). Romeo and Juliette were sex offenders: An analysis of the age of consent and a call for reform. *University of Missouri – Kansas City, Law Review*, 78, 241–250. *Comments:* Many teens with close-in-age sexual behaviors pose little to no danger to the public.

Kloess, J.A., Hamilton-Giachritsis, C.E., & Beech, A.R. (2019). Offense processes of online sexual grooming and abuse of children via internet communication platforms. *Sexual Abuse*, 31, 73–96. *Comments*: N = only 5, but of interest, only 2 engaged in grooming behaviors. "The majority of the interactions...were found to be a direct approach." Victims were between 5 and 11 years of age." Most online perpetrators were apparently not interested in a hands-on sexual crime but appeared to be aroused simply by the electronic communications.

Meier, A.M. (2007). Adolescents' first sex and subsequent mental health. *American Journal of Sociology*, 112, 1811–1847. *Comments:* The age of first sex is not correlated with later mental health. No adverse effects were seen secondary to the age of first sex, frequency of sexual encounters, or age difference if within six years.

Middleton, J.F., Mandeville-Norton, R., & Hayes, E. (2009). Does treatment work with internet sex offenders? Emerging findings from the internet sexual offender treatment programme (i-SOTP). *Journal of Sexual Aggression*, 15, 5–19. *Comments:* Internet communicators involving those over 18 with those under 18 were involved in sexual offender-specific treatment centers. A low rate of reoffending was found in which the age difference of the male exceeded that of the female by at least 9 years.

Nickel, M. (2005). This study evaluated criminal justice handling of statutory rape cases. Taubman Center for Public Policy, Brown University, December 7, 2005, 1–7. *Comments:* There exist wide variations in how differing jurisdictions mete out justice in such cases. Penalties varied across a broad spectrum of possibilities.

Norman-Eady, S. (2003). Statutory rape in the New England states. OLR Research Report, R-0149, 1–6. *Comments:* In many states, age of consent differs by as much as four years, from 14 to 18.

Nunziato, D.C. (2012). Romeo and Juliet online and in trouble: Criminalizing depictions of teen sexuality. *Northwestern Journal of Technology and Intellectual Property*, 57, 56–91. *Comments:* Sexting between teens could lead to charges of *Luring*, and *Communicating with a Minor for Immoral Purposes*. Cases should only should be punishable if no consent existed or if sharing sexually explicit images occurred without consent.

Olszewski, D. (2006). Statutory rape in Wisconsin: History, rationale, and the need for reform. *Marquette Law Review*, 89, 693–700. *Comments:* "Decriminalization could be tied to brief educational programs. We should encourage prosecutors to use rehabilitation (such as educational classes) instead of punishment."

Patchin, J.W., & Hinduja, S. (2020). Sextortion among adolescents: Results from a National Survey of U.S. youth. *Sexual Abuse*, 32, 30–54. *Comments:* N=5,568 middle and high school students. Approximately 5% reported that they had been the victims of sextortion, defined by electronic dissemination of explicit, intimate or embarrassing images of a sexual nature. Males were more likely to target others but, surprisingly, were also more likely to be targeted themselves. "It appears that youth simply do not have much confidence in the ability of parents, educators, law enforcement or other authority figures to meaningfully assist or support them." Those who work with youth were called upon to educate students about the risks associated with sharing explicit materials online and stressing their availability to assist them if they are thus victimized.

Pritchard, J., Worthley, R., Watters, P.A., Spiranovic, C., Hunn, C., & Krone, T. (2022). Effects of internet users attempting to access "barely legal" pornography. *Sexual Abuse*, 34, 106–124. *Comments:* N=419 adult males responding to a "barely legal" porn site. Makes the case for prevention of child sexual exploitation via "online warning messages, which significantly reduced the click-through to 'barely legal' pornography sites." However, the authors were legally limited to accessing postpubescent sites, which they acknowledge was not a totally accurate analog to prepubescent sites.

Smith, B.L., & Kercher, G.A. (2018). Adolescent sexual behavior and the law. Criminal Justice Center, Sam Houston State University, 25–36. *Comments:* "The intent of the laws when they were passed was to protect minors from coercive or involuntary sexual activity. However, it is becoming increasingly clear that many teenagers engage in sexual activity even before they reach the legally defined age of consent. Given the changing mores in this country more and more young people are finding themselves facing sexual assault charges whether or not either party feels victimized." In Oregon no greater than three years difference cannot be a felony, but it can still be charged as a misdemeanor.

Spohn, C.C., & Homey, J. (1996). The impact of rape law reform on the processing of simple and aggravated rape cases. *Journal of Criminal Law and Criminology*, 86, 861–884. *Comments:* There has been an increase in simple rape cases with changes in the laws in Michigan. There has also been an increase in sentences with aggravating factors and priors, but there has been an overall reduction in all sexual crimes in the state over the past ten years.

Tchen, C.M. (1983). Rape reform and the statutory consent defense. *Journal of Criminal Law and Criminology*, 74, 1518–1555. *Comments:* Lack of coercion or force should be key elements in considerations of criminal intent. "Words or actions implying consent are not consistent with rape."

Zillney, L.T., & Zillney, L.A. (2009). *Perverts and predators: The making of sexual offender laws*. Lanham, MD: Rowman and Littlefield Publishers, Inc. *Comments:* "In making outcasts of these low-risk offenders this may create the opposite effect of what was intended. It may limit their reintegration into society, thereby depriving them of the ability to lead productive lives, and may increase the risk of delinquency." The authors review considerable research in criminology which supports the claim that the main factors that discourage recidivism are public reintegration, stress management, and a stable lifestyle.

The General Literature Concerning Sexual Offending

Abel Screening (2015) The Abel Assessment for Sexual Interest-2M (AASI-2). Accessed at: http://abelscreen.com/tests/aasi.html. *Comments:* The first iteration of the Abel viewing test for sexual interest, including viewing times not divulged to the offender and a series of self-ratings of past criminal and non-criminal behaviors.

Aebi, M., Krause, C., Barra, S., Vogt, V., Vertone, L., Mannetsch, M., Imbach, K., Endrass, J., Rossegger, M., Schemeck, K., & Bessler, C. (2022). What kind of therapy works with juveniles who have sexually offended? Two versions of a specialized cognitive behavioral outpatient treatment program. *Sexual Abuse*, 34, 973–1002. *Comments:* A specialized cognitive/behavioral treatment program reduced recidivism to a greater extent than generalized social skills adaptation therapy.

Amron, A., Calkins, C., & Jamison, F. (2019). Between the pew and the pulpit: Can personality measures help identify sexually abusive clergy? *Sexual Abuse*, 31, 686–706. *Comments:* Most personality tests such as the MMPI failed to distinguish between abusing and non-abusing clergy, but one scale, the Aggressive/Sadistic Scale, on the personality segment on the MCMI–III, did identify clergy who had actually sexually abused children in the past.

Baker, T., Zgoba, K., & Gordon, J.A. (2019). Incarcerated for a sex offense: In-person experiences and concerns about reentry. *Sexual Abuse*, 33, 135–156. *Comments:* Being incarcerated for a sexual offense caused considerable concerns about employment and housing after release, fears about being victimized while in prison, but many fewer concerns about re-offending.

Bekkers, L.M.J., Leukfeldt, E.R., & Holt, T.J. (2024). Online communities for child-attracted persons as informal health care: Exploring self-reported wellbeing outcomes. *Sexual Abuse*, 36, 158–184. *Comments:* Online support communities in The Netherlands resulted in the buildup of trust and an enhanced sense of wellbeing among a group of sexual offenders against children. These results had been shown to reduce recidivism in similar offenders in extensive past research results. The authors reported an improvement in mood and a reduction of suicidal thoughts in these offenders. They believe online teletherapy could hold promise in an era in which a shortage of professionals in this field may limit in-person therapy programs.

Blokland, A., & Lussier, P. (2014). *Sex offenders: A criminal career approach*. New York: John Wiley. *Comments:* An overview of antisocial behavior among a variety of sexual offenders.

Bosetti, R.L. (2024). Investigating trauma symptomology as a mediator between childhood maltreatment and sexual and non-sexual delinquency. *Sexual Abuse*, 36, 349–380. *Comments:* Experiencing neglect in childhood was significantly associated with non-sexual delinquency while sexual abuse by itself or combined with other traumas, was especially correlated with sexual delinquency.

Budd, K.M., Mancini, C., & Bierie, D.M. (2019). Parks, playgrounds, and incidents of sexual assault. *Sexual Abuse*, 31, 580–606. *Comments:* "Fewer than 1% of sex offenses were committed at a park/playground location." This calls into question the routine prohibition by supervisors of sexual offenders frequenting such locations.

Bureau of Justice Statistics (2022). Prison inmates, 2009–2022. Washington, D.C. Department of Justice. Accessed at: http://bjs.ojp.usddoj/imdex.cfm.?ty=pbdetail&iid=839. *Comments:* Documents an increase in federal prisoners overall but particularly sexual offenders with CP and entrapment crimes.

Calpbrisi, E.A., & Knight, R.A. (2023). Comparison of community and expert samples in the perceived risk of individuals who have sexually offended. *Sexual Abuse*, 35, 568–595. *Comments:* Estimates of risk among the general population were significantly higher than those of experts in the assessment and treatment of sexual offenders.

Ciardha, C.O., Ildeniz, G. & Karoglu, N. (2022). The prevalence of sexual interest in children and sexually harmful behavior self-reported by men recruited through an online crowdsourcing platform. *Sexual Abuse*, 34, 207–226. *Comments:* Anonymous crowdsourcing of almost 1,000 men revealed almost 20% admitted to some sexual interest in children but many may have interpreted children to include postpubescent females.

Dillien, T., Goethals, K., Sabbe, B., & Brazil, I.A. (2020). Impairment of both reward and punishment learning in males who have sexually offended against a child. *Sexual Abuse*, 32, 931–957. *Comments:* Using a passive avoidance test, sexual offenders (N=57) had difficulty in distinguishing behaviors associated with rewards and demonstrated problems suppressing behaviors associated with punishments compared with non-offenders (N=33). More tailored therapeutic procedures were urged in helping sexual offenders in responding to both positive and negative behaviors.

Dressing, H., Dolling, D., Hermann, D., Kruse, A., Schmitt, E., Bannenberg, B., Whittaker, K., Hoell, A., Voss, E., & Salize, H.J. (2021). Child sexual abuse by Catholic priests, deacons, and male members of religious orders in the authority of the German Bishops' Conference 1946–2014. *Sexual Abuse*, 33, 274–294. *Comments:* The personnel files of 38,156 Catholic priests, deacons and male members of the German Bishops' Conference were examined from 1946 to 2014. Findings included 4.4% of all clerics were alleged to have committed child sexual abuse affecting a total of 3,677 children and adolescents. These findings mirror those from the US. However, the quality of record-keeping, especially in the earliest years of the study was "heterogenous," implying these figures represent an underreporting of actual child sexual abuse prevalence amongst priests.

Dum, C.P., Socia, K.M., Long, B.L., & Yarrison, F. (2020) Would God forgive? Public attitudes toward sex offenders in places of worship. *Sexual Abuse*, 32, 567–590.

Comments: "The stronger an individual's faith, the less accepting they are of registered sex offenders."

Emond, F.C., Nolet, K., Rochat, L., Rouleau, J., & Gagnon, J. (2002). Inhibitory control in sexually coercive men: Behavioral insights using a stop-signal task with neutral, emotional, and erotic stimuli. *Sexual Abuse* 32, 301–319. *Comments:* N=94 college-age men. Poorer inhibitory control was found among male college students who had exhibited sexual coercion in the past than with non-perpetrators.

Hales, S.T., & Gannon, T.A. (2022). Understanding sexual aggression in UK male university students: An empirical assessment of prevalence and psychological risk factors. *Sexual Abuse*, 34, 774–870. *Comments:* Explores factors related to college-age males who self-report sexually aggressive behavior and provides prevention interventions for sexual aggression on campuses.

Hamilton, E., Sanchez, D., & Ferrara, M.L. (2022). Measuring collateral consequences among individuals registered for a sexual offense: Development of a Sexual Offender Collateral Consequences Measure. *Sexual Abuse*, 34, 254–291. *Comments:* A literature review of 19 studies citing examples of the adverse effects of registration, included avoidance of participation in volunteer, social and religious activities, the belief they had been snubbed by former friends and family, and the finding that they were frequently harassed or even assaulted as a result of being on the sexual offender registry.

Harper, C.A., & Hicks, R.A. (2002). The effects of attitudes towards individuals with sexual convictions on professional and student risk judgements. *Sexual Abuse*, 34, 948–972. *Comments:* While it was expected that a population of general college students would hold more negative views toward sexual offenders, the authors were surprised that even forensic professionals, who do not work with sexual offenders, harbored almost equally negative views toward such individuals.

Hartley, M., & Bartels, M. (2002). Public perception of men who have committed intrafamilial and extrafamilial sexual offences against children. *Sexual Abuse*, 34, 1003–1098. *Comments:* Extrafamilial offenders, such as a stranger or a babysitter, were perceived as more dangerous than an intrafamilial abuser, such as that perpetrated by a biological relative or stepfather.

Hatcher, D.L. (2023). *Injustice Inc.* Oakland, CA: University of California Press. *Comments*: A scathing but thorough accounting of how the criminal justice system profits financially from charging, prosecuting, incarcerating, supervising, and managing after-care facilities for all offenders. Frequent court cases are cited in which both state, federal and for-profit corporations earn millions of dollars annually from juvenile and adult cases while inmates suffer, especially under contracts with private corporations.

Holper, L., Mokros, A., & Hebermeyer, E. (2024). Moderators of sexual recidivism as indicator of treatment effectiveness in persons with sexual offense histories: An updated meta-analysis. *Sexual Abuse*, 36, 255–291. *Comments:* Reduction in recidivism was associated with specialized sexual offender-based treatment programs than general clinical providers. Risk level was an appropriate indicator of future offending. The efficacy of more modern specialized techniques was apparent across a broad variety of programs and among a wide assortment of methodologies.

Jahnke, S., Schmidt, A., & Hoyer, J. (2023). Pedohebophilia and perceived non-coercive childhood experiences: Two non-matched case-control studies. *Sexual*

Abuse, 35, 240–374. *Comments:* A substantial number of non-offending male adults showed arousal to post-pubescent females.

Jeglick, E.C., Calkins, C., Kaylor, L., Margoetes, K., Doychak, K., Blasko, B., Chesin, M., & Panza, N. (2023). The nature and scope of educator misconduct in K-12. *Sexual Abuse*, 35, 188–213. *Comments:* Interviews with high school graduates inquired about whether they had experienced any type of sexual abuse during their K-high school years. About 11% reported some type of sexual behavior on the part of teachers or administrators. An excellent follow-up would be to specify the gender of the students and what types of misbehaviors actually occurred, from sexual inuendoes to hands-on crimes. It would also be of note to learn at what age these graduates recall being aware of any type of sexual advances. The authors note that it appears, from prior such surveys, that educator-sexual behaviors toward students has lessened over the years.

Kahn, R.E., Jackson, K., Keiser, K., & Ambroziak, J.S. (2021). Adverse childhood experiences among sexual offenders: Associations with sexual recidivism risk and psychopathology. *Sexual Abuse*, 33, 839–866. *Comments:* Adverse childhood experiences were not associated with recidivism in a sample of 317 sexual offenders.

Kelley, S.M., Kahn, R.E., Mundt, J.C., & Barahal, R.M. (2023). Do sanctions affect undetected sexual offending? *Sexual Abuse*, 35, 624–648. *Comments:* A small sample out of a total of 200 sexual offenders repeated a sexual offense following an initial violation but the vast majority of offenders, under strict scrutiny, did not commit any further violations. The authors concluded that undetected sexual offenses are decreasing and there exists, at present, a high detection rate.

Kitson-Boyce, R., Blagden, N., Winder, B., & Dillion, G. (2019). "This time is different": Preparing for release through a prison-model of CoSA: A phenomological and repertory grid analysis. *Sexual Abuse*, 31, 886–907. *Comments:* Circles of Support and Accountability (CoSA), a support group for sexual offender inmates prior to their release, reduced anxiety, provided support, and strengthened motivation for change. Unfortunately, a comparison group of inmates not participating in the program was not included, limiting interpretation of results, although such support groups prior to release do appear to benefit offenders following incarceration.

Lee, S.C., Hanson, R.K., Calkins, C., & Jeglic, E. (2020). Paraphilia and antisocial motivations for sexual offending may differ for American Whites and Blacks. *Sexual Abuse*, 32, 335–365. *Comments:* White sexual offenders (N=797) appeared more paraphilic than antisocial, while Black sexual offenders (N=788) displayed higher antisociality in this New Jersey study. Although the authors suggested that different treatment techniques might be necessary for the two groups, they could not determine any reasons for the disparity nor specify which treatment modalities might be more effective for either of the groups.

Letourneau, E.J., Roberts, T.W.M., Malone, L., & Son, Y. (2023). No check we won't write: A report on the high cost of sex offender incarceration. *Sexual Abuse*, 32, 54–82. *Comments:* In the US the costs of sexual offenders incarcerated exceeds $84 billion annually. This excludes additional expenses associated with court and administrative fees and, following incarceration, the fees associated with supervision and registration. The authors point out the value in funding research into treatment and prevention of sexual abuse. They put this into the perspective of the hundreds of thousands of dollars devoted to federal financing of medical research by noting that in 2018 just ten million dollars were allotted for sexual offense research.

Leung, P.C., Looman, J., & Abracen, J. (2021). To reoffend or not to reoffend? An investigation of recidivism among individuals with sexual offense histories and psychopathy. *Sexual Abuse*, 33, 88–113. *Comments:* Data from 111 sexual offenders who demonstrated higher scores on a psychopathy assessment instrument were followed for eight years to determine reoffending. Those who were older, had fewer nonsexual crimes in the past, and those who were involved in a stable romantic relationship were less likely to re-offend.

Lowe, G., & Willis, G. (2020). "Sex offender" versus "person": The influence of labels on willingness to volunteer with people who have sexually abused. *Sexual Abuse*, 32, 591–613. *Comments:* Offense-based labels were associated with less willingness to accept a volunteer but neutral language, such as referring to such offenders "as those who have had trouble with sexual behaviors" improved the willingness to allow sexual offenders to participate in volunteer activities.

MacKinnon, C.A. (2016). Rape redefined. *Harvard Law and Policy Review*, 10, 431–477. *Comments:* Rape should be considered if there is a power differential: boss/employee, director/actress, teacher/student, even if no quid pro quo was expected.

Maletzky, B.M. (1980). Assisted covert sensitization. In D.J. Cox & R.J. Daitzman (Eds.), *Exhibitionism: Description, assessment, and treatment* (pp. 187–251). New York: Garland Press. *Comments*: A more detailed description of this technique plus additional cognitive and behavioral methods.

Maletzky, B.M. (1980). Self-referred versus court-referred sexually deviant patients: Success with assisted covert sensitization. *Behavior Therapy*, 11, 306–314. *Comments:* A demonstration that involuntary sexual offenders can be successfully treated and do not reoffend.

Maletzky, B.M. (1985). Assisted covert sensitization. In A.S. Bellack & M. Hersen (Eds.), *Dictionary of behavior therapy techniques* (pp. 10–11). New York: Pergamon Press. *Comments:* A description of this aversive therapy technique.

Maletzky, B.M. (1985). Orgasmic reconditioning. In A.S. Bellack & M. Hersen (Eds.), *Dictionary of behavior therapy techniques* (pp.157–158). New York: Pergamon Press. *Comments:* Descriptions of a variety of cognitive and behavioral techniques in common practice in Clinics treating sexual offenders.

Maletzky, B.M. (1991). *Treating the sexual offender*. Newbury Park, CA: Sage Press. *Comments:* The first textbook for clinicians treating sexual offenders containing a variety of assessment and treatment techniques.

Maletzky, B.M. (1996). Evolution, psychopathology and sexual offending: Aping our ancestors. *Aggression and Violent Behavior*, 1, 369–373. *Comments:* An overview of evolution and psychopathology.

Maletzky, B.M. (2014). Ocular microsaccades in the assessment of sexual offenders. Presented at the Sexual Abuse Conference, Portland OR; January 27, 2014. *Comments:* Presentation of a more accurate viewing test to detect sexual interest in men accused of sexual crimes.

Maletzky, B.M. (2016). *Sexual abuse and the sexual offender. Common man or monster?*London: Routledge Press. *Comments:* The most recent overall text of assessment and treatment of sexual offenders; includes results after treatment for 35,000 sexual offenders over a follow-up period of from 5 to 35 years. Also a discussion of the differences amongst types of sexual offenders and a discussion of the flaws in how the criminal justice system operates when confronted with these distinctions.

Maletzky, B.M. (2019). Maternal immunosuppression and homosexuality. Presented at Grand Rounds, Oregon Health Sciences University, Portland, OR; October 15, 2003. *Comments:* An exposition of one nonexclusive theory for the origins of homosexuality.

Maletzky, B.M. (2000). Exhibitionism. In M. Hersen & M. Biaggio (Eds.), *Effective brief therapy: A clinician's guide* (pp. 229–256). San Diego, CA: Academic Press. *Comments:* The use of cognitive and behavioral therapy for men with exhibitionism.

Maletzky, B.M. (2000). Sexual assault. In V.B. Basselt & M. Hersen (Eds.), *Aggression and violence: An introductory text* (pp. 145–167). Needham Heights, MA: Allyn and Bacon. *Comments:* An overview of the possible genesis of sexually aggressive behavior and its treatment.

Maletzky, B.M. (2002). The paraphilias: Research and treatment update. In J.M. Gorman & P.E. Nathan (Eds.), *A guide to treatments that work*, volume 2 (pp.525–557). London: Oxford University Press. *Comments:* A summary of treatments in common use for sexual offenders and results in terms of recidivism for a large group of offenders.

Maletzky, B.M., & Field, G. (2003). The biological treatment of dangerous sexual offenders: A review and preliminary report of the Oregon pilot depo-Provera program. *Aggression and Violent Behavior*, 8, 391–412. *Comments:* A review of the lack of recidivism in predatory offenders treated with depo-Provera.

Maletzky, B.M, & Steinhauser, C. (1998). The Portland Sexual Abuse Clinic. In W.L. Marshall, Y.M. Fernandez, S. Hudson, & T. Ward (Eds.), *Sourcebook of treatment programs for sexual offenders* (pp. 105–116). New York: Plenum Press. *Comments:* A description of the equipment and operations of a sexual offender treatment facility.

Maletzky, B.M., & Steinhauser, C. (2002), A 25-year follow up of cognitive/behavioral therapy with 7,295 sexual offenders. *Behavior Modification*, 26, 123–147. *Comments:* DOJ records of low recidivism following graduation from a sexual offender treatment program.

Maletzky, B.M., & Steinhauser, C. (2011). An overview of assessment and treatment techniques for sexual offenders: A comprehensive study. *Sexual Abuse: A Journal of Research and Treatment*, 23, 92–123. *Comments:* "Internal barriers may inhibit non-contact offenders from acting-out their deviant fantasies." Meta-analysis of 27 studies; most included mixed offenders. All CP offenders admitted priors in 12.2% of cases but many of these had histories of sexual attraction to children. CPO offenders showed increased social skills, greater self-control, better impulse control and higher intelligence scores. "Even if the rates of prior sexual offenses are included in all sexual offenders (12.2%)...the rate of prior criminal involvement is substantially less than in samples of child molesters."

Maletzky, B.M., Tolan, A., & McFarland, B. (2006). The Oregon depo-Provera Program: A five-year follow-up. *Sexual Abuse: A Journal of Research and Treatment.* 18, 303–316. *Comments:* Absence of re-offense among predatory offenders following hormonal treatment.

Mancini, C., Pickett, J.T., Call, C., Diehl Mcdougle, R., Brubaker, S.J., & Brownstein, H.H. (2019). Sexual assault in the Ivory Tower: Public opinion on university accountability and mandatory reporting. *Sexual Abuse*, 31, 344–365. *Comments:* The majority of the public believes universities can respond to allegations of sexual crimes but they also believe mandatory reporting to public policing authorities are warranted in many cases.

McGibbin, G., Gallois, E., & Humphreys, C. (2024). Perpetration-focused prevention: The perceptions of victim-survivors. *Sexual Abuse* 36, 185–202. *Comments:* Around an initial core of revulsion at the discussion of a sexual crime, sessions with survivors revealed a progression from that of an initial stage through dismissal, congruence, and partial acceptance.

Morrow, E.P. (2020). Cognitive, affective, and general empathy in individuals convicted of a sexual offense: A meta-analysis. *Sexual Abuse*, 32, 883–906. *Comments:* Individuals convicted of a sexual offense did not display significantly lower levels of affective empathy than the general population, but did have lower levels of cognitive empathy. One limitation of these results was the use of solely self-report data. Nonetheless, results indicate that empathy training remains a necessary part in the comprehensive treatment of all sexual offenders.

Muniz, C.N., Poers, R.A., & Leilli, J.A. (2021) The influence of gender on perceptions of culpability and victim status in statutory rape offenses involving teachers. *Sexual Abuse*, 33, 529–551. *Comments:* Both men and women college undergraduates (N=648) were "pro-victim" but students in the male teacher/male student dyad scenarios were assessed as having less responsibility than if the teacher was a male and the victim was a female. Of interest, women, but not men, were more likely to favor some punishment of the student and hence a greater amount of responsibility than did their male peers.

New York Times World Almanac of Facts (2024). U.S. Department of Justice statistics. *Comments*: Cases of rape in 1990 were 103,000 while in 2020 they numbered 103,500, and in 2021 they numbered 107,500. The incidence of sodomy in 2020 was 25,700 while in 2021 this increased slightly to 26,100 cases. However, there was a reduction of all sexual crimes from 2000 to 2023 of 21% excluding internet crimes such as *Luring, Possessing and Distribution of Child Pornography* and *Sexual Exploitation of a Child*, which increased totals of sexually related increases by approximately 30%. Excluding those internet crimes would have reduced the overall rate of sexual offences by about 19%. Whites represented the greatest number of sexual assault convictions in prison (19.6%) followed by Hispanics (15.9%) and African-Americans (9.7%). The Almanac also noted that by the senior year of high school, well over half of male and female students were sexually active.

Oliver, M.E., Marshall, L.E., Marshall, W.L., & Nicholaichuk, T.P. (2020). A long-term outcome assessment on subsequent re-offense rates of a prison-based CBT/RNR sex offender program with strength-based elements. *Sexual Abuse*, 32, 127–153. *Comments:* A Canadian program of over 500 sexual offenders who received in-prison cognitive/behavioral treatment had significantly lower rates of recidivism than a control group over a follow-up period of 29 years.

Rydberg, J., Huebner, B.M., Grommon, E., & Miller, A. (2023). Investigating effect of post-release housing mobility on recidivism: Considering individuals of sexual offenses. *Sexual Abuse* 35, 539–567. *Comments:* Although the general public expressed a punitive stance toward sexual offenders, there was indifference about whether immediate housing was an important factor in offenders following release from incarceration. Of interest, there was significant aversion to housing such offenders in local neighborhoods. The hazard of recidivating correlated in a strong fashion with repeating relocations within both institutional and community populations.

Seung, C.L., Hanson, R.K., & Yoon, S.Y. (2023). Predictive validity of the Static-99R among 8,207 men convicted of sexual crimes in South Korea: A prospective field study. *Sexual Abuse*, 35, 687–715. *Comments*: Validity and reliability were of moderate to high success with this brief test.

Stimson, J.D., Puszkiewicz, K.L., & Lasher, M.P. (2023). Associations between self-regulation, experiences, of childhood adversity, and problematic sexual and aggressive behaviors. *Sexual Abuse*, 35, 31–53. *Comments:* A study of 156 incarcerated sexual offenders showed that among all types of correlations, the most significant was between trauma in childhood and difficulty with impulse control.

Swaby, H., & Lievesley, R. (2023). "Falling through the cracks": A retrospective exploration of the barriers to help-seeking among men convicted of sexual crimes. *Sexual Abuse*, 35, 812–841. *Comments:* A discussion, following structured interviews, describes offenders with sexual proclivities which would be illegal but that are distressing either by prior attempts at ineffective treatment or have never sought treatment for fear of the legal system.

Tamarit, J.M., & Balcells, M. (2022). Between sanctity and real life: Child sexual abuse in the Catholic Church in Spain. *Sexual Abuse*, 34, 806–829. *Comments:* Calls for institutional reforms and emphasizes loneliness and celibacy as aggravating factors in clergy sexual abuse of children.

Volandra, E.W., & Hoksila, W.W. (Eds.) (2023). *Colorizing Restorative Justice.* St. Paul, MN: Living Justice Press. *Comments:* Eighteen Chapters describing the current state of the Criminal Justice System and suggested changes to modernize it while humanizing it as well.

Walker, A.M. (2021). A delicate dance: Ethical and systemic issues in provider-based sex offender treatment. *Sexual Abuse*, 33, 769–792. *Comments:* Discussion of the means by which a balance may be struck between supervisors and treatment providers so as to enhance treatment while remaining aware of the limitations supervisors must, by law, impose on sexual offenders.

Willis, G.M., & Levenson, J.S. (2022). Exploring risk for sexual recidivism through the lens of early trauma. *Sexual Abuse*, 34, 597–619. *Comments*: Correlates risk of sexual offence recidivism with severity of adverse childhood experiences.

Winters, G.M., Jeglic, E.L., &Terry, K.J. (2022). The prevalence of sexual grooming behaviors in a large sample of clergy. *Sexual Abuse*, 34, 93–947. *Comments:* Clergy who molested prepubescent children frequently employed tactics in gaining access to them, and used isolation, development of trust and desensitization, to groom potential child victims of sexual abuse.

Index

Kolibri 360 GmbH
Ferdinand-Jühlke-Straße 7
99095 Erfurt, Deutschland
produktsicherheit@kolibri360.de

»Ich bestehe aus Literatur« Franz Kafka – Mit seinen oft unvollendet gebliebenen, bis heute ihr Rätsel nicht offenbarenden Romanen, Geschichten und Parabeln ist Franz Kafka eine der maßgeblichen Säulenfiguren der modernen Literatur.

Für »Erzählungen von Tieren« hat Kafka-Biograph Reiner Stach alle Erzählungen Kafkas versammelt, in denen Tiere die Protagonisten sind und sogar die Geschichten selbst erzählen. Von tierähnlichen Geschöpfen wie in »Eine Kreuzung« bis hin zu menschenähnlichen Tieren wie in »Josefine, die Sängerin oder das Volk der Mäuse« zeigen die Geschichten, dass das Erzählen durch die Tiere Kafka die Möglichkeit gab, noch deutlicher auf uns Menschen zu verweisen und uns im Tier selbst erblicken zu lassen.

FRANZ KAFKA wurde am 3. Juli 1883 als Sohn jüdischer Eltern in Prag geboren. Nach einem Jurastudium, das er 1906 mit der Promotion abschloss, trat Kafka 1908 in die »Arbeiter-Unfall-Versicherungs-Anstalt« ein, deren Beamter er bis zu seiner frühzeitigen Pensionierung im Jahr 1922 blieb. Im Spätsommer 1917 erlitt Franz Kafka einen Blutsturz; es war der Ausbruch der Tuberkulose, an deren Folgen er am 3. Juni 1924, noch nicht 41 Jahre alt, starb.

Weitere Informationen finden Sie auf www.fischerverlage.de

FRANZ KAFKA

Erzählungen von Tieren

Herausgegeben und
mit einem Nachwort
von Reiner Stach

FISCHER Taschenbuch

Weitere Informationen zu Kafkas Welt:

»Ich bestehe aus Literatur« Franz Kafka

MIX
Papier | Fördert gute Waldnutzung
FSC® C083411

2. Auflage: Juli 2024

Erschienen bei FISCHER Taschenbuch

Franz Kafka, »Die Erzählungen und andere ausgewählte Prosa«. Herausgegeben von Roger Hermes. Frankfurt am Main: S. Fischer Verlag, 2011
Franz Kafka, »Nachgelassene Schriften und Fragmente I«. Herausgegeben von Malcolm Pasley. Frankfurt am Main: S. Fischer Verlag, 1993
Franz Kafka, »Nachgelassene Schriften und Fragmente II«. Herausgegeben von Jost Schillemeit. Frankfurt am Main: S. Fischer Verlag, 1992

Umschlaggestaltung: KOSMOS – Büro für visuelle Kommunikation
Satz: Dörlemann Satz, Lemförde
Druck und Bindung: CPI books GmbH, Leck
ISBN 978-3-596-70964-9

Schakale und Araber

Wir lagerten in der Oase. Die Gefährten schliefen. Ein Araber, hoch und weiß, kam an mir vorüber; er hatte die Kamele versorgt und ging zum Schlafplatz.

Ich warf mich rücklings ins Gras; ich wollte schlafen; ich konnte nicht; das Klagegeheul eines Schakals in der Ferne; ich saß wieder aufrecht. Und was so weit gewesen war, war plötzlich nah. Ein Gewimmel von Schakalen um mich her; in mattem Gold erglänzende, verlöschende Augen; schlanke Leiber, wie unter einer Peitsche gesetzmäßig und flink bewegt.

Einer kam von rückwärts, drängte sich, unter meinem Arm durch, eng an mich, als brauche er meine Wärme, trat dann vor mich und sprach, fast Aug in Aug mit mir:

»Ich bin der älteste Schakal, weit und breit. Ich bin glücklich, dich noch hier begrüßen zu können. Ich hatte schon die Hoffnung fast aufgegeben, denn wir warten unendlich lange auf dich; meine Mutter hat gewartet und ihre Mutter und weiter alle ihre Mütter bis hinauf zur Mutter aller Schakale. Glaube es!«

»Das wundert mich«, sagte ich und vergaß, den Holzstoß anzuzünden, der bereit lag, um mit seinem Rauch die Schakale abzuhalten, »das wundert mich sehr zu hören. Nur zufällig komme ich aus dem hohen Norden und bin auf einer kurzen Reise begriffen. Was wollt ihr denn, Schakale?«

Und wie ermutigt durch diesen vielleicht allzu freundlichen Zuspruch zogen sie ihren Kreis enger um mich; alle atmeten kurz und fauchend.

»Wir wissen«, begann der Älteste, »dass du vom Norden kommst, darauf eben baut sich unsere Hoffnung. Dort ist der Verstand, der hier unter den Arabern nicht zu finden ist. Aus diesem kalten Hochmut, weißt du, ist kein Funken Verstand zu schlagen. Sie töten Tiere, um sie zu fressen, und Aas missachten sie.«

»Rede nicht so laut«, sagte ich, »es schlafen Araber in der Nähe.«

»Du bist wirklich ein Fremder«, sagte der Schakal, »sonst wüsstest du, dass noch niemals in der Weltgeschichte ein Schakal einen Araber gefürchtet hat. Fürchten sollten wir sie? Ist es nicht Unglück genug, dass wir unter solches Volk verstoßen sind?«

»Mag sein, mag sein«, sagte ich, »ich maße mir kein Urteil an in Dingen, die mir so fern liegen; es scheint ein sehr alter Streit; liegt also wohl im Blut; wird also vielleicht erst mit dem Blute enden.«

»Du bist sehr klug«, sagte der alte Schakal; und alle atmeten noch schneller; mit gehetzten Lungen, trotzdem sie doch stillestanden; ein bitterer, zeitweilig nur mit zusammengeklemmten Zähnen erträglicher Geruch entströmte den offenen Mäulern, »du bist sehr klug; das, was du sagst, entspricht unserer alten Lehre. Wir nehmen ihnen also ihr Blut, und der Streit ist zu Ende.«

»Oh!«, sagte ich wilder, als ich wollte, »sie werden sich wehren; sie werden mit ihren Flinten euch rudelweise niederschießen.«

»Du missverstehst uns«, sagte er, »nach Menschenart, die sich also auch im hohen Norden nicht verliert. Wir werden sie doch nicht töten. So viel Wasser hätte der Nil nicht, um uns rein zu waschen. Wir laufen doch schon vor dem bloßen Anblick ihres lebenden Leibes weg, in reinere Luft, in die Wüste, die deshalb unsere Heimat ist.«

Und alle Schakale ringsum, zu denen inzwischen noch viele von fernher gekommen waren, senkten die Köpfe zwischen die Vorderbeine und putzten sie mit den Pfoten; es war, als wollten sie einen Widerwillen verbergen, der so schrecklich war, dass ich am liebsten mit einem hohen Sprung aus ihrem Kreis entflohen wäre.

»Was beabsichtigt ihr also zu tun«, fragte ich und wollte aufstehen; aber ich konnte nicht; zwei junge Tiere hatten sich mir hinten in Rock und Hemd festgebissen; ich musste sitzen bleiben. »Sie halten deine Schleppe«, sagte der alte Schakal erklärend und ernsthaft, »eine Ehrbezeugung.« »Sie sollen mich loslassen!«, rief ich, bald zum Alten, bald zu den Jungen gewendet. »Sie werden es natürlich«, sagte der Alte, »wenn du es verlangst. Es dauert aber ein Weilchen, denn sie haben nach der Sitte tief sich eingebissen und müssen erst langsam die Gebisse voneinander lösen. Inzwischen höre unsere Bitte.« »Euer Verhalten hat mich dafür nicht sehr empfänglich gemacht«, sagte ich. »Lass uns unser Ungeschick nicht entgelten«, sagte er und nahm jetzt zum ersten Mal den Klageton seiner natürlichen Stimme zu Hilfe, »wir sind arme Tiere, wir haben nur das Gebiss; für alles, was wir tun wollen, das Gute und das Schlechte, bleibt uns einzig das Gebiss.« »Was willst du also?«, fragte ich, nur wenig besänftigt.

»Herr«, rief er, und alle Schakale heulten auf; in fernster Ferne schien es mir eine Melodie zu sein. »Herr, du sollst den Streit beenden, der die Welt entzweit. So wie du bist, haben unsere Alten den beschrieben, der es tun wird. Frieden müssen wir haben von den Arabern; atembare Luft; gereinigt von ihnen den Ausblick rund am Horizont; kein Klagegeschrei eines Hammels, den der Araber absticht; ruhig soll alles Getier krepieren; ungestört soll es von uns leergetrunken und bis auf die Knochen gereinigt werden. Reinheit, nichts als Reinheit wollen wir« – und nun weinten, schluchzten alle – »wie erträgst nur du es in dieser Welt, du edles Herz und süßes Eingeweide? Schmutz ist ihr Weiß; Schmutz ist ihr Schwarz; ein Grauen ist ihr Bart; speien muss man beim Anblick ihrer Augenwinkel; und heben sie den Arm, tut sich in der Achselhöhle die Hölle auf. Darum, o Herr, darum, o teurer Herr, mit Hilfe deiner alles vermögenden Hände, mit Hilfe deiner alles vermögenden Hände schneide ihnen mit dieser Schere die Hälse durch!« Und einem Ruck seines Kopfes folgend kam ein Schakal herbei, der an einem Eckzahn eine kleine, mit altem Rost bedeckte Nähschere trug.

»Also endlich die Schere und damit Schluss!«, rief der Araberführer unserer Karawane, der sich gegen den Wind an uns herangeschlichen hatte und nun seine riesige Peitsche schwang.

Alles verlief sich eiligst, aber in einiger Entfernung blieben sie doch, eng zusammengekauert, die vielen Tiere so eng und starr, dass es aussah wie eine schmale Hürde, von Irrlichtern umflogen.

»So hast du, Herr, auch dieses Schauspiel gesehen und gehört«, sagte der Araber und lachte so fröhlich, als es die Zurückhaltung seines Stammes erlaubte. »Du weißt also, was die Tiere wollen?«, fragte ich. »Natürlich, Herr«, sagte er, »das ist doch allbekannt; solange es Araber gibt, wandert diese Schere durch die Wüste und wird mit uns wandern bis ans Ende der Tage. Jedem Europäer wird sie angeboten zu dem großen Werk; jeder Europäer ist gerade derjenige, welcher ihnen berufen scheint. Eine unsinnige Hoffnung haben diese Tiere; Narren, wahre Narren sind sie. Wir lieben sie deshalb; es sind unsere Hunde; schöner als die eurigen. Sieh nur, ein Kamel ist in der Nacht verendet, ich habe es herschaffen lassen.«

Vier Träger kamen und warfen den schweren Kadaver vor uns hin. Kaum lag er da, erhoben die Schakale ihre Stimmen. Wie von Stricken unwiderstehlich jeder Einzelne gezogen, kamen sie, stockend, mit dem Leib den Boden streifend, heran. Sie hatten die Araber vergessen, den Hass vergessen, die alles auslöschende Gegenwart des stark ausdunstenden Leichnams bezauberte sie. Schon hing einer am Hals und fand mit dem ersten Biss die Schlagader. Wie eine kleine rasende Pumpe, die ebenso unbedingt wie aussichtslos einen übermächtigen Brand löschen will, zerrte und zuckte jede Muskel seines Körpers an ihrem Platz. Und schon lagen in gleicher Arbeit alle auf dem Leichnam hoch zu Berg.

Da strich der Führer kräftig mit der scharfen Peitsche

kreuz und quer über sie. Sie hoben die Köpfe; halb in Rausch und Ohnmacht; sahen die Araber vor sich stehen; bekamen jetzt die Peitsche mit den Schnauzen zu fühlen; zogen sich im Sprung zurück und liefen eine Strecke rückwärts. Aber das Blut des Kamels lag schon in Lachen da, rauchte empor, der Körper war an mehreren Stellen weit aufgerissen. Sie konnten nicht widerstehen; wieder waren sie da; wieder hob der Führer die Peitsche; ich fasste seinen Arm.

»Du hast recht, Herr«, sagte er, »wir lassen sie bei ihrem Beruf; auch ist es Zeit aufzubrechen. Gesehen hast du sie. Wunderbare Tiere, nicht wahr? Und wie sie uns hassen!«

Der neue Advokat

Wir haben einen neuen Advokaten, den Dr. Bucephalus. In seinem Äußern erinnert wenig an die Zeit, da er noch Streitross Alexanders von Macedonien war. Wer allerdings mit den Umständen vertraut ist, bemerkt einiges. Doch sah ich letzthin auf der Freitreppe selbst einen ganz einfältigen Gerichtsdiener mit dem Fachblick des kleinen Stammgastes der Wettrennen den Advokaten bestaunen, als dieser, hoch die Schenkel hebend, mit auf dem Marmor aufklingendem Schritt von Stufe zu Stufe stieg.

Im Allgemeinen billigt das Barreau die Aufnahme des Bucephalus. Mit erstaunlicher Einsicht sagt man sich, dass Bucephalus bei der heutigen Gesellschaftsordnung in einer schwierigen Lage ist und dass er deshalb, sowie auch wegen seiner weltgeschichtlichen Bedeutung, jedenfalls Entgegenkommen verdient. Heute – das kann niemand leugnen – gibt es keinen großen Alexander. Zu morden verstehen zwar manche; auch an der Geschicklichkeit, mit der Lanze über den Bankettisch hinweg den Freund zu treffen, fehlt es nicht; und vielen ist Macedonien zu eng, so dass sie Philipp, den Vater, verfluchen – aber niemand, niemand kann nach Indien führen. Schon damals waren Indiens Tore unerreichbar, aber ihre Richtung war durch das Königsschwert bezeichnet. Heute sind die Tore ganz anderswohin und weiter und höher vertragen; niemand zeigt die Richtung; viele halten Schwerter, aber nur, um mit ihnen zu fuchteln; und der Blick, der ihnen folgen will, verwirrt sich.

Vielleicht ist es deshalb wirklich das Beste, sich, wie es Bucephalus getan hat, in die Gesetzbücher zu versenken. Frei, unbedrückt die Seiten von den Lenden des Reiters, bei stiller Lampe, fern dem Getöse der Alexanderschlacht, liest und wendet er die Blätter unserer alten Bücher.

Eine Kreuzung

Ich habe ein eigentümliches Tier, halb Kätzchen, halb Lamm. Es ist ein Erbstück aus meines Vaters Besitz, entwickelt hat es sich aber doch erst in meiner Zeit, früher war es viel mehr Lamm als Kätzchen, jetzt aber hat es von beiden wohl gleichviel. Von der Katze Kopf und Krallen, vom Lamm Größe und Gestalt, von beiden die Augen, die flackernd und mild sind, das Fellhaar, das weich ist und knapp anliegt, die Bewegungen, die sowohl Hüpfen als Schleichen sind, im Sonnenschein auf dem Fensterbrett macht es sich rund und schnurrt, auf der Wiese läuft es wie toll und ist kaum einzufangen, vor Katzen flieht es, Lämmer will es anfallen, in der Mondnacht ist die Dachtraufe sein liebster Weg, Miauen kann es nicht und vor Ratten hat es Abscheu, neben dem Hühnerstall kann es stundenlang auf der Lauer liegen, doch hat es noch niemals eine Mordgelegenheit ausgenutzt, ich nähre es mit süßer Milch, die bekommt ihm bestens, in langen Zügen saugt es sie über seine Raubtierzähne hinweg in sich ein. Natürlich ist es ein großes Schauspiel für Kinder. Sonntagvormittag ist Besuchsstunde, ich habe das Tierchen auf dem Schoß, und die Kinder der ganzen Nachbarschaft stehen um mich herum. Da werden die sonderbarsten Fragen gestellt, die kein Mensch beantworten kann. Ich gebe mir auch keine Mühe, sondern begnüge mich ohne weitere

Erklärungen damit, das zu zeigen, was ich habe. Manchmal bringen die Kinder Katzen mit, einmal haben sie sogar zwei Lämmer gebracht; es kam aber entgegen ihrer Erwartung zu keinen Erkennungsszenen, die Tiere sahen einander ruhig aus Tieraugen an und nahmen offenbar ihr Dasein als göttliche Tatsache gegenseitig hin.

In meinem Schoß kennt das Tier weder Angst noch Verfolgungslust. An mich angeschmiegt fühlt es sich am wohlsten. Es hält zur Familie die es aufgezogen hat. Es ist das wohl nicht irgendeine außergewöhnliche Treue, sondern der richtige Instinkt eines Tieres, das auf der Erde zwar unzählige Verschwägerte, aber vielleicht keinen einzigen nahen Blutsverwandten hat, und dem deshalb der Schutz den es bei uns gefunden hat, heilig ist. Manchmal muss ich lachen, wenn es mich umschnuppert, zwischen den Beinen sich durchwindet und gar nicht von mir zu trennen ist. Nicht genug damit, dass es Lamm und Katze ist, will es fast auch noch ein Hund sein. Ähnliches glaube ich nämlich im Ernst. Es hat beiderlei Unruhe in sich, die von der Katze und die vom Lamm, so verschiedenartig sie sind. Darum ist ihm aber seine Haut zu eng. Vielleicht wäre für das Tier das Messer des Fleischers eine Erlösung, die muss ich ihm aber als einem Erbstück versagen.

Ein Bericht für eine Akademie

Hohe Herren von der Akademie!
Sie erweisen mir die Ehre, mich aufzufordern, der Akademie einen Bericht über mein äffisches Vorleben einzureichen.

In diesem Sinne kann ich leider der Aufforderung nicht nachkommen. Nahezu fünf Jahre trennen mich vom Affentum, eine Zeit, kurz vielleicht am Kalender gemessen, unendlich lang aber durchzugaloppieren, so wie ich es getan habe, streckenweise begleitet von vortrefflichen Menschen, Ratschlägen, Beifall und Orchestralmusik, aber im Grunde allein, denn alle Begleitung hielt sich, um im Bilde zu bleiben, weit vor der Barriere. Diese Leistung wäre unmöglich gewesen, wenn ich eigensinnig hätte an meinem Ursprung, an den Erinnerungen der Jugend festhalten wollen. Gerade Verzicht auf jeden Eigensinn war das oberste Gebot, das ich mir auferlegt hatte; ich, freier Affe, fügte mich diesem Joch. Dadurch verschlossen sich mir aber ihrerseits die Erinnerungen immer mehr. War mir zuerst die Rückkehr, wenn die Menschen gewollt hätten, freigestellt durch das ganze Tor, das der Himmel über der Erde bildet, wurde es gleichzeitig mit meiner vorwärts gepeitschten Entwicklung immer niedriger und enger; wohler und eingeschlossener fühlte ich mich in der Menschenwelt; der Sturm, der mir aus meiner Vergangenheit nachblies, sänftigte sich; heute ist es nur ein

Luftzug, der mir die Fersen kühlt; und das Loch in der Ferne, durch das er kommt und durch das ich einstmals kam, ist so klein geworden, dass ich, wenn überhaupt die Kräfte und der Wille hinreichen würden, um bis dorthin zurückzulaufen, das Fell vom Leib mir schinden müsste, um durchzukommen. Offen gesprochen, so gerne ich auch Bilder wähle für diese Dinge, offen gesprochen: Ihr Affentum, meine Herren, sofern Sie etwas Derartiges hinter sich haben, kann Ihnen nicht ferner sein als mir das meine. An der Ferse aber kitzelt es jeden, der hier auf Erden geht: den kleinen Schimpansen wie den großen Achilles.

In eingeschränktestem Sinn aber kann ich doch vielleicht Ihre Anfrage beantworten, und ich tue es sogar mit großer Freude. Das Erste, was ich lernte, war: den Handschlag geben; Handschlag bezeugt Offenheit; mag nun heute, wo ich auf dem Höhepunkt meiner Laufbahn stehe, zu jenem ersten Handschlag auch das offene Wort hinzukommen. Es wird für die Akademie nichts wesentlich Neues beibringen und weit hinter dem zurückbleiben, was man von mir verlangt hat und was ich beim besten Willen nicht sagen kann – immerhin, es soll die Richtlinie zeigen, auf welcher ein gewesener Affe in die Menschenwelt eingedrungen ist und sich dort festgesetzt hat. Doch dürfte ich selbst das Geringfügige, was folgt, gewiss nicht sagen, wenn ich meiner nicht völlig sicher wäre und meine Stellung auf allen großen Varietébühnen der zivilisierten Welt sich nicht bis zur Unerschütterlichkeit gefestigt hätte:

Ich stamme von der Goldküste. Darüber, wie ich eingefangen wurde, bin ich auf fremde Berichte angewiesen. Eine

Jagdexpedition der Firma Hagenbeck – mit dem Führer habe ich übrigens seither schon manche gute Flasche Rotwein geleert – lag im Ufergebüsch auf dem Anstand, als ich am Abend inmitten eines Rudels zur Tränke lief. Man schoss; ich war der Einzige, der getroffen, wurde; ich bekam zwei Schüsse.

Einen in die Wange; der war leicht; hinterließ aber eine große ausrasierte rote Narbe, die mir den widerlichen, ganz und gar unzutreffenden, förmlich von einem Affen erfundenen Namen Rotpeter eingetragen hat, so als unterschiede ich mich von dem unlängst krepierten, hie und da bekannten, dressierten Affentier Peter nur durch den roten Fleck auf der Wange. Dies nebenbei.

Der zweite Schuss traf mich unterhalb der Hüfte. Er war schwer, er hat es verschuldet, dass ich noch heute ein wenig hinke. Letzthin las ich in einem Aufsatz irgendeines der zehntausend Windhunde, die sich in den Zeitungen über mich auslassen: meine Affennatur sei noch nicht ganz unterdrückt; Beweis dessen sei, dass ich, wenn Besucher kommen, mit Vorliebe die Hosen ausziehe, um die Einlaufstelle jenes Schusses zu zeigen. Dem Kerl sollte jedes Fingerchen seiner schreibenden Hand einzeln weggeknallt werden. Ich, ich darf meine Hosen ausziehen, vor wem es mir beliebt; man wird dort nichts finden als einen wohlgepflegten Pelz und die Narbe nach einem – wählen wir hier zu einem bestimmten Zwecke ein bestimmtes Wort, das aber nicht missverstanden werden wolle – die Narbe nach einem frevelhaften Schuss. Alles liegt offen zutage; nichts ist zu verbergen; kommt es auf Wahrheit an, wirft jeder Großgesinnte die allerfeinsten Manieren ab. Würde dagegen jener Schreiber die Hosen ausziehen, wenn Besuch kommt, so hätte dies allerdings ein anderes Ansehen, und ich will es als Zeichen der Vernunft gelten lassen, dass er es nicht tut. Aber dann mag er mir auch mit seinem Zartsinn vom Halse bleiben!

Nach jenen Schüssen erwachte ich – und hier beginnt allmählich meine eigene Erinnerung – in einem Käfig im Zwischendeck des Hagenbeckschen Dampfers. Es war kein vierwandiger Gitterkäfig; vielmehr waren nur drei Wände an einer Kiste festgemacht; die Kiste also bildete die vierte Wand. Das Ganze war zu niedrig zum Aufrechtstehen und zu schmal zum Niedersitzen. Ich hockte deshalb mit eingebogenen, ewig zitternden Knien, und zwar, da ich zunächst wahrscheinlich niemanden sehen und immer nur im Dunkel sein wollte, zur Kiste gewendet, während sich mir hinten die Gitterstäbe ins Fleisch einschnitten. Man hält eine solche Verwahrung wilder Tiere in der allerersten Zeit für vorteilhaft, und ich kann heute nach meiner Erfahrung nicht leugnen, dass dies im menschlichen Sinn tatsächlich der Fall ist.

Daran dachte ich aber damals nicht. Ich war zum ersten Mal in meinem Leben ohne Ausweg; zumindest geradeaus ging es nicht; geradeaus vor mir war die Kiste, Brett fest an Brett gefügt. Zwar war zwischen den Brettern eine durchlaufende Lücke, die ich, als ich sie zuerst entdeckte, mit dem glückseligen Heulen des Unverstandes begrüßte, aber diese Lücke reichte bei weitem nicht einmal zum Durchstecken des Schwanzes aus und war mit aller Affenkraft nicht zu verbreitern.

Ich soll, wie man mir später sagte, ungewöhnlich wenig

Lärm gemacht haben, woraus man schloss, dass ich entweder bald eingehen müsse oder dass ich, falls es mir gelingt, die erste kritische Zeit zu überleben, sehr dressurfähig sein werde. Ich überlebte diese Zeit. Dumpfes Schluchzen, schmerzhaftes Flöhesuchen, müdes Lecken einer Kokosnuss, Beklopfen der Kistenwand mit dem Schädel, Zungenblecken, wenn mir jemand nahe kam – das waren die ersten Beschäftigungen in dem neuen Leben. In alledem aber doch nur das eine Gefühl: kein Ausweg. Ich kann natürlich das damals affenmäßig Gefühlte heute nur mit Menschenworten nachzeichnen und verzeichne es infolgedessen, aber wenn ich auch die alte Affenwahrheit nicht mehr erreichen kann, wenigstens in der Richtung meiner Schilderung liegt sie, daran ist kein Zweifel.

Ich hatte doch so viele Auswege bisher gehabt und nun keinen mehr. Ich war festgerannt. Hätte man mich angenagelt, meine Freizügigkeit wäre dadurch nicht kleiner geworden. Warum das? Kratz dir das Fleisch zwischen den Fußzehen auf, du wirst den Grund nicht finden. Drück dich hinten gegen die Gitterstange, bis sie dich fast zweiteilt, du wirst den Grund nicht finden. Ich hatte keinen Ausweg, musste mir ihn aber verschaffen, denn ohne ihn konnte ich nicht leben. Immer an dieser Kistenwand – ich wäre unweigerlich verreckt. Aber Affen gehören bei Hagenbeck an die Kistenwand – nun, so hörte ich auf, Affe zu sein. Ein klarer, schöner Gedankengang, den ich irgendwie mit dem Bauch ausgeheckt haben muss, denn Affen denken mit dem Bauch.

Ich habe Angst, dass man nicht genau versteht, was ich unter Ausweg verstehe. Ich gebrauche das Wort in seinem gewöhnlichsten und vollsten Sinn. Ich sage absichtlich nicht Freiheit. Ich meine nicht dieses große Gefühl der Freiheit nach allen Seiten. Als Affe kannte ich es vielleicht, und ich habe Menschen kennen gelernt, die sich danach sehnen. Was mich aber anlangt, verlangte ich Freiheit weder damals noch heute. Nebenbei: mit Freiheit betrügt man sich unter Menschen allzu oft. Und so wie die Freiheit zu den erhabensten Gefühlen zählt, so auch die entsprechende Täuschung zu den erhabensten. Oft habe ich in den Varietés vor meinem Auftreten irgendein Künstlerpaar oben an der Decke an Trapezen hantieren sehen. Sie schwangen sich, sie schaukelten, sie sprangen, sie schwebten einander in die Arme, einer trug den anderen an den Haaren mit dem Gebiss. »Auch das ist Menschenfreiheit«, dachte ich, »selbstherrliche Bewegung.« Du Verspottung der heiligen Natur! Kein Bau würde standhalten vor dem Gelächter des Affentums bei diesem Anblick.

Nein, Freiheit wollte ich nicht. Nur einen Ausweg; rechts, links, wohin immer; ich stellte keine anderen Forderungen; sollte der Ausweg auch nur eine Täuschung sein; die Forderung war klein, die Täuschung würde nicht größer sein. Weiterkommen, weiterkommen! Nur nicht mit aufgehobenen Armen stillestehen, angedrückt an eine Kistenwand.

Heute sehe ich klar: ohne größte innere Ruhe hätte ich nie entkommen können. Und tatsächlich verdanke ich vielleicht alles, was ich geworden bin, der Ruhe, die mich nach den ersten Tagen dort im Schiff überkam. Die Ruhe wiederum aber verdankte ich wohl den Leuten vom Schiff.

Es sind gute Menschen, trotz allem. Gerne erinnere ich mich noch heute an den Klang ihrer schweren Schritte, der damals in meinem Halbschlaf widerhallte. Sie hatten die Gewohnheit, alles äußerst langsam in Angriff zu nehmen. Wollte sich einer die Augen reiben, so hob er die Hand wie ein Hängegewicht. Ihre Scherze waren grob, aber herzlich. Ihr Lachen war immer mit einem gefährlich klingenden aber nichts bedeutenden Husten gemischt. Immer hatten sie im Mund etwas zum Ausspeien, und wohin sie ausspien, war ihnen gleichgültig. Immer klagten sie, dass meine Flöhe auf sie überspringen; aber doch waren sie mir deshalb niemals ernstlich böse; sie wussten eben, dass in meinem Fell Flöhe gedeihen und dass Flöhe Springer sind; damit fanden sie sich ab. Wenn sie dienstfrei waren, setzten sich manchmal einige im Halbkreis um mich nieder; sprachen kaum, sondern gurrten einander nur zu; rauchten, auf Kisten ausgestreckt, die Pfeife; schlugen sich aufs Knie, sobald ich die geringste Bewegung machte; und hie und da nahm einer einen Stecken und kitzelte mich dort, wo es mir angenehm war. Sollte ich heute eingeladen werden, eine Fahrt auf diesem Schiffe mitzumachen, ich würde die Einladung gewiss ablehnen, aber ebenso gewiss ist, dass es nicht nur hässliche Erinnerungen sind, denen ich dort im Zwischendeck nachhängen könnte.

Die Ruhe, die ich mir im Kreis dieser Leute erwarb, hielt mich vor allem von jedem Fluchtversuch ab. Von heute aus gesehen scheint es mir, als hätte ich zumindest geahnt, dass ich einen Ausweg finden müsse, wenn ich leben wolle, dass dieser Ausweg aber nicht durch Flucht zu erreichen sei. Ich weiß nicht mehr, ob Flucht möglich war, aber ich glaube es; einem Affen sollte Flucht immer möglich sein. Mit meinen heutigen Zähnen muss ich schon beim gewöhnlichen Nüsseknacken vorsichtig sein, damals aber hätte es mir wohl im Lauf der Zeit gelingen müssen, das Türschloss durchzubeißen. Ich tat es nicht. Was wäre damit auch gewonnen gewesen? Man hätte mich, kaum war der Kopf hinausgesteckt, wieder eingefangen und in einen noch schlimmeren Käfig gesperrt; oder ich hätte mich unbemerkt zu anderen Tieren, etwa zu den Riesenschlangen mir gegenüber flüchten können und mich in ihren Umarmungen ausgehaucht; oder es wäre mir gar gelungen, mich bis aufs Deck zu stehlen und über Bord zu springen, dann hätte ich ein Weilchen auf dem Weltmeer geschaukelt und wäre ersoffen. Verzweiflungstaten. Ich rechnete nicht so menschlich, aber unter dem Einfluss meiner Umgebung verhielt ich mich so, wie wenn ich gerechnet hätte.

Ich rechnete nicht, wohl aber beobachtete ich in aller Ruhe. Ich sah diese Menschen auf und ab gehen, immer die gleichen Gesichter, die gleichen Bewegungen, oft schien es mir, als wäre es nur einer. Dieser Mensch oder diese Menschen gingen also unbehelligt. Ein hohes Ziel dämmerte mir auf. Niemand versprach mir, dass, wenn ich so wie sie werden würde, das Gitter aufgezogen werde. Solche Versprechungen für scheinbar unmögliche Erfüllungen werden nicht gegeben. Löst man aber die Erfüllungen ein, erscheinen nachträglich auch die Versprechungen genau dort, wo man sie früher vergeblich gesucht hat. Nun war an diesen Menschen an sich nichts, was mich sehr verlockte. Wäre ich ein Anhänger jener erwähnten Freiheit, ich hätte gewiss das Weltmeer dem Ausweg vorgezogen, der sich mir im trüben Blick dieser Menschen zeigte. Jedenfalls aber beobachtete ich sie schon lange vorher, ehe ich an solche Dinge dachte, ja die angehäuften Beobachtungen drängten mich erst in die bestimmte Richtung.

Es war so leicht, die Leute nachzuahmen. Spucken konnte ich schon in den ersten Tagen. Wir spuckten einander dann gegenseitig ins Gesicht; der Unterschied war nur, dass ich mein Gesicht nachher reinleckte, sie ihres nicht. Die Pfeife rauchte ich bald wie ein Alter; drückte ich dann auch noch den Daumen in den Pfeifenkopf, jauchzte das ganze Zwischendeck; nur den Unterschied zwischen der leeren und der gestopften Pfeife verstand ich lange nicht.

Die meiste Mühe machte mir die Schnapsflasche. Der Geruch peinigte mich; ich zwang mich mit allen Kräften; aber es vergingen Wochen, ehe ich mich überwand. Diese inneren Kämpfe nahmen die Leute merkwürdigerweise ernster als irgendetwas sonst an mir. Ich unterscheide die Leute auch in meiner Erinnerung nicht, aber da war einer, der kam immer wieder, allein oder mit Kameraden, bei Tag, bei Nacht, zu den verschiedensten Stunden; stellte sich mit der Flasche vor mich hin und gab mir Unterricht. Er begriff mich nicht, er wollte das Rätsel meines Seins lösen. Er entkorkte langsam die Flasche und blickte mich dann an, um zu prüfen, ob ich verstanden habe; ich gestehe, ich sah ihm immer mit wilder, mit überstürzter Aufmerksamkeit zu; einen solchen Menschenschüler findet kein Menschenlehrer auf dem ganzen Erdenrund; nachdem die Flasche entkorkt war, hob er sie zum Mund; ich mit meinen Blicken ihm nach bis in die Gurgel; er nickt, zufrieden mit mir, und setzt die Flasche an die Lippen; ich, entzückt von allmählicher Erkenntnis, kratze mich quietschend der Länge und Breite nach, wo es sich trifft; er freut sich, setzt die Flasche an und macht einen Schluck; ich, ungeduldig und verzweifelt, ihm nachzueifern, verunreinige mich in meinem Käfig, was wieder ihm große Genugtuung macht; und nun weit die Flasche von sich streckend und im Schwung sie wieder hinaufführend, trinkt er sie, übertrieben lehrhaft zurückgebeugt, mit einem Zuge leer. Ich, ermattet von allzu großem Verlangen, kann nicht mehr folgen und hänge schwach am Gitter, während er den theoretischen Unterricht damit beendet, dass er sich den Bauch streicht und grinst.

Nun erst beginnt die praktische Übung. Bin ich nicht schon allzu erschöpft durch das Theoretische? Wohl, allzu erschöpft. Das gehört zu meinem Schicksal. Trotzdem greife ich, so gut ich kann, nach der hingereichten Flasche; entkorke sie zitternd; mit dem Gelingen stellen sich allmählich neue Kräfte ein; ich hebe die Flasche, vom Original schon kaum zu unterscheiden; setze sie an und – und werfe sie mit Abscheu, mit Abscheu, trotzdem sie leer ist und nur noch der Geruch sie füllt, werfe sie mit Abscheu auf den Boden. Zur Trauer meines Lehrers, zur größeren Trauer meiner selbst; weder ihn, noch mich versöhne ich dadurch, dass ich auch nach dem Wegwerfen der Flasche nicht vergesse, ausgezeichnet meinen Bauch zu streichen und dabei zu grinsen.

Allzu oft nur verlief so der Unterricht. Und zur Ehre meines Lehrers: er war mir nicht böse; wohl hielt er mir manchmal die brennende Pfeife ans Fell, bis es irgendwo, wo ich nur schwer hinreichte, zu glimmen anfing, aber dann löschte er es selbst wieder mit seiner riesigen guten Hand; er war mir nicht böse, er sah ein, dass wir auf der gleichen Seite gegen die Affennatur kämpften und dass ich den schwereren Teil hatte.

Was für ein Sieg dann allerdings für ihn wie für mich, als ich eines Abends vor großem Zuschauerkreis – vielleicht war ein Fest, ein Grammophon spielte, ein Offizier erging sich zwischen den Leuten – als ich an diesem Abend, gerade unbeachtet, eine vor meinem Käfig versehentlich stehen gelassene Schnapsflasche ergriff, unter steigender Aufmerksamkeit der Gesellschaft sie schulgerecht entkorkte, an den Mund setzte und ohne Zögern, ohne Mundverziehen, als Trinker von Fach, mit rund gewälzten Augen, schwappender Kehle, wirklich und wahrhaftig leer trank; nicht mehr als Verzweifelter, sondern als Künstler die Flasche hinwarf; zwar vergaß den Bauch zu streichen; dafür aber, weil ich nicht anders konnte, weil es mich drängte, weil mir die Sinne rauschten, kurz und gut »Hallo!« ausrief, in Menschenlaut ausbrach, mit diesem Ruf in die Menschengemeinschaft sprang und ihr Echo: »Hört nur, er spricht!« wie einen Kuss auf meinem ganzen schweißtriefenden Körper fühlte.

Ich wiederhole: Es verlockte mich nicht, die Menschen nachzuahmen; ich ahmte nach, weil ich einen Ausweg suchte, aus keinem anderen Grund. Auch war mit jenem Sieg noch wenig getan. Die Stimme versagte mir sofort wieder; stellte sich erst nach Monaten ein; der Widerwille gegen die Schnapsflasche kam sogar noch verstärkter. Aber meine Richtung allerdings war mir ein für allemal gegeben.

Als ich in Hamburg dem ersten Dresseur übergeben wurde, erkannte ich bald die zwei Möglichkeiten, die mir offen standen: Zoologischer Garten oder Varieté. Ich zögerte nicht. Ich sagte mir: Setze alle Kraft an, um ins Varieté zu kommen; das ist der Ausweg; Zoologischer Garten ist nur ein neuer Gitterkäfig; kommst du in ihn, bist du verloren.

Und ich lernte, meine Herren. Ach, man lernt, wenn man muss; man lernt, wenn man einen Ausweg will; man lernt rücksichtslos. Man beaufsichtigt sich selbst mit der Peitsche; man zerfleischt sich beim geringsten Widerstand. Die Affennatur raste, sich überkugelnd, aus mir hinaus und weg, so dass mein erster Lehrer selbst davon fast äffisch wurde, bald den Unterricht aufgeben und in eine Heilanstalt gebracht werden musste. Glücklicherweise kam er wieder bald hervor.

Aber ich verbrauchte viele Lehrer, ja sogar einige Lehrer gleichzeitig. Als ich meiner Fähigkeiten schon sicherer geworden war, die Öffentlichkeit meinen Fortschritten folgte, meine Zukunft zu leuchten begann, nahm ich selbst Lehrer auf, ließ sie in fünf aufeinanderfolgenden Zimmern niedersetzen und lernte bei allen zugleich, indem ich ununterbrochen aus einem Zimmer ins andere sprang.

Diese Fortschritte! Dieses Eindringen der Wissensstrahlen von allen Seiten ins erwachende Hirn! Ich leugne nicht: Es beglückte mich. Ich gestehe aber auch ein: Ich überschätzte es nicht, schon damals nicht, wie viel weniger heute. Durch eine Anstrengung, die sich bisher auf der Erde nicht wiederholt hat, habe ich die Durchschnittsbildung eines Europäers erreicht. Das wäre an sich vielleicht gar nichts, ist aber insofern doch etwas, als es mir aus dem Käfig half und mir diesen besonderen Ausweg, diesen Menschenausweg verschaffte.

Es gibt eine ausgezeichnete deutsche Redensart: sich in die Büsche schlagen; das habe ich getan, ich habe mich in die Büsche geschlagen. Ich hatte keinen anderen Weg, immer vorausgesetzt, dass nicht die Freiheit zu wählen war.

Überblicke ich meine Entwicklung und ihr bisheriges Ziel, so klage ich weder, noch bin ich zufrieden. Die Hände in den Hosentaschen, die Weinflasche auf dem Tisch, liege ich halb, halb sitze ich im Schaukelstuhl und schaue aus dem Fenster. Kommt Besuch, empfange ich ihn, wie es sich gebührt. Mein Impresario sitzt im Vorzimmer; läute ich, kommt er und hört, was ich zu sagen habe. Am Abend ist fast immer Vorstellung, und ich habe wohl kaum mehr zu steigernde Erfolge. Komme ich spät nachts von Banketten, aus wissenschaftlichen Gesellschaften, aus gemütlichem Beisammensein nach Hause, erwartet mich eine kleine halbdressierte Schimpansin, und ich lasse es mir nach Affenart bei ihr wohlgehen. Bei Tag will ich sie nicht sehen; sie hat nämlich den Irrsinn des verwirrten dressierten Tieres im Blick; das erkenne nur ich, und ich kann es nicht ertragen.

Im Ganzen habe ich jedenfalls erreicht, was ich erreichen wollte. Man sage nicht, es wäre der Mühe nicht wert gewesen. Im Übrigen will ich keines Menschen Urteil, ich will nur Kenntnisse verbreiten, ich berichte nur, auch Ihnen, hohe Herren von der Akademie, habe ich nur berichtet.

Fragmente zu »Ein Bericht für eine Akademie«

[I]

Wir alle kennen den Rotpeter, so wie ihn die halbe Welt kennt. Aber als er zu einem Gastspiel in unsere Stadt kam, beschloss ich, ihn näher, ihn persönlich kennenzulernen. Es ist nicht schwer vorgelassen zu werden. In großen Städten, wo alles, gewitzt, nur danach verlangt, die Berühmtheiten aus nächster Nähe atmen zu sehen, mag es gewisse Schwierigkeiten haben, in unserer Stadt aber bescheidet man sich, das Staunenswerte vom Parterreplatz aus anzustaunen, ich war daher, wie mir der Hoteldiener sagte, bisher der Einzige, der seinen Besuch angemeldet hatte. Herr Busenau, der Impresario empfing mich überaus freundlich. Ich hatte nicht erwartet, in ihm einen so bescheidenen, ja fast kleinmütigen Mann anzutreffen. Er saß im Vorzimmer der Wohnung Rotpeters und aß eine Eierspeise. Trotzdem Vormittag war, saß er doch schon im Abendfrack, in dem er bei den Vorstellungen erscheint. Kaum erblickte er mich, den fremden bedeutungslosen Gast, sprang er, der Besitzer höchster Orden, der König der Dresseure, der Ehrendoktor der großen Universitäten – sprang er auf, schüttelte mir die Hände, nötigte mich zum Sitzen, wischte seinen Löffel am Tischtuch ab und bot mir ihn freundschaftlichst an, damit ich die

Eierspeise zu Ende esse. Meinen ablehnenden Dank ließ er nicht gelten und wollte nun anfangen, selbst mich zu füttern. Ich hatte Mühe, ihn zu beruhigen und ihn mit Teller und Löffel zurückzudrängen. »Sehr liebenswürdig, dass Sie gekommen sind«, sagte er dann mit stark fremdländischer Betonung, »wirklich liebenswürdig. Auch kommen Sie zu richtiger Stunde, nicht immer, leider nicht immer kann Rotpeter empfangen, es widersteht ihm oft, Menschen zu sehen; dann wird niemand, wer es auch sei, vorgelassen, selbst ich, selbst ich darf dann nur gewissermaßen geschäftlich mit ihm verkehren, auf der Bühne. Aber gleich nach der Vorstellung muss ich verschwinden, er fährt allein nach Hause, sperrt sich in seine Zimmer ab und bleibt so meist wieder bis zum nächsten Abend. Einen großen Reisekorb voll Früchte hat er immer im Schlafzimmer, davon nährt er sich dann in solchen Fällen. Ich aber, der ich ihn natürlich nicht ohne Aufsicht lassen darf, miete immer die gegenüberliegende Wohnung und beobachte ihn hinter Vorhängen.«

[II]
»Wenn ich Ihnen, Rotpeter, hier so gegenübersitze, Sie reden höre, Ihnen zutrinke, wahrhaftig – ob Sie es nun als Kompliment auffassen oder nicht, es ist aber nur die Wahrheit – ich vergesse dann ganz, dass Sie ein Schimpanse sind. Erst nach und nach, wenn ich mich aus den Gedanken zur Wirklichkeit zurückzwinge, zeigen mir wieder die Augen, wessen Gast ich bin.«

»Ja.«

»Sie sind so still geworden, warum denn? Haben mir noch gerade jetzt so staunenswert richtige Urteile über unsere Stadt gesagt und sind jetzt so still.«

»Still?«

»Fehlt Ihnen etwas? Soll ich den Dresseur rufen? Vielleicht sind Sie gewohnt, um diese Stunde eine Mahlzeit einzunehmen?«

»Nein, nein. Es ist auch schon gut. Ich kann Ihnen auch sagen, was es war. Manchmal überkommt mich ein solcher Widerwille vor Menschen, dass ich dem Brechreiz kaum widerstehen kann. Das hat natürlich nichts mit dem Einzelnen zu tun, nichts mit Ihrer liebenswürdigen Gegenwart. Es geht gegen alle Menschen. Es ist das auch nichts Merkwürdiges, sollten Sie zum Beispiel mit Affen ständig zusammenleben, hätten Sie bei aller Selbstbeherrschung gewiss ähnliche Anfälle. Im Übrigen ist es auch nicht eigentlich der Geruch der Mitmenschen, der mich so anwidert, sondern der Menschengeruch, den ich angenommen habe und der sich mit dem Geruch aus meiner alten Heimat mischt. Bitte riechen Sie selbst! Hier auf der Brust! Tiefer die Nase ins Fell! Tiefer, sage ich.«

»Ich kann leider nichts Besonderes riechen. Der gewöhnliche Geruch eines gepflegten Körpers, sonst nichts. Allerdings, die Nasen der Stadtmenschen sind hier nicht maßgebend. Sie wittern natürlich tausenderlei, das an uns vorüberweht.«

»Früher, mein Herr, früher. Das ist vorüber.«

»Da Sie selbst davon beginnen, wage ich die Frage: Wie lange leben Sie eigentlich unter uns?«

»Fünf Jahre, am fünften August werden es fünf Jahre.«

»Unerhörte Leistung. In fünf Jahren das Affentum abwerfen und die ganze Menschheitsentwicklung durchzugaloppieren. Das hat wahrhaftig noch niemand getan. Auf dieser Rennbahn sind Sie ganz allein.«

»Ich weiß, es ist viel, und manchmal geht es auch über meine Begriffe. In ruhigen Stunden aber urteile ich nicht so überschwänglich. Wissen Sie, wie ich gefangen wurde?«

»Was über Sie gedruckt worden ist, habe ich alles gelesen. Sie wurden angeschossen und dann gefangen.«

»Ja, ich bekam zwei Schüsse, hier in die Wange einen, die Wunde war natürlich viel größer, als die Narbe jetzt, und einen Schuss unterhalb der Hüfte. Ich werde die Hose ausziehen, damit Sie auch diese Narbe sehen. Hier also war der Einschuss, das war die entscheidende schwere Wunde, ich fiel vom Baum, und als ich aufwachte, war ich in einem Käfig im Zwischendeck.«

»Im Käfig! Im Zwischendeck! Anders liest man davon, und anders fasst man es auf, wenn man Sie selbst es erzählen hört.«

»Und noch anders, wenn man es selbst erlebt hat, mein Herr. Ich hatte bis dahin nicht gewusst, was es bedeutet: keinen Ausweg haben. Es war kein vierwandiger Gitterkäfig, vielmehr waren nur drei Wände an einer Kiste festgemacht, die Kiste bildete die vierte Wand. Das Ganze war so niedrig dass ich nicht aufrecht stehen konnte, und so schmal, dass ich nicht einmal sitzen konnte. Ich konnte also nur mit eingebogenen Knien dort hocken. In meiner Wut wollte ich niemand sehen und blieb deshalb zur Kiste gewendet, so lauerte ich dort mit zitternden Knien Tage und Nächte, und hinten schnitten sich die Gitterstäbe in mich ein. Man hält eine solche Verwahrung wilder Tiere in der allerersten Zeit für vorteilhaft, und ich kann nach meiner Erfahrung nicht leugnen, dass dies im menschlichen Sinn tatsächlich der Fall ist. Aber am menschlichen Sinn lag mir damals noch nichts. Ich hatte die Kiste vor mir. Öffne die Bretterwand, beiße ein Loch durch, presse dich durch eine Lücke, die in Wirklichkeit kaum den Blick durchlässt und die du bei der ersten Entdeckung mit dem glückseligen Heulen des Unverstands begrüßest. Wohin willst du? Hinter dem Brett fängt der Wald an,

Der Geier

Es war ein Geier, der hackte in meine Füße. Stiefel und Strümpfe hatte er schon aufgerissen, nun hackte er schon in die Füße selbst. Immer schlug er zu, flog dann unruhig mehrmals um mich und setzte dann die Arbeit fort. Es kam ein Herr vorüber, sah ein Weilchen zu und fragte dann, warum ich den Geier dulde. »Ich bin ja wehrlos«, sagte ich, »er kam und fing zu hacken an, da wollte ich ihn natürlich wegtreiben, versuchte ihn sogar zu würgen, aber ein solches Tier hat große Kräfte, auch wollte er mir schon ins Gesicht springen, da opferte ich lieber die Füße. Nun sind sie schon fast zerrissen.« »Dass Sie sich so quälen lassen«, sagte der Herr, »ein Schuss und der Geier ist erledigt.« »Ist das so?« fragte ich, »und wollten Sie das besorgen?« »Gern«, sagte der Herr, »ich muss nur nach Hause gehen und mein Gewehr holen. Können Sie noch eine halbe Stunde warten?« »Das weiß ich nicht«, sagte ich und stand eine Weile starr vor Schmerz, dann sagte ich: »Bitte, versuchen Sie es für jeden Fall.« »Gut«, sagte der Herr, »ich werde mich beeilen.« Der Geier hatte während des Gespräches ruhig zugehört und die Blicke zwischen mir und dem Herrn wandern lassen. Jetzt sah ich, dass er alles verstanden hatte, er flog auf, weit beugte er sich zurück, um genug Schwung zu bekommen, und stieß dann wie ein Speerwerfer den Schnabel durch meinen Mund tief in mich. Zurückfallend fühlte ich befreit, wie er in meinem alle Tiefen füllenden, alle Ufer überfließenden Blut unrettbar ertrank.

Kleine Fabel

»Ach«, sagte die Maus, »die Welt wird enger mit jedem Tag. Zuerst war sie so breit, dass ich Angst hatte, ich lief weiter und war glücklich, dass ich endlich rechts und links in der Ferne Mauern sah, aber diese langen Mauern eilen so schnell aufeinander zu, dass ich schon im letzten Zimmer bin, und dort im Winkel steht die Falle, in die ich laufe.« »Du musst nur die Laufrichtung ändern«, sagte die Katze und fraß sie.

In unserer Synagoge ...

In unserer Synagoge lebt ein Tier in der Größe etwa eines Marders. Es ist oft sehr gut zu sehen, bis auf eine Entfernung von etwa zwei Metern duldet es das Herankommen der Menschen. Seine Farbe ist ein helles Blaugrün. Sein Fell hat noch niemand berührt, es lässt sich also darüber nichts sagen, fast möchte man behaupten, dass auch die wirkliche Farbe des Felles unbekannt ist, vielleicht stammt die sichtbare Farbe nur vom Staub und Mörtel die sich im Fell verfangen haben, die Farbe ähnelt ja auch dem Verputz des Synagogeninnern, nur ist sie ein wenig heller. Es ist, von seiner Furchtsamkeit abgesehen, ein ungemein ruhiges sesshaftes Tier; würde es nicht so oft aufgescheucht werden, es würde wohl den Ort kaum wechseln, sein Lieblingsaufenthalt ist das Gitter der Frauenabteilung, mit sichtbarem Behagen krallt es sich in die Maschen des Gitters, streckt sich und blickt hinab in den Betraum, diese kühne Stellung scheint es zu freuen, aber der Tempeldiener hat den Auftrag, das Tier niemals am Gitter zu dulden, es würde sich an diesen Platz gewöhnen, und das kann man wegen der Frauen, die das Tier fürchten, nicht zulassen. Warum sie es fürchten, ist unklar. Es sieht allerdings beim ersten Anblick erschreckend aus, besonders der lange Hals, das dreikantige Gesicht, die fast waagrecht vorstehenden Oberzähne, über der Oberlippe eine Reihe langer, die Zähne überragender, offenbar ganz harter heller Borstenhaare, das alles kann erschrecken, aber bald muss man erkennen, wie ungefährlich dieser ganze scheinbare Schrecken ist. Vor allem hält es sich ja von den Menschen fern, es ist scheuer als ein Waldtier, es scheint mit nichts als mit dem Gebäude verbunden, und sein persönliches Unglück besteht wohl darin, dass dieses Gebäude eine Synagoge ist, also ein zeitweilig sehr belebter Ort. Könnte man sich mit dem Tier verständigen, könnte man es allerdings damit trösten, dass die Gemeinde unseres Bergstädtchens von Jahr zu Jahr kleiner wird und es ihr schon Mühe macht, die Kosten für die Erhaltung der Synagoge aufzubringen. Es ist nicht ausgeschlossen, dass in einiger Zeit aus der Synagoge ein Getreidespeicher wird oder dergleichen und dass das Tier die Ruhe bekommt, die ihm jetzt schmerzlich fehlt.

Es sind allerdings nur die Frauen, die das Tier fürchten, den Männern ist es längst gleichgültig geworden, eine Generation hat es der andern gezeigt, immer wieder hat man es gesehen, schließlich hat man keinen Blick mehr daran gewendet, und selbst die Kinder, die es zum ersten Mal sehen, staunen nicht mehr. Es ist das Haustier der Synagoge geworden, warum sollte nicht die Synagoge ein besonderes, nirgends sonst vorkommendes Haustier haben? Wären nicht die Frauen, man würde kaum mehr von der Existenz des Tieres wissen. Aber selbst die Frauen haben keine wirkliche Furcht vor dem Tier, es wäre auch zu sonderbar, ein solches Tier tagaus, tagein zu fürchten, jahre- und jahrzehntelang. Sie verteidigen sich zwar damit, dass ihnen das Tier meist viel näher ist als den Männern, und das ist richtig. Hinunter zu den Männern wagt sich das Tier nicht, niemals hat man es noch auf dem Fußboden gesehen. Lässt man es nicht zum Gitter der Frauenabteilung, so hält es sich wenigstens in gleicher Höhe auf der gegenüberliegenden Wand auf. Dort ist ein ganz schmaler Mauervorsprung, kaum zwei Finger breit, er umläuft drei Seiten der Synagoge, auf diesem Vorsprung huscht das Tier manchmal hin und her, meistens aber hockt es ruhig auf einer bestimmten Stelle gegenüber den Frauen. Es ist fast unbegreiflich, wie es diesen schmalen Weg so leicht benützen kann, und die Art, wie es dort oben, am Ende angekommen, wieder wendet, ist sehenswert, es ist doch schon ein sehr altes Tier, aber es zögert nicht, den gewagtesten Luftsprung zu machen, der auch niemals misslingt, in der Luft hat es sich umgedreht, und schon läuft es wieder seinen Weg zurück. Allerdings, wenn man das einige Mal gesehen hat, ist man gesättigt und hat keinen Anlass immerfort hinzustarren. Es ist ja auch weder Furcht noch Neugier, welche die Frauen in Bewegung hält, würden sie sich mehr mit dem Beten beschäftigen, könnten sie das Tier völlig vergessen, die frommen Frauen täten das auch, wenn es die anderen, welche die große Mehrzahl sind, zuließen, diese aber wollen immer gern auf sich aufmerksam machen, und das Tier ist ihnen dafür ein willkommener Vorwand. Wenn sie es könnten und wenn sie es wagten, hätten sie gewiss das Tier noch näher zu sich gelockt, um noch mehr erschrecken zu dürfen. Aber in Wirklichkeit drängt sich ja das Tier gar nicht zu ihnen, es kümmert sich, wenn es nicht angegriffen wird, um sie ebenso wenig wie um die Männer, am liebsten würde es wahrscheinlich in der Verborgenheit bleiben, in der es in den Zeiten außerhalb des Gottesdienstes lebt, offenbar in irgendeinem Mauerloch, das wir noch nicht entdeckt haben. Erst wenn man zu beten anfängt, erscheint es, erschreckt durch den Lärm, will es sehen, was geschehen ist, will es wachsam bleiben, will es frei sein, fähig zur Flucht, vor Angst läuft es hervor, aus Angst macht es seine Kapriolen und wagt sich nicht zurückzuziehen, bis der Gottesdienst zu Ende ist. Die Höhe bevorzugt es natürlich deshalb, weil es dort am sichersten ist, und die besten Laufmöglichkeiten hat es auf dem Gitter und dem Mauervorsprung, aber es ist keineswegs immer dort, manchmal steigt es auch tiefer zu den Männern hinab, der Vorhang der Bundeslade wird von einer glänzenden Messingstange getragen, die scheint das Tier zu locken, oft genug schleicht es hin, dort aber sitzt es immer ruhig, nicht einmal wenn es dort knapp bei der Bundeslade ist, kann man sagen, dass es stört, mit seinen blanken, immer offenen, vielleicht lidlosen Augen scheint es die Gemeinde anzusehen, sieht aber gewiss niemanden an, sondern blickt nur den Gefahren entgegen, von denen es sich bedroht fühlt.

In dieser Hinsicht schien es, wenigstens bis vor kurzem, nicht viel verständiger als unsere Frauen. Was für Gefahren hat es denn zu fürchten? Wer beabsichtigt, ihm etwas zu tun? Lebt es denn nicht seit vielen Jahren völlig sich selbst überlassen? Die Männer kümmern sich nicht um seine Anwesenheit, und die Mehrzahl der Frauen wäre wahrscheinlich unglücklich, wenn es verschwände. Und da es das einzige Tier im Haus ist, hat es also überhaupt keinen Feind. Das hätte es nachgerade im Laufe der Jahre schon durchschauen können. Und der Gottesdienst mit seinem Lärm mag ja für das Tier sehr erschreckend sein, aber er wiederholt sich doch in bescheidenem Ausmaß jeden Tag und gesteigert an den Festtagen, immer regelmäßig und ohne Unterbrechung, auch das ängstlichste Tier hätte sich schon daran gewöhnen können, besonders wenn es sieht, dass es nicht etwa der Lärm von Verfolgern ist, sondern ein Lärm, der es gar nicht betrifft. Und doch diese Angst. Ist es die Erinnerung an längst vergangene oder die Vorahnung künftiger Zeiten? Weiß dieses alte Tier vielleicht mehr, als die drei Generationen, die jeweils in der Synagoge versammelt sind?

Vor vielen Jahren, so erzählt man, soll man wirklich versucht haben, das Tier zu vertreiben. Es ist ja möglich, dass es wahr ist, wahrscheinlicher aber ist es dass es sich nur um erfundene Geschichten handelt. Nachweisbar allerdings ist, dass man damals vom religionsgesetzlichen Standpunkt aus die Frage untersucht hat, ob man ein solches Tier im Gotteshause dulden darf. Man holte die Gutachten verschiedener berühmter Rabbiner ein, die Ansichten waren geteilt, die Mehrheit war für die Vertreibung und Neueinweihung des Gotteshauses, aber es war leicht, von der Ferne zu dekretieren, in Wirklichkeit war es ja unmöglich, das Tier zu vertreiben.

Forschungen eines Hundes

Wie sich mein Leben verändert hat und wie es sich doch nicht verändert hat im Grunde! Wenn ich jetzt zurückdenke und die Zeiten mir zurückrufe, da ich noch inmitten der Hundeschaft lebte, teilnahm an allem, was sie bekümmert, ein Hund unter Hunden, finde ich bei näherem Zusehen doch, dass hier seit jeher etwas nicht stimmte, eine kleine Bruchstelle vorhanden war, ein leichtes Unbehagen inmitten der ehrwürdigsten volklichen Veranstaltungen mich befiel, ja manchmal selbst im vertrauten Kreise, nein, nicht manchmal, sondern sehr oft, der bloße Anblick eines mir lieben Mithundes, der bloße Anblick, irgendwie neu gesehen, mich verlegen, erschrocken, hilflos, ja mich verzweifelt machte. Ich suchte mich gewissermaßen zu begütigen, Freunde, denen ich es eingestand, halfen mir, es kamen wieder ruhigere Zeiten, Zeiten, in denen zwar jene Überraschungen nicht fehlten, aber gleichmütiger aufgenommen, gleichmütiger ins Leben eingefügt wurden, vielleicht traurig und müde machten, aber im Übrigen mich bestehen ließen als einen zwar ein wenig kalten, zurückhaltenden, ängstlichen, rechnerischen, aber alles in allem genommen doch regelrechten Hund. Wie hätte ich auch ohne diese Erholungspausen das Alter erreichen können, dessen ich mich jetzt erfreue, wie hätte ich mich durchringen können zu der

Ruhe, mit der ich die Schrecken meiner Jugend betrachte und die Schrecken des Alters ertrage, wie hätte ich dazu kommen können, die Folgerungen aus meiner, wie ich zugebe, unglücklichen oder, um es vorsichtiger auszudrücken, nicht sehr glücklichen Anlage zu ziehen und fast völlig ihnen entsprechend zu leben. Zurückgezogen, einsam, nur mit meinen kleinen, hoffnungslosen, aber mir unentbehrlichen Untersuchungen beschäftigt, so lebe ich, habe aber dabei von der Ferne den Überblick über mein Volk nicht verloren, oft dringen Nachrichten zu mir, und auch ich lasse hie und da von mir hören. Man behandelt mich mit Achtung, versteht meine Lebensweise nicht, aber nimmt sie mir nicht übel, und selbst junge Hunde, die ich hier und da in der Ferne vorüberlaufen sehe, eine neue Generation, an deren Kindheit ich mich kaum dunkel erinnere, versagen mir nicht den ehrerbietigen Gruß. Man darf eben nicht außer Acht lassen, dass ich trotz meiner Sonderbarkeiten, die offen zu Tage liegen, doch nicht völlig aus der Art schlage. Es ist ja, wenn ich's bedenke, und dies zu tun habe ich Zeit und Lust und Fähigkeit, mit der Hundeschaft überhaupt sonderbar bestellt. Es gibt außer uns Hunden vielerlei Arten von Geschöpfen ringsumher, arme, geringe, stumme, nur auf gewisse Schreie eingeschränkte Wesen, viele unter uns Hunden studieren sie, haben ihnen Namen gegeben, suchen ihnen zu helfen, sie zu veredeln und dergleichen, mir sind sie, wenn sie mich nicht etwa zu stören versuchen, gleichgültig, ich verwechsle sie, ich sehe über sie hinweg, eines aber ist zu auffallend, als dass es mir hätte entgehen können, wie wenig sie nämlich, mit uns Hunden verglichen, zusammenhalten, wie fremd sie aneinander vorübergehen, wie sie weder ein hohes noch ein niedriges Interesse verbindet, wie vielmehr jedes Interesse sie noch mehr voneinander abhält, als es schon der gewöhnliche Zustand der Ruhe mit sich bringt. Wir Hunde dagegen! Man darf doch wohl sagen, dass wir alle förmlich in einem einzigen Haufen leben, alle, so unterschieden wir sonst sind durch die unzähligen und tief gehenden Unterscheidungen, die sich im Laufe der Zeiten ergeben haben. Alle in einem Haufen! Es drängt uns zueinander, und nichts kann uns hindern, diesem Drängen genugzutun, alle unsere Gesetze und Einrichtungen, die wenigen, die ich noch kenne, und die zahllosen, die ich vergessen habe, gehen zurück auf dieses höchste Glück, dessen wir fähig sind, das warme Beisammensein. Nun aber das Gegenspiel hierzu. Kein Geschöpf lebt meines Wissens so weithin zerstreut wie wir Hunde, keines hat so viele, gar nicht übersehbare Unterschiede der Klassen, der Arten, der Beschäftigungen, wir, die wir zusammenhalten wollen – und immer wieder gelingt es uns trotz allem, in überschwänglichen Augenblicken –, gerade wir leben weit voneinander getrennt, in eigentümlichen, schon dem Nebenhund oft unverständlichen Berufen, festhaltend an Vorschriften, die nicht die der Hundeschaft sind, ja eher gegen sie gerichtet. Was für schwierige Dinge das sind, Dinge, an die man lieber nicht rührt – ich verstehe auch diesen Standpunkt, verstehe ihn besser als den meinen – und doch Dinge, denen ich ganz und gar verfallen bin. Warum tue ich es nicht wie die anderen, lebe einträchtig mit meinem Volke und nehme das, was die Eintracht stört, stillschweigend hin, vernachlässige es als kleinen Fehler in der großen Rechnung und bleibe immer zugekehrt dem, was glücklich bindet, nicht dem, was uns immer wieder unwiderstehlich aus dem Volkskreis zerrt. Ich erinnere mich an einen Vorfall aus meiner Jugend, ich war damals in einer jener seligen unerklärlichen Aufregungen, wie sie wohl jeder als Kind erlebt, ich war noch ein ganz junger Hund, alles gefiel mir, alles hatte Bezug zu mir, ich glaubte, dass große Dinge um mich vorgehen, deren Anführer ich sei, denen ich meine Stimme leihen müsse, Dinge, die elend am Boden liegen bleiben müssten, wenn ich nicht für sie lief, für sie meinen Körper schwenkte, nun, Phantasien der Kinder, die mit den Jahren sich verflüchtigen, aber damals waren sie sehr stark, ich war ganz in ihrem Bann, und es geschah dann auch freilich etwas Außerordentliches, was den wilden Erwartungen Recht zu geben schien. An sich war es nichts Außerordentliches, später habe ich solche und noch merkwürdigere Dinge oft genug gesehen, aber damals traf es mich mit dem starken ersten unverwischbaren, für vieles folgende richtunggebenden Eindruck. Ich traf nämlich eine kleine Hundegesellschaft, vielmehr ich traf sie nicht, sie kam auf mich zu. Ich war damals lange durch die Finsternis gelaufen, in Vorahnung großer Dinge, eine Vorahnung, die freilich leicht täuschte, denn ich hatte sie immer, war lange durch die Finsternis gelaufen, kreuz und quer, geführt von nichts anderem als dem unbestimmten Verlangen, machte plötzlich Halt in dem Gefühl, hier sei ich am rechten Ort, sah auf, und es war überheller Tag, nur ein wenig dunstig, ich begrüßte den Morgen mit wirren Lauten, da – als hätte ich sie heraufbeschworen – traten aus irgendwelcher Finsternis unter Hervorbringung eines entsetzlichen Lärms, wie ich ihn noch nie gehört hatte, sieben Hunde ans Licht. Hätte ich nicht deutlich gesehen, dass es Hunde waren und dass sie selbst diesen Lärm mitbrachten, trotzdem ich nicht erkennen konnte, wie sie ihn erzeugten – ich wäre sofort weggelaufen, so aber blieb ich. Damals wusste ich noch fast nichts von der nur dem Hundegeschlecht verliehenen Musikalität, sie war meiner sich erst entwickelnden Aufmerksamkeit entgangen, nur in Andeutungen hatte man mich darauf hinzuweisen versucht, umso überraschender, geradezu niederwerfend waren jene sieben großen Musikkünstler für mich. Sie redeten nicht, sie sangen nicht, sie schwiegen im Allgemeinen fast mit einer gewissen Verbissenheit, aber aus dem leeren Raum zauberten sie die Musik empor. Alles war Musik. Das Heben und Niedersetzen ihrer Füße, bestimmte Wendungen des Kopfes, ihr Laufen und ihr Ruhen, die Stellungen, die sie zueinander einnahmen, die reigenmäßigen Verbindungen, die sie miteinander eingingen, indem etwa einer die Vorderpfoten auf des anderen Rücken stützte und sie es dann alle sieben so durchführten, dass der erste die Last aller andern trug, oder indem sie mit ihren nah am Boden hinschleichenden Körpern verschlungene Figuren bildeten und niemals sich irrten, nicht einmal der letzte, der noch ein wenig unsicher war, nicht immer gleich den Anschluss an die anderen fand, gewissermaßen im Anschlagen der Melodie manchmal schwankte, aber doch unsicher war nur im Vergleich mit der großartigen Sicherheit der anderen und selbst bei viel größerer, ja bei vollkommener Unsicherheit nichts hätte verderben können, wo die anderen, große Meister, den

Takt unerschütterlich hielten. Aber man sah sie ja kaum, man sah sie ja alle kaum. Sie waren hervorgetreten, man hatte sie innerlich begrüßt als Hunde, sehr beirrt war man zwar von dem Lärm, der sie begleitete, aber es waren doch Hunde, Hunde wie ich und du, man beobachtete sie gewohnheitsmäßig, wie Hunde, denen man auf dem Weg begegnet, man wollte sich ihnen nähern, Grüße tauschen, sie waren auch ganz nah, Hunde, zwar viel älter als ich und nicht von meiner langhaarigen wolligen Art, aber doch auch nicht allzu fremd an Größe und Gestalt, recht vertraut vielmehr, viele von solcher oder ähnlicher Art kannte ich, aber während man noch in solchen Überlegungen befangen war, nahm allmählich die Musik überhand, fasste einen förmlich, zog einen hinweg von diesen wirklichen kleinen Hunden und ganz wider Willen, sich sträubend mit allen Kräften, heulend, als würde einem Schmerz bereitet, durfte man sich mit nichts anderem beschäftigen, als mit der von allen Seiten, von der Höhe, von der Tiefe, von überall her kommenden, den Zuhörer in die Mitte nehmenden, überschüttenden, erdrückenden, über seiner Vernichtung noch, in solcher Nähe, dass es schon Ferne war, kaum hörbar noch Fanfaren blasenden Musik. Und wieder wurde man entlassen, weil man schon zu erschöpft, zu vernichtet, zu schwach war, um noch zu hören, man wurde entlassen und sah die sieben kleinen Hunde ihre Prozessionen führen, ihre Sprünge tun, man wollte sie, so ablehnend sie aussahen, anrufen, um Belehrung bitten, sie fragen, was sie denn hier machten - ich war ein Kind und glaubte immer und jeden fragen zu dürfen -, aber kaum setzte ich an, kaum fühlte ich die gute vertraute hündische Verbindung mit den sieben, war wieder ihre Musik da, machte mich besinnungslos, drehte mich im Kreis herum, als sei ich selbst einer der Musikanten, während ich doch nur ihr Opfer war, warf mich hierhin und dorthin, so sehr ich auch um Gnade bat, und rettete mich schließlich vor ihrer eigenen Gewalt, indem sie mich in ein Gewirr von Hölzern drückte, das in jener Gegend ringsum sich erhob, ohne dass ich es bisher bemerkt hatte, mich jetzt fest umfing, den Kopf mir niederduckte und mir, mochte dort im Freien die Musik noch donnern, die Möglichkeit gab, ein wenig zu verschnaufen. Wahrhaftig, mehr als über die Kunst der sieben Hunde – sie war mir unbegreiflich, aber auch gänzlich unanknüpfbar außerhalb meiner Fähigkeiten – wunderte ich mich über ihren Mut, sich dem, was sie erzeugten, völlig und offen auszusetzen, und über ihre Kraft, es, ohne dass es ihnen das Rückgrat brach, ruhig zu ertragen. Freilich erkannte ich jetzt aus meinem Schlupfloch bei genauerer Beobachtung, dass es nicht so sehr Ruhe als äußerste Anspannung war, mit der sie arbeiteten, diese scheinbar so sicher bewegten Beine zitterten bei jedem Schritt in unaufhörlicher ängstlicher Zuckung, starr wie in Verzweiflung sah einer den anderen an, und die immer wieder bewältigte Zunge hing doch gleich wieder schlapp aus den Mäulern. Es konnte nicht Angst wegen des Gelingens sein, was sie so erregte; wer solches wagte, solches zustandebrachte, der konnte keine Angst mehr haben, wovor denn Angst? Wer zwang sie denn zu tun, was sie hier taten? Und ich konnte mich nicht mehr zurückhalten, besonders da sie mir jetzt so unverständlich hilfsbedürftig erschienen, und so rief ich durch allen Lärm meine Fragen laut und fordernd hinaus. Sie aber – unbegreiflich! unbegreiflich! – sie antworteten nicht, taten als wäre ich nicht da, Hunde, die auf Hundeanruf gar nicht antworten, ein Vergehen gegen die guten Sitten, das dem kleinsten wie dem größten Hund unter keinen Umständen verziehen wird. Waren es etwa doch nicht Hunde? Aber wie sollten es denn nicht Hunde sein, hörte ich doch jetzt bei genauerem Hinhorchen sogar leise Zurufe, mit denen sie einander befeuerten, auf Schwierigkeiten aufmerksam machten, vor Fehlern warnten, sah ich doch den letzten kleinsten Hund, dem die meisten Zurufe galten, öfters nach mir hinschielen, so als hätte er viel Lust mir zu antworten, bezwänge sich aber, weil es nicht sein dürfe. Aber warum durfte es nicht sein, warum durfte denn das, was unsere Gesetze bedingungslos immer verlangen, diesmal nicht sein? Das Herz empörte sich in mir, fast vergaß ich die Musik. Diese Hunde hier vergingen sich gegen das Gesetz. Mochten es noch so große Zauberer sein, das Gesetz galt auch für sie, das verstand ich Kind schon ganz genau. Und ich merkte von da aus noch mehr. Sie hatten wirklich Grund zu schweigen, vorausgesetzt, dass sie aus Schuldgefühl schwiegen. Denn wie führten sie sich auf, vor lauter Musik hatte ich es bisher nicht bemerkt, sie hatten ja alle Scham von sich geworfen, die Elenden taten das gleichzeitig Lächerlichste und Unanständigste, sie gingen aufrecht auf den Hinterbeinen. Pfui Teufel! Sie entblößten sich und trugen ihre Blöße protzig zur Schau; sie taten sich darauf zugute, und wenn sie einmal auf einen Augenblick dem guten Trieb gehorchten und die Vorderbeine senkten, erschraken sie förmlich, als sei es ein Fehler, als sei die Natur ein Fehler, hoben wieder schnell die Beine, und ihr Blick schien um Verzeihung dafür zu bitten, dass sie in ihrer Sündhaftigkeit ein wenig hatten innehalten müssen. War die Welt verkehrt? Wo war ich? Was war denn geschehen? Hier durfte ich um meines eigenen Bestandes willen nicht mehr zögern, ich machte mich los aus den umklammernden Hölzern, sprang mit einem Satz hervor und wollte zu den Hunden, ich kleiner Schüler musste Lehrer sein, musste ihnen begreiflich machen, was sie taten, musste sie abhalten vor weiterer Versündigung. »So alte Hunde, so alte Hunde!«, wiederholte ich mir immerfort. Aber kaum war ich frei, und nur noch zwei, drei Sprünge trennten mich von den Hunden, war es wieder der Lärm, der seine Macht über mich bekam. Vielleicht hätte ich in meinem Eifer sogar ihm, den ich doch nun schon kannte, widerstanden, wenn nicht durch alle seine Fülle, die schrecklich war, aber vielleicht doch zu bekämpfen, ein klarer strenger immer sich gleichbleibender, förmlich aus großer Ferne unverändert ankommender Ton, vielleicht die eigentliche Melodie inmitten des Lärms, geklungen und mich in die Knie gezwungen hätte. Ach, was machten doch diese Hunde für eine betörende Musik. Ich konnte nicht weiter, ich wollte sie nicht mehr belehren, mochten sie weiter die Beine spreizen, Sünden begehen und andere zur Sünde des stillen Anschauens verlocken, ich war ein so kleiner Hund, wer konnte so Schweres von mir verlangen, ich machte mich noch kleiner, als ich war, ich winselte, hätten mich damals die Hunde um meine Meinung gefragt, ich hätte ihnen vielleicht recht gegeben. Es dauerte übrigens nicht lange, und sie verschwanden mit allem Lärm und allem Licht in der Finsternis, aus der sie gekommen waren.

Wie ich schon sagte: Dieser ganze Vorfall enthält nichts Außergewöhnliches, im Verlauf eines langen Lebens begegnet einem mancherlei, was aus dem Zusammenhang genommen und mit den Augen eines Kindes angesehen, noch viel erstaunlicher wäre. Überdies kann man es natürlich – wie der treffende Ausdruck lautet – »verreden«, so wie alles, dann zeigt sich, dass hier sieben Musiker zusammengekommen waren, um in der Stille des Morgens Musik zu machen, dass ein kleiner Hund sich hinverirrt hatte, ein lästiger Zuhörer, den sie durch besonders schreckliche oder erhabene Musik, leider vergeblich, zu vertreiben suchten. Er störte sie durch Fragen, hätten sie, die schon durch die bloße Anwesenheit des Fremdlings genug gestört waren, auch noch auf diese Belästigung eingehen und sie durch Antworten vergrößern sollen? Und wenn auch das Gesetz befiehlt, jedem zu antworten, ist denn ein solcher winziger hergelaufener Hund überhaupt ein nennenswerter Jemand. Und vielleicht verstanden sie ihn gar nicht, er lallte ja doch wohl seine Fragen recht unverständlich. Oder vielleicht verstanden sie ihn wohl und antworteten in Selbstüberwindung, aber er, der Kleine, der Musik-Ungewohnte, konnte die Antwort von der Musik nicht sondern. Und was die Hinterbeine betrifft, vielleicht gingen sie wirklich ausnahmsweise nur auf ihnen, es ist eine Sünde, wohl! Aber sie waren allein, sieben Freunde, unter Freunden, im vertraulichen Beisammensein, gewissermaßen in den eigenen vier Wänden, gewissermaßen ganz allein, denn Freunde sind doch keine Öffentlichkeit, und wo keine Öffentlichkeit ist, bringt sie auch ein kleiner neugieriger Straßenhund nicht hervor, in diesem Fall also: Ist es hier nicht so, als wäre nichts geschehen? Ganz so ist es nicht, aber nahezu, und die Eltern sollten ihre Kleinen weniger herumlaufen und dafür besser schweigen und das Alter achten lehren.

Ist man so weit, dann ist der Fall erledigt. Freilich was für die Großen erledigt ist, ist es für die Kleinen noch nicht. Ich lief umher, erzählte und fragte, klagte an und forschte und wollte jeden hinziehen zu dem Ort, wo alles geschehen war, und wollte jedem zeigen, wo ich gestanden hatte und wo die sieben gewesen und wo und wie sie getanzt und musiziert hatten, und wäre jemand mit mir gekommen, statt dass mich jeder abgeschüttelt und ausgelacht hätte, ich hätte dann wohl meine Sündlosigkeit geopfert und mich auch auf die Hinterbeine zu stellen versucht, um alles genau zu verdeutlichen. Nun, einem Kinde nimmt man alles übel, verzeiht ihm aber schließlich auch alles. Ich aber habe dieses kindhafte Wesen behalten und bin darüber ein alter Hund geworden. So wie ich damals nicht aufhörte, jenen Vorfall, den ich allerdings heute viel niedriger einschätze, laut zu besprechen, in seine Bestandteile zu zerlegen, an den Anwesenden zu messen, ohne Rücksicht auf die Gesellschaft, in der ich mich befand, nur immer mit der Sache beschäftigt, die ich lästig fand genau so wie jeder andere, die ich aber – das war der Unterschied – gerade deshalb restlos durch Untersuchung auflösen wollte, um den Blick endlich wieder freizubekommen für das gewöhnliche, ruhige, glückliche Leben des Tages, ganz so wie damals habe ich, wenn auch mit weniger kindlichen Mitteln – aber sehr groß ist der Unterschied nicht – in der Folgezeit gearbeitet und halte auch heute nicht weiter.

Mit jenem Konzert aber begann es. Ich klage nicht darüber, es ist mein eingeborenes Wesen, das hier wirkt und das sich gewiss, wenn das Konzert nicht gewesen wäre, eine andere Gelegenheit gefunden hätte, um durchzubrechen, nur dass es so bald geschah, tat mir früher manchmal leid, es hat mich um einen großen Teil meiner Kindheit gebracht, das glückselige Leben der jungen Hunde, das mancher für sich jahrelang auszudehnen imstande ist, hat für mich nur wenige kurze Monate gedauert. Sei's darum! Es gibt wichtigere Dinge als die Kindheit. Und vielleicht winkt mir im Alter, erarbeitet durch ein hartes Leben, mehr kindliches Glück, als ein wirkliches Kind zu ertragen die Kraft hätte, die ich dann aber haben werde.

Ich begann damals meine Untersuchungen mit den einfachsten Dingen, an Material fehlte es nicht, leider, der Überfluss ist es, der mich in dunklen Stunden verzweifeln lässt. Ich begann zu untersuchen, wovon sich die Hundeschaft nährte. Das ist nun, wenn man will, natürlich keine einfache Frage, sie beschäftigt uns seit Urzeiten, sie ist der Hauptgegenstand unseres Nachdenkens, zahllos sind die Beobachtungen und Versuche und Ansichten auf diesem Gebiet, es ist eine Wissenschaft geworden, die in ihren ungeheuren Ausmaßen nicht nur über die Fassungskraft des Einzelnen, sondern über jene aller Gelehrten insgesamt geht und ausschließlich von niemandem anderen als von der gesamten Hundeschaft und selbst von dieser nur seufzend und nicht ganz vollständig getragen werden kann, immer wieder abbröckelt in altem längst besessenem Gut und mühselig ergänzt werden muss, von den Schwierigkeiten und kaum zu erfüllenden Voraussetzungen neuer Forschung ganz zu schweigen. Das alles wende man mir nicht ein, das alles weiß ich, wie nur irgendein Durchschnittshund, es fällt mir nicht ein, mich in die wahre Wissenschaft zu mengen, ich habe alle Ehrfurcht vor ihr, die ihr gebührt, aber sie zu vermehren fehlt es mir an Wissen und Fleiß und Ruhe und – nicht zuletzt, besonders seit einigen Jahren – auch an Appetit. Ich schlinge das Essen herunter, wenn ich es finde, aber der geringsten vorgängigen geordneten landwirtschaftlichen Betrachtung ist es mir nicht wert. Mir genügt in dieser Hinsicht der Extrakt aller Wissenschaft, die kleine Regel, mit welcher die Mütter die Kleinen von ihren Brüsten ins Leben entlassen: »Mache alles nass, soviel du kannst.« Und ist hier nicht wirklich fast alles enthalten? Was hat die Forschung, von unseren Urvätern angefangen, entscheidend Wesentliches dem hinzuzufügen? Einzelheiten, Einzelheiten, und wie unsicher ist alles, diese Regel aber wird bestehen, solange wir Hunde sind. Sie betrifft unsere Hauptnahrung; gewiss, wir haben noch andere Hilfsmittel, aber im Notfall, und wenn die Jahre nicht zu schlimm sind, könnten wir von dieser Hauptnahrung leben, diese Hauptnahrung finden wir auf der Erde, die Erde aber braucht unser Wasser, nährt sich von ihm, und nur für diesen Preis gibt sie uns unsere Nahrung, deren Hervorkommen man allerdings, dies ist auch nicht zu vergessen, durch bestimmte Sprüche, Gesänge, Bewegungen beschleunigen kann. Das ist aber meiner Meinung nach alles, von dieser Seite her ist über diese Sache Grundsätzliches nicht mehr zu sagen. Hierin bin ich auch einig mit der großen Mehrzahl der Hundeschaft und von allen in dieser Hinsicht ketzerischen Ansichten wende ich mich streng ab. Wahrhaftig, es geht mir nicht um Besonderheiten, um Rechthaberei, ich bin glücklich, wenn ich mit den Volksgenossen übereinstimmen kann, und in diesem Falle geschieht es. Meine eigenen Untersuchungen gehen aber in anderer Richtung. Der Augenschein lehrt mich, dass die Erde, wenn sie nach den Regeln der Wissenschaft besprengt und bearbeitet wird, die Nahrung hergibt, und zwar in solcher Qualität, in solcher Menge, auf solche Art, an solchen Orten, zu solchen Stunden, wie es die gleichfalls von der Wissenschaft ganz oder teilweise festgestellten Gesetze verlangen. Das nehme ich hin, meine Frage aber ist: »Woher nimmt die Erde diese Nahrung?« Eine Frage, die man im Allgemeinen nicht zu verstehen vorgibt und auf die man mir besten Falls antwortet: »Hast du nicht genug zu essen, werden wir dir von dem unsern geben.« Man beachte diese Antwort. Ich weiß: Es gehört nicht zu den Vorzügen der Hundeschaft, dass wir Speisen, die wir einmal erlangt haben, zur Verteilung bringen. Das Leben ist schwer, die Erde spröde, die Wissenschaft reich an Erkenntnissen, aber arm genug an praktischen Erfolgen; wer Speise hat, behält sie; das ist nicht Eigennutz, sondern das Gegenteil, ist Hundegesetz, ist einstimmiger Volksbeschluss, hervorgegangen aus Überwindung der Eigensucht, denn die Besitzenden sind ja immer in der Minderzahl. Und darum ist jene Antwort: »Hast du nicht genug zu essen, werden wir dir von dem unsern geben« eine ständige Redensart, ein Scherzwort, eine Neckerei. Ich habe das nicht vergessen. Aber eine umso größere Bedeutung hatte es für mich, dass man mir gegenüber, damals als ich mich mit meinen Fragen in der Welt umhertrieb, den Spaß beiseite ließ; man gab mir zwar noch immer nichts zu essen – woher hätte man es gleich nehmen sollen? Und wenn man es gerade zufällig hatte, vergaß man natürlich in der Raserei des Hungers jede andere Rücksicht, aber das Angebot meinte man ernst, und hie und da bekam ich dann wirklich eine Kleinigkeit, wenn ich schnell genug dabei war, sie an mich zu reißen. Wie kam es, dass man sich zu mir so besonders verhielt? Mich schonte, mich bevorzugte. Weil ich ein magerer schwacher Hund war, schlecht genährt und zu wenig um Ernährung besorgt? Aber es laufen viel schlecht genährte Hunde herum, und man nimmt ihnen selbst die elendste Nahrung vor dem Mund weg, wenn man es kann, oft nicht aus Gier, sondern meist aus Grundsatz. Nein, man bevorzugte mich, ich konnte es nicht so sehr mit Einzelheiten belegen, als dass ich vielmehr den bestimmten Eindruck dessen hatte. Waren es also meine Fragen, über die man sich freute, die man für besonders klug ansah? Nein, man freute sich nicht und hielt sie alle für dumm. Und doch konnten es nur die Fragen sein, die mir die Aufmerksamkeit erwarben. Es war, als wolle man lieber das Ungeheuerliche tun, mir den Mund mit Essen zustopfen – man tat es nicht, aber man wollte es – als meine Frage dulden. Aber dann hätte man mich doch besser verjagen können und meine Fragen sich verbitten. Nein, das wollte man nicht, man wollte zwar meine Fragen nicht hören, aber gerade wegen dieser meiner

Fragen wollte man mich nicht verjagen. Es war, so sehr ich ausgelacht, als dummes kleines Tier behandelt, hin- und hergeschoben wurde, eigentlich die Zeit meines größten Ansehens, niemals hat sich später etwas Derartiges wiederholt, überall hatte ich Zutritt, nichts wurde mir verwehrt, unter dem Vorwand rauer Behandlung wurde mir eigentlich geschmeichelt. Und alles also doch nur wegen meiner Fragen, wegen meiner Ungeduld, wegen meiner Forschungsbegierde. Wollte man mich damit einlullen, ohne Gewalt, fast liebend mich von einem falschen Wege abbringen, von einem Wege, dessen Falschheit doch nicht so über allem Zweifel stand, dass sie erlaubt hätte Gewalt anzuwenden, auch hielt eine gewisse Achtung und Furcht von Gewaltanwendung ab. Ich ahnte schon damals etwas Derartiges, heute weiß ich es genau, viel genauer als die, welche es damals taten, es ist wahr, man hat mich ablocken wollen von meinem Wege. Es gelang nicht, man erreichte das Gegenteil, meine Aufmerksamkeit verschärfte sich. Es stellte sich mir sogar heraus, dass ich es war, der die anderen verlocken wollte, und dass mir tatsächlich die Verlockung bis zu einem gewissen Grad gelang. Erst mit der Hilfe der Hundeschaft begann ich, meine eigenen Fragen zu verstehen. Wenn ich zum Beispiel fragte: Woher nimmt die Erde diese Nahrung?, kümmerte mich denn dabei, wie es den Anschein haben konnte, die Erde, kümmerten mich etwa der Erde Sorgen? Nicht im Geringsten, das lag mir wie ich bald erkannte, völlig fern, mich kümmerten nur die Hunde, gar nichts sonst. Denn was gibt es außer den Hunden? Wen kann man sonst anrufen in der weiten, leeren Welt? Alles Wissen, die Gesamtheit aller

Fragen und aller Antworten ist in den Hunden enthalten. Wenn man nur dieses Wissen wirksam, wenn man es nur an den hellen Tag bringen könnte, wenn sie nur nicht so unendlich viel mehr wüssten, als sie zugestehen, als sie sich selbst zugestehen. Noch der redseligste Hund ist verschlossener, als es die Orte zu sein pflegen, wo die besten Speisen sind. Man umschleicht den Mithund, man schäumt von Begierde, man prügelt sich selbst mit dem eigenen Schwanz, man fragt, man bittet, man heult, man beißt und erreicht – nun erreicht das, was man auch ohne jede Anstrengung erreichen würde: liebevolles Anhören, freundliche Berührungen, ehrenvolle Beschnupperungen, innige Umarmungen, mein und dein Heulen mischt sich in eins, alles ist darauf gerichtet, im Entzücken Vergessen zu finden, aber das eine, das man vor allem erreichen wollte: Eingeständnis des Wissens, das bleibt versagt, auf diese Bitte, ob stumm, ob laut, antworten besten Falls, wenn man die Verlockung schon aufs äußerste getrieben hat, nur stumpfe Mienen, schiefe Blicke, verhängte, trübe Augen. Es ist nicht viel anders, als es damals war, da ich als Kind die Musikerhunde anrief und sie schwiegen. Nun könnte man sagen: »du beschwerst dich über deine Mithunde, über ihre Schweigsamkeit hinsichtlich der entscheidenden Dinge, du behauptest, sie wüssten mehr, als sie eingestehen, mehr als sie im Leben gelten lassen wollen, und dieses Verschweigen, dessen Grund und Geheimnis sie natürlich auch noch mitverschweigen, vergifte das Leben, mache es dir unerträglich, du müssest es ändern oder es verlassen, mag sein, aber du bist doch selbst ein Hund, hast auch das Hundewissen, nun, sprich es aus, nicht nur in Form der Frage, sondern als Antwort. Wenn du es aussprichst, wer wird dir widerstehen? Der große Chor der Hundeschaft wird einfallen, als hätte er darauf gewartet. Dann hast du Wahrheit, Klarheit, Eingeständnis, soviel du nur willst. Das Dach dieses niedrigen Lebens, dem du so Schlimmes nachsagst, wird sich öffnen, und wir werden alle, Hund bei Hund, aufsteigen in die hohe Freiheit. Und sollte das Letzte nicht gelingen, sollte es schlimmer werden als bisher, sollte die ganze Wahrheit unerträglicher sein als die halbe, sollte sich bestätigen, dass die Schweigenden als Erhalter des Lebens im Rechte sind, sollte aus der leisen Hoffnung, die wir jetzt noch haben, völlige Hoffnungslosigkeit werden, des Versuches ist das Wort doch wert, da du, so wie du leben darfst, nicht leben willst. Nun also, warum machst du den anderen ihre Schweigsamkeit zum Vorwurf und schweigst selbst?« Leichte Antwort: Weil ich ein Hund bin. Im Wesentlichen genau so wie die anderen fest verschlossen, Widerstand leistend den eigenen Fragen, hart aus Angst. Frage ich denn, genau genommen, zumindest seitdem ich erwachsen bin, die Hundeschaft deshalb, dass sie mir antwortet? Habe ich so törichte Hoffnungen? Sehe ich die Fundamente unseres Lebens, ahne ihre Tiefe, sehe die Arbeiter beim Bau, bei ihrem finsteren Werk und erwarte noch immer, dass auf meine Fragen hin alles dies beendigt, zerstört, verlassen wird? Nein, das erwarte ich wahrhaftig nicht mehr. Mit meinen Fragen hetze ich nur noch mich selbst, will mich anfeuern durch das Schweigen, das allein ringsum mir noch antwortet. Wie lange wirst du es ertragen, dass die Hundeschaft, wie du dir durch deine Forschungen immer mehr zu Bewusstsein bringst, schweigt und immer schweigen wird? Wie lange wirst du es ertragen, so lautet über allen Einzelfragen meine eigentliche Lebensfrage; sie ist nur an mich gestellt und belästigt keinen anderen. Leider kann ich sie leichter beantworten als die Einzelfragen: Ich werde es voraussichtlich aushalten bis zu meinem natürlichen Ende, den unruhigen Fragen widersteht immer mehr die Ruhe des Alters. Ich werde wahrscheinlich schweigend, von Schweigen umgeben, friedlich sterben, und ich sehe dem nahezu gefasst entgegen. Ein bewunderungswürdig starkes Herz, eine vorzeitig nicht abzunützende Lunge sind uns Hunden wie aus Bosheit mitgegeben, wir widerstehen allen Fragen, selbst dem eigenen, Bollwerk des Schweigens, das wir sind.

Immer mehr in letzter Zeit überdenke ich mein Leben, suche den entscheidenden alles verschuldenden Fehler, den ich vielleicht begangen habe, und kann ihn nicht finden. Und ich muss ihn doch begangen haben, denn hätte ich ihn nicht begangen und hätte trotzdem durch die redliche Arbeit eines langen Lebens, das, was ich wollte, nicht erreicht, so wäre bewiesen, dass das, was ich wollte, unmöglich war, und völlige Hoffnungslosigkeit würde daraus folgen. Sieh das Werk deines Lebens! Zuerst die Untersuchungen hinsichtlich der Frage: Woher nimmt die Erde die Nahrung für uns. Ein junger Hund, im Grunde natürlich gierig und lebenslustig, verzichtete ich auf alle Genüsse, wich allen Vergnügungen im Bogen aus, vergrub vor Verlockungen den Kopf zwischen den Beinen und machte mich an die Arbeit. Es war keine Gelehrtenarbeit, weder was die Gelehrsamkeit, noch was die Methode, noch was die Absicht betrifft. Das waren wohl Fehler, aber entscheidend können sie nicht gewesen sein. Ich habe wenig gelernt, denn ich kam frühzeitig von der Mutter fort, gewöhnte mich bald an Selbständigkeit, führte ein freies Leben, und allzu frühe Selbständigkeit ist dem systematischen Lernen feindlich. Aber ich habe viel gesehen, gehört, mit vielen Hunden der verschiedensten Arten und Berufe gesprochen, und alles, wie ich glaube, nicht schlecht aufgefasst und die Einzelbeobachtungen nicht schlecht verbunden, das hat ein wenig die Gelehrsamkeit ersetzt, außerdem aber ist Selbständigkeit, mag sie für das Lernen ein Nachteil sein, für eigene Forschung ein großer Vorzug. Sie war in meinem Fall umso nötiger, als ich nicht die eigentliche Methode der Wissenschaft befolgen konnte, nämlich die Arbeiten der Vorgänger zu benützen und mit den zeitgenössischen Forschern mich zu verbinden. Ich war völlig auf mich allein angewiesen, begann mit dem allerersten Anfang und mit dem für die Jugend beglückenden, für das Alter dann aber äußerst niederdrückenden Bewusstsein, dass der zufällige Schlusspunkt, den ich setzen werde, auch der endgültige sein müsse. War ich wirklich so allein mit meinen Forschungen, jetzt und seit jeher? Ja und nein. Es ist unmöglich, dass nicht immer und auch heute einzelne Hunde hier und dort in meiner Lage waren und sind. So schlimm kann es mit mir nicht stehen. Ich bin kein Haar breit außerhalb des Hundewesens. Jeder Hund hat wie ich den Drang, zu fragen, und ich habe wie jeder Hund den Drang, zu schweigen. Jeder hat den Drang, zu fragen. Hätte ich denn sonst durch meine Fragen auch nur die leichten Erschütterungen erreichen können, die mir oft mit Entzücken, übertriebenem Entzücken allerdings zu sehen vergönnt war. Und dass ich den Drang, zu schweigen, habe, bedarf leider keines besonderen Beweises. Ich bin also grundsätzlich nicht anders als jeder andere Hund, darum wird mich trotz aller Meinungsverschiedenheiten und Abneigungen im Grunde jeder anerkennen, und ich werde es mit jedem Hund nicht anders tun. Nur die Mischung der Elemente ist verschieden, ein persönlich sehr großer, volklich bedeutungsloser Unterschied. Und nun sollte die Mischung dieser immer vorhandenen Elemente innerhalb der Vergangenheit und Gegenwart niemals ähnlich der meinen ausgefallen sein, und wenn man meine Mischung unglücklich nennen will, nicht auch noch viel unglücklicher? Das wäre gegen alle übrige Erfahrung. In den sonderbarsten Berufen sind wir Hunde beschäftigt, Berufe, an die man gar nicht glauben würde, wenn man nicht die vertrauenswürdigsten Nachrichten darüber hätte. Ich denke hier am liebsten an das Beispiel der Lufthunde. Als ich zum ersten Mal von einem hörte, lachte ich, ließ es mir auf keine Weise einreden. Wie? Es sollte einen Hund von allerkleinster Art geben, nicht viel größer als mein Kopf, auch im hohen Alter nicht größer, und dieser Hund, natürlich schwächlich, dem Anschein nach ein künstliches, unreifes, übersorgfältig frisiertes Gebilde, unfähig, einen ehrlichen Sprung zu tun, dieser Hund sollte, wie man erzählte, meistens hoch in der Luft sich fortbewegen, dabei aber keine sichtbare Arbeit machen, sondern ruhen. Nein, solche Dinge mir einreden wollen, das hieß doch, die Unbefangenheit eines jungen Hundes gar zu sehr ausnützen, glaubte ich. Aber kurz darauf hörte ich von anderer Seite von einem andern Lufthund erzählen. Hatte man sich vereinigt, mich zum Besten zu halten? Dann aber sah ich die Musikerhunde, und von dieser Zeit an hielt ich alles für möglich, kein Vorurteil beschränkte meine Fassungskraft, den unsinnigsten Gerüchten ging ich nach, verfolgte sie, soweit ich konnte, das Unsinnigste erschien mir in diesem unsinnigen Leben wahrscheinlicher als das Sinnvolle und für meine Forschung besonders ergiebig. So auch die Lufthunde. Ich erfuhr vielerlei über sie, es gelang mir zwar bis heute, keinen zu sehen, aber von ihrem Dasein bin ich schon längst fest überzeugt, und in meinem Weltbild haben sie ihren wichtigen Platz. Wie meistens so auch hier ist es natürlich nicht die Kunst, die mich vor allem nachdenklich macht. Es ist wunderbar, wer kann das leugnen, dass diese Hunde in der Luft zu schweben imstande sind, im Staunen darüber bin ich mit der Hundeschaft einig. Aber viel wunderbarer ist für mein Gefühl die Unsinnigkeit, die schweigende Unsinnigkeit dieser Existenzen. Im Allgemeinen wird sie gar nicht begründet, sie schweben in der Luft, und dabei bleibt es, das Leben geht weiter seinen Gang, hie und da spricht man von Kunst und Künstlern, das ist alles. Aber warum, grundgütige Hundeschaft, warum nur schweben diese Hunde? Was für einen Sinn hat ihr Beruf? Warum ist kein Wort der Erklärung von ihnen zu bekommen? Warum schweben sie dort oben, lassen die Beine, den Stolz des Hundes, verkümmern, sind getrennt von der nährenden Erde, säen nicht und ernten doch, werden angeblich sogar auf Kosten der Hundeschaft besonders gut genährt. Ich kann mir schmeicheln, dass ich durch meine Fragen in diese Dinge doch ein wenig Bewegung gebracht habe. Man beginnt zu begründen, eine Art Begründung zusammenzuhaspeln, man beginnt und wird allerdings auch über diesen Beginn nicht hinausgehen. Aber etwas ist es doch. Und es zeigt sich dabei zwar nicht die Wahrheit – niemals wird man so weit kommen –, aber doch etwas von der tiefen Verwurzelung der Lüge. Alle unsinnigen Erscheinungen unseres Lebens und die unsinnigsten ganz besonders lassen sich nämlich begründen. Nicht vollständig natürlich – das ist der teuflische Witz –, aber um sich gegen peinliche Fragen zu schützen, reicht's hin. Die Lufthunde wieder als Beispiel genommen. Sie sind nicht hochmütig, wie man zunächst glauben könnte, sie sind vielmehr der Mithunde besonders bedürftig, versucht man, sich in ihre Lage zu versetzen, versteht man's. Sie müssen ja, wenn sie es schon nicht offen tun können – das wäre Verletzung der Schweigepflicht –, so doch auf irgendeine andere Art für ihre Lebensweise Verzeihung zu erlangen suchen oder wenigstens von ihr ablenken, sie vergessen machen, sie tun das, wie man mir erzählt, durch eine fast unerträgliche Geschwätzigkeit. Immerfort haben sie zu erzählen, teils von ihren philosophischen Überlegungen, mit denen sie sich, da sie auf körperliche Anstrengung völlig verzichtet haben, fortwährend beschäftigen können, teils von den Beobachtungen, die sie von ihrem erhöhten Standort aus machen. Und trotzdem sie sich, was bei einem solchen Lotterleben selbstverständlich ist, durch Geisteskraft nicht sehr auszeichnen und ihre Philosophie so wertlos ist wie ihre Beobachtungen und die Wissenschaft kaum etwas davon verwenden kann und überhaupt auf so jämmerliche Hilfsquellen nicht angewiesen ist, trotzdem wird man, wenn man fragt, was die Lufthunde überhaupt sollen, immer wieder zur Antwort bekommen, dass sie zur Wissenschaft viel beitragen. »Das ist richtig«, sagt man darauf, »aber ihre Beiträge sind wertlos und lästig.« Die weitere Antwort ist Achselzucken, Ablenkung, Ärger oder Lachen, und in einem Weilchen, wenn man wieder fragt, erfährt man doch wiederum, dass sie zur Wissenschaft beitragen, und schließlich, wenn man nächstens gefragt wird und sich nicht sehr beherrscht, antwortet man das Gleiche. Und vielleicht ist es auch gut, nicht allzu hartnäckig zu sein und sich zu fügen, die schon bestehenden Lufthunde nicht in ihrer Lebensberechtigung anzuerkennen, was unmöglich ist, aber doch zu dulden. Aber mehr darf man nicht verlangen, das ginge zu weit, und man verlangt es doch. Man verlangt die Duldung immer neuer Lufthunde, die heraufkommen. Man weiß gar nicht genau, woher sie kommen. Vermehren sie sich durch Fortpflanzung? Haben sie denn noch die Kraft dazu, sie sind ja nicht viel mehr als ein schönes Fell, was soll sich hier fortpflanzen? Und wenn das Unwahrscheinliche möglich wäre, wann sollte es geschehen? Immer sieht man sie doch allein, selbstgenügsam oben in der Luft, und wenn sie einmal zu laufen sich herablassen, geschieht es nur ein kleines Weilchen lang, paar gezierte Schritte und immer wieder nur streng allein und in angeblichen Gedanken, von denen sie sich, selbst wenn sie sich anstrengen, nicht losreißen können, wenigstens behaupten sie das. Wenn sie sich aber nicht fortpflanzen, wäre es denkbar, dass sich Hunde finden, welche freiwillig das ebenerdige Leben aufgeben, freiwillig Lufthunde werden und um den

Preis der Bequemlichkeit und einer gewissen Kunstfertigkeit dieses öde Leben dort auf den Kissen wählen? Das ist nicht denkbar, weder Fortpflanzung noch freiwilliger Anschluss ist denkbar. Die Wirklichkeit aber zeigt, dass es doch immer wieder neue Lufthunde gibt; daraus ist zu schließen, dass, mögen auch die Hindernisse unserem Verstande unüberwindbar scheinen, eine einmal vorhandene Hundeart, sei sie auch noch so sonderbar, nicht ausstirbt, zumindest nicht leicht, zumindest nicht ohne dass in jeder Art etwas wäre, das sich lange erfolgreich wehrt. Muss ich das, wenn es für eine so abseitige sinnlose äußerlich allersonderbarste, lebensunfähige Art wie die der Lufthunde gilt, nicht auch für meine Art annehmen? Dabei bin ich äußerlich gar nicht sonderbar, gewöhnlicher Mittelstand, der wenigstens hier in der Gegend sehr häufig ist, durch nichts besonders hervorragend, durch nichts besonders verächtlich, in meiner Jugend und noch teilweise im Mannesalter, solange ich mich nicht vernachlässigte und viel Bewegung machte, war ich sogar ein recht hübscher Hund, besonders meine Vorderansicht wurde gelobt, die schlanken Beine, die schöne Kopfhaltung, aber auch mein grau-weißgelbes, nur in den Haarspitzen sich ringelndes Fell war sehr gefällig, das alles ist nicht sonderbar, sonderbar ist nur mein Wesen, aber auch dieses, wie ich niemals außer Acht lassen darf, im allgemeinen Hundewesen wohl begründet. Wenn nun sogar der Lufthund nicht allein bleibt, hier und dort in der großen Hundewelt immer wieder sich einer findet und sie sogar aus dem Nichts immer wieder neuen Nachwuchs holen, dann kann auch ich die Zuversicht haben, dass ich nicht verlassen bin. Freilich ein besonderes

Schicksal müssen meine Artgenossen haben, und ihr Dasein wird mir niemals sichtbar helfen, schon deshalb nicht, weil ich sie kaum je erkennen werde. Wir sind die, welche das Schweigen drückt, welche es förmlich aus Lufthunger durchbrechen wollen, den andern scheint im Schweigen wohl zu sein, zwar hat es nur diesen Anschein, so wie bei den Musikhunden, die scheinbar ruhig musizierten, in Wirklichkeit aber sehr aufgeregt waren, aber dieser Anschein ist stark, man versucht ihm beizukommen, er spottet jedes Angriffs. Wie helfen sich nun meine Artgenossen? Wie sehen ihre Versuche, dennoch zu leben, aus? Das mag verschieden sein. Ich habe es mit meinen Fragen versucht, so lange ich jung war. Ich könnte mich also vielleicht an die halten, welche viel fragen, und da hätte ich dann meine Artgenossen. Ich habe auch das eine Zeitlang mit Selbstüberwindung versucht, mit Selbstüberwindung, denn mich kümmern ja vor allem die, welche antworten sollen, die, welche mir immerfort mit Fragen, die ich meist nicht beantworten kann, dazwischenfahren, sind mir widerwärtig. Und dann, wer fragt denn nicht gern, solange er jung ist, wie soll ich aus den vielen Fragern die richtigen herausfinden. Eine Frage klingt wie die andere, auf die Absicht kommt es an, die aber ist verborgen, oft auch dem Frager. Und überhaupt, das Fragen ist ja eine Eigentümlichkeit der Hundeschaft, alle fragen durcheinander, es ist, als sollte damit die Spur der richtigen Frager verwischt werden. Nein, unter den Fragern, den Jungen, finde ich meine Artgenossen nicht, und unter den Schweigern, den Alten, zu denen ich jetzt gehöre, ebenso wenig. Aber was sollen denn die Fragen, ich bin ja mit ihnen gescheitert, wahrscheinlich sind meine Genossen viel klüger als ich und wenden ganz andere vortreffliche Mittel an, um dieses Leben zu ertragen, Mittel freilich, die wie ich aus eigenem hinzufüge, vielleicht ihnen zur Not helfen, beruhigen, einschläfern, artverwandelnd wirken, aber in der Allgemeinheit ebenso ohnmächtig sind, wie die meinen, denn soviel ich auch ausschaue, einen Erfolg sehe ich nicht. Ich fürchte, an allem andern werde ich meine Artgenossen eher erkennen, als am Erfolg. Wo sind dann aber meine Artgenossen? Ja das ist die Klage, das ist sie eben. Wo sind sie? Überall und nirgends. Vielleicht ist es mein Nachbar, drei Sprünge weit von mir, wir rufen einander oft zu, er kommt auch zu mir herüber, ich zu ihm nicht. Ist er mein Artgenosse? Ich weiß nicht, ich erkenne zwar nichts dergleichen an ihm, aber möglich ist es. Möglich ist es, aber doch ist nichts unwahrscheinlicher; wenn er fern ist, kann ich zum Spiel mit Zuhilfenahme aller Phantasie manches mich verdächtig Anheimelnde an ihm herausfinden, steht er dann aber vor mir, sind alle meine Erfindungen zum Lachen. Ein alter Hund, noch etwas kleiner als ich, der ich kaum Mittelgröße habe, braun, kurzhaarig, mit müde hängendem Kopf, mit schlürfenden Schritten, das linke Hinterbein schleppt er überdies infolge einer Krankheit ein wenig nach. So nah wie mit ihm verkehre ich schon seit lange mit niemandem, ich bin froh, dass ich ihn doch noch leidlich ertrage, und wenn er fortgeht, schreie ich ihm die freundlichsten Dinge nach, freilich nicht aus Liebe, sondern zornig auf mich, weil ich ihn, wenn ich ihm nachsehe, doch wieder nur ganz abscheulich finde, wie er sich wegschleicht mit dem nachschleppenden Fuß und dem viel zu niedrigen Hinterteil. Manchmal ist mir, als wollte ich mich selbst verspotten, wenn ich ihn in Gedanken meinen Genossen nenne. Auch in unseren Gesprächen verrät er nichts von irgendeiner Genossenschaft, zwar ist er klug und, für unsere Verhältnisse hier, gebildet genug, und ich könnte viel von ihm lernen, aber suche ich Klugheit und Bildung? Wir unterhalten uns gewöhnlich über örtliche Fragen, und ich staune dabei, durch meine Einsamkeit in dieser Hinsicht hellsichtiger gemacht, wie viel Geist selbst für einen gewöhnlichen Hund, selbst bei durchschnittlich nicht allzu ungünstigen Verhältnissen nötig ist, um sein Leben zu fristen und sich vor den größten üblichen Gefahren zu schützen. Die Wissenschaft gibt zwar die Regeln, aber sie auch nur von der Ferne und in den gröbsten Hauptzügen zu verstehen, ist gar nicht leicht, und wenn man sie verstanden hat, kommt erst das eigentlich Schwere, sie nämlich auf die örtlichen Verhältnisse anzuwenden, hier kann kaum jemand helfen, fast jede Stunde gibt neue Aufgaben und jedes neue Fleckchen Erde seine besonderen; dass er für die Dauer irgendwo eingerichtet ist und dass sein Leben nun gewissermaßen von selbst verläuft, kann niemand von sich behaupten, nicht einmal ich, dessen Bedürfnisse sich förmlich von Tag zu Tag verringern. Und alle diese unendliche Mühe – zu welchem Zweck? Doch nur um sich immer weiter zu vergraben im Schweigen und um niemals und von niemand mehr herausgeholt werden zu können. Man rühmt oft den allgemeinen Fortschritt der Hundeschaft durch die Zeiten und meint damit wohl hauptsächlich den Fortschritt der Wissenschaft. Gewiss, die Wissenschaft schreitet fort, das ist unaufhaltsam, sie schreitet sogar mit

Beschleunigung fort, immer schneller, aber was ist daran zu rühmen? Es ist so, wie wenn man jemanden deshalb rühmen wollte, weil er mit zunehmenden Jahren älter wird und infolgedessen immer schneller der Tod sich nähert. Das ist ein natürlicher und überdies ein hässlicher Vorgang, an dem ich nichts zu rühmen finde. Ich sehe nur Verfall, wobei ich aber nicht meine, dass frühere Generationen im Wesen besser waren, sie waren nur jünger, das war ihr großer Vorzug, ihr Gedächtnis war noch nicht so überlastet wie das heutige, es war noch leichter, sie zum Sprechen zu bringen, und wenn es auch niemandem gelungen ist, die Möglichkeit war größer, diese größere Möglichkeit ist ja das, was uns beim Anhören jener alten, doch eigentlich einfältigen Geschichten so erregt. Hie und da hören wir ein andeutendes Wort und möchten fast aufspringen, fühlten wir nicht die Last der Jahrhunderte auf uns. Nein, was ich auch gegen meine Zeit einzuwenden habe, die früheren Generationen waren nicht besser als die neueren, ja in gewissem Sinn waren sie viel schlechter und schwächer. Die Wunder gingen freilich auch damals nicht frei über die Gassen zum beliebigen Einfangen, aber die Hunde waren, ich kann es nicht anders ausdrücken, noch nicht so hündisch wie heute, das Gefüge der Hundeschaft war noch locker, das wahre Wort hätte damals noch eingreifen, den Bau bestimmen, umstimmen, nach jedem Wunsche ändern, in sein Gegenteil verkehren können, und jenes Wort war da, war zumindest nahe, schwebte auf der Zungenspitze, jeder konnte es erfahren, wo ist es heute hingekommen, heute könnte man schon ins Gekröse greifen und würde es nicht finden. Unsere Generation ist vielleicht verloren, aber sie ist unschuldiger als die damalige. Das Zögern meiner Generation kann ich verstehen, es ist ja auch gar kein Zögern mehr, es ist das Vergessen eines vor tausend Nächten geträumten und tausendmal vergessenen Traumes, wer will uns gerade wegen des tausendsten Vergessens zürnen? Aber auch das Zögern unserer Urväter glaube ich zu verstehen, wir hätten wahrscheinlich nicht anders gehandelt, fast möchte ich sagen, wohl uns, dass nicht wir es waren, die die Schuld auf uns laden mussten, dass wir vielmehr in einer schon von anderen verfinsterten Welt in fast schuldlosem Schweigen dem Tode zueilen dürfen. Als unsere Urväter abirrten, dachten sie wohl kaum an ein endloses Irren, sie sahen ja förmlich noch den Kreuzweg, es war leicht, wann immer zurückzukehren, und wenn sie zurückzukehren zögerten, so nur deshalb, weil sie noch eine kurze Zeit sich des Hundelebens freuen wollten, es war noch gar kein eigentliches Hundeleben, und schon schien es ihnen berauschend schön, wie musste es erst später werden, wenigstens noch ein kleines Weilchen später, und so irrten sie weiter. Sie wussten nicht, was wir bei Betrachtung des Geschichtsverlaufs ahnen können, dass die Seele sich früher wandelt als das Leben und dass sie, als sie das Hundeleben zu freuen begann, schon eine recht althündische Seele haben mussten und gar nicht mehr so nahe dem Ausgangspunkt waren, wie ihnen schien oder wie ihr in allen Hundefreuden schwelgendes Auge sie glauben machen wollte. Wer kann heute noch von Jugend sprechen. Sie waren die eigentlichen jungen Hunde, aber ihr einziger Ehrgeiz war leider darauf gerichtet, alte Hunde zu werden, etwas, was ihnen freilich nicht misslingen konnte, wie alle folgenden Generationen beweisen und unsere, die letzte, am besten. – Über alle diese Dinge rede ich natürlich mit meinem Nachbar nicht, aber ich muss oft an sie denken, wenn ich ihm gegenübersitze, diesem typisch alten Hund, oder die Schnauze in sein Fell vergrabe, das schon einen Anhauch jenes Geruches hat, den abgezogene Felle haben. Es wäre sinnlos, über jene Dinge zu reden, übrigens mit ihm wie mit jedem anderen. Ich weiß, wie das Gespräch verlaufen würde. Er hätte einige kleine Einwände hie und da, schließlich würde er zustimmen – Zustimmung ist die beste Waffe – und die Sache wäre begraben, warum sie also überhaupt erst aus ihrem Grab bemühen? Und trotz allem, es gibt doch vielleicht eine über bloße Worte hinausgehende tiefere Übereinstimmung mit meinem Nachbar. Ich kann nicht aufhören, das zu behaupten, trotzdem ich keine Beweise dafür habe und vielleicht dabei nur einer einfachen Täuschung unterliege, weil er eben seit langem der Einzige ist, mit dem ich verkehre, und ich mich also an ihn halten muss. »Bist du doch vielleicht mein Genosse? Auf deine Art? Und schämst dich, weil dir alles misslungen ist? Sieh, mir ist es ebenso gegangen. Wenn ich allein bin, heule ich darüber, komm, zu zweit ist es süßer.« So denke ich manchmal und sehe ihn dabei fest an. Er senkt dann den Blick nicht, aber auch zu entnehmen ist ihm nichts, stumpf sieht er mich an und wundert sich, warum ich schweige und unsere Unterhaltung unterbrochen habe. Aber vielleicht ist gerade dieser Blick seine Art zu fragen, und ich enttäusche ihn, so wie er mich enttäuscht. In meiner Jugend hätte ich ihn, wenn mir damals nicht andere Fragen wichtiger gewesen wären und ich allein mir reichlich genügt hätte, vielleicht laut gefragt, hätte eine matte Zustimmung bekommen, also weniger als heute, da er schweigt. Aber schweigen nicht alle ebenso? Was hindert mich zu glauben, dass alle meine Genossen sind, dass ich nicht nur hie und da einen Mitforscher hatte, der mit seinen winzigen Ergebnissen versunken und vergessen ist und zu dem ich auf keine Weise mehr gelangen kann durch das Dunkel der Zeiten oder das Gedränge der Gegenwart, dass ich vielmehr in allen seit jeher Genossen habe, die sich alle bemühen nach ihrer Art, alle erfolglos nach ihrer Art, alle schweigend oder listig plappernd nach ihrer Art, wie es diese hoffnungslose Forschung mit sich bringt. Dann hätte ich mich aber auch gar nicht absondern müssen, hätte ruhig unter den anderen bleiben können, hätte nicht wie ein unartiges Kind durch die Reihen der Erwachsenen mich hinausdrängen müssen, die ja ebenso hinaus wollen wie ich und an denen mich nur ihr Verstand beirrt, der ihnen sagt, dass niemand hinauskommt und dass alles Drängen töricht ist.

Solche Gedanken sind allerdings deutlich die Wirkung meines Nachbars, er verwirrt mich, er macht mich ganz melancholisch; und ist für sich fröhlich genug, wenigstens höre ich ihn, wenn er in seinem Bereich ist, schreien und singen, dass es mir lästig ist. Es wäre gut, auch auf diesen letzten Verkehr zu verzichten, nicht vagen Träumereien nachzugehen, wie sie jeder Hundeverkehr, so abgehärtet man zu sein glaubt, unvermeidlich erzeugt und die kleine Zeit, die mir bleibt, ausschließlich für meine Forschungen zu verwenden. Ich werde, wenn er nächstens kommt, mich verkriechen und schlafend stellen und das so lange wiederholen, bis er ausbleibt.

Auch ist in meine Forschungen Unordnung gekommen, ich lasse nach, ich ermüde, ich trotte nur noch mechanisch, wo ich begeistert lief. Ich denke zurück an die Zeit, als ich die Frage: »Woher nimmt die Erde unsere Nahrung?« zu untersuchen begann. Freilich lebte ich damals mitten im Volk, drängte mich dorthin, wo es am dichtesten war, wollte alle zu Zeugen meiner Arbeiten machen, diese Zeugenschaft war mir sogar wichtiger als meine Arbeit, da ich ja noch irgendeine allgemeine Wirkung erwartete. Davon erhielt ich natürlich eine große Befeuerung, die nun für mich Einsamen vorbei ist. Damals aber war ich so stark, dass ich etwas tat, was unerhört ist, allen unseren Grundsätzen widerspricht und an das sich gewiss jeder Augenzeuge von damals als an etwas Unheimliches erinnert. Ich fand in der Wissenschaft, die sonst zu grenzenloser Spezialisierung strebt, in einer Hinsicht eine merkwürdige Vereinfachung. Sie lehrt, dass in der Hauptsache die Erde unsere Nahrung hervorbringt, und gibt dann, nachdem sie diese Voraussetzung gemacht hat, die Methoden an, mit welchen sich die verschiedenen Speisen in bester Art und größter Fülle erreichen lassen. Nun ist es freilich richtig, dass die Erde die Nahrung hervorbringt, daran kann kein Zweifel sein, aber so einfach, wie es gewöhnlich dargestellt wird, jede weitere Untersuchung ausschließend, ist es nicht. Man nehme doch nur die primitivsten Vorfälle her, die sich täglich wiederholen. Wenn wir gänzlich untätig wären, wie ich es nun schon fast bin, nach flüchtiger Bodenbearbeitung uns zusammenrollen würden und warten, was kommt, so würden wir allerdings, vorausgesetzt dass sich überhaupt etwas ergeben würde, die Nahrung auf der Erde finden. Aber das ist doch nicht der Regelfall. Wer sich nur ein wenig Unbefangenheit gegenüber der Wissenschaft bewahrt hat – und deren sind freilich wenige, denn die Kreise, welche die Wissenschaft zieht, werden immer größer –, wird, auch wenn er gar nicht auf besondere Beobachtungen ausgeht, leicht erkennen, dass der Hauptteil der Nahrung, die dann auf der Erde liegt, von oben herabkommt, wir fangen ja je nach unserer Geschicklichkeit und Gier das meiste sogar ab, ehe es die Erde berührt. Damit sage ich noch nichts gegen die Wissenschaft, die Erde bringt ja auch diese Nahrung natürlich hervor, ob sie die eine aus sich heraufzieht oder die andere aus der Höhe herabruft, ist ja vielleicht kein wesentlicher Unterschied, und die Wissenschaft, welche festgestellt hat, dass in beiden Fällen Bodenbearbeitung nötig ist, muss sich vielleicht mit jenen Unterscheidungen nicht beschäftigen, heißt es doch: »Hast du den Fraß im Maul, so hast du für diesmal alle Fragen gelöst.« Nur scheint es mir, dass die Wissenschaft sich in verhüllter Form doch wenigstens teilweise mit diesen Dingen beschäftigt, da sie ja doch zwei Hauptmethoden der Nahrungsbeschaffung kennt, nämlich die eigentliche Bodenbearbeitung und dann die Ergänzungs- und Verfeinerungsarbeit in Form von Spruch, Tanz und Gesang. Ich finde darin eine zwar nicht vollständige, aber doch genug deutliche, meiner Unterscheidung entsprechende Zweiteilung. Die Bodenbearbeitung dient meiner Meinung nach zur Erzielung von beiderlei Nahrung und bleibt immer unentbehrlich, Spruch, Tanz und Gesang aber betreffen weniger die Bodennahrung im engeren Sinn, sondern dienen hauptsächlich dazu, die Nahrung von oben herabzuziehen. In dieser Auffassung bestärkt mich die Tradition. Hier scheint das Volk, die Wissenschaft richtigzustellen, ohne es zu wissen und ohne dass die Wissenschaft sich zu wehren wagt. Wenn wie die Wissenschaft will, jene Zeremonien nur dem Boden dienen sollten, etwa um ihm die Kraft zu geben, die Nahrung von oben zu holen, so müssten sie sich doch folgerichtig völlig am Boden vollziehen, dem Boden müsste alles zugeflüstert, vorgesungen, vorgetanzt werden. Die Wissenschaft verlangt wohl auch meines Wissens nichts anderes. Und nun das Merkwürdige, das Volk richtet sich mit allen seinen Zeremonien in die Höhe. Es ist das keine Verletzung der Wissenschaft, sie verbietet es nicht, lässt dem Landwirt darin die Freiheit, sie denkt bei ihren Lehren nur an den Boden, und führt der Landwirt ihre auf den Boden sich beziehenden Lehren aus, ist sie zufrieden, aber ihr Gedankengang sollte meiner Meinung nach eigentlich mehr verlangen. Und ich, der ich niemals tiefer in die Wissenschaft eingeweiht worden bin, kann mir gar nicht vorstellen, wie die Gelehrten es dulden können, dass unser Volk, leidenschaftlich wie es nun einmal ist, die Zaubersprüche aufwärts ruft, unsere alten Volksgesänge in die Lüfte klagt und Sprungtänze aufführt, als ob es sich den Boden vergessend für immer emporschwingen wollte. Von der Betonung dieser Widersprüche ging ich aus, ich beschränkte mich, wann immer nach den Lehren der Wissenschaft die Erntezeit sich näherte, völlig auf den Boden, ich scharrte ihn im Tanz, ich verdrehte den Kopf, um nur dem Boden möglichst nahe zu sein, ich machte mir später eine Grube für die Schnauze und sang so und deklamierte, dass nur der Boden es hörte und niemand sonst neben oder über mir. Die Forschungsergebnisse waren gering, manchmal bekam ich das Essen nicht, und schon wollte ich jubeln über meine Entdeckung, aber dann kam das Essen doch wieder, so als wäre man zuerst beirrt gewesen durch meine sonderbare Aufführung, erkenne aber jetzt den Vorteil, den sie bringe, und verzichte gern auf meine Schreie und Sprünge, oft kam das Essen sogar reichlicher als früher, aber dann blieb es doch auch wieder gänzlich aus. Ich machte mit einem Fleiß, der an jungen Hunden bisher unbekannt gewesen war, genaue Aufstellungen aller meiner Versuche, glaubte schon, hier und da eine Spur zu finden, die mich weiterführen könnte, aber dann verlief sie sich doch wieder ins Unbestimmte. Es kam mir hierbei unstreitig auch meine ungenügende wissenschaftliche Vorbereitung in die Quere. Wo hatte ich die Bürgschaft, dass zum Beispiel das Ausbleiben des Essens nicht durch mein Experiment, sondern durch unwissenschaftliche Bodenbearbeitung bewirkt war, und traf das zu, dann waren alle meine Schlussfolgerungen haltlos. Unter gewissen Bedingungen hätte ich ein fast ganz präzises Experiment erreichen können, wenn es mir nämlich gelungen wäre, ganz ohne Bodenbearbeitung einmal nur durch aufwärts gerichtete Zeremonie das Herabkommen des Essens und dann durch ausschließliche Bodenzeremonie das Ausbleiben des Essens zu erreichen. Ich versuchte auch Derartiges, aber ohne festen Glauben und nicht mit vollkommenen Versuchsbedingungen, denn meiner unerschütterlichen

Meinung nach ist wenigstens eine gewisse Bodenbearbeitung immer nötig, und selbst wenn die Ketzer, die es nicht glauben, recht hätten, ließe es sich doch nicht beweisen, da die Bodenbesprengung unter einem Drang geschieht und sich in gewissen Grenzen gar nicht vermeiden lässt. Ein anderes allerdings etwas abseitiges Experiment glückte mir besser und machte einiges Aufsehen. Anschließend an das übliche Abfangen der Nahrung aus der Luft beschloss ich, die Nahrung zwar nicht niederfallen zu lassen, sie aber auch nicht abzufangen. Zu diesem Zwecke machte ich immer, wenn die Nahrung kam, einen kleinen Luftsprung, der aber so berechnet war, dass er nicht ausreichte; meistens fiel sie ja dann doch stumpf-gleichgültig zu Boden, und ich warf mich wütend auf sie, in der Wut nicht nur des Hungers, sondern auch der Enttäuschung. Aber in vereinzelten Fällen geschah doch etwas anderes, etwas eigentlich Wunderbares, die Speise fiel nicht, sondern folgte mir in der Luft, die Nahrung verfolgte den Hungrigen. Es geschah nicht lange, eine kurze Strecke nur, dann fiel sie doch oder verschwand gänzlich, oder – der häufigste Fall – meine Gier beendete vorzeitig das Experiment, und ich fraß die Sache auf. Immerhin, ich war damals glücklich, durch meine Umgebung ging ein Raunen, man war unruhig und aufmerksam geworden, ich fand meine Bekannten zugänglicher meinen Fragen, in ihren Augen sah ich irgendein Hilfe suchendes Leuchten, mochte es auch nur der Widerschein meiner eigenen Blicke sein, ich wollte nichts anderes, ich war zufrieden. Bis ich dann freilich erfuhr – und die anderen erfuhren es mit mir –, dass dieses Experiment in der Wissenschaft längst beschrieben ist, viel großartiger schon gelungen ist als mir, zwar schon lange nicht gemacht worden ist wegen der Schwierigkeit der Selbstbeherrschung, die es verlangt, aber wegen seiner angeblichen wissenschaftlichen Bedeutungslosigkeit auch nicht wiederholt werden muss. Es beweise nur das, was man schon wusste, dass der Boden die Nahrung nicht nur gerade abwärts von oben holt, sondern auch schräg, ja sogar in Spiralen. Da stand ich nun, aber entmutigt war ich nicht, dazu war ich noch zu jung, im Gegenteil, ich wurde dadurch aufgemuntert zu der vielleicht größten Leistung meines Lebens. Ich glaubte nicht der wissenschaftlichen Entwertung meines Experiments, aber hier hilft kein Glauben, sondern nur der Beweis, und den wollte ich antreten und wollte damit auch dieses ursprünglich etwas abseitige Experiment ins volle Licht, in den Mittelpunkt der Forschung stellen. Ich wollte beweisen, dass, wenn ich vor der Nahrung zurückwich, nicht der Boden sie schräg zu sich herabzog, sondern ich es war, der sie hinter mir her lockte. Dieses Experiment konnte ich allerdings nicht weiter ausbauen, den Fraß vor sich zu sehen und dabei wissenschaftlich experimentieren, das hält man für die Dauer nicht aus. Aber ich wollte etwas anderes tun, ich wollte, solange ich es aushielt, völlig fasten, allerdings dabei auch jeden Anblick der Nahrung, jede Verlockung vermeiden. Wenn ich mich so zurückzog, mit geschlossenen Augen liegen blieb Tag und Nacht, weder um das Aufheben noch um das Abfangen der Nahrung mich kümmerte und wie ich nicht zu behaupten wagte, aber leise hoffte, ohne alle sonstige Maßnahmen nur auf die unvermeidliche unrationelle Bodenbesprengung hin, und stilles Aufsagen der Sprüche und Lieder (den Tanz wollte ich unterlassen, um mich nicht zu schwächen) die Nahrung von oben selbst herabkäme und, ohne sich um den Boden zu kümmern, an mein Gebiss klopfen würde, um eingelassen zu werden - wenn dies geschah, dann war die Wissenschaft zwar nicht widerlegt, denn sie hat genug Elastizität für Ausnahmen und Einzelfälle, aber was würde das Volk sagen, das glücklicherweise nicht so viel Elastizität hat? Denn es würde das ja auch kein Ausnahmsfall von der Art sein, wie sie die Geschichte überliefert, dass etwa einer wegen körperlicher Krankheit oder wegen Trübsinn sich weigert, die Nahrung vorzubereiten, zu suchen, aufzunehmen und dann die Hundeschaft in Beschwörungsformeln sich vereinigt und dadurch ein Abirren der Nahrung von ihrem gewöhnlichen Weg geradewegs in das Maul des Kranken erreicht. Ich war dagegen in voller Kraft und Gesundheit, mein Appetit so prächtig, dass er mich tagelang hinderte, an etwas anderes zu denken als an ihn, ich unterzog mich, mochte man es glauben oder nicht, dem Fasten freiwillig, war selbst imstande für das Herabkommen der Nahrung zu sorgen und wollte es auch tun, brauchte also auch keine Hilfe der Hundeschaft und verbat sie mir sogar auf das Entschiedenste. Ich suchte mir einen geeigneten Ort in einem entlegenen Gebüsch, wo ich keine Essgespräche, kein Schmatzen und Knochenknacken hören würde, fraß mich noch einmal völlig satt und legte mich dann hin. Ich wollte womöglich die ganze Zeit mit geschlossenen Augen verbringen; solange kein Essen kommen sollte, würde es für mich ununterbrochen Nacht sein, mochte es Tage und Wochen dauern. Dabei durfte ich allerdings, dies war eine große Erschwerung, wenig oder am besten gar nicht schlafen, denn ich musste ja nicht nur die Nahrung herabbeschwören, sondern auch auf der Hut sein, dass ich die Ankunft der Nahrung nicht etwa gar verschlafe, andererseits wiederum war Schlaf sehr willkommen, denn schlafend würde ich viel länger hungern können als im Wachen. Aus diesen Gründen beschloss ich, die Zeit vorsichtig einzuteilen und viel zu schlafen, aber immer nur ganz kurze Zeit. Ich erreichte dies dadurch, dass ich den Kopf im Schlaf immer auf einen schwachen Ast stützte, der bald einknickte und mich dadurch weckte. So lag ich, schlief oder wachte, träumte oder sang still für mich hin. Die erste Zeit verging ereignislos, noch war es vielleicht dort, woher die Nahrung kommt, irgendwie unbemerkt geblieben, dass ich mich hier gegen den üblichen Verlauf der Dinge stemmte, und so blieb alles still. Ein wenig störte mich in meiner Anstrengung die Befürchtung, dass die Hunde mich vermissen, bald auffinden und etwas gegen mich unternehmen würden. Eine zweite Befürchtung war, dass auf die bloße Besprengung hin, der Boden, trotzdem es ein nach der Wissenschaft unfruchtbarer Boden war, die sogenannte Zufallsnahrung hergeben und ihr Geruch mich verführen würde. Aber vorläufig geschah nichts dergleichen, und ich konnte weiterhungern. Abgesehen von diesen Befürchtungen war ich zunächst ruhig, wie ich es an mir noch nie bemerkt hatte. Trotzdem ich hier eigentlich an der Aufhebung der Wissenschaft arbeitete, erfüllte mich Behagen und fast die sprichwörtliche Ruhe des wissenschaftlichen Arbeiters. In meinen Träumereien erlangte ich von der Wissenschaft Verzeihung, es fand sich in ihr auch ein Raum für meine Forschungen, trostreich klang es mir in den Ohren, dass ich, mögen auch meine Forschungen noch so erfolgreich werden und besonders dann, keineswegs für das Hundeleben verloren sei, die Wissenschaft sei mir freundlich geneigt, sie selbst werde die Deutung meiner Ergebnisse vornehmen, und dieses Versprechen bedeute schon die Erfüllung selbst, ich werde, während ich mich bisher im Innersten ausgestoßen fühlte und die Mauern meines Volkes berannte wie ein Wilder, in großen Ehren aufgenommen werden, die ersehnte Wärme versammelter Hundeleiber werde mich umströmen, hochgepriesen werde ich auf den Schultern meines Volkes schwanken. Merkwürdige Wirkung des ersten Hungerns. Meine Leistung erschien mir so groß, dass ich aus Rührung und aus Mitleid mit mir selbst dort in dem stillen Gebüsch zu weinen anfing, was allerdings nicht ganz verständlich war, denn wenn ich den verdienten Lohn erwartete, warum weinte ich dann? Wohl nur aus Behaglichkeit. Niemals hat mir mein Weinen gefallen. Immer nur wenn mir behaglich war, selten genug, habe ich geweint. Damals ging es freilich bald vorüber. Die schönen Bilder verflüchtigten sich allmählich mit dem Ernsterwerden des Hungers, es dauerte nicht lange, und ich war, nach schneller Verabschiedung aller Phantasien und aller Rührung, völlig allein mit dem in den Eingeweiden brennenden Hunger. »Das ist der Hunger«, sagte ich mir damals unzählige Mal, so als wollte ich mich glauben machen, Hunger und ich seien noch immer zweierlei, und ich könnte ihn abschütteln wie einen lästigen Liebhaber, aber in Wirklichkeit waren wir höchst schmerzlich eines, und wenn ich mir erklärte: »Das ist der Hunger«, so war es eigentlich der Hunger, der sprach und sich damit über mich lustig machte. Eine böse, böse Zeit! Mich schauert, wenn ich an sie denke, freilich nicht nur wegen des Leides, das ich damals durchlebt habe, sondern vor allem deshalb, weil ich damals nicht fertig geworden bin, weil ich dieses Leiden noch einmal werde durchkosten müssen, wenn ich etwas erreichen will, denn das Hungern halte ich noch heute für das letzte und stärkste Mittel meiner Forschung. Durch das Hungern geht der Weg, das Höchste ist nur der höchsten Leistung erreichbar, wenn es erreichbar ist, und diese höchste Leistung ist bei uns freiwilliges Hungern. Wenn ich also jene Zeiten durchdenke – und für mein Leben gern wühle ich in ihnen –, durchdenke ich auch die Zeiten, die mir drohen. Es scheint, dass man fast ein Leben verstreichen lassen muss, ehe man sich von einem solchen Versuch erholt, meine ganzen Mannesjahre trennen mich von jenem Hungern, aber erholt bin ich noch nicht. Ich werde, wenn ich nächstens das Hungern beginne, vielleicht mehr Entschlossenheit haben als früher, infolge meiner größeren Erfahrung und besserer Einsicht in die Notwendigkeit des Versuches, aber meine Kräfte sind geringer noch von damals her, zumindest werde ich schon ermatten in der bloßen Erwartung der bekannten Schrecken. Mein schwächerer Appetit wird mir nicht helfen, er entwertet nur ein wenig den Versuch und wird mich wahrscheinlich noch zwingen, länger zu hungern, als es damals nötig gewesen wäre. Über diese und andere Voraussetzungen glaube ich, mir klar zu sein, an Vorversuchen hat es ja nicht gefehlt in dieser langen Zwischenzeit, oft genug habe ich das Hungern förmlich angebissen, war aber noch nicht stark zum Äußersten, und die unbefangene Angriffslust der Jugend ist natürlich für immer dahin. Sie schwand schon damals inmitten des Hungerns. Mancherlei Überlegungen quälten mich. Drohend erschienen mir unsere Urväter. Ich halte sie zwar, wenn ich es auch öffentlich nicht zu sagen wage, für schuld an allem, sie haben das Hundeleben verschuldet, und ich könnte also ihren Drohungen leicht mit Gegendrohungen antworten, aber vor ihrem Wissen beuge ich mich, es kam aus Quellen, die wir nicht mehr kennen, deshalb würde ich auch, sosehr es mich gegen sie anzukämpfen drängt, niemals ihre Gesetze geradezu überschreiten, nur durch die Gesetzeslücken, für die ich eine besondere Witterung habe, schwärme ich aus. Hinsichtlich des Hungerns berufe ich mich auf das berühmte Gespräch, im Laufe dessen einer unserer Weisen die Absicht aussprach, das Hungern zu verbieten, worauf ein Zweiter davon abriet mit der Frage: »Wer wird denn jemals hungern?« und der Erste sich überzeugen ließ und das Verbot zurückhielt. Nun entsteht aber wieder die Frage: »Ist nun das Hungern nicht eigentlich doch verboten?« Die große Mehrzahl der Kommentatoren verneint sie, sieht das Hungern für freigegeben an, hält es mit dem zweiten Weisen und befürchtet deshalb auch von einer irrtümlichen Kommentierung keine schlimmen Folgen. Dessen hatte ich mich wohl vergewissert, ehe ich mit dem Hungern begann. Nun aber, als ich mich im Hunger krümmte, schon in einiger Geistesverwirrung immerfort bei meinen Hinterbeinen Rettung suchte und sie verzweifelt leckte, kaute, aussaugte bis zum After hinauf, erschien mir die allgemeine Deutung jenes Gespräches ganz und gar falsch, ich verfluchte die kommentatorische Wissenschaft, ich verfluchte mich, der ich mich von ihr hatte irreführen lassen, das Gespräch enthielt ja, wie ein Kind erkennen musste – freilich ein hungerndes –, mehr als nur ein einziges Verbot des Hungerns, der erste Weise wollte das Hungern verbieten, was ein Weiser will, ist schon geschehen, das Hungern war also verboten, der zweite Weise stimmte ihm nicht nur zu, sondern hielt das Hungern sogar für unmöglich, wälzte also auf das erste Verbot noch ein zweites, das Verbot der Hundenatur selbst, der Erste erkannte dies an und hielt das ausdrückliche Verbot zurück, das heißt, er gebot den Hunden nach Darlegung alles dessen, Einsicht zu üben und sich selbst das Hungern zu verbieten. Also ein dreifaches Verbot statt des üblichen einen, und ich hatte es verletzt. Nun hätte ich ja wenigstens jetzt verspätet gehorchen und zu hungern aufhören können, aber mitten durch den Schmerz ging auch eine Verlockung, weiter zu hungern, und ich folgte ihr, lüstern wie einem unbekannten Hund. Ich konnte nicht aufhören, vielleicht war ich auch schon zu schwach, um aufzustehen und in bewohnte Gegenden mich zu retten. Ich wälzte mich hin und her auf der Waldstreu, schlafen konnte ich nicht mehr, ich hörte überall Lärm, die während meines bisherigen Lebens schlafende Welt schien durch mein Hungern erwacht zu sein, ich bekam die Vorstellung, dass ich nie mehr werde fressen können, denn dadurch musste ich die freigelassen lärmende Welt wieder zum Schweigen bringen, und das würde ich nicht imstande sein, den größten Lärm allerdings hörte ich in meinem Bauche, ich legte oft das Ohr an ihn und muss entsetzte Augen gemacht haben, denn ich konnte kaum glauben, was ich hörte. Und da es nun zu arg wurde, schien der Taumel auch meine Natur zu ergreifen, sie machte sinnlose Rettungsversuche, ich begann, Speisen zu riechen, auserlesene Speisen, die ich längst nicht mehr gegessen hatte, Freuden meiner Kindheit, ja, ich roch den Duft der Brüste meiner Mutter; ich vergaß meinen Entschluss, Gerüchen Widerstand leisten zu wollen, oder richtiger, ich vergaß ihn nicht, mit dem Entschluss, so als sei es ein Entschluss, der dazugehöre, schleppte ich mich nach allen Seiten, immer nur paar Schritte und schnupperte, so als suchte ich die Speisen nur, um mich vor ihnen zu hüten. Dass ich nichts fand, enttäuschte mich nicht, die Speisen waren da, nur waren sie immer paar Schritte zu weit, die Beine knickten mir vorher ein. Gleichzeitig allerdings wusste ich, dass gar nichts da war, dass ich die kleinen Bewegungen nur machte aus Angst vor dem endgültigen Zusammenbrechen auf einem Platz, den ich nicht mehr verlassen würde. Die letzten Hoffnungen schwanden, die letzten Verlockungen, elend würde ich hier zugrundegehen, was sollten meine Forschungen, kindliche Versuche aus kindlich glücklicher Zeit, hier und jetzt war Ernst, hier hätte die Forschung ihren Wert beweisen können, aber wo war sie? Hier war nur ein hilflos ins Leere schnappender Hund, der zwar noch krampfhaft eilig, ohne es zu wissen, immerfort den Boden besprengte, aber in seinem Gedächtnis aus dem ganzen Wust der Zaubersprüche nicht das Geringste mehr auftreiben konnte, nicht einmal das Verschen, mit dem sich die Neugeborenen unter ihre Mutter ducken. Es war mir, als sei ich hier nicht durch einen kurzen Lauf von den Brüdern getrennt, sondern unendlich weit fort von allen, und als stürbe ich eigentlich gar nicht durch Hunger, sondern infolge meiner Verlassenheit. Es war doch ersichtlich, dass sich niemand um mich kümmerte, niemand unter der Erde, niemand auf ihr, niemand in der Höhe, ich ging an ihrer Gleichgültigkeit zugrunde, ihre Gleichgültigkeit sagte: Er stirbt, und so würde es geschehen. Und stimmte ich nicht bei? Sagte ich nicht das Gleiche? Hatte ich nicht diese Verlassenheit gewollt? Wohl, ihr Hunde, aber nicht um hier so zu enden, sondern um zur Wahrheit hinüberzukommen, aus dieser Welt der Lüge, wo sich niemand findet, von dem man Wahrheit erfahren kann, auch von mir nicht, eingeborenem Bürger der Lüge. Vielleicht war die Wahrheit gar nicht mehr allzu weit, nur für mich zu weit, der ich versagte und starb. Vielleicht war sie nicht allzu weit, und ich also nicht so verlassen wie ich dachte, nicht von den anderen verlassen, nur von mir, der ich versagte und starb. Doch man stirbt nicht so eilig, wie ein nervöser Hund glaubt. Ich fiel nur in Ohnmacht, und als ich aufwachte und die Augen erhob, stand ein fremder Hund vor mir. Ich fühlte keinen Hunger, ich war sehr kräftig, in den Gelenken federte es meiner Meinung nach, wenn ich auch keinen Versuch machte, es durch Aufstehen zu erproben. Ich sah an und für sich nicht mehr als sonst, ein schöner aber nicht allzu ungewöhnlicher Hund stand vor mir, das sah ich, nichts anderes, und doch glaubte ich, mehr an ihm zu sehen als sonst. Unter mir lag Blut, im ersten Augenblick dachte ich, es sei Speise, ich merkte aber gleich, dass es Blut war, das ich ausgebrochen hatte. Ich wandte mich davon ab und dem fremden Hunde zu. Er war mager, hochbeinig, braun, hier und da weiß gefleckt und hatte einen schönen, starken, forschenden Blick. »Was machst du hier?«, sagte er, »du musst von hier fortgehen.« »Ich kann jetzt nicht fortgehen«, sagte ich, ohne weitere Erklärung, denn wie hätte ich ihm alles erklären sollen, auch schien er in Eile zu sein. »Bitte, geh fort«, sagte er und hob unruhig ein Bein nach dem andern. »Lass mich«, sagte ich, »geh und kümmere dich nicht um mich, die anderen kümmern sich auch nicht um mich.« »Ich bitte dich um deinetwillen«, sagte er. »Bitte mich, aus welchem Grunde du willst«, sagte ich, »ich kann nicht gehen, selbst wenn ich wollte.« »Daran fehlt es nicht«, sagte er lächelnd. »Du kannst gehen. Eben weil du schwach zu sein scheinst, bitte ich dich, dass du jetzt langsam fortgehst, zögerst du, wirst du später laufen müssen.« »Lass das meine Sorge sein«, sagte ich. »Es ist auch meine«, sagte er, traurig wegen meiner Hartnäckigkeit, und wollte nun offenbar mich also schon vorläufig hier lassen, aber die Gelegenheit benützen und sich liebend an mich heranmachen. Zu anderer Zeit hätte ich es gerne geduldet von dem Schönen, damals aber, ich begriff es nicht, fasste mich ein Entsetzen davor, »Weg«, schrie ich, umso lauter, als ich mich anders nicht verteidigen konnte. »Ich lasse dich ja«, sagte er, langsam zurücktretend. »Du bist sonderbar. Gefalle ich dir denn nicht?« »Du wirst mir gefallen, wenn du fortgehst und mich in Ruhe lässt«, sagte ich, aber ich war meiner nicht mehr so sicher, wie ich ihn glauben machen wollte. Irgendetwas sah oder hörte ich an ihm mit meinen durch das Hungern geschärften Sinnen, es war erst in den Anfängen, es wuchs, es näherte sich, und ich wusste schon: Dieser Hund hat allerdings die Macht dich fortzutreiben, wenn du dir jetzt auch noch nicht vorstellen kannst, wie du dich jemals wirst erheben können. Und ich sah ihn, der auf meine grobe Antwort nur sanft den Kopf geschüttelt hatte, mit immer größerer Begierde an. »Wer bist du?«, fragte ich. »Ich bin ein Jäger«, sagte er. »Und warum willst du mich nicht hier lassen?« fragte ich. »Du störst mich«, sagte er. »Ich kann nicht jagen, wenn du hier bist.« »Versuch es«, sagte ich, »vielleicht wirst du doch jagen können.« »Nein«, sagte er, »es tut mir leid, aber du musst fort.« »Lass heute das Jagen!«, bat ich. »Nein«, sagte er, »ich muss jagen.« »Ich muss fortgehen, du musst jagen«, sagte ich, »lauter müssen. Verstehst du es, warum wir müssen?« »Nein«, sagte er, »es ist daran aber auch nichts zu verstehen, es sind selbstverständliche natürliche Dinge.« »Doch nicht«, sagte ich, »es tut dir ja leid, dass du mich verjagen musst, und dennoch tust du es.« »So ist es«, sagte er. »So ist es«, wiederholte ich ärgerlich »das ist keine Antwort. Welcher Verzicht fiele dir leichter, der Verzicht auf die Jagd, oder darauf mich wegzutreiben?« »Der Verzicht auf die Jagd«, sagte er ohne Zögern. »Nun also«, sagte ich, »hier ist doch ein Widerspruch.« »Was für ein Widerspruch denn?«, sagte er. »Du lieber kleiner Hund, verstehst du denn wirklich nicht dass ich muss? Verstehst du denn das Selbstverständliche nicht?« Ich antwortete nichts mehr, denn ich merkte – und neues Leben durchfuhr mich dabei, Leben wie es der Schrecken gibt – ich merkte an unfassbaren Einzelheiten, die vielleicht niemand außer mir hätte merken können, dass der Hund aus der Tiefe der Brust zu einem Gesange anhob. »Du wirst singen«, sagte ich. »Ja«, sagte er ernst, »ich werde singen, bald, aber noch nicht.« »Du beginnst schon«, sagte ich. »Nein«, sagte er, »noch nicht. Aber mach dich bereit.« »Ich höre es schon, trotzdem du es leugnest«, sagte ich zitternd. Er schwieg. Und ich glaubte damals, etwas zu erkennen, was kein Hund je vor mir erfahren hat, wenigstens findet sich in der Überlieferung nicht die leiseste Andeutung dessen, und ich versenkte eilig in unendlicher Angst und Scham das Gesicht in der Blutlache vor mir. Ich glaubte nämlich zu erkennen, dass der Hund schon sang, ohne es noch zu wissen, ja mehr noch, dass die Melodie, von ihm getrennt, nach eigenem Gesetz durch die Lüfte schwebte und über ihn hinweg, als gehöre er nicht dazu, nach mir, nur nach mir hin zielte. Heute leugne ich natürlich alle derartigen Erkenntnisse und schreibe sie meiner damaligen Überreiztheit zu, aber wenn es auch ein Irrtum war, so hat er doch eine gewisse Großartigkeit, ist die einzige, wenn auch nur scheinbare Wirklichkeit, die ich aus der Hungerzeit in diese Welt herübergerettet habe, und zeigt zumindest, wie weit bei völligem Außersichsein wir gelangen können. Und ich war wirklich völlig außer mir. Unter gewöhnlichen Umständen wäre ich schwer krank gewesen, unfähig mich zu rühren, aber der Melodie, die nun bald der Hund als die seine zu übernehmen schien, konnte ich nicht widerstehen. Immer stärker wurde sie; ihr Wachsen hatte vielleicht keine Grenzen, und schon jetzt sprengte sie mir fast das Gehör. Das Schlimmste aber war, dass sie nur meinetwegen vorhanden zu sein schien, diese Stimme, vor deren Erhabenheit der Wald verstummte, nur meinetwegen, wer war ich, der ich noch immer hierzubleiben wagte und mich vor ihr breitmachte in meinem Schmutz und Blut. Schlotternd erhob ich mich, sah an mir herab, »dieses wird doch nicht laufen«, dachte ich noch, aber schon flog ich von der Melodie gejagt in den herrlichsten Sprüngen dahin. Meinen Freunden erzählte ich nichts, gleich bei meiner Ankunft hätte ich wahrscheinlich alles erzählt, aber da war ich zu schwach, später schien es mir wieder nicht mitteilbar. Andeutungen, die zu unterdrücken ich mich nicht bezwingen konnte, verloren sich spurlos in den Gesprächen. Körperlich erholte ich mich übrigens in wenigen Stunden, geistig trage ich noch heute die Folgen.

Meine Forschungen aber erweiterte ich auf die Musik der Hunde. Die Wissenschaft war gewiss auch hier nicht untätig, die Wissenschaft von der Musik ist, wenn ich gut berichtet bin, vielleicht noch umfangreicher als jene von der Nahrung und jedenfalls fester begründet. Es ist das dadurch zu erklären, dass auf diesem Gebiet leidenschaftsloser gearbeitet werden kann als auf jenem, und dass es sich hier mehr um bloße Beobachtungen und Systemisierungen handelt, dort dagegen vor allem um praktische Folgerungen. Damit hängt zusammen, dass der Respekt vor der Musikwissenschaft größer ist als vor der Nahrungswissenschaft, die erstere aber niemals so tief ins Volk dringen konnte wie die zweite. Auch ich stand der Musikwissenschaft, ehe ich die Stimme im Wald gehört hatte, fremder gegenüber als irgendeiner anderen. Zwar hatte mich schon das Erlebnis mit den Musikhunden auf sie hingewiesen, aber ich war damals noch zu jung, auch ist es nicht leicht, an diese Wissenschaft auch nur heranzukommen, sie gilt als besonders schwierig und schließt sich vornehm gegen die Menge ab. Auch war zwar die Musik bei jenen Hunden das zunächst Auffallendste gewesen, aber wichtiger als die Musik schien mir ihr verschwiegenes Wesen, für ihre schreckliche Musik fand sich vielleicht überhaupt keine Ähnlichkeit anderswo, ich konnte sie eher vernachlässigen, aber ihr Wesen begegnete mir von damals an in allen Hunden überall. In das Wesen der Hunde einzudringen, schienen mir aber Forschungen über die Nahrung am geeignetsten und ohne Umweg zum Ziele führend. Vielleicht hatte ich darin Unrecht. Ein Grenzgebiet der beiden Wissenschaften lenkte allerdings schon damals meinen Verdacht auf sich. Es ist die Lehre von dem die Nahrung herabrufenden Gesang. Wieder ist es hier für mich sehr störend, dass ich auch in die Musikwissenschaft niemals ernstlich eingedrungen bin und mich in dieser Hinsicht bei weitem nicht einmal zu den von der Wissenschaft immer besonders verachteten Halbgebildeten rechnen kann. Dies muss mir immer gegenwärtig bleiben. Vor einem Gelehrten würde ich, ich habe leider dafür Beweise, auch in der leichtesten wissenschaftlichen Prüfung sehr schlecht bestehen. Das hat natürlich, von den schon erwähnten Lebensumständen abgesehen, seinen Grund zunächst in meiner wissenschaftlichen Unfähigkeit, geringen Denkkraft, schlechtem Gedächtnis, und vor allem in dem Außerstandesein, das wissenschaftliche Ziel mir immer vor Augen zu halten. Das alles gestehe ich mir offen ein, sogar mit einer gewissen Freude. Denn der tiefere Grund meiner wissenschaftlichen Unfähigkeit scheint mir ein Instinkt und wahrlich kein schlechter Instinkt zu sein. Wenn ich bramarbasieren wollte, könnte ich sagen, dass gerade dieser Instinkt meine wissenschaftlichen Fähigkeiten zerstört hat, denn es wäre doch eine zumindest sehr merkwürdige Erscheinung, dass ich, der ich in den gewöhnlichen täglichen Lebensdingen, die gewiss nicht die einfachsten sind, einen erträglichen Verstand zeige und vor allem, wenn auch nicht die Wissenschaft, so doch die Gelehrten sehr gut verstehe, was an meinen Resultaten nachprüfbar ist, von vornherein unfähig gewesen sein sollte, die Pfote auch nur zur ersten Stufe der Wissenschaft zu erheben. Es war der Instinkt, der mich vielleicht gerade um der Wissenschaft willen, aber einer anderen Wissenschaft, als sie heute geübt wird, einer allerletzten Wissenschaft, die Freiheit höher schätzen ließ als alles andere. Die Freiheit! Freilich die Freiheit, wie sie heute möglich ist, ein kümmerliches Gewächs. Aber immerhin Freiheit, immerhin ein Besitz.

Der Bau

Ich habe den Bau eingerichtet, und er scheint wohlgelungen. Von außen ist eigentlich nur ein großes Loch sichtbar, dieses führt aber in Wirklichkeit nirgends hin, schon nach paar Schritten stößt man auf natürliches festes Gestein, ich will mich nicht dessen rühmen, diese List mit Absicht ausgeführt zu haben, es war vielmehr der Rest eines der vielen vergeblichen Bauversuche, aber schließlich schien es mir vorteilhaft, dieses eine Loch unverschüttet zu lassen. Freilich manche List ist so fein, dass sie sich selbst umbringt, das weiß ich besser als irgendwer sonst, und es ist gewiss auch kühn, durch dieses Loch überhaupt auf die Möglichkeit aufmerksam zu machen, dass hier etwas Nachforschungswertes vorhanden ist. Doch verkennt mich, wer glaubt, dass ich feige bin und etwa nur aus Feigheit meinen Bau anlege. Wohl tausend Schritte von diesem Loch entfernt liegt, von einer abhebbaren Moosschicht verdeckt, der eigentliche Zugang zum Bau, er ist so gesichert, wie eben überhaupt auf der Welt etwas gesichert werden kann, gewiss, es kann jemand auf das Moos treten oder hineinstoßen, dann liegt mein Bau frei da, und wer Lust hat – allerdings sind wohlgemerkt auch gewisse nicht allzu häufige Fähigkeiten dazu nötig –, kann eindringen und für immer alles zerstören. Das weiß ich wohl, und mein Leben hat selbst jetzt auf seinem Höhepunkt kaum eine völlig ruhige Stunde, dort an jener Stelle im dunkeln Moos bin ich sterblich, und in meinen Träumen schnuppert dort oft eine lüsterne Schnauze unaufhörlich herum. Ich hätte, wird man meinen, auch dieses wirkliche Eingangsloch zuschütten können, oben in dünner Schicht mit fester, weiter unten mit lockerer Erde, so dass es mir immer nur wenig Mühe gegeben hätte, mir immer wieder von neuem den Ausweg zu erarbeiten. Es ist aber doch nicht möglich, gerade die Vorsicht verlangt, dass ich eine sofortige Auslaufmöglichkeit habe, gerade die Vorsicht verlangt, wie leider so oft, das Risiko des Lebens; das alles sind recht mühselige Rechnungen, und die Freude des scharfsinnigen Kopfes an sich selbst ist manchmal die alleinige Ursache dessen, dass man weiterrechnet. Ich muss die sofortige Auslaufmöglichkeit haben, kann ich denn trotz aller Wachsamkeit nicht von ganz unerwarteter Seite angegriffen werden? Ich lebe im innersten meines Baues in Frieden, und inzwischen bohrt sich langsam und still der Gegner von irgendwoher an mich heran, ich will nicht sagen, dass er besseren Spürsinn hat als ich, vielleicht weiß er ebenso wenig von mir wie ich von ihm, aber es gibt leidenschaftliche Räuber, die blindlings die Erde durchwühlen, und bei der ungeheuren Ausdehnung meines Baues haben selbst sie Hoffnung, irgendwo auf einen meiner Wege zu stoßen, freilich, ich habe den Vorteil in meinem Haus zu sein, alle Wege und Richtungen genau zu kennen, der Räuber kann sehr leicht mein Opfer werden und ein süß schmeckendes, aber ich werde alt, es gibt viele, die kräftiger sind als ich, und meiner Gegner gibt es unzählige, es könnte geschehen, dass ich vor einem Feind fliehe und dem andern in die Fänge laufe, ach, was könnte nicht alles geschehen, jedenfalls aber muss ich die Zuversicht haben, dass irgendwo vielleicht ein leicht erreichbarer, völlig offener Ausgang ist, wo ich, um hinauszukommen, gar nicht mehr zu arbeiten habe, so dass ich nicht etwa, während ich dort verzweifelt grabe, sei es auch in leichter Aufschüttung, plötzlich - bewahre mich der Himmel - die Zähne des Verfolgers in meinen Schenkeln spüre. Und es sind nicht nur die äußeren Feinde die mich bedrohen, es gibt auch solche im Innern der Erde, ich habe sie noch nie gesehen, aber die Sagen erzählen von ihnen, und ich glaube fest an sie. Es sind Wesen der inneren Erde, nicht einmal die Sage kann sie beschreiben, selbst wer ihr Opfer geworden ist, hat sie kaum gesehen, sie kommen, man hört das Kratzen ihrer Krallen knapp unter sich in der Erde, die ihr Element ist, und schon ist man verloren. Hier gilt auch nicht, dass man in seinem Haus ist, vielmehr ist man in ihrem Haus. Vor ihnen rettet mich auch jener Ausweg nicht, wie er mich ja wahrscheinlich überhaupt nicht rettet, sondern verdirbt, aber eine Hoffnung ist er, und ich kann ohne ihn nicht leben.

Außer diesem großen Weg verbinden mich mit der Außenwelt noch ganz enge, ziemlich ungefährliche Wege, die mir gut atembare Luft verschaffen, sie sind von den Waldmäusen angelegt, ich habe es verstanden, sie in meinen Bau richtig einzubeziehen, sie bieten mir auch die Möglichkeit weitreichender Witterung und geben mir so Schutz, auch kommt durch sie allerlei kleines Volk zu mir, das ich verzehre, so dass ich eine gewisse, für einen bescheidenen Lebensunterhalt ausreichende Niederjagd haben kann, ohne überhaupt meinen Bau zu verlassen, das ist natürlich sehr wertvoll.

Das schönste an meinem Bau ist aber seine Stille, freilich sie ist trügerisch, plötzlich einmal kann sie unterbrochen werden und alles ist zu ende, vorläufig aber ist sie noch da, stundenlang kann ich durch meine Gänge schleichen und höre nichts als manchmal das Rascheln irgendeines Kleintiers, das ich dann gleich zwischen meinen Zähnen auch zur Ruhe bringe, oder das Rieseln der Erde, das mir die Notwendigkeit irgendeiner Ausbesserung anzeigt, sonst ist es still. Die Waldluft weht herein, es ist gleichzeitig warm und kühl, manchmal strecke ich mich aus und drehe mich in dem Gang rundum vor Behagen. Schön ist es für das nahende Alter einen solchen Bau zu haben, sich unter Dach gebracht zu haben, wenn der Herbst beginnt.

Alle hundert Meter etwa habe ich die Gänge zu kleinen runden Plätzen erweitert, dort kann ich mich bequem zusammenrollen, mich an mir wärmen und ruhen. Dort schlafe ich den süßen Schlaf des Friedens, des beruhigten Verlangens, des erreichten Zieles, des Hausbesitzes. Ich weiß nicht, ob es eine Gewohnheit aus alten Zeiten ist oder ob doch die Gefahren auch dieses Hauses stark genug sind, mich zu wecken, regelmäßig von Zeit zu Zeit schrecke ich auf aus tiefem Schlaf und lausche, lausche in die Stille, die hier unverändert herrscht bei Tag und Nacht, lächle beruhigt und sinke mit gelösten Gliedern in noch tieferen Schlaf. Arme Wanderer, ohne Haus, auf Landstraßen, in Wäldern, bestenfalls verkrochen in einem Blätterhaufen oder in einem Rudel der Genossen, ausgeliefert allem Verderben des Himmels und der Erde. Ich liege hier auf einem allseits gesicherten Platz – mehr als fünfzig solcher Art gibt es in meinem Bau –, und zwischen Hindämmern und bewusstlosem Schlaf vergehen mir die Stunden, die ich nach meinem Belieben dafür wähle.

Nicht ganz in der Mitte des Baues, wohlerwogen für den Fall der äußersten Gefahr, nicht geradezu einer Verfolgung, aber einer Belagerung, liegt der Hauptplatz. Während alles andere vielleicht mehr eine Arbeit angestrengtesten Verstandes als des Körpers ist, ist dieser Burgplatz das Ergebnis allerschwerster Arbeit meines Körpers in allen seinen Teilen. Einige Male wollte ich in der Verzweiflung körperlicher Ermüdung von allem ablassen, wälzte mich auf dem Rücken und fluchte dem Bau, schleppte mich hinaus und ließ den Bau offen daliegen, konnte es ja tun, da ich nicht mehr zu ihm zurückkehren wollte, bis ich dann nach Stunden oder Tagen reuig zurückkam, fast einen Gesang erhoben hätte über die Unverletztheit des Baus und in aufrichtiger Fröhlichkeit mit der Arbeit von neuem begann. Die Arbeit am Burgplatz erschwerte sich auch unnötig, unnötig will sagen, dass der Bau von der Mehrarbeit keinen eigentlichen Nutzen hatte, dadurch, dass gerade an der Stelle, wo der Platz plangemäß sein sollte, die Erde recht locker und sandig war, die Erde musste dort geradezu festgehämmert werden, um den großen schön gewölbten und gerundeten Platz zu bilden. Für eine solche Arbeit aber habe ich nur die Stirn. Mit der Stirn also bin ich tausend und tausend Mal tage- und nächtelang gegen die Erde angerannt, war glücklich, wenn ich sie mir blutig schlug, denn dies war ein Beweis der beginnenden Festigung der Wand, und habe mir auf diese Weise, wie man mir vielleicht zugestehen wird, meinen Burgplatz wohl verdient.

Auf diesem Burgplatz sammle ich meine Vorräte, alles, was ich über meine augenblicklichen Bedürfnisse hinaus innerhalb des Baues erjage, und alles, was ich von meinen Jagden außer dem Hause mitbringe, häufe ich hier auf. Der Platz ist so groß, dass ihn Vorräte für ein halbes Jahr nicht füllen. Infolgedessen kann ich sie wohl ausbreiten, zwischen ihnen herumgehen, mit ihnen spielen, mich an der Menge und an den verschiedenen Gerüchen freuen und immer einen genauen Überblick über das Vorhandene haben. Ich kann dann auch immer Neuordnungen vornehmen und entsprechend der Jahreszeit die nötigen Vorausberechnungen und Jagdpläne machen. Es gibt Zeiten, in denen ich so wohl versorgt bin, dass ich aus Gleichgültigkeit gegen das Essen überhaupt das Kleinzeug, das hier herumhuscht, gar nicht berühre, was allerdings aus anderen Gründen vielleicht unvorsichtig ist. Die häufige Beschäftigung mit Verteidigungsvorbereitungen bringt es mit sich, dass meine Ansichten hinsichtlich der Ausnützung des Baues für solche Zwecke sich ändern oder entwickeln, in kleinem Rahmen allerdings. Es scheint mir dann manchmal gefährlich, die Verteidigung ganz auf dem Burgplatz zu basieren, die Mannigfaltigkeit des Baues gibt mir doch auch mannigfaltigere Möglichkeiten, und es scheint mir der Vorsicht entsprechender, die Vorräte ein wenig zu verteilen und auch manche kleinen Plätze mit ihnen zu versorgen, dann bestimme ich etwa jeden dritten Platz zum Reservevorratsplatz oder jeden vierten Platz zu einem Haupt- und jeden zweiten zu einem Nebenvorratsplatz und dergleichen. Oder ich schalte manche Wege zu Täuschungszwecken überhaupt aus der Behäufung mit Vorräten aus, oder ich wähle ganz sprunghaft, je nach ihrer Lage zum Hauptausgang, nur wenige Plätze. Jeder solcher neue Plan verlangt allerdings schwere Lastträgerarbeit, ich muss die neue Berechnung vornehmen und trage dann die Lasten hin und her. Freilich kann ich das in Ruhe ohne Übereilung machen, und es ist nicht gar so schlimm, die guten Dinge im Maule zu tragen, sich auszuruhen, wo man will, und was einem gerade schmeckt zu naschen. Schlimmer ist es, wenn es mir manchmal, gewöhnlich beim Aufschrecken aus dem Schlaf, scheint, dass die gegenwärtige Aufteilung ganz und gar verfehlt ist, große Gefahren herbeiführen kann und sofort eiligst ohne Rücksicht auf Schläfrigkeit und Müdigkeit richtiggestellt werden muss, dann eile ich, dann fliege ich, dann habe ich keine Zeit zu Berechnungen, der ich gerade einen neuen ganz genauen Plan ausführen will, fasse willkürlich, was mir unter die Zähne kommt, schleppe, trage, seufze, stöhne, stolpere, und nur irgendeine beliebige Veränderung des gegenwärtigen mir so übergefährlich scheinenden Zustandes will mir schon genügen. Bis allmählich mit völligem Erwachen die Ernüchterung kommt, ich die Übereilung kaum verstehe, tief den Frieden meines Hauses einatme, den ich selbst gestört habe, zu meinem Schlafplatz zurückkehre, in neugewonnener Müdigkeit sofort einschlafe und beim Erwachen als unwiderleglichen Beweis der schon fast traumhaft erscheinenden Nachtarbeit etwa noch eine Ratte an den Zähnen hängen habe. Dann gibt es wieder Zeiten, wo mir die Vereinigung aller Vorräte auf einem Platz das Allerbeste scheint. Was können mir die Vorräte auf den kleinen Plätzen helfen, wie viel lässt sich denn dort überhaupt unterbringen, und was man immer auch hinbringt, es verstellt den Weg und wird mich vielleicht einmal bei der Verteidigung, beim Laufen eher hindern. Außerdem ist es zwar dumm, aber wahr, dass das Selbstbewusstsein darunter leidet, wenn man nicht alle Vorräte beisammen sieht und so mit einem einzigen Blick weiß, was man besitzt. Kann nicht auch bei diesen vielen Verteilungen vieles verloren gehen? Ich kann nicht immerfort durch meine Kreuz- und Quergänge galoppieren, um zu sehen, ob alles in richtigem Stande ist. Der Grundgedanke einer Verteilung der Vorräte ist ja richtig, aber eigentlich nur dann, wenn man mehrere Plätze von der Art meines Burgplatzes hat. Mehrere solche Plätze! Freilich! Aber wer kann das schaffen? Auch sind sie im Gesamtplan meines Baues jetzt nachträglich nicht mehr unterzubringen. Zugeben aber will ich, dass darin ein Fehler des Baues liegt, wie überhaupt dort immer ein Fehler ist, wo man von irgendetwas nur ein Exemplar besitzt. Und ich gestehe auch ein, dass in mir während des ganzen Baues dunkel im Bewusstsein, aber deutlich genug, wenn ich den guten Willen gehabt hätte, die Forderung nach mehreren Burgplätzen lebte, ich habe ihr nicht nachgegeben, ich fühlte mich zu schwach für die ungeheure Arbeit, ja, ich fühlte mich zu schwach, mir die Notwendigkeit der Arbeit zu vergegenwärtigen, irgendwie tröstete ich mich mit Gefühlen von nicht minderer Dunkelheit, nach denen das, was sonst nicht hinreichen würde, in meinem Fall einmal, ausnahmsweise, gnadenweise, wahrscheinlich weil der Vorsehung an der Erhaltung meiner Stirn, des Stampfhammers, besonders gelegen ist, hinreichen werde. Nun, so habe ich nur einen Burgplatz, aber die dunklen Gefühle, dass der eine diesmal hinreichen werde, haben sich verloren. Wie es auch sei, ich muss mich mit dem einen begnügen, die kleinen Plätze können ihn unmöglich ersetzen, und so fange ich dann, wenn diese Anschauung in mir gereift ist, wieder an, alles aus den kleinen Plätzen zum Burgplatz zurückzuschleppen. Für einige Zeit ist es mir dann ein großer Trost, alle Plätze und Gänge frei zu haben, zu sehen, wie auf dem Burgplatz sich die Mengen des Fleisches häufen und.weithin bis in die äußersten Gänge die Mischung der vielen Gerüche senden, von denen jedes in seiner Art mich entzückt und die ich aus der Ferne genau zu sondern imstande bin. Dann pflegen besonders friedliche Zeiten zu kommen, in denen ich meine Schlafplätze langsam, allmählich von den äußeren Kreisen nach innen verlege, immer tiefer in die Gerüche tauche, bis ich es nicht mehr ertrage und eines Nachts auf den Burgplatz stürze, mächtig unter den Vorräten aufräume und bis zur vollständigen Selbstbetäubung mit dem Besten, was ich habe, mich fülle. Glückliche, aber gefährliche Zeiten, wer sie auszunützen verstünde, könnte mich leicht, ohne sich zu gefährden, vernichten. Auch hier wirkt das Fehlen eines zweiten oder dritten Burgplatzes schädigend mit, die große einmalige Gesamtanhäufung ist es, die mich verführt. Ich suche mich verschiedentlich dagegen zu schützen, die Verteilung auf die kleinen Plätze ist ja auch eine derartige Maßnahme, leider führt sie, wie andere ähnliche Maßnahmen, durch Entbehrung zu noch größerer Gier, die dann mit Überrennung des

Verstandes, die Verteidigungspläne zu ihren Zwecken willkürlich ändert.

Nach solchen Zeiten pflege ich, um mich zu sammeln, den Bau zu revidieren und, nachdem die nötigen Ausbesserungen vorgenommen sind, ihn öfters, wenn auch immer nur für kürzere Zeit zu verlassen. Die Strafe, ihn lange zu entbehren, scheint mir selbst dann zu hart, aber die Notwendigkeit zeitweiliger Ausflüge sehe ich ein. Es hat immer eine gewisse Feierlichkeit, wenn ich mich dem Ausgang nähere. In den Zeiten des häuslichen Lebens weiche ich ihm aus, vermeide sogar den Gang, der zu ihm führt, in seinen letzten Ausläufern zu begehen, es ist auch gar nicht leicht, dort herumzuwandern, denn ich habe dort ein kleines tolles Zickzackwerk von Gängen angelegt; dort fing mein Bau an, ich durfte damals noch nicht hoffen, ihn je so beenden zu können, wie er in meinem Plane dastand, ich begann halb spielerisch an diesem Eckchen, und so tobte sich dort die erste Arbeitsfreude in einem Labyrinthbau aus, der mir damals die Krone aller Bauten schien, den ich aber heute wahrscheinlich richtiger als allzu kleinliche, des Gesamtbaues nicht recht würdige Bastelei beurteile, die zwar theoretisch vielleicht köstlich ist – hier ist der Eingang zu meinem Haus, sagte ich damals ironisch zu den unsichtbaren Feinden und sah sie sämtlich schon in dem Eingangslabyrinth ersticken –, in Wirklichkeit aber eine viel zu dünnwandige Spielerei darstellt, die einem ernsten Angriff oder einem verzweifelt um sein Leben kämpfenden Feind kaum widerstehen wird. Soll ich diesen Teil deshalb umbauen? Ich zögere die Entscheidung hinaus, und es wird wohl schon so bleiben, wie es ist. Abgesehen von der großen Arbeit, die ich mir damit zumuten würde, wäre es auch die gefährlichste, die man sich denken kann, damals als ich den Bau begann, konnte ich dort verhältnismäßig ruhig arbeiten, das Risiko war nicht viel größer als irgendwann sonst, heute aber hieße es, fast mutwillig die Welt auf den ganzen Bau aufmerksam machen zu wollen, heute ist es nicht mehr möglich. Es freut mich fast, eine gewisse Empfindsamkeit für dieses Erstlingswerk ist ja auch vorhanden. Und wenn ein großer Angriff kommen sollte, welcher Grundriss des Eingangs könnte mich retten? Der Eingang kann täuschen, ablenken, den Angreifer quälen, das tut auch dieser zur Not. Aber einem wirklich großen Angriff muss ich gleich mit allen Mitteln des Gesamtbaues und mit allen Kräften des Körpers und der Seele zu begegnen suchen – das ist ja selbstverständlich. So mag also dieser Eingang schon bleiben. Der Bau hat so viele von der Natur ihm aufgezwungene Schwächen, mag er auch noch diesen von meinen Händen geschaffenen und wenn auch erst nachträglich, so doch genau erkannten Mangel behalten. Mit dem allen ist freilich nicht gesagt, dass mich dieser Fehler nicht von Zeit zu Zeit oder vielleicht immer doch beunruhigt. Wenn ich bei meinen gewöhnlichen Spaziergängen diesem Teil des Baues ausweiche, so geschieht es hauptsächlich deshalb, weil mir sein Anblick unangenehm ist, weil ich nicht immer einen Mangel des Baues in Augenschein nehmen will, wenn dieser Mangel schon in meinem Bewusstsein nur allzu sehr rumort. Mag der Fehler dort oben am Eingang unausrottbar bestehen, ich aber mag, solange es sich vermeiden lässt, von seinem Anblick verschont bleiben. Gehe ich nur in der Richtung zum

Ausgang, sei ich auch noch durch Gänge und Plätze von ihm getrennt, glaube ich schon, in die Atmosphäre einer großen Gefahr zu geraten, mir ist manchmal, als verdünne sich mein Fell, als könnte ich bald mit bloßem kahlen Fleisch dastehen und in diesem Augenblick vom Geheul meiner Feinde begrüßt werden. Gewiss, solche ungesunde Gefühle bringt schon an und für sich der Ausgang selbst hervor, das Aufhören des häuslichen Schutzes, aber es ist doch auch dieser Eingangsbau, der mich besonders quält. Manchmal träume ich, ich hätte ihn umgebaut, ganz und gar geändert, schnell, mit Riesenkräften, in einer Nacht, von niemandem bemerkt, und nun sei er uneinnehmbar, der Schlaf, in dem mir das geschieht, ist der süßeste von allen, Tränen der Freude und Erlösung glitzern noch an meinen Barthaaren, wenn ich erwache.

Die Pein dieses Labyrinthes muss ich also auch körperlich überwinden, wenn ich ausgehe, und es ist mir ärgerlich und rührend zugleich, wenn ich mich manchmal in meinem eigenen Gebilde für einen Augenblick verirre und das Werk sich also noch immer anzustrengen scheint, mir, dessen Urteil schon längst feststeht, doch noch seine Existenzberechtigung zu beweisen. Dann aber bin ich unter der Moosdecke, der ich manchmal Zeit lasse – solange rühre ich mich nicht aus dem Hause –, mit dem übrigen Waldboden zusammenzuwachsen, und nun ist nur noch ein Ruck des Kopfes nötig, und ich bin in der Fremde. Diese kleine Bewegung wage ich lange nicht auszuführen, hätte ich nicht wieder das Eingangslabyrinth zu überwinden, gewiss würde ich heute davon ablassen und wieder zurückwandern. Wie?

Dein Haus ist geschützt, in sich abgeschlossen, du lebst in Frieden, warm, gut genährt, Herr, alleiniger Herr über eine Vielzahl von Gängen und Plätzen, und alles dieses willst du hoffentlich nicht opfern, aber doch gewissermaßen preisgeben, hast zwar die Zuversicht, es zurückzugewinnen, aber lässt dich doch darauf ein, ein hohes, ein allzu hohes Spiel zu spielen. Es gäbe vernünftige Gründe dafür? Nein, für etwas Derartiges kann es keine vernünftigen Gründe geben. Aber dann hebe ich doch vorsichtig die Falltür und bin draußen; lasse sie vorsichtig sinken und jage, so schnell ich kann, weg von dem verräterischen Ort.

Aber im Freien bin ich eigentlich nicht, zwar drücke ich mich nicht mehr durch die Gänge, sondern jage im offenen Wald, fühle in meinem Körper neue Kräfte, für die im Bau gewissermaßen kein Raum ist, nicht einmal auf dem Burgplatz, und wäre er zehnmal größer, auch ist die Ernährung draußen eine bessere, die Jagd zwar schwieriger, der Erfolg seltener, aber das Ergebnis in jeder Hinsicht höher zu bewerten, das alles leugne ich nicht und verstehe es wahrzunehmen und zu genießen, zumindest so gut wie jeder andere, aber wahrscheinlich viel besser, denn ich jage nicht wie ein Landstreicher aus Leichtsinn oder Verzweiflung, sondern zweckvoll und ruhig. Auch bin ich nicht dem freien Leben bestimmt und ausgeliefert, sondern ich weiß, dass meine Zeit gemessen ist, dass ich nicht endlos hier jagen muss, sondern dass mich, gewissermaßen wenn ich will und des Lebens hier müde bin, jemand zu sich rufen wird, dessen Einladung ich nicht werde widerstehen können. Und so kann ich diese Zeit hier ganz auskosten und sorgenlos verbringen, vielmehr, ich könnte es und kann es doch nicht. Zuviel beschäftigt mich der Bau. Schnell bin ich vom Eingang fortgelaufen, bald aber komme ich zurück. Ich suche mir ein gutes Versteck und belauere den Eingang meines Hauses – diesmal von außen – tage- und nächtelang. Mag man es töricht nennen, es macht mir aber eine unsagbare Freude, mehr noch, es beruhigt mich. Mir ist dann, als stehe ich nicht vor meinem Haus, sondern vor mir selbst, während ich schlafe, und hätte das Glück gleichzeitig tief zu schlafen und dabei mich scharf bewachen zu können. Ich bin gewissermaßen ausgezeichnet, die Gespenster der Nacht nicht nur in der Hilflosigkeit und Vertrauensseligkeit des Schlafes zu sehen, sondern ihnen gleichzeitig in Wirklichkeit bei voller Kraft des Wachseins in ruhiger Urteilsfähigkeit zu begegnen. Und ich finde, dass es merkwürdiger Weise nicht so schlimm mit mir steht, wie ich oft glaubte und wie ich wahrscheinlich wieder glauben werde, wenn ich in mein Haus hinabsteige. In dieser Hinsicht – wohl auch in anderer, aber in dieser besonders – sind diese Ausflüge wahrhaftig unentbehrlich. Gewiss, so sorgfältig ich den Eingang abseitsliegend gewählt habe – der Gesamtplan legte mir allerdings darin gewisse Einschränkungen auf – der Verkehr, der sich dort vollzieht, ist doch, wenn man die Beobachtungen etwa einer Woche zusammenfasst, sehr groß, aber so ist es vielleicht überhaupt in allen bewohnbaren Gegenden, und wahrscheinlich ist es sogar besser, einem größeren Verkehr sich auszusetzen, der infolge seiner Größe sich selbst mit weiterreißt, als in völliger Einsamkeit dem ersten besten langsam suchenden Eindringling ausgeliefert zu sein. Hier gibt es viele Feinde und noch mehr Helfershelfer der Feinde, aber sie bekämpfen sich auch gegenseitig und jagen in diesen Beschäftigungen am Bau vorbei. Niemanden habe ich in der ganzen Zeit geradezu am Eingang forschen sehen, zu meinem und zu seinem Glück, denn ich hätte mich, besinnungslos vor Sorge um den Bau, gewiss an seine Kehle geworfen. Freilich, es kam auch Volk, in dessen Nähe ich nicht zu bleiben wagte und vor denen ich, wenn ich sie nur in der Ferne ahnte, fliehen musste, über ihr Verhalten zum Bau dürfte ich mich eigentlich mit Sicherheit nicht äußern, doch genügt es wohl zur Beruhigung, dass ich bald zurückkam, niemanden von ihnen mehr vorfand und den Eingang unverletzt. Es gab glückliche Zeiten, in denen ich mir fast sagte, dass die Gegnerschaft der Welt gegen mich vielleicht aufgehört oder sich beruhigt habe oder dass die Macht des Baues mich heraushebe aus dem bisherigen Vernichtungskampf. Der Bau schützt vielleicht mehr, als ich jemals gedacht habe oder im Innern des Baues zu denken wage. Es ging so weit, dass ich manchmal den kindischen Wunsch bekam, überhaupt nicht mehr in den Bau zurückzukehren, sondern hier in der Nähe des Eingangs mich einzurichten, mein Leben in der Beobachtung des Eingangs zu verbringen und immerfort mir vor Augen zu halten und darin mein Glück zu finden, wie fest mich der Bau, wäre ich darin, zu sichern imstande wäre. Nun es gibt ein schnelles Aufschrecken aus kindischen Träumen. Was ist es denn für eine Sicherung, die ich hier beobachte? Darf ich denn die Gefahr, in welcher ich im Bau bin, überhaupt nach den Erfahrungen beurteilen, die ich hier draußen mache. Haben denn meine Feinde überhaupt die richtige Witterung, wenn ich nicht im Bau bin? Einige Witterung von mir haben sie gewiss, aber die volle nicht. Und ist nicht erst der Bestand der vollen Witterung die Voraussetzung der normalen Gefahr? Es sind also nur Halb- und Zehntelversuche, die ich hier anstelle, geeignet, mich zu beruhigen und durch falsche Beruhigung aufs höchste zu gefährden. Nein, ich beobachte doch nicht wie ich glaubte meinen Schlaf, vielmehr bin ich es der schläft, während der Verderber wacht. Vielleicht ist er unter denen, die achtlos am Eingang vorüberschlendern, sich immer nur vergewissern, nicht anders als ich, dass die Tür noch unverletzt ist und auf ihren Angriff wartet, und nur vorübergehen, weil sie wissen, dass der Hausherr nicht im Innern ist oder weil sie vielleicht gar wissen, dass er unschuldig nebenan im Gebüsche lauert. Und ich verlasse meinen Beobachtungsplatz und bin satt des Lebens im Freien, mir ist, als könnte ich nichts mehr hier lernen, nicht jetzt und nicht später. Und ich habe Lust, Abschied zu nehmen von allem hier, hinabzusteigen in den Bau und niemals mehr zurückzukommen, die Dinge ihren Lauf nehmen zu lassen und sie durch unnütze Beobachtungen nicht aufzuhalten. Aber verwöhnt dadurch, dass ich so lange alles gesehen habe, was über dem Eingang vor sich ging, ist es mir jetzt sehr quälend, die an sich geradezu Aufsehen machende Prozedur des Hinabsteigens durchzuführen und nicht zu wissen, was im ganzen Umkreis hinter meinem Rücken und dann hinter der wieder eingefügten Falltür geschehen wird. Ich versuche es zunächst in stürmischen Nächten mit dem schnellen Hineinwerfen der Beute, das scheint zu gelingen, aber ob es wirklich gelungen ist, wird sich erst zeigen, wenn ich selbst hineingestiegen bin, es wird sich zeigen, aber nicht mehr mir oder auch mir, aber zu spät. Ich lasse also ab davon und steige nicht ein. Ich grabe, natürlich in genügender Entfernung vom wirklichen Eingang, einen Versuchsgraben, er ist nicht länger als ich selbst bin und auch von einer Moosdecke abgeschlossen. Ich krieche in den Graben, decke ihn hinter mir zu, warte sorgfältig berechnete kürzere und längere Zeiten zu verschiedenen Tagesstunden, werfe dann das Moos ab, komme hervor und registriere meine Beobachtungen. Ich mache die verschiedensten Erfahrungen, guter und schlimmer Art, ein allgemeines Gesetz oder eine unfehlbare Methode des Hinabsteigens finde ich aber nicht. Ich bin infolgedessen glücklich, noch nicht in den wirklichen Eingang hinabgestiegen zu sein, und verzweifelt, es doch bald tun zu müssen. Ich bin nicht ganz fern von dem Entschluss, in die Ferne zu gehen, das alte trostlose Leben wieder aufzunehmen, das gar keine Sicherheit hatte, das eine einzige ununterscheidbare Fülle von Gefahren war und infolgedessen die einzelne Gefahr nicht so genau sehen und fürchten ließ, wie es mich der Vergleich zwischen meinem sicheren Bau und dem sonstigen Leben immerfort lehrt. Gewiss, ein solcher Entschluss wäre eine völlige Narrheit, hervorgerufen nur durch allzu langes Leben in der sinnlosen Freiheit, noch gehört der Bau mir, ich habe nur einen Schritt zu tun und bin gesichert. Und ich reiße mich los von allen Zweifeln und laufe geradewegs bei hellem Tag auf die Tür zu, um sie nun ganz gewiss zu heben, aber ich kann es doch nicht, ich überlaufe sie und werfe mich mit Absicht in ein Dornengebüsch, um mich zu strafen, zu strafen für eine Schuld, die ich nicht kenne. Denn allerdings muss ich mir letzten Endes sagen, dass ich doch recht habe und dass es wirklich unmöglich ist, hinabzusteigen, ohne das Teuerste was ich habe, allen ringsherum, auf dem Boden, auf den Bäumen, in den Lüften wenigstens für ein Weilchen offen preiszugeben. Und die Gefahr ist keine eingebildete, sondern eine sehr wirkliche. Es muss ja kein eigentlicher Feind sein, dem ich die Lust errege mir zu folgen, es kann recht gut irgendeine beliebige kleine Unschuld, irgendein widerliches kleines Wesen sein, welches aus Neugier mir nachgeht und damit, ohne es zu wissen, zur Führerin der Welt gegen mich wird, es muss auch das nicht sein, vielleicht ist es – und das ist nicht weniger schlimm als das andere, in mancher Hinsicht ist es das schlimmste – vielleicht ist es irgendjemand von meiner Art, ein Kenner und Schätzer von Bauten, irgendein Waldbruder, ein Liebhaber des Friedens, aber ein wüster Lump, der wohnen will, ohne zu bauen. Wenn er doch jetzt käme, wenn er doch mit seiner schmutzigen Gier den Eingang entdeckte, wenn er doch daran zu arbeiten begänne, das Moos zu heben, wenn es ihm doch gelänge, wenn er doch sich flink hineinzwängte und schon darin so weit verschwunden wäre, dass nur sein Hinterer für einen Augenblick gerade noch auftauchte, wenn das alles doch geschähe, damit ich endlich in einem Rasen hinter ihm her, frei von allen Bedenken ihn anspringen könnte, ihn zerbeißen, zerfleischen, zerreißen und austrinken und seinen Kadaver gleich zur anderen Beute stopfen könnte, vor allem aber, das wäre die Hauptsache, endlich wieder in meinem Bau wäre, gern diesmal sogar das Labyrinth bewundern wollte, zunächst aber die Moosdecke über mich ziehen und ruhen wollte, ich glaube, den ganzen noch übrigen Rest meines Lebens. Aber es kommt niemand, und ich bleibe auf mich allein angewiesen. Ich verliere, immerfort nur mit der Schwierigkeit der Sache beschäftigt, viel von meiner Ängstlichkeit, ich weiche dem Eingang auch äußerlich nicht mehr aus, ihn in Kreisen zu umstreichen wird meine Lieblingsbeschäftigung, es ist schon fast so, als sei ich der Feind und spioniere die passende Gelegenheit aus, um mit Erfolg einzubrechen. Hätte ich doch irgendjemanden, dem ich vertrauen könnte, den ich auf meinen Beobachtungsposten stellen könnte, dann könnte ich wohl getrost hinabsteigen. Ich würde mit ihm, dem ich vertraue, vereinbaren, dass er die Situation bei meinem Hinabsteigen und eine lange Zeit hinterher genau beobachtet, im Falle von gefährlichen Anzeichen an die Moosdecke klopft, sonst aber nicht. Damit wäre über mir völlig reiner Tisch gemacht, es bliebe kein Rest, höchstens mein Vertrauensmann. Denn wird er nicht eine Gegenleistung verlangen, wird er nicht wenigstens den Bau ansehen wollen, schon dieses, jemanden freiwillig in meinen Bau zu lassen, wäre mir äußerst peinlich, ich habe ihn für mich, nicht für Besucher gebaut, ich glaube, ich würde ihn nicht einlassen; selbst um den Preis, dass er es mir ermöglicht, in den Bau zu kommen, würde ich ihn nicht einlassen. Aber ich könnte ihn gar nicht einlassen, denn entweder müsste ich ihn allein hinablassen, und das ist doch außerhalb jeder Vorstellbarkeit, oder wir müssten gleichzeitig hinabsteigen, wodurch dann eben der Vorteil, den er mir bringen soll, hinter mir Beobachtungen anzustellen, verloren ginge. Und wie ist es mit dem Vertrauen? Kann ich dem, welchem ich Aug in Aug vertraue, noch ebenso vertrauen, wenn ich ihn nicht sehe und wenn die Moosdecke uns trennt. Es ist verhältnismäßig leicht, jemandem zu vertrauen, wenn man ihn gleichzeitig überwacht oder wenigstens überwachen kann, es ist vielleicht sogar möglich, jemandem aus der Ferne zu vertrauen, aber aus dem Innern des Baues, also einer anderen Welt heraus, jemandem außerhalb völlig zu vertrauen, ich glaube, das ist unmöglich. Aber solche Zweifel sind noch nicht einmal nötig, es genügt ja schon die Überlegung, dass während oder nach meinem Hinabsteigen alle die unzähligen Zufälle des Lebens den Vertrauensmann hindern können, seine Pflicht zu erfüllen, und was für unberechenbare Folgen kann seine kleinste Verhinderung für mich haben. Nein, fasst man alles zusammen, muss ich es gar nicht beklagen, dass ich allein bin und niemanden habe, dem ich vertrauen kann. Ich verliere dadurch gewiss keinen Vorteil und erspare mir wahrscheinlich Schaden. Vertrauen aber kann ich nur mir und dem Bau. Das hätte ich früher bedenken und für den Fall, der mich jetzt so beschäftigt, Vorsorge treffen sollen. Es wäre am Beginne des Baues wenigstens zum Teil möglich gewesen. Ich hätte den ersten Gang so anlegen müssen, dass er, in gehörigem Abstand voneinander zwei Eingänge gehabt hätte, so dass ich durch den einen Eingang mit aller unvermeidlichen Umständlichkeit hinabgestiegen wäre, rasch den Anfangsgang bis zum zweiten Eingang durchlaufen, die Moosdecke dort, die zu dem Zwecke entsprechend hätte eingerichtet sein müssen, ein wenig gelüftet und von dort aus die Lage einige Tage und Nächte zu überblicken versucht hätte. So allein wäre es richtig gewesen, zwar verdoppeln zwei Eingänge die Gefahr, aber dieses Bedenken hätte hier schweigen müssen, zumal der eine Eingang, der nur als Beobachtungsplatz gedacht war, ganz eng hätte sein können. Und damit verliere ich mich in technische Überlegungen, ich fange wieder einmal meinen Traum eines ganz vollkommenen Baues zu träumen an, das beruhigt mich ein wenig, entzückt sehe ich mit geschlossenen Augen klare und weniger klare Baumöglichkeiten, um unbemerkt aus- und einschlüpfen zu können. Wenn ich so daliege und daran denke, bewerte ich diese Möglichkeiten sehr hoch, aber doch nur als technische Errungenschaften, nicht als wirkliche Vorteile, denn dieses ungehinderte Aus- und Einschlüpfen, was soll es? Es deutet auf unruhigen Sinn, auf unsichere Selbsteinschätzung, auf unsaubere Gelüste, schlechte Eigenschaften, die noch viel schlechter werden angesichts des Baus der doch dasteht und Frieden einzugießen vermag, wenn man sich ihm nur völlig öffnet. Nun bin ich freilich jetzt außerhalb seiner und suche eine Möglichkeit der Rückkehr, dafür wären die nötigen technischen Einrichtungen sehr erwünscht. Aber vielleicht doch nicht gar so sehr. Heißt es nicht in der augenblicklichen nervösen Angst den Bau sehr unterschätzen, wenn man ihn nur als eine Höhlung ansieht, in die man sich mit möglichster Sicherheit verkriechen will. Gewiss, er ist auch diese sichere Höhlung oder sollte es sein, und wenn ich mir vorstelle, ich sei mitten in einer Gefahr, dann will ich mit zusammengebissenen Zähnen und mit aller Kraft des Willens, dass der Bau nichts anderes sei als das für meine Lebensrettung bestimmte Loch und dass er diese klar gestellte

Aufgabe mit möglichster Vollkommenheit erfülle, und jede andere Aufgabe bin ich bereit, ihm zu erlassen. Nun verhält es sich aber so, dass er in Wirklichkeit – und für die hat man in der großen Not keinen Blick, und selbst in ungefährdeten Zeiten muss man sich diesen Blick erst erwerben – zwar viel Sicherheit gibt, aber durchaus nicht genug, hören denn jemals die Sorgen völlig in ihm auf, es sind andere, stolzere, inhaltsreichere, oft weit zurückgedrängte Sorgen, aber ihre verzehrende Wirkung ist vielleicht die gleiche wie jene der Sorgen, die das Leben draußen bereitet. Hätte ich den Bau nur zu meiner Lebenssicherung aufgeführt, wäre ich zwar nicht betrogen, aber das Verhältnis zwischen der ungeheuren Arbeit und der tatsächlichen Sicherung, wenigstens soweit ich sie zu empfinden imstande bin und soweit ich von ihr profitieren kann, wäre ein für mich nicht günstiges. Es ist sehr schmerzlich, sich das einzugestehen, aber es muss geschehen, gerade angesichts des Eingangs dort, der sich jetzt gegen mich, den Erbauer und Besitzer, abschließt, ja förmlich verkrampft. Aber der Bau ist eben nicht nur ein Rettungsloch! Wenn ich auf dem Burgplatz stehe, umgeben von den hohen Fleischvorräten, das Gesicht zugewendet den zehn Gängen, die von hier ausgehen, jeder besonders dem Gesamtplan entsprechend gesenkt oder gehoben, gestreckt oder gerundet, sich erweiternd oder sich verengend und alle gleichmäßig still und leer und bereit, jeder in seiner Art, mich weiterzuführen zu den vielen Plätzen und auch alle diese still und leer – dann liegt mir der Gedanke an Sicherheit fern, dann weiß ich genau, dass hier meine Burg ist, die ich durch Kratzen und Beißen, Stampfen und Stoßen dem widerspenstigen Boden abgewonnen habe, meine Burg, die auf keine Weise jemandem anderen angehören kann und die so sehr mein ist, dass ich hier letzten Endes ruhig von meinem Feind auch die tödliche Verwundung annehmen kann, denn mein Blut versickert hier in meinem Boden und geht nicht verloren. Und was ist denn auch anderes als dies der Sinn der schönen Stunden, die ich halb friedlich schlafend, halb fröhlich wachend in den Gängen zu verbringen pflege, in diesen Gängen, die ganz genau für mich berechnet sind, für wohliges Strecken, kindliches Sichwälzen, träumerisches Daliegen, seliges Entschlafen. Und die kleinen Plätze, jeder mir wohlbekannt, jeder trotz völliger Gleichheit von mir mit geschlossenen Augen schon nach dem Schwung der Wände deutlich unterschieden, sie umfangen mich friedlich und warm, wie kein Nest keinen Vogel umfängt. Und alles, alles still und leer.

Wenn es aber so ist, warum zögere ich dann, warum fürchte ich den Eindringling mehr, als die Möglichkeit, vielleicht niemals meinen Bau wiederzusehen? Nun, dieses letztere ist glücklicherweise eine Unmöglichkeit, es wäre gar nicht nötig, mir durch Überlegungen erst klar zu machen, was mir der Bau bedeutet, ich und der Bau gehören so zusammen, dass ich ruhig, ruhig bei aller meiner Angst, mich hier niederlassen könnte, gar nicht versuchen müsste, mich zu überwinden, um den Eingang entgegen allen Bedenken zu öffnen, es würde durchaus genügen, wenn ich untätig warte, denn nichts kann uns auf die Dauer trennen, und irgendwie komme ich schließlich ganz gewiss hinab. Aber freilich, wie viel Zeit kann bis dahin vergehen, und wie viel kann in dieser

Zeit sich ereignen, hier oben sowohl wie dort unten. Und es liegt doch nur an mir, diesen Zeitraum zu verkürzen und das Notwendige gleich zu tun.

Und nun, schon denkunfähig von Müdigkeit, mit hängendem Kopf, unsicheren Beinen, halb schlafend, mehr tastend als gehend nähere ich mich dem Eingang, hebe langsam das Moos, steige langsam hinab, lasse aus Zerstreutheit den Eingang überflüssig lange unbedeckt, erinnere mich dann an das Versäumte, steige wieder hinauf, um es nachzuholen, aber warum denn hinaufsteigen?, nur die Moosdecke soll ich zuziehen, gut, so steige ich wieder hinunter, und nun endlich ziehe ich die Moosdecke zu. Nur in diesem Zustand, ausschließlich in diesem Zustand kann ich diese Sache ausführen. Dann also liege ich unter dem Moos oben auf der eingebrachten Beute, umflossen von Blut und Fleischsäften, und könnte den ersehnten Schlaf zu schlafen beginnen. Nichts stört mich, niemand ist mir gefolgt, über dem Moos scheint es wenigstens bis jetzt ruhig zu sein, und selbst wenn es nicht ruhig wäre, ich glaube, ich könnte mich jetzt nicht mit Beobachtungen aufhalten, ich habe den Ort gewechselt, aus der Oberwelt bin ich in meinen Bau gekommen, und ich fühle die Wirkung dessen sofort. Es ist eine neue Welt, die neue Kräfte gibt, und was oben Müdigkeit ist, gilt hier nicht als solche. Ich bin von einer Reise zurückgekehrt, besinnungslos müde von den Strapazen, aber das Wiedersehen der alten Wohnung, die Einrichtungsarbeit, die mich erwartet, die Notwendigkeit, schnell alle Räume wenigstens oberflächlich zu besichtigen, vor allem aber eiligst zum Burgplatz vorzudringen, das alles verwandelt meine Müdigkeit in Unruhe und Eifer, es ist, als hätte ich während des Augenblicks, da ich den Bau betrat, einen langen und tiefen Schlaf getan. Die erste Arbeit ist sehr mühselig und nimmt mich ganz in Anspruch: die Beute nämlich durch die engen und schwachwandigen Gänge des Labyrinthes zu bringen. Ich drücke vorwärts mit allen Kräften, und es geht auch, aber mir viel zu langsam; um es zu beschleunigen, reiße ich einen Teil der Fleischmassen zurück und dränge mich über sie hinweg, durch sie hindurch, nun habe ich bloß einen Teil vor mir, nun ist es leichter, ihn vorwärtszubringen, aber ich bin derart mitten darin in der Fülle des Fleisches hier in den engen Gängen, durch die es mir, selbst wenn ich allein bin, nicht immer leicht wird durchzukommen, dass ich recht gut in meinen eigenen Vorräten ersticken könnte, manchmal kann ich mich schon nur durch Fressen und Trinken vor ihrem Andrang bewahren. Aber der Transport gelingt, ich beende ihn in nicht zu langer Zeit, das Labyrinth ist überwunden, aufatmend stehe ich in einem regelrechten Gang, treibe die Beute durch einen Verbindungsgang in einen für solche Fälle besonders vorgesehenen Hauptgang, der in starkem Gefälle zum Burgplatz hinabführt. Nun ist es keine Arbeit mehr, nun rollt und fließt das Ganze fast von selbst hinab. Endlich auf meinem Burgplatz! Endlich werde ich ruhen dürfen. Alles ist unverändert, kein größeres Unglück scheint geschehen zu sein, die kleinen Schäden, die ich auf den ersten Blick bemerke, werden bald verbessert sein. Nur noch vorher die lange Wanderung durch die Gänge, aber das ist keine Mühe, das ist ein Plaudern mit Freunden, so wie ich es tat in alten Zeiten oder – ich bin noch gar nicht so alt, aber für vieles trübt sich die Erinnerung schon völlig – wie ich es tat oder wie ich hörte, dass es zu geschehen pflegt. Ich beginne jetzt mit dem zweiten Gang, absichtlich langsam, nachdem ich den Burgplatz gesehen habe, habe ich endlose Zeit, immer innerhalb des Baues habe ich endlose Zeit, denn alles, was ich dort tue, ist gut und wichtig und sättigt mich gewissermaßen. Ich beginne mit dem zweiten Gang, und breche die Revision in der Mitte ab und gehe zum dritten Gang über und lasse mich von ihm zum Burgplatz zurückführen und muss nun allerdings wieder den zweiten Gang von neuem vornehmen und spiele so mit der Arbeit und vermehre sie und lache vor mich hin und freue mich und werde ganz wirr von der vielen Arbeit, aber lasse nicht von ihr ab. Euretwegen ihr Gänge und Plätze, und du vor allem Burgplatz, bin ich ja gekommen, habe mein Leben für nichts geachtet, nachdem ich lange Zeit die Dummheit hatte, seinetwegen zu zittern und die Rückkehr zu euch zu verzögern. Was kümmert mich die Gefahr jetzt, da ich bei euch bin. Ihr gehört zu mir, ich zu euch, verbunden sind wir, was kann uns geschehen. Mag sich oben auch das Volk schon drängen und die Schnauze bereit sein, die das Moos durchstoßen wird. Und mit seiner Stummheit und Leere begrüßt nun auch mich der Bau und bekräftigt, was ich sage.

Nun aber überkommt mich doch eine gewisse Lässigkeit, und auf einem Platz, der zu meinen Lieblingen gehört, rolle ich mich ein wenig zusammen, noch lange habe ich nicht alles besichtigt, aber ich will ja auch noch weiter besichtigen bis zum Ende, ich will hier nicht schlafen, nur der Lockung gebe ich nach, mich hier so einzurichten, wie wenn ich schlafen wollte, nachsehen will ich, ob das hier noch immer so gut gelingt wie früher. Es gelingt, aber mir gelingt es nicht mich loszureißen, ich bleibe hier in tiefem Schlaf. Ich habe wohl sehr lange geschlafen, erst aus dem letzten von selbst schon sich auflösenden Schlaf werde ich geweckt, der Schlaf muss nun schon sehr leicht sein, denn ein an sich kaum hörbares Zischen weckt mich. Ich verstehe es sofort, das Kleinzeug, viel zu wenig von mir beaufsichtigt, viel zu sehr von mir geschont, hat in meiner Abwesenheit irgendwo einen neuen Weg gebohrt, dieser Weg ist mit einem alten zusammengestoßen, die Luft verfängt sich dort, und das ergibt das zischende Geräusch. Was für ein unaufhörlich tätiges Volk das ist und wie lästig sein Fleiß. Ich werde genau horchend an den Wänden meines Ganges durch Versuchsgrabungen den Ort der Störung erst feststellen müssen und dann erst das Geräusch beseitigen können. Übrigens kann der neue Graben, wenn er den Verhältnissen des Baues irgendwie entspricht, als neue Luftzuführung mir auch willkommen sein. Aber auf die Kleinen will ich nun viel besser achten als bisher, keines darf geschont werden.

Da ich große Übung in solchen Untersuchungen habe, wird es wohl nicht lange dauern, und ich kann gleich damit beginnen, es liegen zwar noch andere Arbeiten vor, aber diese ist die dringendste, es soll still sein in meinen Gängen. Dieses Geräusch ist übrigens ein verhältnismäßig unschuldiges; ich habe es gar nicht gehört, als ich kam, trotzdem es gewiss schon vorhanden war; ich musste erst wieder völlig heimisch werden, um es zu hören, es ist gewissermaßen nur mit dem Ohr des wirklichen sein Amt ausübenden Hausbesitzers hörbar. Und es ist nicht einmal ständig, wie sonst solche Geräusche zu sein pflegen, es macht große Pausen, das geht offenbar auf Anstauungen des Luftstromes zurück. Ich beginne die Untersuchung, aber es gelingt mir nicht, die Stelle, wo man eingreifen müsste, zu finden, ich mache zwar einige Grabungen, aber nur aufs Geratewohl, natürlich ergibt sich so nichts, und die große Arbeit des Grabens und die noch größere des Zuschüttens und Ausgleichens ist vergeblich. Ich komme gar nicht dem Ort des Geräusches näher, immer klingt es unverändert dünn in regelmäßigen Pausen, einmal wie Zischen, einmal eher wie Pfeifen. Nun ich könnte es auch vorläufig auf sich beruhen lassen, es ist zwar sehr störend, aber an der von mir angenommenen Herkunft des Geräusches kann kaum ein Zweifel sein, es wird sich also kaum verstärken, im Gegenteil, es kann auch geschehen – bisher habe ich allerdings niemals so lange gewartet –, dass solche Geräusche im Laufe der Zeit durch die weitere Arbeit der kleinen Bohrer von selbst verschwinden, und abgesehen davon, oft bringt ein Zufall leicht auf die Spur der Störung, während systematisches Suchen lange versagen kann. So tröste ich mich und wollte viel lieber weiter durch die Gänge schweifen und die Plätze besuchen, von denen ich noch viele nicht einmal wiedergesehen habe und dazwischen immer ein wenig mich auf dem Burgplatz tummeln, aber es lässt mich doch nicht, ich muss weitersuchen. Viel Zeit, viel Zeit, die besser verwendet werden könnte, kostet mich das kleine Volk. Bei solchen Gelegenheiten ist es gewöhnlich das technische Problem, das mich lockt, ich stelle mir zum Beispiel nach dem Geräusch, das mein Ohr in allen seinen Feinheiten zu unterscheiden die Übung hat, ganz genau, aufzeichenbar, die Veranlassung vor, und nun drängt es mich nachzuprüfen, ob die Wirklichkeit dem entspricht. Mit gutem Grund, denn solange hier eine Feststellung nicht erfolgt ist, kann ich mich auch nicht sicher fühlen, selbst wenn es sich nur darum handeln würde zu wissen, wohin ein Sandkorn, das eine Wand herabfällt, rollen wird. Und gar ein solches Geräusch, das ist in dieser Hinsicht eine gar nicht unwichtige Angelegenheit. Aber wichtig oder unwichtig, wie sehr ich auch suche, ich finde nichts, oder vielmehr, ich finde zu viel. Gerade auf meinem Lieblingsplatz musste dies geschehen, denke ich, gehe recht weit von dort weg, fast in die Mitte des Weges zum nächsten Platz, das Ganze ist eigentlich ein Scherz, so als wollte ich beweisen, dass nicht etwa gerade mein Lieblingsplatz allein mir diese Störung bereitet hat, sondern dass es Störungen auch anderwärts gibt, und ich fange lächelnd an zu horchen, höre aber bald zu lächeln auf, denn, wahrhaftig, das gleiche Zischen gibt es auch hier. Es ist ja nichts, manchmal glaube ich, niemand außer mir würde es hören, ich höre es freilich jetzt mit dem durch die Übung geschärften Ohr immer deutlicher, trotzdem es in Wirklichkeit überall ganz genau das gleiche Geräusch ist, wie ich mich durch Vergleichen überzeugen kann. Es wird auch nicht stärker, wie ich erkenne, wenn ich, ohne direkt an der Wand zu horchen, mitten im Gang lausche. Dann kann ich überhaupt nur mit Anstrengung, ja mit Versenkung hie und da den Hauch eines Lautes mehr erraten als hören. Aber gerade dieses Gleichbleiben an allen Orten stört mich am meisten, denn es lässt sich mit meiner ursprünglichen Annahme nicht in Übereinstimmung bringen. Hätte ich den Grund des Geräusches richtig erraten, hätte es in größter Stärke von einem bestimmten Ort, der eben zu finden gewesen wäre, ausstrahlen und dann immer kleiner werden müssen. Wenn aber meine Erklärung nicht zutraf, was war es sonst? Es bestand noch die Möglichkeit, dass es zwei Geräuschzentren gab, dass ich bis jetzt nur weit von den Zentren gehorcht hatte und dass, wenn ich mich dem einen Zentrum näherte, zwar seine Geräusche zunahmen, aber infolge Abnehmens der Geräusche des andern Zentrums das Gesamtergebnis für das Ohr immer ein annähernd gleiches blieb. Fast glaubte ich schon, wenn ich genau hinhorchte, Klangunterschiede, die der neuen Annahme entsprachen, wenn auch nur sehr undeutlich zu erkennen. Jedenfalls musste ich das Versuchsgebiet viel weiter ausdehnen, als ich bisher getan hatte. Ich gehe deshalb den Gang abwärts bis zum Burgplatz und beginne dort zu horchen. Sonderbar, das gleiche Geräusch auch hier. Nun, es ist ein Geräusch, erzeugt durch die Grabungen irgendwelcher nichtiger Tiere, die die Zeit meiner Abwesenheit in infamer Weise ausgenützt haben, jedenfalls liegt ihnen irgendeine gegen mich gerichtete Absicht fern, sie sind nur mit ihrem Werk beschäftigt, und solange ihnen nicht ein Hindernis in den Weg kommt, halten sie die einmal genommene Richtung ein, das alles weiß ich, trotzdem ist es mir unbegreiflich und erregt mich und verwirrt mir den für die Arbeit sehr notwendigen Verstand, dass sie es gewagt haben, bis an den Burgplatz heranzugehen. Ich will in der Hinsicht nicht unterscheiden: War es die immerhin bedeutende Tiefe, in welcher der Burgplatz liegt, war es seine große Ausdehnung und die ihr entsprechende starke Luftbewegung, welche die Grabenden abschreckte, oder war einfach die Tatsache, dass es der Burgplatz war, durch irgendwelche Nachrichten bis an ihren stumpfen Sinn gedrungen, die Feierlichkeit des Ortes, Grabungen hatte ich jedenfalls bisher in den Wänden des Burgplatzes nicht beobachtet. Tiere kamen zwar, angezogen von den kräftigen Ausdünstungen in Mengen her, hier hatte ich meine beste Jagd, aber sie hatten sich irgendwo oben in meine Gänge durchgegraben und kamen dann, beklommen zwar, aber mächtig angezogen, die Gänge herabgelaufen. Nun aber bohrten sie also auch in den Wänden. Hätte ich doch wenigstens die wichtigsten Pläne meines Jünglings- und frühen Mannesalters ausgeführt oder vielmehr hätte ich die Kraft gehabt, sie auszuführen, denn an dem Willen hat es nicht gefehlt. Einer dieser Lieblingspläne war es gewesen, den Burgplatz loszulösen von der ihn umgebenden Erde, das heißt, seine Wände nur in einer etwa meiner Höhe entsprechenden Dicke zu belassen, darüber hinaus aber rings um den Burgplatz bis auf ein kleines von der Erde leider nicht loslösbares Fundament einen Hohlraum im Ausmaß der Wand zu schaffen. In diesem Hohlraum hatte ich mir immer, und wohl kaum mit Unrecht, den schönsten Aufenthaltsort vorgestellt, den es für mich geben könnte. Auf dieser Rundung hängen, hinauf sich ziehen, hinab zu gleiten, sich überschlagen und wieder Boden unter den Füßen haben und alle diese Spiele förmlich auf dem Körper des Burgplatzes spielen und doch nicht in seinem eigentlichen Raum; den Burgplatz meiden können, die Augen ausruhen lassen können von ihm, die Freude, ihn zu sehen, auf eine spätere Stunde verschieben und doch ihn nicht entbehren müssen, sondern ihn förmlich fest zwischen den Krallen halten, etwas, was unmöglich ist, wenn man nur den einen gewöhnlichen offenen Zugang zu ihm hat; vor allem aber ihn bewachen können, für die Entbehrung seines Anblickes also derart entschädigt werden, dass man gewiss, wenn man zwischen dem Aufenthalt im Burgplatz oder im Hohlraum zu wählen hätte, den Hohlraum wählte für alle Zeit seines Lebens, nur immer dort auf- und abzuwandern und den Burgplatz zu schützen. Dann gäbe es keine Geräusche in den Wänden, keine frechen Grabungen bis an den Platz heran, dann wäre dort der Friede gewährleistet, und ich wäre sein Wächter, nicht die Grabungen des kleinen Volkes hätte ich mit Widerwillen zu behorchen, sondern mit Entzücken etwas, was mir jetzt völlig entgeht: das Rauschen der Stille auf dem Burgplatz. Aber alles dieses Schöne besteht nun eben nicht, und ich muss an meine Arbeit, fast muss ich froh sein, dass sie nun auch in direkter Beziehung zum Burgplatz steht, denn das beflügelt mich. Ich brauche freilich, wie sich immer mehr herausstellt, alle meine Kräfte zu dieser Arbeit, die zuerst eine ganz geringfügige schien. Ich horche jetzt die Wände des Burgplatzes ab, und wo ich horche, hoch und tief, an den Wänden oder am Boden, an den Eingängen oder im Innern, überall, überall das gleiche Geräusch. Und wie viel Zeit, wie viel Anspannung erfordert dieses lange Horchen auf das pausenweise Geräusch. Einen kleinen Trost zur Selbsttäuschung kann man, wenn man will, darin finden, dass man hier auf dem Burgplatz, wenn man das Ohr vom Erdboden entfernt, zum Unterschied von den Gängen wegen der Größe des Platzes gar nichts hört. Nur zum Ausruhen, zum Selbstbesinnen mache ich häufig diese Versuche, horche angestrengt und bin glücklich, nichts zu hören. Aber im Übrigen, was ist denn geschehen? Vor dieser Erscheinung versagen meine ersten Erklärungen völlig. Aber auch andere Erklärungen, die sich mir anbieten, muss ich bald ablehnen. Man könnte daran denken, dass das, was ich höre, eben das Kleinzeug selbst bei seiner Arbeit ist. Das würde aber aller Erfahrung widersprechen; was ich nie gehört habe, trotzdem es immer vorhanden war, kann ich doch nicht plötzlich zu hören anfangen. Meine Empfindlichkeit gegen Störungen ist vielleicht im Bau größer geworden mit den Jahren, aber das Gehör ist doch keineswegs schärfer geworden. Es ist eben das Wesen des Kleinzeugs, dass man es nicht hört, hätte ich es denn sonst jemals geduldet; auf die Gefahr hin zu verhungern, hätte ich es ausgerottet. Aber vielleicht, auch dieser Gedanke schleicht sich mir ein, handelt es sich hier um ein Tier, das ich noch nicht kenne. Möglich wäre es, zwar beobachte ich schon lange und sorgfältig genug das Leben hier unten, aber die Welt ist mannigfaltig, und an schlimmen Überraschungen fehlt es niemals. Aber es wäre ja nicht ein einzelnes Tier, es müsste eine große Herde sein, die plötzlich in mein Gebiet eingefallen wäre, eine große Herde kleiner Tiere, die zwar, da sie überhaupt hörbar sind, über dem Kleinzeug stehen, aber es doch nur wenig überragen, denn das Geräusch ihrer Arbeit ist an sich nur gering. Es könnten also unbekannte Tiere sein, eine Herde auf der Wanderschaft, die nur vorüberziehen, die mich stören, aber deren Zug bald ein Ende nehmen wird. So könnte ich also eigentlich warten und müsste keine schließlich überflüssige Arbeit tun. Aber wenn es fremde Tiere sind, warum bekomme ich sie nicht zu sehen. Nun habe ich schon viele Grabungen gemacht, um eines von ihnen zu fassen, aber ich finde keines. Es fällt mir ein, dass es vielleicht ganz winzige Tiere sind, viel kleiner als die, welche ich kenne, und dass nur das Geräusch, welches sie machen, ein größeres ist. Ich untersuche deshalb die ausgegrabene Erde, ich werfe die Klumpen in die Höhe, dass sie in allerkleinste Teilchen zerfallen, aber die Lärmmacher sind nicht darunter. Ich sehe langsam ein, dass ich durch solche kleine Zufallsgrabungen nichts erreichen kann, ich durchwühle damit nur die Wände meines Baues, scharre hier und dort in Eile, habe keine Zeit, die Löcher zuzuschütten, an vielen Stellen sind schon Erdhaufen, die den Weg und Ausblick verstellen, freilich stört mich das alles nur nebenbei, ich kann jetzt weder wandern noch umherschauen noch ruhen, öfters bin ich schon für ein Weilchen in irgendeinem Loch bei der Arbeit eingeschlafen, die eine Pfote eingekrallt oben in der Erde, von der ich im letzten Halbschlaf ein Stück niederreißen wollte. Ich werde nun meine Methode ändern. Ich werde in der Richtung zum Geräusch hin einen regelrechten großen Graben bauen und nicht früher zu graben aufhören, bis ich, unabhängig von allen Theorien, die wirkliche Ursache des Geräusches finde. Dann werde ich sie beseitigen, wenn es in meiner Kraft ist, wenn aber nicht, werde ich wenigstens Gewissheit haben. Diese Gewissheit wird mir entweder Beruhigung oder Verzweiflung bringen, aber wie es auch sein wird, dieses oder jenes, es wird zweifellos und berechtigt sein. Dieser Entschluss tut mir wohl, alles was ich bisher getan habe, kommt mir übereilt vor, in der Aufregung der Rückkehr, noch nicht frei von den Sorgen der Oberwelt, noch nicht völlig aufgenommen in den Frieden des Baues, überempfindlich dadurch gemacht, dass ich ihn solange hatte entbehren müssen, habe ich mich durch eine, zugegebenerweise sonderbare Erscheinung, um jede Besinnung bringen lassen. Was ist es denn? Ein leichtes Zischen, in langen Pausen nur hörbar, ein Nichts, an das man sich, ich will nicht sagen, gewöhnen könnte, nein gewöhnen könnte man sich daran nicht, das man aber, ohne vorläufig geradezu etwas dagegen zu unternehmen, eine Zeitlang beobachten könnte, beobachten, das heißt, alle paar Stunden gelegentlich hinhorchen und das Ergebnis geduldig registrieren, aber nicht wie ich das Ohr die Wände entlang schleifen und fast bei jedem Hörbarwerden des Geräusches die Erde aufreißen, nicht um eigentlich etwas zu finden, sondern um etwas der inneren Unruhe Entsprechendes zu tun. Das wird jetzt anders werden, hoffe ich. Und hoffe es auch wieder nicht – wie ich mit geschlossenen Augen wütend über mich selbst mir eingestehe –, denn die Unruhe zittert in mir noch genau so wie seit Stunden, und wenn mich der Verstand nicht zurückhielte, würde ich wahrscheinlich am liebsten an irgendeiner Stelle, gleichgültig ob etwas dort zu hören ist oder nicht, stumpfsinnig, trotzig nur des Grabens wegen zu graben anfangen, schon fast ähnlich dem Kleinzeug, welches entweder ganz ohne Sinn gräbt oder nur weil es die Erde frisst. Der neue vernünftige Plan lockt mich und lockt mich nicht. Es ist nichts gegen ihn einzuwenden, ich wenigstens weiß keinen Einwand, er muss, soweit ich es verstehe, zum Ziele führen. Und trotzdem glaube ich ihm nicht im Grunde, glaube ihm so wenig, dass ich nicht einmal die möglichen Schrecken seines Ergebnisses fürchte, nicht einmal an ein schreckliches Ergebnis glaube ich, ja es scheint mir, ich hätte, schon seit dem ersten Auftreten des Geräusches, an ein solches konsequentes Graben gedacht, und nur weil ich kein Vertrauen dazu hatte, bisher damit nicht begonnen. Trotzdem werde ich natürlich den Graben beginnen, es bleibt mir keine andere Möglichkeit, aber ich werde nicht gleich beginnen, ich werde die Arbeit ein wenig aufschieben, wenn der Verstand wieder zu Ehren kommen soll, soll es ganz geschehen, ich werde mich nicht in diese Arbeit stürzen. Jedenfalls werde ich vorher die Schäden gutmachen, die ich durch meine Wühlarbeit dem Bau verursacht habe; das wird nicht wenig Zeit kosten, aber es ist notwendig; wenn der neue Graben wirklich zu einem Ziel führen sollte, wird er wahrscheinlich lang werden, und wenn er zu keinem Ziel führen sollte, wird er endlos sein, jedenfalls bedeutet diese Arbeit ein längeres Fernbleiben vom Bau, kein so schlimmes wie jenes auf der Oberwelt, ich kann die Arbeit, wann ich will, unterbrechen und zu Besuch nach Hause gehen, und selbst wenn ich das nicht tue, wird die Luft des Burgplatzes zu mir hinwehen und bei der Arbeit mich umgeben, aber eine Entfernung vom Bau und die Preisgabe an ein ungewisses Schicksal bedeutet es dennoch, deshalb will ich hinter mir den Bau in guter Ordnung zurücklassen, es soll nicht heißen, dass ich, der ich um seine Ruhe kämpfe, selbst sie gestört und nicht gleich wiederhergestellt habe. So beginne ich denn damit, die Erde in die Löcher zurückzuscharren, eine Arbeit, die ich genau kenne, die ich unzählige Mal fast ohne das Bewusstsein einer Arbeit getan habe und die ich, besonders was das letzte Pressen und Glätten betrifft – es ist gewiss kein bloßes Selbstlob, es ist einfach Wahrheit –, unübertrefflich auszuführen imstande bin. Diesmal aber wird es mir schwer, ich bin zu zerstreut, immer wieder mitten in der Arbeit drücke ich das Ohr an die Wand und horche und lasse gleichgültig unter mir die kaum gehobene Erde wieder in den Hang zurückrieseln. Die letzten Verschönerungsarbeiten, die eine stärkere Aufmerksamkeit erfordern, kann ich kaum leisten. Hässliche Buckel, störende Risse bleiben, nicht zu reden davon, dass sich auch im Ganzen der alte Schwung einer derart geflickten Wand nicht wieder einstellen will. Ich suche mich damit zu trösten, dass es nur eine vorläufige Arbeit ist. Wenn ich zurückkomme, der Friede wieder verschafft ist, werde ich alles endgültig verbessern, im Fluge wird sich das dann alles machen lassen. Ja, in Märchen geht alles im Fluge, und zu den Märchen gehört auch dieser Trost. Besser wäre es, gleich jetzt vollkommene Arbeit zu tun, viel nützlicher, als sie immer wieder zu unterbrechen, sich auf Wanderschaft durch die Gänge zu begeben und neue Geräuschstellen festzustellen; was wahrhaftig sehr leicht ist, denn es erfordert nichts, als an einem beliebigen Orte stehen zu bleiben und zu horchen. Und noch weitere unnütze Entdeckungen mache ich. Manchmal scheint es mir, als habe das Geräusch aufgehört, es macht ja lange Pausen, manchmal überhört man ein solches Zischen, allzu sehr klopft das eigene Blut im Ohr, dann schließen sich zwei Pausen zu einer zusammen, und ein Weilchen lang glaubt man, das Zischen sei für immer zu

Ende. Man horcht nicht mehr weiter, man springt auf, das ganze Leben macht eine Umwälzung, es ist, als öffnete sich die Quelle, aus welcher die Stille des Baues strömt. Man hütet sich, die Entdeckung gleich nachzuprüfen, man sucht jemanden, dem man sie vorher unangezweifelt anvertrauen könnte, man galoppiert deshalb zum Burgplatz, man erinnert sich, da man mit allem, was man ist, zu neuem Leben erwacht ist, dass man schon lange nichts gegessen hat, man reißt irgendetwas von den unter der Erde halb verschütteten Vorräten hervor und schlingt daran noch, während man zu dem Ort der unglaublichen Entdeckung zurückläuft, man will sich zuerst nur nebenbei, nur flüchtig während des Essens von der Sache nochmals überzeugen, man horcht, aber das flüchtigste Hinhorchen zeigt sofort, dass man sich schmählich geirrt hat, unerschüttert zischt es dort weit in der Ferne. Und man speit das Essen aus und möchte es in den Boden stampfen, und man geht zu seiner Arbeit zurück, weiß gar nicht zu welcher, irgendwo, wo es nötig zu sein scheint, und solcher Orte gibt es genug, fängt man mechanisch etwas zu tun an, so als sei nur der Aufseher gekommen, und man müsse ihm eine Komödie vorspielen. Aber kaum hat man ein Weilchen derart gearbeitet, kann es geschehen, dass man eine neue Entdeckung macht. Das Geräusch scheint stärker geworden, nicht viel stärker natürlich, hier handelt es sich immer nur um feinste Unterschiede, aber ein wenig stärker doch, deutlich dem Ohre erkennbar. Und dieses Stärkerwerden scheint ein Näherkommen, noch viel deutlicher, als man das Stärker-Werden hört, sieht man förmlich den Schritt, mit dem es näher kommt. Man springt von der Wand zurück, man sucht mit einem Blick, alle Möglichkeiten zu übersehen, welche diese Entdeckung zur Folge haben wird. Man hat das Gefühl, als hätte man den Bau niemals eigentlich zur Verteidigung gegen einen Angriff eingerichtet, die Absicht hatte man, aber entgegen aller Lebenserfahrung schien einem die Gefahr eines Angriffs und daher die Einrichtungen der Verteidigung fernliegend oder nicht fernliegend (wie wäre das möglich!), aber im Rang tief unter den Einrichtungen für ein friedliches Leben, denen man deshalb im Bau überall den Vorzug gab. Vieles hätte in jener Richtung eingerichtet werden können, ohne den Grundplan zu stören, es ist in einer eigentlich unverständlichen Weise versäumt worden. Ich habe viel Glück gehabt in allen diesen Jahren, das Glück hat mich verwöhnt, unruhig war ich gewesen, aber Unruhe innerhalb des Glücks führt zu nichts. Was jetzt zunächst zu tun wäre, wäre eigentlich, den Bau genau auf die Verteidigung und auf alle bei ihr vorstellbaren Möglichkeiten hin zu besichtigen, einen Verteidigungs- und einen zugehörigen Bauplan auszuarbeiten und dann mit der Arbeit gleich, frisch wie ein Junger, zu beginnen. Das wäre die notwendige Arbeit, für die es, nebenbei gesagt natürlich viel zu spät ist, aber die notwendige Arbeit wäre es, und keineswegs die Grabung irgendeines großen Forschungsgrabens, der eigentlich nur den Zweck hat, verteidigungslos mich mit allen meinen Kräften auf das Aufsuchen der Gefahr zu verlegen, in der närrischen Befürchtung, sie könne nicht genug bald selbst herankommen. Ich verstehe plötzlich meinen früheren Plan nicht, ich kann in dem ehemals verständigen nicht den geringsten Verstand finden, wieder lasse ich die Arbeit und lasse auch das Horchen, ich will jetzt keine weiteren Verstärkungen entdecken, ich habe genug der Entdeckungen, ich lasse alles, ich wäre schon zufrieden, wenn ich nur den inneren Widerstreit beruhigte. Wieder lasse ich mich von meinen Gängen wegführen, komme in immer entferntere, seit meiner Rückkehr noch nicht gesehene, von meinen Scharrpfoten noch völlig unberührte, deren Stille aufwacht bei meinem Kommen und sich über mich senkt. Ich gebe mich nicht hin, ich eile hindurch, ich weiß gar nicht, was ich suche, wahrscheinlich nur Zeitaufschub. Ich irre so weit ab, dass ich bis zum Labyrinth komme, es lockt mich, an der Moosdecke zu horchen, so ferne Dinge, für den Augenblick so ferne, haben mein Interesse. Ich dringe bis hinauf vor und horche. Tiefe Stille; wie schön es hier ist, niemand kümmert sich dort um meinen Bau, jeder hat seine Geschäfte, die keine Beziehung zu mir haben, wie habe ich es angestellt, das zu erreichen. Hier an der Moosdecke ist vielleicht jetzt die einzige Stelle in meinem Bau, wo ich stundenlang vergebens horchen kann. Eine völlige Umkehrung der Verhältnisse im Bau, der bisherige Ort der Gefahr ist ein Ort des Friedens geworden, der Burgplatz aber ist hineingerissen worden in den Lärm der Welt und ihrer Gefahren. Noch schlimmer, auch hier ist in Wirklichkeit kein Frieden, hier hat sich nichts verändert, ob still, ob lärmend, die Gefahr lauert wie früher über dem Moos, aber ich bin unempfindlich gegen sie geworden, allzu sehr in Anspruch genommen bin ich von dem Zischen in meinen Wänden. Bin ich davon in Anspruch genommen? Es wird stärker, es kommt näher, ich aber schlängele mich durch das Labyrinth und lagere mich hier oben unter dem Moos, es ist ja fast, als überließe ich dem Zischer schon das Haus, zufrieden, wenn ich nur hier oben ein wenig Ruhe habe. Dem Zischer? Habe ich etwa eine neue bestimmte Meinung über die Ursache des Geräusches? Das Geräusch stammt doch wohl von den Rinnen, welche das Kleinzeug gräbt? Ist das nicht meine bestimmte Meinung? Von ihr scheine ich doch noch nicht abgegangen zu sein. Und wenn es nicht direkt von den Rinnen stammt, so irgendwie indirekt. Und wenn es gar nicht mit ihnen zusammenhängen sollte, dann lässt sich von vornherein wohl gar nichts annehmen, und man muss warten, bis man die Ursache wirklich findet oder sie selbst sich zeigt. Mit Annahmen spielen könnte man freilich auch noch jetzt, es ließe sich zum Beispiel sagen, dass irgendwo in der Ferne ein Wassereinbruch stattgefunden hat und das, was mir Zischen oder Pfeifen scheint, wäre dann eigentlich ein Rauschen. Aber abgesehen davon dass ich in dieser Hinsicht gar keine Erfahrungen habe – das Grundwasser, das ich zuerst gefunden habe, habe ich gleich abgeleitet und es ist nicht wiedergekommen in diesem sandigen Boden – abgesehen davon ist es eben ein Zischen und in ein Rauschen nicht umzudeuten. Aber was helfen alle Mahnungen zur Ruhe, die Einbildungskraft will nicht stillstehen, und ich halte tatsächlich dabei zu glauben – es ist zwecklos, sich das selbst abzuleugnen –, das Zischen stamme von einem Tier, und zwar nicht von vielen und kleinen, sondern von einem einzigen Großen. Es spricht manches dagegen: dass das Geräusch überall zu hören ist und immer in gleicher Stärke, und überdies regelmäßig bei Tag und Nacht. Gewiss, zuerst musste man eher dazu neigen, viele kleine Tiere anzunehmen, da ich sie aber bei meinen Grabungen hätte finden müssen und nichts gefunden habe, bleibt nur die Annahme der Existenz des großen Tieres, zumal das, was der Annahme zu widersprechen scheint, bloß Dinge sind, welche das Tier nicht unmöglich, sondern nur über alle Vorstellbarkeit hinaus gefährlich machen. Nur deshalb habe ich mich gegen diese Annahme gewehrt. Ich lasse von dieser Selbsttäuschung ab. Schon lange spiele ich mit dem Gedanken, dass es deshalb selbst auf große Entfernung hin zu hören ist, weil es rasend arbeitet, es gräbt sich so schnell durch die Erde, wie ein Spaziergänger im freien Gange geht, die Erde zittert rings in seinem Graben, auch wenn er schon vorüber ist, dieses Nachzittern und das Geräusch der Arbeit selbst vereinigen sich in der großen Entfernung, und ich, der ich nur das letzte Verebben des Geräusches höre, höre es überall gleich. Dabei wirkt mit, dass das Tier nicht auf mich zugeht, darum ändert sich das Geräusch nicht, es liegt vielmehr ein Plan vor, dessen Sinn ich nicht durchschaue, ich nehme nur an, dass das Tier, wobei ich gar nicht behaupten will, dass es von mir weiß, mich einkreist, wohl einige Kreise hat es schon um meinen Bau gezogen, seitdem ich es beobachte. Und jetzt wird nun das Geräusch doch stärker, die Kreise also enger. Viel zu denken gibt mir die Art des Geräusches, das Zischen oder Pfeifen. Wenn ich in meiner Art an der Erde kratze und scharre, ist es doch ganz anders anzuhören. Ich kann mir das Zischen nur so erklären, dass das Hauptwerkzeug des Tieres nicht seine Krallen sind, mit denen es vielleicht nur nachhilft, sondern seine Schnauze oder sein Rüssel, die allerdings abgesehen von ihrer offenbar ungeheuren Kraft wohl auch irgendwelche Schärfen haben. Wahrscheinlich bohrt es mit einem einzigen mächtigen Stoß den Rüssel in die Erde und reißt ein großes Stück heraus, während dieser Zeit höre ich nichts, das ist die Pause, dann aber zieht es wieder Luft ein zum neuen Stoß, dieses Einziehen der Luft, das ein die Erde erschütternder Lärm sein muss, nicht nur wegen der Kraft des Tieres, sondern auch wegen seiner Eile, seines Arbeitseifers, diesen Lärm höre ich dann als leises Zischen. Gänzlich unverständlich bleibt mir allerdings seine Fähigkeit, unaufhörlich zu arbeiten, vielleicht enthalten die kleinen Pausen auch die Gelegenheit für ein winziges Ausruhen, aber zu einem wirklichen großen Ausruhen ist es scheinbar noch nicht gekommen, Tag und Nacht gräbt es, immer in gleicher Kraft und Frische, seinen eiligst auszuführenden Plan vor Augen, den zu verwirklichen es alle Fähigkeiten besitzt. Nun, einen solchen Gegner habe ich nicht erwarten können. Aber abgesehen von seinen Eigentümlichkeiten ereignet sich jetzt doch nur etwas, was ich eigentlich immer zu befürchten gehabt hätte, etwas, wogegen ich immer Vorbereitungen hätte treffen sollen: Es kommt jemand heran. Wie kam es nur, dass so lange Zeit alles still und glücklich verlief? Wer hat die Wege der Feinde gelenkt, dass sie den großen Bogen machten um meinen Besitz? Warum wurde ich so lange beschützt, um jetzt so geschreckt zu werden? Was waren alle kleinen Gefahren, mit deren Durchdenken ich die Zeit hinbrachte gegen diese eine! Hoffte ich, als Besitzer des Baues die Übermacht zu haben gegen jeden, der käme? Eben als Besitzer dieses großen empfindlichen Werkes bin ich wohlverstanden gegenüber jedem ernsteren Angriff wehrlos, das Glück seines Besitzes hat mich verwöhnt, die Empfindlichkeit des Baues hat mich empfindlich gemacht, seine Verletzungen schmerzen mich, als wären es die meinen. Eben dieses hätte ich voraussehen müssen, nicht nur an meine eigene Verteidigung denken – und wie leichthin und ergebnislos habe ich selbst das getan –, sondern an die Verteidigung des Baues. Es müsste vor allem Vorsorge dafür getroffen sein, dass einzelne Teile des Baues und möglichst viele einzelne Teile, wenn sie von jemandem angegriffen werden, durch Erdverschüttungen, die in kürzester Zeit erzielbar sein müssten, von den weniger gefährdeten Teilen getrennt werden, und zwar durch solche Erdmassen und derart wirkungsvoll getrennt werden könnten, dass der Angreifer gar nicht ahnte, dass dahinter erst der eigentliche Bau ist. Noch mehr, diese Erdverschüttungen müssten geeignet sein, nicht nur den Bau zu verbergen, sondern auch den Angreifer zu begraben. Nicht den kleinsten Anlauf zu etwas Derartigem habe ich gemacht, nichts, gar nichts ist in dieser Richtung geschehen, leichtsinnig wie ein Kind bin ich gewesen, meine Mannesjahre habe ich mit kindlichen Spielen verbracht, selbst mit den Gedanken an die Gefahren habe ich nur gespielt, an die wirklichen Gefahren wirklich zu denken, habe ich versäumt. Und an Mahnungen hat es nicht gefehlt. Etwas, was an das jetzige heranreichen würde, ist allerdings nicht geschehen, aber doch immerhin etwas Ähnliches in den Anfangszeiten des Baues. Der Hauptunterschied war eben, dass es die Anfangszeiten des Baues waren. Ich arbeitete damals förmlich als kleiner Lehrling noch am ersten Gang, das Labyrinth war erst in grobem Umriss entworfen, einen kleinen Platz hatte ich schon ausgehöhlt, aber er war im Ausmaß und in der Wandbehandlung ganz misslungen, kurz, alles war derartig am Anfang, dass es überhaupt nur als Versuch gelten konnte, als etwas, das man, wenn einmal die Geduld reißt, ohne großes Bedauern plötzlich liegen lassen könnte. Da geschah es, dass ich einmal in der Arbeitspause – ich habe in meinem Leben immer zu viel Arbeitspausen gemacht – zwischen meinen Erdhaufen lag und plötzlich ein Geräusch in der Ferne hörte. Jung wie ich war, wurde ich dadurch mehr neugierig als ängstlich. Ich ließ die Arbeit und verlegte mich aufs Horchen, immerhin horchte ich und lief nicht oben unter das Moos, um mich dort zu strecken und nicht horchen zu müssen. Wenigstens horchte ich. Ich konnte recht wohl unterscheiden, dass es sich um ein Graben handelte, ähnlich dem meinen, etwas schwächer klang es wohl, aber wie viel davon der Entfernung zuzurechnen war, konnte man nicht wissen. Ich war gespannt, aber sonst kühl und ruhig. Vielleicht bin ich in einem fremden Bau, dachte ich, und der Besitzer gräbt sich jetzt an mich heran. Hätte sich die Richtigkeit dieser Annahme herausgestellt, wäre ich, da ich niemals eroberungssüchtig oder angriffslustig gewesen bin, weggezogen, um anderswo zu bauen. Aber freilich, ich war noch jung, und ich hatte noch keinen Bau, ich konnte noch kühl und ruhig sein. Auch der weitere Verlauf der Sache brachte mir keine wesentliche Aufregung, nur zu deuten war er nicht leicht. Wenn der, welcher dort grub, wirklich zu mir hinstrebte, weil er mich graben gehört hatte, so war es, wenn er, wie es jetzt tatsächlich geschah, die Richtung änderte, nicht festzustellen, ob er dies tat, weil ich durch meine Arbeitspause ihm jeden Anhaltspunkt für seinen Weg nahm, oder vielmehr, weil er selbst seine Absicht änderte. Vielleicht aber hatte ich mich überhaupt getäuscht, und er hatte sich niemals geradezu gegen mich gerichtet, jedenfalls verstärkte sich das Geräusch noch eine Zeitlang, so als nähere er sich, ich Junge wäre damals vielleicht gar nicht damit unzufrieden gewesen, den Graber plötzlich aus der Erde hervortreten zu sehen, es geschah aber nichts dergleichen, von einem bestimmten Punkte an begann sich das Graben abzuschwächen, es wurde leiser und leiser, so als schwenke der Graber allmählich von seiner ersten Richtung ab, und auf einmal brach es ganz ab, so als habe er sich jetzt zu einer völlig entgegengesetzten Richtung entschlossen und rücke geradewegs von mir weg in die Ferne. Lange horchte ich ihm noch in die Stille nach, ehe ich wieder zu arbeiten begann. Nun, diese Mahnung war deutlich genug, aber bald vergaß ich sie, und auf meine Baupläne hat sie kaum einen Einfluss gehabt. Zwischen damals und heute liegt mein Mannesalter, ist es aber nicht so, als liege gar nichts dazwischen, noch immer mache ich eine große Arbeitspause und horche an der Wand, und der Graber hat neuerlich seine Absicht geändert, er hat kehrtgemacht, er kommt zurück von seiner Reise, er glaubt, er hätte mir inzwischen genug Zeit gelassen, mich für seinen Empfang einzurichten. Aber auf meiner Seite ist alles weniger eingerichtet, als es damals war, der große Bau steht da, wehrlos, und ich bin kein kleiner Lehrling mehr, sondern ein alter Baumeister, und was ich an Kräften noch habe, versagt mir, wenn es zur Entscheidung kommt. Aber wie alt ich auch bin, es scheint mir, dass ich recht gern noch älter wäre, als ich bin, so alt, dass ich mich gar nicht mehr erheben könnte von meinem Ruhelager unter dem Moos. Denn in Wirklichkeit ertrage ich es hier doch nicht, erhebe mich und jage als hätte ich mich hier statt mit Ruhe mit neuen Sorgen erfüllt, wieder hinunter ins Haus. Wie standen die Dinge zuletzt? Das Zischen war schwächer geworden? Nein es war stärker geworden. Ich horche an zehn beliebigen Stellen und merke die Täuschung deutlich, das Zischen ist gleich geblieben, nichts hat sich geändert. Dort drüben gehen keine Veränderungen vor sich, dort ist man ruhig und über die Zeit erhaben, hier aber rüttelt jeder Augenblick am Horcher. Und ich gehe wieder den langen Weg zum Burgplatz zurück, alles ringsherum scheint mit mir erregt, scheint mich anzusehen, scheint dann auch gleich wieder wegzusehen, um mich nicht zu stören und strengt sich doch wieder an, von meinen Mienen die rettenden Entschlüsse abzulesen. Ich schüttele den Kopf, ich habe noch keine. Auch zum Burgplatz gehe ich nicht, um dort irgendeinen Plan auszuführen. Ich komme an der Stelle vorüber, wo ich den Forschungsgraben hatte anlegen wollen, ich prüfe sie nochmals, es wäre eine gute Stelle gewesen, der Graben hätte in der Richtung geführt, in welcher die meisten kleinen Luftzuführungen liegen, die mir die Arbeit sehr erleichtert hätten, vielleicht hätte ich gar nicht sehr weit graben müssen, hätte mich gar nicht herangraben müssen an den Ursprung des Geräusches, vielleicht hätte das Horchen an den Zuführungen genügt. Aber keine Überlegung ist stark genug, um mich zu dieser Grabungsarbeit aufzumuntern. Dieser Graben soll mir Gewissheit bringen? Ich bin so weit, dass ich Gewissheit gar nicht haben will. Auf dem Burgplatz wähle ich ein schönes Stück enthäuteten roten Fleisches aus und verkrieche mich damit in einen der Erdhaufen, dort wird jedenfalls Stille sein, soweit es hier überhaupt eigentliche Stille noch gibt. Ich lecke und nasche am Fleisch, denke abwechselnd einmal an das fremde Tier, das in der Ferne seinen Weg zieht, und dann wieder daran, dass ich, solange ich noch die Möglichkeit habe, ausgiebigst meine Vorräte genießen sollte. Dieses Letztere ist wahrscheinlich der einzige ausführbare Plan, den ich habe. Im Übrigen suche ich den Plan des Tiers zu enträtseln. Ist es auf Wanderschaft, oder arbeitet es in seinem eigenen Bau? Ist es auf Wanderschaft, dann wäre vielleicht eine Verständigung mit ihm möglich. Wenn es wirklich bis zu mir durchbricht, gebe ich ihm einiges von meinen Vorräten, und es wird weiterziehen. Wohl, es wird weiterziehen. In meinem Erdhaufen kann ich natürlich von allem träumen, auch von Verständigung, trotzdem ich genau weiß, dass es etwas Derartiges nicht gibt und dass wir in dem Augenblick, wenn wir einander sehen, ja wenn wir einander nur in der Nähe ahnen, gleich besinnungslos, keiner früher keiner später, mit einem neuen anderen Hunger, auch wenn wir sonst völlig satt sind, Krallen und Zähne gegeneinander auftun werden. Und wie immer, so auch hier mit vollem Recht, denn wer, wenn er auch auf Wanderschaft ist, würde angesichts des Baues seine Reise- und Zukunftspläne nicht ändern. Aber vielleicht gräbt das Tier in seinem eigenen Bau, dann kann ich von einer Verständigung nicht einmal träumen. Selbst wenn es ein so sonderbares Tier wäre, dass sein Bau eine Nachbarschaft vertragen würde, mein Bau verträgt sie nicht, zumindest eine hörbare Nachbarschaft verträgt er nicht. Nun scheint das Tier freilich sehr weit entfernt, wenn es sich nur noch ein wenig weiter zurückziehen würde, würde wohl auch das Geräusch verschwinden, vielleicht könnte dann noch alles gut werden wie in den alten Zeiten, es wäre dann nur eine böse, aber wohltätige Erfahrung, sie würde mich zu den verschiedensten Verbesserungen anregen, wenn ich Ruhe habe und die Gefahr nicht unmittelbar drängt, bin ich noch zu allerlei ansehnlicher Arbeit sehr wohl fähig. Vielleicht verzichtet das Tier angesichts der ungeheuren Möglichkeiten, die es bei seiner Arbeitskraft zu haben scheint, auf die Ausdehnung seines Baues in der Richtung gegen den meinen und entschädigt sich auf einer anderen Seite dafür. Auch das lässt sich natürlich nicht durch Verhandlungen erreichen, sondern nur durch den eigenen Verstand des Tieres oder durch einen Zwang, der von meiner Seite ausgeübt würde. In beider Hinsicht wird entscheidend sein, ob und was das Tier von mir weiß. Je mehr ich darüber nachdenke, desto unwahrscheinlicher scheint es mir, dass das Tier mich überhaupt gehört hat, es ist möglich wenn auch mir unvorstellbar, dass es sonst irgendwelche Nachrichten über mich hat, aber gehört hat es mich wohl nicht. Solange ich nichts von ihm wusste, kann es mich überhaupt nicht gehört haben, denn da verhielt ich mich still, es gibt nichts Stilleres als das Wiedersehen mit dem Bau, dann als ich die Versuchsgrabungen machte, hätte es mich wohl hören können, trotzdem meine Art zu graben sehr wenig Lärm macht; wenn es mich aber gehört hätte, hätte doch auch ich etwas davon bemerken müssen, es hätte doch wenigstens in der Arbeit öfters innehalten müssen und horchen, aber alles blieb unverändert, das

Josefine, die Sängerin oder das Volk der Mäuse

Unsere Sängerin heißt Josefine. Wer sie nicht gehört hat, kennt nicht die Macht des Gesanges. Es gibt niemanden, den ihr Gesang nicht fortreißt, was umso höher zu bewerten ist, als unser Geschlecht im Ganzen Musik nicht liebt. Stiller Frieden ist uns die liebste Musik; unser Leben ist schwer, wir können uns, auch wenn wir einmal alle Tagessorgen abzuschütteln versucht haben, nicht mehr zu solchen, unserem sonstigen Leben so fernen Dingen erheben, wie es die Musik ist. Doch beklagen wir es nicht sehr; nicht einmal so weit kommen wir; eine gewisse praktische Schlauheit, die wir freilich auch äußerst dringend brauchen, halten wir für unseren größten Vorzug, und mit dem Lächeln dieser Schlauheit pflegen wir uns über alles hinwegzutrösten, auch wenn wir einmal - was aber nicht geschieht - das Verlangen nach dem Glück haben sollten, das von der Musik vielleicht ausgeht. Nur Josefine macht eine Ausnahme; sie liebt die Musik und weiß sie auch zu vermitteln; sie ist die Einzige; mit ihrem Hingang wird die Musik - wer weiß wie lange - aus unserem Leben verschwinden.

Ich habe oft darüber nachgedacht, wie es sich mit dieser Musik eigentlich verhält. Wir sind doch ganz unmusikalisch; wie kommt es, dass wir Josefinens Gesang verstehen oder, da

Josefine unser Verständnis leugnet, wenigstens zu verstehen glauben. Die einfachste Antwort wäre, dass die Schönheit dieses Gesanges so groß ist, dass auch der stumpfste Sinn ihr nicht widerstehen kann, aber diese Antwort ist nicht befriedigend. Wenn es wirklich so wäre, müsste man vor diesem Gesang zunächst und immer das Gefühl des Außerordentlichen haben, das Gefühl, aus dieser Kehle erklinge etwas, was wir nie vorher gehört haben und das zu hören wir auch gar nicht die Fähigkeit haben, etwas, was zu hören uns nur diese eine Josefine und niemand sonst befähigt. Gerade das trifft aber meiner Meinung nach nicht zu, ich fühle es nicht und habe auch bei andern nichts dergleichen bemerkt. Im vertrauten Kreis gestehen wir einander offen, dass Josefinens Gesang als Gesang nichts Außerordentliches darstellt.

Ist es denn überhaupt Gesang? Trotz unserer Unmusikalität haben wir Gesangsüberlieferungen; in den alten Zeiten unseres Volkes gab es Gesang; Sagen erzählen davon, und sogar Lieder sind erhalten, die freilich niemand mehr singen kann. Eine Ahnung dessen, was Gesang ist, haben wir also, und dieser Ahnung nun entspricht Josefinens Kunst eigentlich nicht. Ist es denn überhaupt Gesang? Ist es nicht vielleicht doch nur ein Pfeifen? Und Pfeifen allerdings kennen wir alle, es ist die eigentliche Kunstfertigkeit unseres Volkes, oder vielmehr gar keine Fertigkeit, sondern eine charakteristische Lebensäußerung. Alle pfeifen wir, aber freilich denkt niemand daran, das als Kunst auszugeben, wir pfeifen, ohne darauf zu achten, ja, ohne es zu merken, und es gibt sogar viele unter uns, die gar nicht wissen, dass das Pfeifen zu unseren Eigentümlichkeiten gehört. Wenn es also wahr wäre, dass Josefine nicht singt, sondern nur pfeift und vielleicht gar, wie es mir wenigstens scheint, über die Grenzen des üblichen Pfeifens kaum hinauskommt – ja vielleicht reicht ihre Kraft für dieses übliche Pfeifen nicht einmal ganz hin, während es ein gewöhnlicher Erdarbeiter ohne Mühe den ganzen Tag über neben seiner Arbeit zustandebringt – wenn das alles wahr wäre, dann wäre zwar Josefinens angebliche Künstlerschaft widerlegt, aber es wäre dann erst recht das Rätsel ihrer großen Wirkung zu lösen.

Es ist aber eben doch nicht nur Pfeifen, was sie produziert. Stellt man sich recht weit von ihr hin und horcht, oder noch besser, lässt man sich in dieser Hinsicht prüfen, singt also Josefine etwa unter anderen Stimmen und setzt man sich die Aufgabe, ihre Stimme zu erkennen, dann wird man unweigerlich nichts anderes heraushören, als ein gewöhnliches, höchstens durch Zartheit oder Schwäche ein wenig auffallendes Pfeifen. Aber steht man vor ihr, ist es doch nicht nur ein Pfeifen; es ist zum Verständnis ihrer Kunst notwendig, sie nicht nur zu hören, sondern auch zu sehen. Selbst wenn es nur unser tagtägliches Pfeifen wäre, so besteht hier doch schon zunächst die Sonderbarkeit, dass jemand sich feierlich hinstellt, um nichts anderes als das Übliche zu tun. Eine Nuss aufknacken ist wahrhaftig keine Kunst, deshalb wird es auch niemand wagen, ein Publikum zusammenzurufen und vor ihm, um es zu unterhalten, Nüsse knacken. Tut er es dennoch und gelingt seine Absicht, dann kann es sich eben doch nicht nur um bloßes Nüsseknacken handeln. Oder es handelt sich um Nüsseknacken, aber es stellt sich heraus, dass wir über diese Kunst hinweggesehen haben, weil wir sie glatt beherrschten, und dass uns dieser neue Nussknacker erst ihr eigentliches Wesen zeigt, wobei es dann für die Wirkung sogar nützlich sein könnte, wenn er etwas weniger tüchtig im Nüsseknacken ist als die Mehrzahl von uns.

Vielleicht verhält es sich ähnlich mit Josefinens Gesang; wir bewundern an ihr das, was wir an uns gar nicht bewundern; übrigens stimmt sie in letzterer Hinsicht mit uns völlig überein. Ich war einmal zugegen, als sie jemand, wie dies natürlich öfters geschieht, auf das allgemeine Volkspfeifen aufmerksam machte, und zwar nur ganz bescheiden, aber für Josefine war es schon zu viel. Ein so freches, hochmütiges Lächeln, wie sie es damals aufsetzte, habe ich noch nicht gesehen; sie, die äußerlich eigentlich vollendete Zartheit ist, auffallend zart selbst in unserem an solchen Frauengestalten reichen Volk, erschien damals geradezu gemein; sie mochte es übrigens in ihrer großen Empfindlichkeit auch gleich selbst fühlen und fasste sich. Jedenfalls leugnet sie also jeden Zusammenhang zwischen ihrer Kunst und dem Pfeifen. Für die, welche gegenteiliger Meinung sind, hat sie nur Verachtung und wahrscheinlich uneingestandenen Hass. Das ist nicht gewöhnliche Eitelkeit, denn diese Opposition, zu der auch ich halb gehöre, bewundert sie gewiss nicht weniger, als es die Menge tut, aber Josefine will nicht nur bewundert, sondern genau in der von ihr bestimmten Art bewundert sein, an Bewunderung allein liegt ihr nichts. Und wenn man vor ihr sitzt, versteht man sie; Opposition treibt man nur in der Ferne; wenn man vor ihr sitzt, weiß man: Was sie hier pfeift, ist kein Pfeifen.

Da Pfeifen zu unseren gedankenlosen Gewohnheiten gehört, könnte man meinen, dass auch in Josefinens Auditorium gepfiffen wird; es wird uns wohl bei ihrer Kunst, und wenn uns wohl ist, pfeifen wir; aber ihr Auditorium pfeift nicht, es ist mäuschenstill, so als wären wir des ersehnten Friedens teilhaftig geworden, von dem uns zumindest unser eigenes Pfeifen abhält, schweigen wir. Ist es ihr Gesang, der uns entzückt, oder nicht vielmehr die feierliche Stille, von der das schwache Stimmchen umgeben ist? Einmal geschah es, dass irgendein törichtes kleines Ding während Josefinens Gesang in aller Unschuld auch zu pfeifen anfing. Nun, es war ganz dasselbe, was wir auch von Josefine hörten; dort vorne das trotz aller Routine immer noch schüchterne Pfeifen und hier im Publikum das selbstvergessene kindliche Gepfeife; den Unterschied zu bezeichnen, wäre unmöglich gewesen; aber doch zischten und pfiffen wir gleich die Störerin nieder, trotzdem es gar nicht nötig gewesen wäre, denn sie hätte sich gewiss auch sonst in Angst und Scham verkrochen, während Josefine ihr Triumphpfeifen anstimmte und ganz außer sich war mit ihren ausgespreizten Armen und dem gar nicht mehr höher dehnbaren Hals.

So ist sie übrigens immer, jede Kleinigkeit, jeden Zufall, jede Widerspenstigkeit, ein Knacken im Parkett, ein Zähneknirschen, eine Beleuchtungsstörung hält sie für geeignet, die Wirkung ihres Gesanges zu erhöhen; sie singt ja ihrer Meinung nach vor tauben Ohren; an Begeisterung und Beifall fehlt es nicht, aber auf wirkliches Verständnis, wie sie es meint, hat sie längst verzichten gelernt. Da kommen ihr denn alle Störungen sehr gelegen; alles, was sich von außen her der Reinheit ihres Gesanges entgegenstellt, in leichtem

Kampf, ja ohne Kampf, bloß durch die Gegenüberstellung besiegt wird, kann dazu beitragen, die Menge zu erwecken, sie zwar nicht Verständnis, aber ahnungsvollen Respekt zu lehren.

Wenn ihr aber nun das Kleine so dient, wie erst das Große. Unser Leben ist sehr unruhig, jeder Tag bringt Überraschungen, Beängstigungen, Hoffnungen und Schrecken, dass der Einzelne unmöglich dies alles ertragen könnte, hätte er nicht jederzeit bei Tag und Nacht den Rückhalt der Genossen; aber selbst so wird es oft recht schwer; manchmal zittern selbst tausend Schultern unter der Last, die eigentlich nur für einen bestimmt war. Dann hält Josefine ihre Zeit für gekommen. Schon steht sie da, das zarte Wesen, besonders unterhalb der Brust beängstigend vibrierend, es ist, als hätte sie alle ihre Kraft im Gesang versammelt, als sei allem an ihr, was nicht dem Gesange unmittelbar diene, jede Kraft, fast jede Lebensmöglichkeit entzogen, als sei sie entblößt, preisgegeben, nur dem Schutze guter Geister überantwortet, als könne sie, während sie so, sich völlig entzogen, im Gesange wohnt, ein kalter Hauch im Vorüberwehen töten. Aber gerade bei solchem Anblick pflegen wir angeblichen Gegner uns zu sagen: »Sie kann nicht einmal pfeifen; so entsetzlich muss sie sich anstrengen, um nicht Gesang – reden wir nicht von Gesang – aber um das landesübliche Pfeifen einigermaßen sich abzuzwingen.« So scheint es uns, doch ist dies, wie erwähnt, ein zwar unvermeidlicher, aber flüchtiger, schnell vorübergehender Eindruck. Schon tauchen auch wir in das Gefühl der Menge, die warm, Leib an Leib, scheu atmend horcht.

Und um diese Menge unseres fast immer in Bewegung befindlichen, wegen oft nicht sehr klarer Zwecke hin- und herschießenden Volkes um sich zu versammeln, muss Josefine meist nichts anderes tun, als mit zurückgelegtem Köpfchen, halboffenem Mund, der Höhe zugewandten Augen jene Stellung einnehmen, die darauf hindeutet, dass sie zu singen beabsichtigt. Sie kann dies tun, wo sie will, es muss kein weithin sichtbarer Platz sein, irgendein verborgener, in zufälliger Augenblickslaune gewählter Winkel ist ebenso gut brauchbar. Die Nachricht, dass sie singen will, verbreitet sich gleich, und bald zieht es in Prozessionen hin. Nun, manchmal treten doch Hindernisse ein, Josefine singt mit Vorliebe gerade in aufgeregten Zeiten, vielfache Sorgen und Nöte zwingen uns dann zu vielerlei Wegen, man kann sich beim besten Willen nicht so schnell versammeln, wie es Josefine wünscht, und sie steht dort diesmal in ihrer großen Haltung vielleicht eine Zeitlang ohne genügende Hörerzahl – dann freilich wird sie wütend, dann stampft sie mit den Füßen, flucht ganz unmädchenhaft, ja sie beißt sogar. Aber selbst ein solches Verhalten schadet ihrem Ruf nicht; statt ihre übergroßen Ansprüche ein wenig einzudämmen, strengt man sich an, ihnen zu entsprechen; es werden Boten ausgeschickt, um Hörer herbeizuholen; es wird vor ihr geheim gehalten, dass das geschieht; man sieht dann auf den Wegen im Umkreis Posten aufgestellt, die den Herankommenden zuwinken, sie möchten sich beeilen; dies alles so lange, bis dann schließlich doch eine leidliche Anzahl beisammen ist.

Was treibt das Volk dazu, sich für Josefine so zu bemühen? Eine Frage, nicht leichter zu beantworten als die nach

Josefinens Gesang, mit der sie ja auch zusammenhängt. Man könnte sie streichen und gänzlich mit der zweiten Frage vereinigen, wenn sich etwa behaupten ließe, dass das Volk wegen des Gesanges Josefine bedingungslos ergeben ist. Dies ist aber eben nicht der Fall; bedingungslose Ergebenheit kennt unser Volk kaum; dieses Volk, das über alles die freilich harmlose Schlauheit liebt, das kindliche Wispern, den freilich unschuldigen, bloß die Lippen bewegenden Tratsch, ein solches Volk kann immerhin nicht bedingungslos sich hingeben, das fühlt wohl auch Josefine, das ist es, was sie bekämpft mit aller Anstrengung ihrer schwachen Kehle.

Nur darf man freilich bei solchen allgemeinen Urteilen nicht zu weit gehen, das Volk ist Josefine doch ergeben, nur nicht bedingungslos. Es wäre zum Beispiel nicht fähig, über Josefine zu lachen. Man kann es sich eingestehen: an Josefine fordert manches zum Lachen auf; und an und für sich ist uns das Lachen immer nah; trotz allem Jammer unseres Lebens ist ein leises Lachen bei uns gewissermaßen immer zu Hause; aber über Josefine lachen wir nicht. Manchmal habe ich den Eindruck, das Volk fasse sein Verhältnis zu Josefine derart auf, dass sie, dieses zerbrechliche, schonungsbedürftige, irgendwie ausgezeichnete, ihrer Meinung nach durch Gesang ausgezeichnete Wesen ihm anvertraut sei, und es müsse für sie sorgen; der Grund dessen ist niemandem klar, nur die Tatsache scheint festzustehen. Über das aber, was einem anvertraut ist, lacht man nicht; darüber zu lachen, wäre Pflichtverletzung; es ist das Äußerste an Boshaftigkeit, was die Boshaftesten unter uns Josefine zufügen, wenn sie manchmal sagen: »Das Lachen vergeht uns, wenn wir Josefine sehen.«

So sorgt also das Volk für Josefine in der Art eines Vaters, der sich eines Kindes annimmt, das sein Händchen – man weiß nicht recht, ob bittend oder fordernd – nach ihm ausstreckt. Man sollte meinen, unser Volk tauge nicht zur Erfüllung solcher väterlichen Pflichten, aber in Wirklichkeit versieht es sie, wenigstens in diesem Falle, musterhaft; kein Einzelner könnte es, was in dieser Hinsicht das Volk als Ganzes zu tun imstande ist. Freilich, der Kraftunterschied zwischen dem Volk und dem Einzelnen ist so ungeheuer, es genügt, dass es den Schützling in die Wärme seiner Nähe zieht, und er ist beschützt genug. Zu Josefine wagt man allerdings von solchen Dingen nicht zu reden. »Ich pfeife auf eueren Schutz«, sagt sie dann. »Ja, ja, du pfeifst«, denken wir. Und außerdem ist es wahrhaftig keine Widerlegung, wenn sie rebelliert, vielmehr ist das durchaus Kindesart und Kindesdankbarkeit, und Art des Vaters ist es, sich nicht daran zu kehren.

Nun spricht aber doch noch anderes mit herein, das schwerer aus diesem Verhältnis zwischen Volk und Josefine zu erklären ist. Josefine ist nämlich der gegenteiligen Meinung, sie glaubt, sie sei es, die das Volk beschütze. Aus schlimmer politischer oder wirtschaftlicher Lage rettet uns angeblich ihr Gesang, nichts weniger als das bringt er zuwege, und wenn er das Unglück nicht vertreibt, so gibt er uns wenigstens die Kraft, es zu ertragen. Sie spricht es nicht so aus und auch nicht anders, sie spricht überhaupt wenig, sie ist schweigsam unter den Plappermäulern, aber aus ihren Augen blitzt es, von ihrem geschlossenen Mund – bei uns können nur wenige den Mund geschlossen halten, sie kann es – ist es abzulesen. Bei jeder schlechten Nachricht – und an manchen Tagen überrennen sie einander, falsche und halbrichtige darunter – erhebt sie sich sofort, während es sie sonst müde zu Boden zieht, erhebt sich und streckt den Hals und sucht den Überblick über ihre Herde wie der Hirt vor dem Gewitter. Gewiss, auch Kinder stellen ähnliche Forderungen in ihrer wilden, unbeherrschten Art, aber bei Josefine sind sie doch nicht so unbegründet wie bei jenen. Freilich, sie rettet uns nicht und gibt uns keine Kräfte, es ist leicht, sich als Retter dieses Volkes aufzuspielen, das leidensgewohnt, sich nicht schonend, schnell in Entschlüssen, den Tod wohl kennend, nur dem Anscheine nach ängstlich in der Atmosphäre von Tollkühnheit, in der es ständig lebt, und überdies ebenso fruchtbar wie wagemutig – es ist leicht, sage ich, sich nachträglich als Retter dieses Volkes aufzuspielen, das sich noch immer irgendwie selbst gerettet hat, sei es auch unter Opfern, über die der Geschichtsforscher – im Allgemeinen vernachlässigen wir Geschichtsforschung gänzlich – vor Schrecken erstarrt. Und doch ist es wahr, dass wir gerade in Notlagen noch besser als sonst auf Josefinens Stimme horchen. Die Drohungen, die über uns stehen, machen uns stiller, bescheidener, für Josefinens Befehlshaberei gefügiger; gern kommen wir zusammen, gern drängen wir uns aneinander, besonders weil es bei einem Anlass geschieht, der ganz abseits liegt von der quälenden Hauptsache; es ist, als tränken wir noch schnell – ja, Eile ist nötig, das vergisst Josefine allzu oft – gemeinsam einen Becher des

Friedens vor dem Kampf. Es ist nicht so sehr eine Gesangsvorführung als vielmehr eine Volksversammlung, und zwar eine Versammlung, bei der es bis auf das kleine Pfeifen vorne völlig still ist; viel zu ernst ist die Stunde, als dass man sie verschwätzen wollte.

Ein solches Verhältnis könnte nun freilich Josefine gar nicht befriedigen. Trotz all ihres nervösen Missbehagens, welches Josefine wegen ihrer niemals ganz geklärten Stellung erfüllt, sieht sie doch, verblendet von ihrem Selbstbewusstsein, manches nicht und kann ohne große Anstrengung dazu gebracht werden, noch viel mehr zu übersehen, ein Schwarm von Schmeichlern ist in diesem Sinne, also eigentlich in einem allgemein nützlichen Sinne, immerfort tätig – aber nur nebenbei, unbeachtet, im Winkel einer Volksversammlung zu singen, dafür würde sie, trotzdem es an sich gar nicht wenig wäre, ihren Gesang gewiss nicht opfern.

Aber sie muss es auch nicht, denn ihre Kunst bleibt nicht unbeachtet. Trotzdem wir im Grunde mit ganz anderen Dingen beschäftigt sind und die Stille durchaus nicht nur dem Gesange zuliebe herrscht und mancher gar nicht aufschaut, sondern das Gesicht in den Pelz des Nachbars drückt und Josefine also dort oben sich vergeblich abzumühen scheint, dringt doch – das ist nicht zu leugnen – etwas von ihrem Pfeifen unweigerlich auch zu uns. Dieses Pfeifen, das sich erhebt, wo allen anderen Schweigen auferlegt ist, kommt fast wie eine Botschaft des Volkes zu dem Einzelnen; das dünne Pfeifen Josefinens mitten in den schweren Entscheidungen ist fast wie die armselige Existenz unseres Volkes mitten im Tumult der feindlichen Welt. Josefine behauptet sich, dieses Nichts an Stimme, dieses Nichts an Leistung behauptet sich und schafft sich den Weg zu uns, es tut wohl, daran zu denken. Einen wirklichen Gesangskünstler, wenn einer einmal sich unter uns finden sollte, würden wir in solcher Zeit gewiss nicht ertragen und die Unsinnigkeit einer solchen Vorführung einmütig abweisen. Möge Josefine beschützt werden vor der Erkenntnis, dass die Tatsache, dass wir ihr zuhören, ein Beweis gegen ihren Gesang ist. Eine Ahnung dessen hat sie wohl, warum würde sie sonst so leidenschaftlich leugnen, dass wir ihr zuhören, aber immer wieder singt sie, pfeift sie sich über diese Ahnung hinweg.

Aber es gäbe auch sonst noch immer einen Trost für sie: Wir hören ihr doch auch gewissermaßen wirklich zu, wahrscheinlich ähnlich, wie man einem Gesangskünstler zuhört; sie erreicht Wirkungen, die ein Gesangskünstler vergeblich bei uns anstreben würde und die nur gerade ihren unzureichenden Mitteln verliehen sind. Dies hängt wohl hauptsächlich mit unserer Lebensweise zusammen.

In unserem Volke kennt man keine Jugend, kaum eine winzige Kinderzeit. Es treten zwar regelmäßig Forderungen auf, man möge den Kindern eine besondere Freiheit, eine besondere Schonung gewährleisten, ihr Recht auf ein wenig Sorglosigkeit, ein wenig sinnloses Sichherumtummeln, auf ein wenig Spiel, dieses Recht möge man anerkennen und ihm zur Erfüllung verhelfen; solche Forderungen treten auf, und fast jedermann billigt sie, es gibt nichts, was mehr zu billigen wäre, aber es gibt auch nichts, was in der Wirklichkeit unseres Lebens weniger zugestanden werden könnte, man billigt die Forderungen, man macht Versuche in ihrem Sinn, aber bald ist wieder alles beim Alten. Unser Leben ist eben derart, dass ein Kind, sobald es nur ein wenig läuft und die Umwelt ein wenig unterscheiden kann, ebenso für sich sorgen muss wie ein Erwachsener; die Gebiete, auf denen wir aus wirtschaftlichen Rücksichten zerstreut leben müssen, sind zu groß, unserer Feinde sind zu viele, die uns überall bereiteten Gefahren zu unberechenbar - wir können die Kinder vom Existenzkampfe nicht fernhalten, täten wir es, es wäre ihr vorzeitiges Ende. Zu diesen traurigen Gründen kommt freilich auch ein erhebender: die Fruchtbarkeit unseres Stammes. Eine Generation - und jede ist zahlreich - drängt die andere, die Kinder haben nicht Zeit, Kinder zu sein. Mögen bei anderen Völkern die Kinder sorgfältig gepflegt werden, mögen dort Schulen für die Kleinen errichtet sein, mögen dort aus diesen Schulen täglich die Kinder strömen, die Zukunft des Volkes, so sind es doch immer lange Zeit Tag für Tag die gleichen Kinder, die dort hervorkommen. Wir haben keine Schulen, aber aus unserem Volke strömen in allerkürzesten Zwischenräumen die unübersehbaren Scharen unserer Kinder, fröhlich zischend oder piepsend, solange sie noch nicht pfeifen können, sich wälzend oder kraft des Druckes weiterrollend, solange sie noch nicht laufen können, täppisch durch ihre Masse alles mit sich fortreißend, solange sie noch nicht sehen können, unsere Kinder! Und nicht wie in jenen Schulen die gleichen Kinder, nein, immer, immer wieder neue, ohne Ende, ohne Unterbrechung, kaum erscheint ein Kind, ist es nicht mehr Kind, aber schon drängen hinter ihm die neuen Kindergesichter ununterscheidbar in ihrer Menge und Eile, rosig vor Glück. Freilich, wie schön dies auch sein mag und wie sehr uns andere darum auch mit Recht beneiden mögen, eine wirkliche Kinderzeit können wir eben unseren Kindern nicht geben. Und das hat seine Folgewirkungen. Eine gewisse unerstorbene, unausrottbare Kindlichkeit durchdringt unser Volk; im geraden Widerspruch zu unserem Besten, dem untrüglichen praktischen Verstande, handeln wir manchmal ganz und gar töricht, und zwar eben in der Art, wie Kinder töricht handeln, sinnlos, verschwenderisch, großzügig, leichtsinnig und dies alles oft einem kleinen Spaß zuliebe. Und wenn unsere Freude darüber natürlich nicht mehr die volle Kraft der Kinderfreude haben kann, etwas von dieser lebt darin noch gewiss. Von dieser Kindlichkeit unseres Volkes profitiert seit jeher auch Josefine.

Aber unser Volk ist nicht nur kindlich, es ist gewissermaßen auch vorzeitig alt, Kindheit und Alter machen sich bei uns anders als bei anderen. Wir haben keine Jugend, wir sind gleich Erwachsene, und Erwachsene sind wir dann zu lange, eine gewisse Müdigkeit und Hoffnungslosigkeit durchzieht von da aus mit breiter Spur das im Ganzen doch so zähe und hoffnungsstarke Wesen unseres Volkes. Damit hängt wohl auch unsere Unmusikalität zusammen; wir sind zu alt für Musik, ihre Erregung, ihr Aufschwung passt nicht für unsere Schwere, müde winken wir ihr ab; wir haben uns auf das Pfeifen zurückgezogen; ein wenig Pfeifen hie und da, das ist das Richtige für uns. Wer weiß, ob es nicht Musiktalente unter uns gibt; wenn es sie aber gäbe, der Charakter der Volksgenossen müsste sie noch vor ihrer Entfaltung unterdrücken. Dagegen mag Josefine nach ihrem Belieben pfeifen oder singen oder wie sie es nennen will, das stört uns nicht, das entspricht uns, das können wir wohl vertragen; wenn darin etwas von Musik enthalten sein sollte, so ist es auf die möglichste Nichtigkeit reduziert; eine gewisse Musiktradition wird gewahrt, aber ohne dass uns dies im Geringsten beschweren würde.

Aber Josefine bringt diesem so gestimmten Volke noch mehr. Bei ihren Konzerten, besonders in ernster Zeit, haben nur noch die ganz Jungen Interesse an der Sängerin als solcher, nur sie sehen mit Staunen zu, wie sie ihre Lippen kräuselt, zwischen den niedlichen Vorderzähnen die Luft ausstößt, in Bewunderung der Töne, die sie selbst hervorbringt, erstirbt und dieses Hinsinken benützt, um sich zu neuer, ihr immer unverständlicher werdender Leistung anzufeuern, aber die eigentliche Menge hat sich – das ist deutlich zu erkennen – auf sich selbst zurückgezogen. Hier in den dürftigen Pausen zwischen den Kämpfen träumt das Volk, es ist, als lösten sich dem Einzelnen die Glieder, als dürfte sich der Ruhelose einmal nach seiner Lust im großen warmen Bett des Volkes dehnen und strecken. Und in diese Träume klingt hie und da Josefinens Pfeifen; sie nennt es perlend, wir nennen es stoßend; aber jedenfalls ist es hier an seinem Platze, wie nirgends sonst, wie Musik kaum jemals den auf sie wartenden Augenblick findet. Etwas von der armen kurzen Kindheit ist darin, etwas von verlorenem, nie wieder aufzufindendem Glück, aber auch etwas vom tätigen heutigen Leben ist darin, von seiner kleinen, unbegreiflichen und dennoch bestehenden und nicht zu ertötenden Munterkeit. Und dies alles ist wahrhaftig nicht mit großen Tönen gesagt, sondern leicht, flüsternd, vertraulich, manchmal ein wenig heiser. Natürlich ist es ein Pfeifen. Wie denn nicht? Pfeifen ist die Sprache unseres Volkes, nur pfeift mancher sein Leben lang und weiß es nicht, hier aber ist das Pfeifen freigemacht von den Fesseln des täglichen Lebens und befreit auch uns für eine kurze Weile. Gewiss, diese Vorführungen wollten wir nicht missen.

Aber von da bis zu Josefinens Behauptung, sie gebe uns in solchen Zeiten neue Kräfte usw. usw., ist noch ein sehr weiter Weg. Für gewöhnliche Leute allerdings, nicht für Josefinens Schmeichler. »Wie könnte es anders sein« - sagen sie in recht unbefangener Keckheit - »wie könnte man anders den großen Zulauf, besonders unter unmittelbar drängender Gefahr, erklären, der schon manchmal sogar die genügende, rechtzeitige Abwehr eben dieser Gefahr verhindert hat.« Nun, dies letztere ist leider richtig, gehört aber doch nicht zu den Ruhmestiteln Josefinens, besonders wenn man hinzufügt, dass, wenn solche Versammlungen unerwartet vom Feind gesprengt wurden, und mancher der unsrigen dabei sein Leben lassen musste, Josefine, die alles verschuldet, ja, durch ihr Pfeifen den Feind vielleicht angelockt hatte, immer im Besitz des sichersten Plätzchens war und unter dem Schutze ihres Anhanges sehr still und eiligst als Erste verschwand. Aber auch dieses wissen im Grunde alle, und dennoch eilen sie wieder hin, wenn Josefine nächstens nach ihrem Belieben irgendwo, irgendwann zum Gesange sich erhebt. Daraus könnte man schließen, dass Josefine fast außerhalb des Gesetzes steht, dass sie tun darf, was sie will, selbst wenn es die Gesamtheit gefährdet, und dass ihr alles verziehen wird. Wenn dies so wäre, dann wären auch Josefinens Ansprüche völlig verständlich, ja, man könnte gewissermaßen in dieser Freiheit, die ihr das Volk geben würde, in diesem außerordentlichen, niemand sonst gewährten, die Gesetze eigentlich widerlegenden Geschenk ein Eingeständnis dessen sehen, dass das Volk Josefine, wie sie es behauptet, nicht versteht, ohnmächtig ihre Kunst anstaunt, sich ihrer nicht würdig fühlt, dieses Leid, das es Josefine tut, durch eine geradezu verzweifelte Leistung auszugleichen strebt und, so wie ihre Kunst außerhalb seines Fassungsvermögens ist, auch ihre Person und deren Wünsche außerhalb seiner Befehlsgewalt stellt. Nun, das ist allerdings ganz und gar nicht richtig, vielleicht kapituliert im Einzelnen das Volk zu schnell vor Josefine, aber wie es bedingungslos vor niemandem kapituliert, also auch nicht vor ihr.

Schon seit langer Zeit, vielleicht schon seit Beginn ihrer Künstlerlaufbahn, kämpft Josefine darum, dass sie mit Rücksicht auf ihren Gesang von jeder Arbeit befreit werde; man solle ihr also die Sorge um das tägliche Brot und alles, was sonst mit unserem Existenzkampf verbunden ist, abnehmen und es – wahrscheinlich – auf das Volk als Ganzes überwälzen. Ein schnell Begeisterter – es fanden sich auch solche – könnte schon allein aus der Sonderbarkeit dieser Forderung, aus der Geistesverfassung, die eine solche Forderung auszudenken imstande ist, auf deren innere Berechtigung schließen. Unser Volk zieht aber andere Schlüsse und lehnt ruhig die Forderung ab. Es müht sich auch mit der Widerlegung der Gesuchsbegründung nicht sehr ab. Josefine weist zum Beispiel darauf hin, dass die Anstrengung bei der Arbeit ihrer

Stimme schade, dass zwar die Anstrengung bei der Arbeit gering sei im Vergleich zu jener beim Gesang, dass sie ihr aber doch die Möglichkeit nehme, nach dem Gesang sich genügend auszuruhen und für neuen Gesang sich zu stärken, sie müsse sich dabei gänzlich erschöpfen und könne trotzdem unter diesen Umständen ihre Höchstleistung niemals erreichen. Das Volk hört sie an und geht darüber hinweg. Dieses so leicht zu rührende Volk ist manchmal gar nicht zu rühren. Die Abweisung ist manchmal so hart, dass selbst Josefine stutzt, sie scheint sich zu fügen, arbeitet wie sich's gehört, singt, so gut sie kann, aber das alles nur eine Weile, dann nimmt sie den Kampf mit neuen Kräften – dafür scheint sie unbeschränkt viele zu haben – wieder auf.

Nun ist es ja klar, dass Josefine nicht eigentlich das anstrebt, was sie wörtlich verlangt. Sie ist vernünftig, sie scheut die Arbeit nicht, wie ja Arbeitsscheu überhaupt bei uns unbekannt ist, sie würde auch nach Bewilligung ihrer Forderung gewiss nicht anders leben als früher, die Arbeit würde ihrem Gesang gar nicht im Wege stehen, und der Gesang allerdings würde auch nicht schöner werden – was sie anstrebt, ist also nur die öffentliche, eindeutige, die Zeiten überdauernde, über alles bisher Bekannte sich weit erhebende Anerkennung ihrer Kunst. Während ihr aber fast alles andere erreichbar scheint, versagt sich ihr dieses hartnäckig. Vielleicht hätte sie den Angriff gleich anfangs in andere Richtung lenken sollen, vielleicht sieht sie jetzt selbst den Fehler ein, aber nun kann sie nicht mehr zurück, ein Zurückgehen hieße sich selbst untreu werden, nun muss sie schon mit dieser Forderung stehen oder fallen.

Hätte sie wirklich Feinde, wie sie sagt, sie könnten diesem Kampfe, ohne selbst den Finger rühren zu müssen, belustigt zusehen. Aber sie hat keine Feinde, und selbst wenn mancher hie und da Einwände gegen sie hat, dieser Kampf belustigt niemanden. Schon deshalb nicht, weil sich hier das Volk in seiner kalten richterlichen Haltung zeigt, wie man es sonst bei uns nur sehr selten sieht. Und wenn einer auch diese Haltung in diesem Falle billigen mag, so schließt doch die bloße Vorstellung, dass sich einmal das Volk ähnlich gegen ihn selbst verhalten könnte, jede Freude aus. Es handelt sich eben auch bei der Abweisung, ähnlich wie bei der Forderung, nicht um die Sache selbst, sondern darum, dass sich das Volk gegen einen Volksgenossen derart undurchdringlich abschließen kann und umso undurchdringlicher, als es sonst für eben diesen Genossen väterlich und mehr als väterlich, demütig sorgt.

Stünde hier an Stelle des Volkes ein Einzelner: Man könnte glauben, dieser Mann habe die ganze Zeit über Josefine nachgegeben unter dem fortwährenden brennenden Verlangen, endlich der Nachgiebigkeit ein Ende zu machen; er habe übermenschlich viel nachgegeben im festen Glauben, dass das Nachgeben trotzdem seine richtige Grenze finden werde; ja, er habe mehr nachgegeben, als nötig war, nur um die Sache zu beschleunigen, nur, um Josefine zu verwöhnen und zu immer neuen Wünschen zu treiben, bis sie dann wirklich diese letzte Forderung erhob; da habe er nun freilich, kurz, weil längst vorbereitet, die endgültige Abweisung vorgenommen. Nun, so verhält es sich ganz gewiss nicht, das Volk braucht solche Listen nicht, außerdem ist seine Verehrung für Josefine aufrichtig und erprobt, und Josefinens Forderung ist allerdings so stark, dass jedes unbefangene Kind ihr den Ausgang hätte voraussagen können; trotzdem mag es sein, dass in der Auffassung, die Josefine von der Sache hat, auch solche Vermutungen mitspielen und dem Schmerz der Abgewiesenen eine Bitternis hinzufügen.

Aber mag sie auch solche Vermutungen haben, vom Kampf abschrecken lässt sie sich dadurch nicht. In letzter Zeit verschärft sich sogar der Kampf; hat sie ihn bisher nur durch Worte geführt, fängt sie jetzt an, andere Mittel anzuwenden, die ihrer Meinung nach wirksamer, unserer Meinung nach für sie selbst gefährlicher sind.

Manche glauben, Josefine werde deshalb so dringlich, weil sie sich alt werden fühle, die Stimme Schwächen zeige, und es ihr daher höchste Zeit zu sein scheine, den letzten Kampf um ihre Anerkennung zu führen. Ich glaube daran nicht. Josefine wäre nicht Josefine, wenn dies wahr wäre. Für sie gibt es kein Altern und keine Schwächen ihrer Stimme. Wenn sie etwas fordert, so wird sie nicht durch äußere Dinge, sondern durch innere Folgerichtigkeit dazu gebracht. Sie greift nach dem höchsten Kranz, nicht, weil er im Augenblick gerade ein wenig tiefer hängt, sondern weil es der höchste ist; wäre es in ihrer Macht, sie würde ihn noch höher hängen.

Diese Missachtung äußerer Schwierigkeiten hindert sie allerdings nicht, die unwürdigsten Mittel anzuwenden. Ihr Recht steht ihr außer Zweifel; was liegt also daran, wie sie es erreicht; besonders da doch in dieser Welt, so wie sie sich ihr darstellt, gerade die würdigen Mittel versagen müssen. Vielleicht hat sie sogar deshalb den Kampf um ihr Recht aus dem

Gebiet des Gesanges auf ein anderes ihr wenig teures verlegt. Ihr Anhang hat Aussprüche von ihr in Umlauf gebracht, nach denen sie sich durchaus fähig fühlt, so zu singen, dass es dem Volk in allen seinen Schichten bis in die versteckteste Opposition hinein eine wirkliche Lust wäre, wirkliche Lust nicht im Sinne des Volkes, welches ja behauptet, diese Lust seit jeher bei Josefinens Gesang zu fühlen, sondern Lust im Sinne von Josefinens Verlangen. Aber, fügt sie hinzu, da sie das Hohe nicht fälschen und dem Gemeinen nicht schmeicheln könne, müsse es eben bleiben, wie es sei. Anders aber ist es bei ihrem Kampf um die Arbeitsbefreiung, zwar ist es auch ein Kampf um ihren Gesang, aber hier kämpft sie nicht unmittelbar mit der kostbaren Waffe des Gesanges, jedes Mittel, das sie anwendet, ist daher gut genug.

So wurde zum Beispiel das Gerücht verbreitet, Josefine beabsichtige, wenn man ihr nicht nachgebe, die Koloraturen zu kürzen. Ich weiß nichts von Koloraturen, habe in ihrem Gesange niemals etwas von Koloraturen bemerkt. Josefine aber will die Koloraturen kürzen, vorläufig nicht beseitigen, sondern nur kürzen. Sie hat angeblich ihre Drohung wahr gemacht, mir allerdings ist kein Unterschied gegenüber ihren früheren Vorführungen aufgefallen. Das Volk als Ganzes hat zugehört wie immer, ohne sich über die Koloraturen zu äußern, und auch die Behandlung von Josefinens Forderung hat sich nicht geändert. Übrigens hat Josefine, wie in ihrer Gestalt, unleugbar auch in ihrem Denken manchmal etwas recht Graziöses. So hat sie zum Beispiel nach jener Vorführung, so als sei ihr Entschluss hinsichtlich der Koloraturen gegenüber dem Volk zu hart oder zu plötzlich gewesen, erklärt, nächstens werde sie die Koloraturen doch wieder vollständig singen. Aber nach dem nächsten Konzert besann sie sich wieder anders, nun sei es endgültig zu Ende mit den großen Koloraturen, und vor einer für Josefine günstigen Entscheidung kämen sie nicht wieder. Nun, das Volk hört über alle diese Erklärungen, Entschlüsse und Entschlussänderungen hinweg, wie ein Erwachsener in Gedanken über das Plaudern eines Kindes hinweghört, grundsätzlich wohlwollend, aber unerreichbar.

Josefine aber gibt nicht nach. So behauptete sie zum Beispiel neulich, sie habe sich bei der Arbeit eine Fußverletzung zugezogen, die ihr das Stehen während des Gesanges beschwerlich mache; da sie aber nur stehend singen könne, müsse sie jetzt sogar die Gesänge kürzen. Trotzdem sie hinkt und sich von ihrem Anhang stützen lässt, glaubt niemand an eine wirkliche Verletzung. Selbst die besondere Empfindlichkeit ihres Körperchens zugegeben, sind wir doch ein Arbeitsvolk, und auch Josefine gehört zu ihm; wenn wir aber wegen jeder Hautabschürfung hinken wollten, dürfte das ganze Volk mit Hinken gar nicht aufhören. Aber mag sie sich wie eine Lahme führen lassen, mag sie sich in diesem bedauernswerten Zustand öfters zeigen als sonst, das Volk hört ihren Gesang dankbar und entzückt wie früher, aber wegen der Kürzung macht es nicht viel Aufhebens.

Da sie nicht immerfort hinken kann, erfindet sie etwas anderes, sie schützt Müdigkeit vor, Missstimmung, Schwäche. Wir haben nun außer dem Konzert auch ein Schauspiel. Wir sehen hinter Josefine ihren Anhang, wie er sie bittet und beschwört zu singen. Sie wollte gern, aber sie kann nicht.

Man tröstet sie, umschmeichelt sie, trägt sie fast auf den schon vorher ausgesuchten Platz, wo sie singen soll. Endlich gibt sie mit undeutbaren Tränen nach, aber wie sie mit offenbar letztem Willen zu singen anfangen will, matt, die Arme nicht wie sonst ausgebreitet, sondern am Körper leblos herunterhängend, wobei man den Eindruck erhält, dass sie vielleicht ein wenig zu kurz sind – wie sie so anstimmen will, nun, da geht es doch wieder nicht, ein unwilliger Ruck des Kopfes zeigt es an, und sie sinkt vor unseren Augen zusammen. Dann allerdings rafft sie sich doch wieder auf und singt, ich glaube, nicht viel anders als sonst, vielleicht wenn man für feinste Nuancen das Ohr hat, hört man ein wenig außergewöhnliche Erregung heraus, die der Sache aber nur zugute kommt. Und am Ende ist sie sogar weniger müde als vorher, mit festem Gang, soweit man ihr huschendes Trippeln so nennen kann, entfernt sie sich, jede Hilfe des Anhangs ablehnend und mit kalten Blicken die ihr ehrfurchtsvoll ausweichende Menge prüfend.

So war es letzthin, das Neueste aber ist, dass sie zu einer Zeit, wo ihr Gesang erwartet wurde, verschwunden war. Nicht nur der Anhang sucht sie, viele stellen sich in den Dienst des Suchens, es ist vergeblich; Josefine ist verschwunden, sie will nicht singen, sie will nicht einmal darum gebeten werden, sie hat uns diesmal völlig verlassen. Sonderbar, wie falsch sie rechnet, die Kluge, so falsch, dass man glauben sollte, sie rechne gar nicht, sondern werde nur weiter getrieben von ihrem Schicksal, das in unserer Welt nur ein sehr trauriges werden kann. Selbst entzieht sie sich dem Gesang, selbst zerstört sie die Macht, die sie über die Gemüter erworben hat. Wie konnte sie nur diese Macht erwerben, da sie diese Gemüter so wenig kennt. Sie versteckt sich und singt nicht, aber das Volk, ruhig, ohne sichtbare Enttäuschung, herrisch, eine in sich ruhende Masse, die förmlich, auch wenn der Anschein dagegen spricht, Geschenke nur geben, niemals empfangen kann, auch von Josefine nicht, dieses Volk zieht weiter seines Weges.

Mit Josefine aber muss es abwärts gehen. Bald wird die Zeit kommen, wo ihr letzter Pfiff ertönt und verstummt. Sie ist eine kleine Episode in der ewigen Geschichte unseres Volkes, und das Volk wird den Verlust überwinden. Leicht wird es uns ja nicht werden; wie werden die Versammlungen in völliger Stummheit möglich sein? Freilich, waren sie nicht auch mit Josefine stumm? War ihr wirkliches Pfeifen nennenswert lauter und lebendiger, als die Erinnerung daran sein wird? War es denn noch bei ihren Lebzeiten mehr als eine bloße Erinnerung? Hat nicht vielmehr das Volk in seiner Weisheit Josefinens Gesang, eben deshalb, weil er in dieser Art unverlierbar war, so hoch gestellt?

Vielleicht werden wir also gar nicht sehr viel entbehren, Josefine aber, erlöst von der irdischen Plage, die aber ihrer Meinung nach Auserwählten bereitet ist, wird fröhlich sich verlieren in der zahllosen Menge der Helden unseres Volkes, und bald, da wir keine Geschichte treiben, in gesteigerter Erlösung vergessen sein wie alle ihre Brüder.

Kafkas Tierwelt

Reiner Stach

Kafkas Tiere, so scheint es auf den ersten Blick, greifen auf eine reiche literarische Tradition zurück. Seine »Kleine Fabel« sogar schon im Titel, denn Fabeln mit sprechenden Tieren kannten bereits die Sumerer, und dass diese imaginären Wesen uns vor keine großen Rätsel stellen, war von jeher beabsichtigt. Fabeln nutzen Allegorien wie den schlauen Fuchs, die dumme Gans oder die verräterische Schlange, und selbst schon Kindern ist leicht begreiflich zu machen, dass diese Tiere hier für etwas anderes stehen, für eine menschliche Eigenschaft oder für eine moralische Idee.

Es dauerte bis ins 19. Jahrhundert, ehe sich die satirische und phantastische Literatur von diesem didaktischen Korsett vollends befreien konnte und mit äußerst unterhaltsamen Experimenten in Neuland vorstieß. So sind etwa E.T.A. Hoffmanns sprechender Hund Berganza und sein gebildeter Kater Murr keine bloß allegorischen Figuren mehr, sie entwickeln literarisches Eigengewicht. Auch dienten Tiere nun häufiger der Absicht des Autors, den Leser emotional und moralisch besonders intensiv anzufassen. Das bekannteste Beispiel in der deutschen Literatur ist vermutlich die Erzählung »Krambambuli« von Marie von Ebner-Eschenbach, in der ein Hund sich als äußerst treu erweist und dann genau diese Eigenschaft mit seinem Leben bezahlen muss. Insbesondere die Stummheit des Tieres hat hier offenkundig auch eine ästhetische Funktion, es ist eine sprechende Stummheit. Das wohl neueste, international rezipierte Beispiel in dieser Tradition ist George Saunders' »Fuchs 8«, dessen kindlich-tierischer Erzähler die Menschen um eine Erklärung für ihr zerstörerisches Verhalten bittet.

Aber auch dort, wo nach wie vor die Dynamik der Allegorie oder des Symbols die Szene beherrscht, entwickelt das Tier in der Literatur der Moderne häufig ein Eigenleben, das sich noch vor aller Auslegung ästhetisch rezipieren lässt. So zum Beispiel in Hemingways Erzählung »Der alte Mann und das Meer«, wo mächtige Fische für die unbezwingbare Überlegenheit der Natur über den Menschen stehen, ähnlich wie auch schon in Melvilles »Moby-Dick«, worauf Hemingway natürlich anspielt.

Solche einfach übersetzbaren Bilder finden sich gelegentlich auch in Kafkas Prosa. In der Erzählung »Ein Hungerkünstler« nimmt ein Asket in einem öffentlich ausgestellten Käfig wochenlang keine Nahrung zu sich, so lange, bis das gelangweilte Publikum ihn vergisst. Am Ende stirbt der Mann, und den Käfig bewohnt fortan ein junger Panther, der reine Vitalität repräsentiert und den die Leute daher weit interessanter finden. Kafka nutzt hier die Energie der Tiermetapher, um einen maximalen sinnlichen Kontrast zur Todesnähe des Asketen zu erzeugen.

Auch geheimnisvollere, schwerer zu entziffernde Tiererscheinungen gibt es bei Kafka. Etwa im »Schloss«-Roman die Krähen, die hoch oben den Turm des Schlosses umkreisen. Große schwarze Vögel über einer Schneelandschaft –

sehr poetisch ist das, aber was könnten wir sonst darüber sagen? Oder in der Erzählung »Ein Landarzt«, in der ein von weit hergerufener Arzt hilflos am Bett seines jungen Patienten sitzt, ringsumher die Familie, die ein Wunder von ihm erwartet. Plötzlich werden von außen die Fenster aufgestoßen, zwei Pferdeköpfe erscheinen im Zimmer und betrachten den Jungen. So etwas geschieht sonst nur im Traum, keine einfache Deutung bietet sich hier an, aber eben darum ist das Bild besonders stark.

Solche Motive finden sich in vielfacher Variation in den Literaturen der Welt. Tiere sind per se symbolträchtig, weil sie komplexe, starke, teils auch atavistische Regungen auslösen, noch ehe das bewusste Verständnis einsetzt – die Kunstgeschichte liefert dafür nicht weniger wirkungsmächtige Beispiele. Aber von dieser allgemeinen Motivgeschichte grenzen sich einige von Kafkas Einfällen doch so energisch ab, dass ein bloßer Rekurs auf literarische Traditionen wenig hilfreich wäre. Er weist seinen Tieren eine verblüffende Autonomie zu und reserviert ihnen eine weitläufige Etage seines Werks.

Die in diesem Band abgedruckten Erzählungen beschränken sich nicht auf den symbolischen oder metaphorischen Gebrauch von Tiererscheinungen. Vielmehr stammen ihre Protagonisten selbst aus der Tierwelt, als Wesen mit nicht immer eindeutiger Identität (»Eine Kreuzung« und »In unserer Synagoge …«), als jähe Verkörperung einer Überlieferung (»Der neue Advokat« und »Der Geier«), doch stets in Tiergestalt, geheimnisvoll handelnd, oft intensiv denkend, sogar sprechend. In vier der Texte kommen Menschen überhaupt nicht vor. Und in drei dieser Erzählungen (»Ein Bericht für eine Akademie«, »Forschungen eines Hundes«, »Der Bau«) ist das Tier, der Protagonist, identisch mit dem Ich-Erzähler. Diese Tiere selbst also erzählen davon, wie es ist, ein Tier zu sein, und sie tun dies so reflektiert, ja abgeklärt, dass wir versucht sind, in ihnen Gesprächspartner zu sehen.

Freilich verzichtet Kafka keineswegs darauf, auch das Tiermotiv mit Schockeffekten aufzuladen. Es sind keine Märchentiere, denen wir hier begegnen, vielmehr Wesen, die auf unheimliche Weise die Barriere zwischen Mensch und Tier überwinden oder sogar gänzlich ignorieren. Das ist eine erzählerische Idee, die zu Beginn des 20. Jahrhunderts das Unbehagen, ja den Widerstand des Lesers zweifellos heftiger provozierte als heute. Denn in der Epoche, in der Kafka aufwuchs, galt jene Grenzlinie noch als so offensichtlich und unverrückbar, dass allein der Gedanke, der Mensch sei auf irgendeine Weise aus dem Tierreich hervorgegangen und es handele sich im Grunde um Verwandte, vielen Menschen nicht nur als beleidigend, sondern auch als absurd erschien.

Gewiss, der Nutzen von Zuchttieren war hochgeschätzt, und auch den Unterhaltungswert – sei es von Haustieren, sei es im Zirkus – ließ man sich gerne etwas kosten. Doch der inferiore Status der Tiere schien ein für allemal geklärt. Es war unumstößliches Recht, sie nach Gutdünken lenken, dressieren, jagen, einsperren, bestrafen, am Ende auch schlachten und essen zu dürfen. In der moralischen Rechnung des Menschen kamen sie, wenn überhaupt, nur als ganz marginaler Posten vor. Zwar gab es erste organisierte Bestrebungen zum Tierschutz schon ab Mitte des 19. Jahrhunderts; doch dabei standen keineswegs die Rechte von Tieren, sondern die Vermeidung »unnötigen« Leids im Fokus. Eine kulturell relevante Veränderung in der Wertschätzung von Tieren hatte das noch keineswegs zur Folge – weswegen auch Bezeichnungen von Tieren nach wie vor als herabwürdigende Adjektive oder als Schimpfworte gebraucht wurden, weitaus häufiger, als das heutzutage zu hören ist.

Auch Kafkas Vater Hermann nahm dieses Ventil in Anspruch, gewohnheitsmäßig und kreativ, wie sein Sohn uns insbesondere im »Brief an den Vater« überliefert. Als einmal einer seiner Angestellten sich zu lange krankmeldete, polterte er: »Er soll krepieren, der kranke Hund!« Wenn jemand am Esstisch kleckerte, hieß es: »Du bist ein großes Schwein!« Und wenn das Essen nicht schmeckte, wurde die Köchin als »Vieh« abqualifiziert.[1] Am schlimmsten jedoch eine Szene, die den erwachsenen Kafka unmittelbar betraf. Er hatte einen Freund für eine halbe Stunde mit nach Hause gebracht, den armen und entsprechend schlecht gekleideten ostjüdischen Schauspieler Jizchak Löwy. Der auf soziale Hierarchien empfindlich bedachte Hermann Kafka fand es höchst unpassend, dass sein Sohn sich mit solchen Menschen abgab: »Wer sich mit Hunden zu Bett legt, steht mit Wanzen auf.« So sein Kommentar, den Kafka noch nach Jahren im Ohr hatte.[2]

Wann er zum ersten Mal den Gedanken der Identifikation mit einem Tier hatte, wissen wir nicht, da Kafkas Jugendschriften nicht überliefert sind. Ein Indiz dafür, dass er das literarische Potenzial dieser Idee zunächst noch gar nicht erkannte, findet sich jedoch in der Fragment gebliebenen

Erzählung »Hochzeitsvorbereitungen auf dem Lande«, in der unversehens ein Menschen-Käfer erscheint: »Ich habe, wie ich im Bett liege, die Gestalt eines großen Käfers, eines Hirschkäfers oder eines Maikäfers glaube ich. [...] Und ich lisple eine kleine Zahl Worte, das sind Anordnungen an meinen traurigen Körper, der knapp bei mir steht und gebeugt ist. Bald bin ich fertig, er verbeugt sich, er geht flüchtig, und alles wird er aufs Beste vollführen, während ich ruhe.«[3] Dies ist das früheste überlieferte Menschen-Tier in Kafkas Werk: der große Käfer im Bett, denkend und sprechend. Doch etwa sechs Jahre vor der Niederschrift der »Verwandlung«, in der der Handelsvertreter Samsa als riesiges Insekt erwacht und in dieser Gestalt auch den Tod findet, hat das Bild noch keinerlei existenzielles Gewicht, es reiht sich ein in die Abfolge tagträumerischer Halluzinationen, wie sie für das Frühwerk so charakteristisch sind. Jener Käfer existiert nur im spielerischen Konjunktiv, und er verschwindet folgenlos. Aber offenbar blieb sein Bild aufbewahrt bis zu dem Augenblick, da Kafka ihm höhere Aufgaben zuwies.

Der Geniestreich der »Verwandlung« besteht vor allem darin, dass hier etwas völlig Phantastisches völlig plausibel wird. Kafka präsentiert uns eine gewöhnliche kleinbürgerliche Familienkonstellation, zu deren Beschreibung die realistische Literatur schon vielfache Muster bereithielt. Doch auf keines dieser Muster greift Kafka zurück. Stattdessen übersetzt er die psychosoziale in eine schockierend körperliche Konstellation, so dass die beschreibenden Abstrakta, die hier nahe lägen – Unterwerfung, Demütigung, Entfremdung –, weder vom Erzähler noch von den Figuren ausgesprochen werden müssen. Vielmehr gewinnen sie eine unmittelbare, bezwingende Körperlichkeit, sie werden dadurch schicksalhaft und unwiderlegbar. Gregor Samsa ist anders, auf einfachste, überaus sichtbare Weise, und allein dies zerstört jede moralische Ambivalenz. Denn keinem Menschen ist es zuzumuten, mit diesem »Anderen«, diesem Ungeheuer, unter einem Dach zu leben.

Viel ist bereits publiziert worden über die biographischen Hintergründe dieser Erzählung. Sie sind unbestreitbar und gut dokumentiert, da wir gerade über diese Epoche in Kafkas Leben – die letzten Monate des Jahres 1912 – durch zahlreiche Briefe und Tagebucheinträge besonders genaue Einblicke gewinnen. Offensichtlich ist in dieser Phase, dass ihm seine widersprüchliche Haltung gegenüber der eigenen Familie immer problematischer wird. So stark auch sein Wunsch ist, am Leben der Familie teilzunehmen, so wenig gelingt es ihm, die intellektuelle Distanz aufzuheben. Er bleibt Beobachter, Zaungast der eigenen Familie, die ihn nicht versteht und die sein mangelndes Engagement fortwährend beklagt. Irgendwann muss Kafka zu der Auffassung gelangt sein, dass eine solche Position nicht nur moralisch unhaltbar ist, sondern auch etwas zutiefst Unmenschliches hat. »Oft – und im innersten vielleicht ununterbrochen – zweifle ich daran ein Mensch zu sein«, so schreibt er an Felice Bauer am 7. Juli 1913. Und am folgenden Tag noch kälter: »Winde ich mich nicht seit Monaten vor Dir wie etwas Giftiges? [...] Ich bin kein Mensch«.[4] Die Verlobte dürfte darauf, wie es ihre Art war, beschwichtigend und ausweichend reagiert haben. Dass Kafka Derartiges nicht aus einer Laune heraus schrieb, hat sie wohl erst viel später verstanden, vielleicht erst nach Lektüre der »Verwandlung«, dem öffentlichen Aufblühen von Kafkas Tiermetaphorik.

Die erste große Erzählung, in der die Perspektive auf die Seite des Tieres wechselt, die erste Tiererzählung im engeren Sinne also, ist »Ein Bericht für eine Akademie« vom April 1917. Hier schildert ein Menschenaffe seinen allmählichen, zunächst erzwungenen, dann aber auch ehrgeizigen Übergang in die Welt der Menschen. Dieser Übergang wird möglich durch harte Dressur, durch die Nachahmung menschlicher Gewohnheiten, schließlich durch das Erlernen der menschlichen Sprache. Dass es mit diesem Lernprozess seine vitale Freiheit einbüßt, ja, dass es sogar die Erinnerung an diese Freiheit am Ende verlieren wird, ist dem Tier durchaus bewusst. Der Gewinn, der ihm dafür zuteil wird, ist der vergängliche Ruhm, den es bei zahlreichen Auftritten im Varieté erntet, seine Privilegien als lebendiges Kuriosum. Soziale Bindungen an die Menschen entstehen auf diese Weise jedoch nicht. Weder findet der Affe Freunde unter den Menschen, noch ist je die Rede davon, dass er an den Sorgen der Menschen tieferes Interesse gewinnt. Er denkt und redet in menschlichen Begriffen, doch seine Position entspricht sehr genau der des Haustiers, das die Menschen fortwährend beobachtet, gelegentlich imitiert und sich auch gerne von ihnen ernähren lässt, ohne sie jedoch zu verstehen oder auch nur verstehen zu wollen.

Trotz des gänzlich anderen Sujets sind die Parallelen zur »Verwandlung« offenkundig: Erneut geht es um die randständige Position des Beobachters, der neben, aber nicht mit der Gemeinschaft lebt: ein fragwürdiger Status, über den diese Menschen-Tiere trotz aller Anstrengungen nicht hinauskommen, ebenso wenig wie ihr Erfinder. Denn auch Kafka musste sich sagen, dass er ein selbstverständliches menschliches Interesse, insbesondere für die Sorgen der eigenen Familie, niemals aufbringen konnte, allenfalls ein Interesse aus Neugier. Während die anderen darin Kälte und Eigennutz sahen, verspürte er selbst einen generalisierten Mangel an Zugehörigkeit, ein tiefes Defizit, das dann auch im »Brief an den Vater« thematisiert wird.

Für die weitere Entfaltung von Kafkas Werk ist nun bedeutsam, dass die Tierfigur in »Ein Bericht für eine Akademie« an Autonomie gewonnen hat. Während sich der autobiografische Hintergrund der »Verwandlung« geradezu aufdrängt, sind bei der Affengeschichte auch andere Lektüren möglich, und so ist es nicht überraschend, dass dieser Text zuerst in Martin Bubers kulturzionistischer Zeitschrift »Der Jude« abgedruckt wurde und nicht etwa in einem literarischen Journal. Denn das aussichtslose Bemühen um Assimilation und infolgedessen auch die generelle Fragwürdigkeit der Assimilation als soziale Leitidee – dies war in den frühen Jahren des Zionismus eines der wesentlichen strittigen Themen, mit denen sich die junge Bewegung vom liberalen Judentum absetzte.

Die Affengeschichte als Assimilationstragödie wird noch plausibler durch eine zweite, kürzere Erzählung mit sprechenden Tieren, die kurz zuvor entstand und in der schon der Titel auf eine politische Bedeutungsschicht verweist: »Schakale und Araber«. Hier nähern sich die Tiere in scheinbarer Ehrerbietung einem europäischen Reisenden und bitten ihn darum, den Arabern die Hälse durchzuschneiden: mit Hilfe einer rostigen Nähschere, die sie ihm aufdrängen. Nur so könne das Volk der Schakale erlöst werden. Später erfährt der Reisende von den Arabern, dass die Schakale diese Geschichte jedem Beliebigen erzählen und dass man sie sehr leicht zufriedenstellen kann, indem man ihre hungrigen Mäuler stopft. Für Martin Bubers Leser gewiss eine bittere Pille, denn die Gleichsetzung von Juden mit Schakalen drängt sich hier auf, und die absurde messianische Erwartung und penetrante Unterwürfigkeit der Schakale bietet den denkbar schärfsten Gegensatz zu der völlig gelassenen, überlegenen Vitalität der Araber. Trotzdem war Buber bereit, auch diese Geschichte neben der Affenerzählung abzudrucken, unter dem gemeinsamen, ganz unpolitischen Obertitel »Zwei Tiergeschichten«.

Es scheint, als habe Kafka erst im Jahr 1917 entdeckt, dass das sprechende und denkende Tier eine ungeheuer variationsreich nutzbare Figur ist. Als sei er von der Eigendynamik dieser Vorstellung mitgerissen worden, als habe die Tiermetapher, oder das Tiersymbol, unter seiner Feder neue Sinnoptionen geradezu angesaugt. Wie stets bei diesem Autor war das ein überaus sinnlicher Vorgang. Denn der Brennstoff seiner Imaginationskraft waren vor allem Bilder, Kafka war angewiesen auf visuellen Input, und seine Aufmerksamkeit, sein literarisches Interesse und der Grad an schöpferischer Konzentration waren in hohem Maß davon abhängig.

So ist es kaum verwunderlich, dass er im Herbst 1917 auch den Wechsel von der Großstadt in die karge dörfliche Idylle im nordwestböhmischen Zürau, wo er bei seiner Schwester Ottla lebte, zunächst einmal bildhaft verarbeitete. Während die Freunde – aufs Äußerste besorgt wegen Kafkas Tuberkuloseerkrankung – sich in Mahnungen ergingen und auf vernünftige medizinische Entscheidungen drängten, sah sich Kafka im Dorf in aller Ruhe um und ließ die neuen Bilder in sich eindringen. Und als erstes betrachtete er die Tiere. Von Gänsen, Mäusen und Katzen ist in seinen Briefen aus Zürau ausführlich die Rede, von Füchsen, Ziegen, Schweinen und Kühen. An Felix Weltsch schrieb er Mitte Oktober 1917: »Ich lese im Ganzen nicht viel, das Leben auf dem Dorf ist mir so entsprechend. Hat man erst einmal das Gefühl mit allen seinen Unannehmlichkeiten überwunden, in einem nach neueren Prinzipien eingerichteten Tiergarten zu wohnen, in welchem den Tieren volle Freiheit gegeben ist, dann gibt es kein behaglicheres und vor allem kein freieres Leben als auf dem Dorf«.[5]

Auch die Physiognomie der Tiere betrachtete er genau und machte sich einen Spaß daraus, in ihnen menschliche Züge zu suchen. So wenige Tage zuvor in einem Brief an Elsa Brod, die ihm eine Porträt-Postkarte des Prager Varietédirektors Rolf Wagner geschickt hatte: »Ich will ihn durch den Vergleich mit einem Schwein gar nicht beschimpfen, aber an Merkwürdigkeit, Entschiedenheit, Selbstvergessenheit, Süßigkeit und was noch zu seinem Amt gehört, steht er in der Weltordnung vielleicht doch mit dem Schwein in einer Reihe. Haben Sie schon ein Schwein in der Nähe so genau angesehn, wie Wagner? Es ist erstaunlich.«[6]

Wonach eine eindringliche Beschreibung der Schweine

folgt. Die Heiterkeit dieses Briefautors muss dem Ehepaar Brod geradezu unheimlich gewesen sein. Doch Kafka wusste noch eine Steigerung: »Diese Ziegen also sind äußerlich vollkommen jüdische Typen, meistens Ärzte, doch gibt es auch Annäherungen an Advokaten, polnische Juden und vereinzelt auch jüdische Mädchen. Besonders Dr. Mühlstein, der Arzt, der mich behandelt, ist stark unter ihnen vertreten. Das aus drei jüdischen Ärzten bestehende Konsilium, das ich heute gefüttert habe, war so mit mir zufrieden, dass es sich abends kaum forttreiben lassen wollte, um gemolken zu werden.«[7]

Es schien, als wollte Kafka die Freunde mit literarischen Späßen bloß unterhalten. Doch der Anblick von Tieren, die im Dorf weit tiefer ins Leben der Menschen integriert waren, die oft den Menschen in großer Zahl umgaben und die sich auch entschieden autonomer bewegten als die fast immer vereinzelt erscheinenden Stadttiere – dieser während eines Dreivierteljahrs, bis ins Frühjahr 1918 täglich erneuerte Anblick hatte sich in Kafkas Imagination offenbar eingegraben. Ein Indiz dafür ist, dass auch seine literarischen Tierfiguren von nun an vollends autonom werden und die Szene ganz allein beherrschen. »Forschungen eines Hundes«, »Der Bau« und »Josefine, die Sängerin oder das Volk der Mäuse« – diese drei Erzählungen brauchen keinen menschlichen Souffleur mehr.

Auch an ästhetischer Autonomie gewinnen Kafkas Tiere. Das Ungeziefer ist verhältnismäßig leicht als Metapher dechiffrierbar, ebenso der Menschenaffe, für den es ja charakteristisch ist, dass er den Menschen »nachäfft«, wie die geläufige Redewendung besagt. Eine Metapher übrigens, die Kafka auch im Alltag verwendete, etwa in einem Brief an Felice Bauer, in dem er ihr erklärt, auf einem der frühen Familienfotos sei er als Affe seiner Eltern porträtiert.[8] Solche einfachen semantischen Überlegungen sind bei den späten Tierfiguren jedoch nicht mehr hilfreich, und warum Kafka jeweils diese und nicht eine andere Spezies wählte, das lässt sich nicht mehr allein mit metaphorischen Entsprechungen begründen.

Schließlich beobachten wir – ein weiteres Indiz für die anhaltende Wirkung des Dorflebens –, dass Kafka die Bandbreite der Themen, auf der er seine Tierfiguren agieren lässt, immer mehr erweitert, dass er damit vordringt bis in Bereiche wie Anthropologie und Erkenntnistheorie. Diese Tendenz machte sich auch schon vor den Zürauer Erlebnissen bemerkbar, doch nun verstärkt sie sich in einem Maße, dass sogar das Moment des Erzählerischen selbst bedeutend an Gewicht verliert gegenüber den Verästelungen der Reflexion. Ein naheliegendes Beispiel bietet das allgegenwärtige Phänomen der Verblendung, ein Thema, das bereits in den beiden von Buber veröffentlichten »Tiergeschichten« aufleuchtete. Verblendet sind die Schakale, die sich die eigene Befreiung nur als Ergebnis einer erlösenden Intervention vorstellen können, verblendet ist aber auch der Menschenaffe. Saturiert und mäßig zufrieden erscheint er am Ende seines Berichts, während er doch – für jeden Leser offenkundig – in eine existenzielle Sackgasse geraten ist, aus der es keine Umkehr gibt.

Kafkas »Forschungen eines Hundes« (1922) – deren Erzähler wiederum ein Tier ist – geht über dieses psychologische Moment noch einen Schritt hinaus. Denn der Wille zu rückhaltloser Erkenntnis ist hier durchaus vorhanden, wie ja bereits der Titel der Erzählung klarstellt. Doch scheitert dieser Wille an Erkenntnisschranken, die für diesen Hund, für alle seine Hundegenossen und selbst für die Intellektuellen unter ihnen unüberwindlich sind. Das führt zu komischen Effekten, die Kafka sichtlich ausgekostet hat. So werden erstaunliche Begegnungen mit ganz besonderen Hunden erwähnt, etwa eine Truppe von »Musikhunden«, die Tanzschritte machen und die auf zwei Beinen gehen, während dazu Musik erklingt. Und es werden typische Probleme der Hundephilosophie erörtert, wie zum Beispiel die Frage: Woher kommt eigentlich unsere Nahrung? Was hat es zu bedeuten, dass sie meistens von oben zu uns kommt?

Liest man die Erzählung zum ersten Mal, so drängt sich zuerst die gewöhnliche Tierkomik auf, die allein schon aus dem Gefälle zum Menschen resultiert; so etwa, wenn von der »Hundeschaft« die Rede ist, oder vom Volk der Hunde, das eigene Überlieferungen hat. Das sind große menschliche Begriffe, übertragen auf Tiere – ein Missverhältnis, das erheiternd wirkt. Sehr bald wird jedoch deutlich, dass die eigentliche Komik, auf die der Text abzielt, eine Ebene tiefer verborgen ist. Denn alle diese seltsamen Erfahrungen und Probleme, mit deren Reflexion sich der Hundeerzähler quält, sind nur deshalb so rätselhaft, weil er nicht zur Kenntnis nehmen will, dass es eine weitere kluge Spezies gibt, Menschen nämlich, was die tierische Autonomie entschieden relativiert. So kommt auch die Nahrung keineswegs vom

Himmel herabgeflogen, wie die Hunde-Philosophen annehmen, sondern sie wird den Hunden von Menschen zugeworfen. Und die Musikhunde sind natürlich dressierte Hunde, denen man das Gehen auf zwei Beinen beigebracht hat; die Musik dazu ist menschengemacht.

Die Komik entsteht hier also aus dem Kontrast zwischen den sehr verständigen Ausführungen des Hundes und seiner offensichtlichen Verblendung. Seine Welt ist rätselhaft, weil er das Nächstliegende ausblendet, weil seinem Denken und daher auch seinen »Forschungen« eine ganze Dimension fehlt. Es ist nicht unwahrscheinlich, dass auch auf diesen Text die Erinnerungen an den Zürauer »Tiergarten« einwirkten, denn auch dort war ja die Freiheit der Tiere vor allem eine gestische: Scheinbar taten sie, was sie wollten. Tatsächlich jedoch war diese Freiheit eingebettet in die unaufhebbare Abhängigkeit vom Menschen, es war der Mensch, der die Grenzen definierte, der über Leben und Tod der Tiere entschied.

Auch in der Erzählung »Der Bau« von 1923 lässt sich die erkenntniskritische Perspektive klar ausmachen. Der Erzähler ist hier ein Tier, das die Erde durchwühlt, vermutlich ein Dachs, und erneut gibt es keine durchgängig erzählbare Handlung, sondern der Text wird im Wesentlichen von Reflexionen getragen. Die erzählerische Raffinesse jedoch besteht darin, dass uns die Überlegungen dieses Tieres, anders als die des Hundes, zunächst vollkommen plausibel erscheinen. Der Dachs hat Fressfeinde, und da er nicht pausenlos wachsam sein kann, denkt er über Maßnahmen nach, um dieser Gefahr auch langfristig zu begegnen. So kommt er auf die Idee, ein ausgedehntes unterirdisches Labyrinth zu bauen, eine verborgene Festung, die ihm genügend Verstecke wie auch Nahrungsreserven bietet. Mit Enthusiasmus macht er sich an die Arbeit, stolz erläutert er seinen Bau und berichtet von seinen Fortschritten bei dessen unablässiger Perfektionierung. Das beeindruckt, trotz des zur Schau gestellten Übereifers und entgegen dem naheliegenden Einwand, dass der Dachs hier etwas feiert, was doch ohnehin in seiner Natur liegt – als stünde es ihm frei, auch *ohne* Dachsbau zu leben.

Allmählich geht dem Leser jedoch auf, dass das Tier völlig diesem Bau verfallen ist, im Denken wie im Handeln. Es gibt in seiner Welt nur mehr ihn selbst, seinen Bau und seine Phantasien über mögliche Angriffe von außen. Aus Sicherheitsdenken wird Sicherheitswahn, und diese aufkeimende Paranoia wird konsequent von innen erzählt, ganz aus der Perspektive des paranoiden Tiers selbst. Das heißt, nicht anders als bei der Hundegeschichte muss sich der Leser irgendwann aus der beschränkten Perspektive des tierischen Erzählers lösen, wenn er nicht am Ende selbst zum Opfer von dessen Verblendung werden will. Wobei »Der Bau« in dieser Hinsicht die schwierigere Leseübung ist, denn wo genau ist der Punkt, an dem die Pläne des Tiers, die ja stets gut begründet sind, in wahnhaftes Denken übergehen?

Am Ende vernimmt das Tier ein leises Geräusch, das auf einen sich heranarbeitenden Feind hindeutet, doch dieser Feind ist nicht zu orten, überall im Bau ist das Geräusch mit gleicher Stärke zu vernehmen. Und während das inzwischen völlig verblendete Tier in Verzweiflung gerät, fällt es dem

Leser nicht allzu schwer, die einzig mögliche Erklärung zu finden: Das Tier selbst trägt das Geräusch mit sich herum, es kommt aus ihm selbst, aus dem eigenen Körper, als Anzeichen irgendeiner Fehlfunktion, einer beginnenden Krankheit. Und davor kann auch die scheinbar sicherste Festung ihn nicht retten.

Spätestens an diesem Punkt wird klar, dass es hier um eine Form von *existenzieller* Verblendung geht. Alles Denken und Handeln des Tieres wird von einem einzigen Ziel beherrscht: den vorzeitigen Tod zu vermeiden. Da dies ein durchaus sinnvolles Ziel ist, kann das Tier sich bis zum Ende darüber hinwegtäuschen, dass seine Strategie schwerwiegende Nachteile hat, zuallererst die damit einhergehende Isolation: Das Tier mauert sich ein, lässt aus Sicherheitsgründen selbst Artgenossen nicht in seinen Bau. Damit verzichtet es nicht nur auf die Freuden der sozialen Gemeinschaft, sondern auch auf jede Form von Supervision. Niemand ist da, der es vor dem völligen Abgleiten in die Paranoia bewahren könnte; niemand, der es daran erinnern könnte, dass es – selbst wenn seine Festung Bestand haben sollte – unweigerlich in seinem Bau sterben wird. Und es wird dort sterben, ohne je gelebt zu haben. Denn ein Leben, das sich in Vorsichtsmaßnahmen erschöpft, ist kein Leben, das diesen Namen verdient.

Auf Tierkomik verzichtet Kafka hier fast völlig. Stattdessen nutzt er die Tiermetapher, um die leibliche Verletzlichkeit, das Ausgesetztsein alles Lebendigen zu akzentuieren, ganz ohne die zahllosen Hilfsmittel und Ablenkungen, die dem Menschen zur Verfügung stehen. Überdies macht »Der

Bau« deutlich, wie sehr die Tiergeschichte Kafkas Streben nach ästhetischer Reduktion entgegenkommt. Die Möglichkeit, einen Text aus einem einzigen Sinnbild heraus zu entfalten, entsprach seiner Arbeitsweise sichtlich besser als das Entwerfen umfangreicher Plots mit zahlreichen Akteuren. Die relative Armut an Handlung und den Vorrang, manchmal sogar die Dominanz reflektierender Passagen hat Kafka dafür in Kauf genommen. Das wird an seiner letzten Tiererzählung vielleicht am deutlichsten: »Josefine, die Sängerin oder das Volk der Mäuse«, verfasst nur etwa zwei Monate vor seinem Tod: ein Text, der nahezu ohne Handlung auskommt.

Er besteht im Wesentlichen aus Mitteilungen über Wirken und Schicksal einer weiblichen Maus, die sich zur großen Sängerin berufen fühlt, die jedoch feststellen muss, dass ihr Publikum aus Banausen besteht. Niemand weiß ihre künstlerischen Leistungen zu würdigen, und alles endet in Verbitterung. Der Erzähler freilich, ebenfalls eine Maus, weiß die fragwürdigen Ansprüche der Diva gelassen einzuordnen, und er macht sich Gedanken über die eigentümliche Geschichtslosigkeit des Mäusevolks, das die exaltierte Josefine sehr bald schon vergessen wird.

Auch in diesem neuen Kontext – der Problematisierung der künstlerischen Existenz, der sein letzter Erzählband »Ein Hungerkünstler« gewidmet ist – wollte also Kafka auf das ästhetische Potenzial der Tierwelt nicht verzichten. Allein schon die Tatsache, dass eine Künstlerin, die sich selbst als verkanntes Genie sieht, nur wenige Zentimeter groß ist, ist von bezwingender Komik. Und ihr angeblicher Gesang ist in

Wahrheit ein Pfeifen, das sich, je genauer man hinhört, desto weniger vom gewöhnlichen Pfeifen aller übrigen Mäuse unterscheidet. Was von der Kunst hier übrig bleibt, ist kaum mehr als ein Anspruch, eine Pose und ein bescheidener Unterhaltungswert, den man, sollte die Künstlerin eines Tages abtreten, durch andere Zerstreuungen leicht ersetzen kann. Ein ziemlich gelassener Abschied ist das, bedenkt man, welche Opfer Kafka seiner eigenen Kunst gebracht hat, und es ist ein Abschied aus einer für ihn neuen Perspektive: der Perspektive des Publikums.

Kafkas Umgang mit Tiermetaphern und Tiersymbolen ist virtuos. Deren Plastizität, ihre schier grenzenlose Wandlungsfähigkeit hat er in nie dagewesener Weise ausgeschöpft, und seine tierischen Kreationen gewinnen eine Plausibilität, die erschreckend sein kann. Nichts aber deutet darauf hin, dass Kafka im Jahr vor seinem Tod damit schon an ein Ende gelangt war, weder mit seinem Interesse an Tieren, noch an seiner Lust, sie in Literatur zu verwandeln. Im Gegensatz zu den Romanen, die sämtlich Fragment geblieben waren, befreiten die Tierphantasien Kafka von der Notwendigkeit, komplexe Handlungen und Dramaturgien zu erfinden und erzählerisch auch durchzuhalten. Dennoch ließen sie Raum für das Phantastische, das Komische, das Sinnliche, aber auch für die Wege und Irrwege der menschlichen Reflexion. Vor allem nach den ländlichen Erfahrungen in Zürau wurde Kafka im Umgang mit literarischen Tierphantasien freier, lockerer, spielerischer. Er entfernte sich immer weiter von der Schuld-und-Strafe-Thematik, die man so lange als den Kern seines Werks betrachtet hat. Und schließlich, in der Mäuse-geschichte, gelingt ihm das zuvor Unvorstellbare. In einem Text, in dem es, aus Kafkas Sicht, um Sein oder Nicht-Sein geht, nämlich um die Rechtfertigung oder Verurteilung eines Lebens, das ganz und gar der Kunst geweiht ist – in einem solchen Text entschließt er sich, das Urteil entspannt dem Leser zu überlassen.

---

1 Franz Kafka, »Brief an den Vater«, in: »Zur Frage der Gesetze und andere Schriften aus dem Nachlaß«, Frankfurt am Main (Fischer Taschenbuch Verlag) 2008, S. 10–66, hier S. 32, 20f., 19.

2 Franz Kafka, »Tagebücher«, Bd. 1: 1909–1912, Frankfurt am Main (Fischer Taschenbuch Verlag) 2008, S. 174 (Eintrag vom 3. November 1911). Vgl. den »Brief an den Vater«, a.a.O., S. 18: »Ohne ihn zu kennen, verglichst Du ihn in einer schrecklichen Weise, die ich schon vergessen habe, mit Ungeziefer und wie so oft für Leute, die mir lieb waren, hattest Du automatisch das Sprichwort von den Hunden und Flöhen bei der Hand.«

3 Franz Kafka, »Hochzeitsvorbereitungen auf dem Lande«, in: »Beschreibung eines Kampfes und andere Schriften aus dem Nachlaß«, Frankfurt am Main (Fischer Taschenbuch Verlag) 2008, S. 14–46, hier S. 18f.

4 Franz Kafka, »Briefe 1913–März 1914«, hrsg. von Hans-Gerd Koch, Frankfurt am Main (S. Fischer) 1999, S. 234.

5 Franz Kafka, »Briefe April 1914–1917«, hrsg. von Hans-Gerd Koch, Frankfurt am Main (S. Fischer) 2005, S. 345 (um den 11. Oktober 1917).

6 Ebd., S. 339 (2. oder 3. Oktober 1917).

7 Ebd., S. 340.

8 Franz Kafka, »Briefe 1900–1912«, hrsg. von Hans-Gerd Koch, Frankfurt am Main (S. Fischer) 1999, S. 280 (28. November 1912).

Entstehung und Überlieferung

Schakale und Araber

Niederschrift zwischen Mitte Januar und Mitte Februar 1917 (›Oktavheft B‹). Erstmals veröffentlicht in: »Der Jude. Eine Monatsschrift«, 2. Jg., Oktober 1917.

Der neue Advokat

Niederschrift im Februar 1917 (›Oktavheft B‹). Erstmals veröffentlicht in der bibliophilen expressionistischen Zweimonatsschrift »Marsyas«, Berlin, 1. Jg., Heft 1, September 1917.

Eine Kreuzung

Niederschrift wahrscheinlich Ende März 1917 (›Oktavheft D‹). Erstmals veröffentlicht in: »Die literarische Welt«, Berlin, 27. März 1931.

Ein Bericht für eine Akademie

Niederschrift Mitte April 1917 (›Oktavheft D‹). Erstmals veröffentlicht in: »Der Jude. Eine Monatsschrift«, 2. Jg., November 1917.

Die beiden hier wiedergegebenen Fragmente entstanden kurz vor der vollendeten Erzählung. In ihnen erprobte Kafka zunächst andere Erzählperspektiven, ehe er sich dazu entschied, das Tier monologisch erzählen zu lassen.

Der Geier

Titel von Max Brod. Niederschrift im September/Oktober 1920 (›Konvolut 1920‹). Erstmals veröffentlich in: »Beschreibung eines Kampfes. Novellen, Skizzen, Aphorismen aus dem Nachlaß« (= Band V der »Gesammelten Schriften«), hrsg. von Max Brod in Gemeinschaft mit Heinz Politzer, Prag (Verlag Heinrich Mercy Sohn) 1936.

Kleine Fabel

Titel von Max Brod. Niederschrift um den 24. Oktober 1920 (›Konvolut 1920‹). Erstmals veröffentlicht in: »Beim Bau der Chinesischen Mauer. Ungedruckte Erzählungen und Prosa aus dem Nachlaß«, hrsg. von Max Brod und Hans-Joachim Schoeps, Berlin (Gustav Kiepenheuer Verlag) 1931.

In unserer Synagoge ...

Unvollendet, im Manuskript ohne Titel. Niederschrift wahrscheinlich 1922 (›Hungerkünstler-Heft‹). Erstmals veröffentlicht in: »Tagebücher und Briefe« (= Band VI der »Gesammelten Schriften«), hrsg. von Max Brod in Gemeinschaft mit Heinz Politzer, Prag (Verlag Heinrich Mercy Sohn) 1937.

Forschungen eines Hundes

Unvollendet, Titel von Max Brod. Niederschrift von Sommer bis Oktober 1922 (›Hungerkünstler-Heft‹ / ›Zwölftes Tagebuch-Heft‹). Erstmals veröffentlicht in: »Beim Bau der Chinesischen Mauer. Ungedruckte Erzählungen und Prosa aus dem Nachlaß«, hrsg. von Max Brod und Hans-Joachim Schoeps, Berlin (Gustav Kiepenheuer Verlag) 1931.

Der Bau
Unvollendet überliefert, Titel von Max Brod. Niederschrift November bis Dezember 1923. Erstmals veröffentlicht in der Zweimonatsschrift »Witiko. Zeitschrift für Kunst und Dichtung«, Eger, Mai 1928.

Josefine, die Sängerin oder das Volk der Mäuse
Niederschrift Ende März/Anfang April 1924. Erstmals veröffentlicht in der Osterbeilage der Prager Presse, 20. April 1924 (unter dem Titel »Josefine, die Sängerin«), danach in dem Band »Ein Hungerkünstler. Vier Geschichten«, erschienen Ende August 1924 im Verlag Die Schmiede, Berlin.

Editorische Notiz

Die Textgrundlage des vorliegenden Bandes sind die folgenden Ausgaben, in modernisierter Rechtschreibung:

Franz Kafka, »Die Erzählungen und andere ausgewählte Prosa«. Herausgegeben von Roger Hermes. Frankfurt am Main: S. Fischer Verlag, 2011

Franz Kafka, »Nachgelassene Schriften und Fragmente I«. Herausgegeben von Malcolm Pasley. Frankfurt am Main: S. Fischer Verlag, 1993

Franz Kafka, »Nachgelassene Schriften und Fragmente II«. Herausgegeben von Jost Schillemeit. Frankfurt am Main: S. Fischer Verlag, 1992

Inhalt